Periodicals of Queen Victoria's Empire

Periodicals of Queen Victoria's Empire: An Exploration

Edited by
J. Don Vann
and
Rosemary T. VanArsdel

UNIVERSITY OF TORONTO PRESS
Toronto and Buffalo

ISBN 0-8020-0810-0

Printed on acid–free paper

Canadian Cataloguing in Publication Data

Main entry under title:

Periodicals of Queen Victoria's Empire

Includes index.
ISBN 0-8020-0810-0

1. English periodicals – Great Britain –
Colonies – History – 19th century. 2. Press –
Great Britain – Colonies – History – 19th
century. I. Vann, J. Don (Jerry Don), 1938–
II. VanArsdel, Rosemary T.

PN5124.P4P47 1996   052.09171'241   C96-930419-6

University of Toronto Press acknowledges the financial assistance to its
publishing program of the Canada Council and the Ontario Arts Council.

Dedicated to the memory of
Paul P. VanArsdel, Jr, MD, 1926–1994
Professor of Medicine
University of Washington
and a steadfast supporter of
Victorian periodicals research

Contents

Acknowledgments

Preparation of the material in this book has taken both the editors and the chapter contributors into new and unexplored territory, and along the way we have had to rely on help from individuals and institutions around the world. The editors are pleased to acknowledge assistance so freely and generously given.

Perhaps our greatest debt is to T.A. Barringer, librarian, the Royal Commonwealth Society Collection, now housed at the University of Cambridge Library, formerly at 18 Northumberland Avenue, London. Her knowledge of the collection is vast and remarkable; her perseverance, not only in locating materials, but also in answering our numerous questions, has been invaluable. Dr N. Merrill Distad, and his wife, Linda, graciously critiqued parts of the manuscript, and it was Merrill who suggested the final choice for the title of the book.

Others who have helped, through correspondence and consultation, include: Margaret Calder, chief librarian, Alexander Turnbull Library, Wellington, New Zealand; Eppie D. Edwards, National Library of Jamaica, Kingston; David Halliday and Madeline Kresge, of Grey Matter, Seattle, Washington, for electronic reproduction; Verna P. Moll for library advice about the West Indies; Frances Salmon, librarian, University of the West Indies, Kingston; Y.C. Wan, curator, Hung On-To Memorial Library, University of Hong Kong; and Dolores Vann, who gave valuable assistance with the index.

Helpful libraries and institutions include: Alexander Turnbull Library, Wellington; British Library; British Library Newspaper Library, Colindale; Commonwealth Institute Library, London; India Office Library, London; Institute of Commonwealth Studies, London; Library, University of Malta, Msida; Library, University of the West Indies, Mona, Kingston; National

Library of Australia, Canberra; National Library of Calcutta; National Library of Jamaica; National Library of Malta, Valletta; National Library of Singapore; National University of Singapore; School of African and Oriental Studies, London; University of London Library, Senate House, London; University of the Witwatersrand Library, Johannesburg; the Map Collection, University of Washington Libraries, and its acting head, Kathryn Womble.

Finally, the editors would like to express their appreciation to Suzanne Rancourt, Karen Boersma, Barbara Porter, and Judy Williams of the University of Toronto Press for their advice and wise counsel in the preparation of this text.

J. DON VANN

ROSEMARY T. VANARSDEL

Periodicals of Queen Victoria's Empire

Introduction

Research in periodical literature over the past thirty years has demonstrated conclusively that the nineteenth century in Britain was uniquely the age of the periodical. It has also shown that the circulation of periodicals and newspapers was wider and more influential than that of books in Victorian society. (See Vann and VanArsdel, *Victorian Periodicals and Victorian Society*, University of Toronto Press 1994). The question which occurs to the student of Empire is whether or not this was equally true in Britain's colonies. Did the custom of periodical publication follow the colonists to their new lands, and, if so, was this literature as pervasive and as important as it was in Britain? What functions did periodicals serve in colonial life? The chapters in this book attempt to provide the answers to these and many other questions.

The essays vary in length and sophistication, largely because of the differences in resources – particularly secondary sources – available to authors; some were doing pioneering work merely by assembling checklists, while others were drawing on a wealth of bibliographies, biographies, and studies of movements, groups of periodicals, or even individual periodicals, to produce richly packed bibliographical essays. While this collection presents a more varied quality of work than many edited volumes, the variety reflects accurately the state of research in each field. This in itself makes an important scholarly statement and also, indirectly, suggests territory for further research.

One important thing to remember about this book is that it is exploratory. It is exploratory in the sense that it is investigating, largely for the first time, what existed in periodical literature in English in the far-flung colonial societies; and in the sense that it is discovering what guides are available to this literature. As Ronald Warwick states in the Introduction to *Commonwealth Literature Periodicals* (1979), 'Any bibliography which deals with a subject not previously covered is, in a sense, an initial step' (xvii). This book represents a first step, important because without it there would be no further steps. Each of the chapters discusses reference works available to aid the researcher, but also the gaping holes that need to be filled. There are some useful and remarkable bibliographies of periodicals, such as the ones for Southern Africa, Malta, Ceylon, Malaya, Australia, and the West Indies, but they are far from complete. On the other hand, almost no studies of individual periodicals have been carried out. There are few studies of editors or journalists, few sweeping studies of the press as a whole, and there are areas, such as India, where virtually no references exist. A word needs to be said about Canada. Although N. Merrill Distad claims that 'neither newspapers nor magazines have attracted the amount of scholarly attention in Canada that their importance warrants' (63), his chapter stands in stark contrast to the others. The resources available, and the technology, bibliographies, dictionaries, directories, indexes, finding aids, and biographies, if not studies of individual periodicals, indicate how much more basic reference material Canadian researchers have to work with than those in India, for instance, where the researcher faces a paucity of secondary sources. One hopes that eventually, partially by means of the guidelines suggested in this volume, the resources available for each area may be developed more equally.

A large step toward that goal is occurring late in the twentieth century by means of new, electronic technology. It is now possible, through the Internet, to access databases in some former colonies. Among these are the National Library of Canada's AMICUS, the National Library of Australia and the Australian Bibliographic Network, and in South Africa, the University of Pretoria and the University of Natal-Durban. New Zealand has the New Zealand Bibliographic Network (NZBN), which links most public, university, government, and special libraries in the country to a central bibliographic database, managed by the National Library of New Zealand. Singapore has the Singapore Integrated Library Automation Service (SILAS), which is a 'national bibliographic network with a union catalogue for its participating libraries' (*World Encyclopedia*, 778). India has a system, INFLIBNET, under development. The University of Sydney has announced a new project, in co-operation with the Library of New South Wales, the National Library of Australia, and Monash University Library, to digitize the full contents, both text and images, of all periodicals published in Australia from 1840 to 1845. This material will be made available through the Internet. Hong Kong, with neither a national library nor a national bibliographic centre, does not, as yet, have a system; nor do Cyprus, Malta, Ceylon (Sri Lanka), or the West Indies. More technology will surely be developed in other parts of the world in years to come.

In considering the potential for power wielded by the colonial press, it is interesting to note the following quotation from the *Colonial Magazine* for January 1840, remarkable for its perceptiveness and for its early date. The editor, Robert Montgomery, insisted vehemently on the fundamental importance to a society of its periodical literature:

Periodicals are amongst the peculiar characteristics of the present age: emanating from the womb of circumstances, and imbued with the vitality of existing events, they direct the current of living thought into active energy, and give a form, a tone, and a hue to society, which, in a concentrated state, is productive of momentous results. ... Hence periodical literature is an instrument of vast but almost unseen power, which may be employed for the dissemination of good or evil, according to the conduct and motives of those who wield that singular element of social life – 'the press.'

One interesting way to observe the power generated by study of the press is to look at the ways that studies of periodical publishing intersect with other areas of human endeavour. An example of this is the development of Empire. When the period of primary colonization occurred during the nineteenth century, for example, the press was influential in providing the 'contact point' between the settlers, or colonists, and the native people and/or the people of previous European arrivals. In almost every colony, periodical literature also faced, head-on, the problems of multilingualism: in Canada, it was English and French; in Southern Africa, English and Dutch and Afrikaans; in New Zealand, English and Maori; in India, English and Hindi; in Malta, English and Greek; and in Southeast Asia, English and Chinese, Tamil, and Malay. Sometimes, facing pages were bound together to provide the same copy in different languages; in some instances identical editions of the same copy were produced in the different tongues; occasionally two or three translations were bound together. In each case, however, it was an effort on the part of native populations to emulate the British form of journalism.

The power of the press also interacts with and informs the modern scholars who use it today for studying the past. Reference librarians world-wide, as well as scholars researching colonial and post-colonial history, the histories and literatures of individual countries, labour and gender issues, or the history of periodicals and publishing in general in the nineteenth-century British empire, all make use of the treasures of knowledge locked in the pages of the periodical press.

The colonial territory surveyed has largely been determined by following the organizational guide of *Commonwealth Literature Periodicals*: Australia, Canada, India, New Zealand, Southern Africa, and 'Outposts' of Empire, including Ceylon (now Sri Lanka), Cyprus, Hong Kong, Malaya and Singapore, Malta, and the West Indies. The editors are keenly aware that the coverage for the continent of Africa is less than exhaustive. However, they are not alone in experiencing difficulties in bringing material from East, West, and North Africa under bibliographic control. In its fifteenth year of publication, the editors of the *Journal of Commonwealth Literature* expressed frustration: owing to lack of compilers, 'Once again we have had to go to press without [a bibliographic] entry for West Africa' (*JCL* 17:2 [1982], ed. note). It is to be hoped that in the future, with better communication and new technology, this deficiency may be remedied.

The beginnings of the press in different colonies followed different timetables and conditions of settlement, but the story is often the same – an old press, with some type, ink, and paper optimistically included among a shipload of settlers. In Australia, the first newspaper, the *Sydney Gazette and New South Wales Advertiser*, appeared 5 March 1803, fifteen years after the first boatload of settlers arrived in 1788. The first magazine, the *Australia Magazine*, was published in May 1821, in Sydney, edited by a group of Methodist ministers.

Canada was in an almost constant process of growth. The Act of Union (1840) united Upper (Ontario) and Lower (Quebec) Canada. The British North America Act of 1867 created the Dominion of Canada by uniting the Canadas with New Brunswick and Nova Scotia. The Dominion expanded to include Rupert's Land (1869), which yielded the provinces of Manitoba (1870), Alberta, and Saskatchewan (both 1905), as well as the Northwest Territories. Other additions filled in the map: British Columbia in 1871, Prince Edward Island in 1873, and Newfoundland in 1949. It was the function of periodicals to serve as essentially political tools 'in the creation of representative government in the provinces' (Distad, 62).

In India, the home of a very ancient civilization, the newspaper was unknown until the end of the eighteenth century. Before that, news was transmitted orally, through people mingling in bazaars, a surprisingly effective and widespread system, and by means of 'akhbars,' or handwritten native Indian newsletters. When the system of journals did take hold, however, it moved swiftly. The first Western-style journal, the *Bengal Gazette*, was founded in 1780 by an Englishman, James Augustus Hicky, and was followed quickly by six others between 1780 and 1786.

The first installation of printing presses in New Zealand, in 1814, was coincident with the arrival of its first missionaries. The importance of the press to colonists is well illustrated by the circumstances of the founding of the *New Zealand Gazette*: the colonists set up the first issue in London before sailing in 1839, and the second issue on the beach in Wellington Harbour on 18 April 1840.

The chapter on Southern Africa begins with newspapers at the time of the first British occupation of the Cape in 1795, although the first literary magazine, the *South African Journal*, did not begin publication until 1824. Thus the author must make use of the very early material in the Cape newspapers, which 'were often the only vehicle for comment and literary expression.' Early Cape newspapers contained 'a good deal in the way of occasional verses and articles of general interest' often becoming a combination of 'news journal and literary magazine' (Cheadle, 243, 244).

Circumstances surrounding the beginnings of the English-language press in the other 'Outposts' of Empire are still shrouded in mystery because so little research has been done; indeed, there are almost no research aids to guide scholars in this field. The same initiating impulses were probably at work here as in the other colonies: presses and missionaries arrived first, and later either trained or aspiring journalists took over to meet the demands of settlers for information and exchange of ideas.

Cyprus and Malta, however, present slightly different situations. The Cyprus weekly, the *Owl*, remarked in September 1888 that no English journal had been published in the more than ten years of British occupation, so British journalism in Cyprus started much later than in other parts of the colonial world. Malta, on the other hand, experienced British presence from 1799 onwards; British journalism was an influence from 1813 forward (see entry for *Malta Government Gazette*), and it tended to deal with more sophisticated subject matter than in Cyprus, such as poetry, natural history, Arabic inscriptions, music, science, dress, and classical subjects. The concerns of Cyprus journalism were largely governmental and colonial; columns often advocated judicial reform and abolition of military rule.

The essays seek to identify colonial periodicals that were locally produced, written in English, published at weekly or longer intervals (fortnightly, monthly, quarterly, or other), during the time-frame of 1800–

1900, containing news, poetry, fiction, criticism, commentary on the arts, news from home, shipping and commodity news, and so on. They also seek to identify what guides are available to this literature, and to point out where further work needs to be done.

Two editorial problems immediately confront the researcher trying to investigate colonial periodical literature. The first is establishing the distinction between newspapers and periodicals; chapter authors comment on this difficulty repeatedly. Distad notes trenchantly, 'few tangible objects are as elusive of precise definition as the periodical magazine' (71). Elizabeth Webby says of Australia that this distinction is hard to make, particularly in the early days, because while newspapers came first, they were weeklies with much general material 'such as serialized novels and poetry' (21). J. Reginald Tye comments that 'nineteenth-century New Zealand newspapers tended to be hybrid, containing matter customarily associated with magazines' (210). Brian D. Cheadle observes that the dividing line between periodicals and newspapers is tenuous, particularly in the early South Africa, and concludes: 'Periodicals form a continuum with many other kinds of serial publication [gazettes, bulletins, government reports, annuals, and so on] and it is important not to lose sight of the full range' (244).

In Canada, for example, newspapers originally dominated the periodical press, growing to enormous power and size. The history of Canadian magazines, on the other hand, was plagued with problems similar to those of Australia and India, such as a small population base and wide geographic dispersal of population; in addition, Canada suffered linguistic fragmentation and a lower literacy base among francophones as well as inadequate copyright protection and foreign (American) competition for readership, advertising revenue, and editorial talent. Indeed, Distad comments, 'the history of Canadian magazines before 1901 is largely a story of attrition and failure' (63).

The *Catalogue* of the British Library addresses this problem by bringing all these artifacts together under the category 'Periodical Publications,' for the very reason that they refuse to fall into convenient groupings. Almost always scholars find weekly, fortnightly, or monthly publications that defy simple classification. The researcher will often encounter a journal, in the monthly octavo format, with a heavy, coloured-paper cover, looking like a magazine, but containing the news stories one would expect to find in a tabloid or broadsheet publication. Consequently, the editors have tended in this book to take the liberal, or all-inclusive, view in defining the genre, and to give full credit for whatever literary work appeared. In some cases a 'sampling' of extant newspapers has been given here so the reader can get a sense of what was available to the contemporary public. School and college magazines have also been included occasionally in this collection because they were important in stimulating youthful creative talent, which sometimes moved on to less parochial journals.

The second large editorial problem is the prevalence of broken runs among surviving copies. Ideally, the entry for each periodical should contain the following information: title, subtitle, frequency of appearance, volume numbers and dates, place of publication, price, editor, comments about contents, location. In reality, however, because of inadequate periodical archives, it is not always possible to reconstruct all the facts; the general rule has been to give whatever pertinent information is known. It should be pointed out that the exigencies of personal survival, particularly in the 'outposts' of Empire, were such that the effort required to preserve periodicals probably was often neglected. Not until 1900, for instance, did the 'Registration of Newspapers Act' require legal deposit of every issue of every newspaper in Barbados; for Malta, systematic collection began with the Public Libraries Ordinance of 1925; while it was not until 1971 that the 'Printed Publications Act' required publishers to deposit books published in Bermuda, a book being defined loosely as 'every part or division of a book, pamphlet, newspaper, or sheet of printed matter.' Further evidence of careless preservation of periodicals is to be found in Proctor's *Colonial British Newspapers, A Bibliography and Directory* (1977), where it is noted that of nineteen newspapers listed for the nineteenth century, copies in broken runs are extant for only ten, while the remaining nine are known to have existed only because they were mentioned in other newspapers.

Ronald Warwick, in his Introduction to *Commonwealth Literature Periodicals*, says that he encountered similar difficulties: 'In many instances the requisite information was not available or could not be ascertained ... The vagaries of periodical numbering (notorious in the case of literary magazines), irregularity of appearance, together with the reliance on secondary and frequently conflicting information [have made it] necessary in some cases to opt for the consensus' (xvi).

It cannot be stressed too often that many of these periodicals are arcane, many without any publication information at all (including dates), often available only in broken sets, in indifferent condition, and exceedingly difficult to locate. Readers should bear in mind that no style sheets existed for the preparation of publication information for nineteenth-century periodicals, and hence often the material the twentieth-century scholar might like to have simply does not exist. The colonial world was often too busy establishing itself in the present to have the leisure to document its periodical literature properly for posterity.

The one exception to this difficulty is Canada, where over the last four decades considerable progress has been made. With the help of the Canadian Library Association, and after the late 1970s the Canadian Institute for Historical Microreproductions, many early periodicals have been microfilmed. In addition, each province has attempted to create a union list of newspapers produced within its borders, thus providing, at a single stroke, a significant archive for researchers of the future. Canada is far in advance of its counterparts in the former Empire and surely points the way for other nations, if only funding and labour to do the job could be secured.

The different functions which periodicals served in the individual colonies is another topic which immediately engages readers' attention. Australia, because of its size, found that the spread of newspapers was ensured by the need for advertisements for goods and land. This was the distinguishing factor for readers in choosing between the local and the imported, British press, and also made weekly publication more desirable than monthly or quarterly, because the advertising gave the papers more revenue. Canadian periodicals played an important role in informing the electorate in the widely scattered provinces (each faced with solving complex political issues), and also in attempts to unite a vast geographic area. Because of the size and the power of Canada's periodical press, Canadian journalism developed distinct types of editorial personalities as the century progressed beginning with printers who became proprietors; politicians who advanced their public careers through their roles as editors and pulishers, or, conversely, editors who became politicians; some editors built their journals so well they became business magnates; while the final stages of journalistic evolution saw development of a new class of 'professional' editors and journalists. Study of such categories sheds light on the interesting and unusual personalities who contributed to the evolution of the Canadian periodical press. In India, journalism was closely linked to the colonization process. If, as the British believed, colonization must be based on intellectual as well as political power, then journalism had two purposes: to strengthen the colonization process, and to shape Indian opinion. The English-language press in India also had a dual personality: the British and the native. The *Brahmanical Magazine* (1821), for instance, owned and edited by an Indian, Ram Mohan Roy, but conducted in English, sought religious reform of Indian customs that it saw as pernicious, such as the caste system, child marriage, and suttee; this represented another attempt to educate Indian opinion. In New Zealand, periodicals were regarded as essential for transmitting news to arriving settlers. Tye comments that 'the pioneer press had a function to perform, principally to inform and act as a forum for political debate among the influential educated settlers' (209). In the Caribbean area, colonial periodical literature seemed to come into being for three very utilitarian reasons: exchange of information, such as births, deaths, marriages, shipping information, and communication among various colonies; cultural identity, because each area prided itself on developing and maintaining a genteel culture of its own; and dissemination of the always important 'news from home' and the rest of Europe.

In colonies such as Ceylon, and Malaya and Singapore, the press clearly played a role in the colonization process: journals served as agents to facilitate colonial administration, to promote the study of English, and to help to 'transplant successfully English social and political institutions' ('Outposts,' 306). On Malta and Cyprus periodicals supplied a vital link with home for colonial administrators who felt uneasy in foreign societies where, often, they formed only a small proportion of the population. In addition, on Cyprus the journalistic mission was often seen as providing a cultural bridge between the English and Greek populations. Repeatedly, the journals pleaded for harmony between the two dominant groups, and called for 'good understanding between governors and governed,' and 'a bridge of intercourse and good understanding between English and native Greeks' (*Hellenic Times* 1:1 [March 1884]).

In transplanting their culture, the colonists often brought familiar artifacts with them, one of which was the re-embodiment of the British humour magazine *Punch*. Its style was particularly popular in New Zealand, where eleven journals bearing 'Punch' in the titles were established between 1855 and 1900. There were also six in Australia, four in Canada, and one each in South Africa, India, and Hong Kong. These were, quite apart from general magazines, devoted to humour, satire, and ridicule, and were definite attempts to duplicate the style of *Punch*.

The push for freedom of the press assumed more importance in some societies. In Australia, after a few early skirmishes with the government, the principle of freedom of the press was firmly established by the 1830s, and 'papers rose and fell according to commercial pressures alone' (Webby, 23). Two adversaries plagued a free press in Canada. From earliest times and well into the 1830s, many 'early publications were dependent upon government contracts and patronage for their very survival' (Distad, 67), thus creating an inevitable conflict of interest. Not until the development of better technology and an increase in advertising revenues was it possible to cast off this yoke. The second obstacle, confronting intellectuals in French-speaking areas, was the monolithic and occasionally censorious Roman Catholic church in Quebec (Distad, 106). In India, on the other hand, development of the press was stifled because of restrictive laws imposed by the British. In 1789, after sharp criticism of colonial administration in the press, the British Parliament introduced a series of regulations designed to control the press. These regulations were not lifted until 1835, and had the effect of slowing early growth among periodicals. New Zealand's early problems with press freedom had a somewhat different character. From the time of settlement, in the 1840s, there was a sharp division between the interests and expectations of the colonists and official government policies.

Turbulence and ill-feeling developed where journals were government-controlled. In South Africa, a fierce struggle was waged over the banning of the *South African Commercial Advertiser* by the governor of the Cape, Lord Charles Somerset (1767–1831), after it had reported on a legal case which reflected badly on the Cape administration. Rather than submit to the demand that each issue should be censored, the editor, George Greig, discontinued publication and brought out a broadsheet explaining the stoppage of the paper. He then returned to England, and, going over Somerset's head, obtained permission to publish free from government censorship. In 1827, the aggrieved Somerset again suppressed the paper, and it reappeared only after there was a new colonial minister and a new governor at the Cape. The root of the problem appeared to be tension between the colonists and an autocratic governor.

On Cyprus the presence of the press was not large, and though its concerns were mainly the cessation of military rule and judicial reform, no effort was exerted to stifle journalism. On Malta the press was free. In the other 'Outposts' of Empire, no research has been carried out on this subject.

The role of missionaries and the religious press is a vast and almost totally neglected area for periodicals research. Missionaries, representing a variety of faiths, were everywhere, and frequently carried with them one of their most valuable tools, the printing press, which gave them an additional means to spread their message. In Australia the first magazine published was edited by Methodist missionaries, but no studies have been done on the practical effects of the missionary press there. Brahma Chaudhuri states flatly that missionaries were 'the most influential force in periodical publication in India,' first, by establishing the printing presses, and, second, by introducing newspapers and periodicals in both English and the vernacular. However, because the East India

Company disliked the idea of allowing missionaries into India, a strong anti-missionary sentiment developed in both India and Britain. Wars of pamphlets ensued between such groups as the secular followers of Ram Mohan Roy and the missionaries who wanted 'to promote the religious and moral improvement of the people of India' (178). The *Calcutta Christian Observer* (1832), published by the Baptists, made an important contribution by devoting one-third of the periodical to Indian literature in translation, thus providing an immense fund of interesting and important information on the languages, literature, and culture of India. In New Zealand, the arrival of the missionaries coincided with the introduction of the printing press in the colony, and it should not be forgotten that their sponsoring organizations often supplied the subsidies needed to ensure a journal's survival. In the early days of the colony, missionary representatives of the Anglicans, Presbyterians, Congregationalists, Catholics, and Methodists were present in New Zealand, and there were even some missions devoted solely to the Maori population. In Tye's words, 'there is a pronounced dichotomy in the orientation of New Zealand periodicals between the secularism of most newspapers and popular journals and the denominational underpinning of a significant number of weekly and monthly periodicals' (218). Cheadle laments that there has been no authoritative study of the many missionary presses in Southern Africa.

The role of the missionary was less pronounced in areas such as Cyprus and Malta, where cultures were firmly rooted in the traditions of the Greek Orthodox and Roman Catholic churches and in ancient mysticism. The missionary presence was definitely felt in Hong Kong, as part of the great missionary movement in China, and to a lesser extent in Ceylon, and Malaya and Singapore, although there was a strong effort to convert the population to Christianity. In Canada, periodicals tended to grow most rapidly in the larger centres of population, which were not the primary focus of missionaries. It was, however, to the efforts of missionaries that Canada's native-language periodical press owed its beginnings.

As the century progressed, many individual national events acted to shape the forces of journalism in the separate colonies. Despite its slow start, by 1850 India boasted thirty-eight periodicals in circulation, and in the second half of the century experienced 'rapid growth of periodicals devoted partly or wholly to literature' (Chaudhuri, 179). The Mutiny of 1856–7 had far-reaching consequences for journalism because it created a distinction between the English language and the Indian vernacular languages and injected a 'racial colour' into British thinking. These events gave rise to the Indian nationalist movement, which was reflected in its periodicals. Chaudhuri maintains that any close examination of Indian periodicals will reveal that they were closely associated with 'socio-religious movements, educational and literary upheavals, and national awakenings' (182). There were, however, general problems which affected Indian journals: the need to maintain high quality to compete with imported British journals; the limited readership and circulation; the short life-span of journals; and often the need for subventions from a church or institution in order to survive.

By contrast, early Australian periodicals chose not to deal with political and controversial questions, considered too divisive for a population scattered over a large area that was trying to unite. Instead, they concentrated on biography, theology, philosophy, religious intelligence, and poetry. The debate intensified over whether it was desirable to encourage contributions from local writers, even if they 'fell short,' or to reprint 'better' material from Britain. By the end of the century, Australian journals had moved decidedly from amateur to professional: most material was original and local; editorship had changed from volunteer clergymen and lawyers to trained writers; journals had moved from being expensive, luxury items to being cheaper and more affordable; and they had moved from unillustrated and unadorned format to illustrations.

Development of Southern African periodicals was certainly dominated by the many political and societal divisions needing to be reconciled. Besides journals published by the British in English, there were periodicals in Dutch, Afrikaans, and the vernacular languages. Despite excluding parish magazines and university and school magazines, Cheadle provides 300 items in his list and concludes, 'there are many more nineteenth-century periodicals than might have been supposed,' 'certainly far more than have ever been comprehensively and independently listed in a convenient form' (Cheadle, 260). In his assessment he concludes that it was impossible to sustain a serious literary magazine after the demise of the *Cape Monthly Magazine* in 1881, and questions whether, because of Southern Africa's proximity to Britain, it was easier to import literary journals than to originate them.

In the beginning, New Zealand periodicals suffered from a variety of ills. In the absence of copyright law, 'purloined' material was common, copy was scarce, typesetting was poor, the paper was subject to disintegration, circulation was low, and costs were high. By 1866, however, the first illustrated weekly appeared from Dunedin, *Illustrated New Zealander*, which covered music, theatre, and sport, and carried fiction and poetry. Twenty-five years later, in 1891, the *Auckland Weekly, New Zea-*

land *Graphic and Lady's Journal* appeared, and was considered the 'most outstanding illustrated journal of the Victorian era.' Tye comments: 'with its publication one has the sensation that New Zealand had emerged from colonial dependence, yet with an appreciation of the colony as part of a great Empire, in an age of self-determined bourgeois affluence, reconciled to the environment, but with a sense of freedom from insurgent Maoridom' (216). Apropos of 'insurgent Maoridom,' however, it is worth noting that Tye's discussion of Maori periodicals is unique; nowhere else in print has any attempt ever been made to list and analyse Maori periodical literature.

It was the move to the west and north and the attempts to unite a vast country that gave shape and form to Canada's journalism. By mid-century 'an increase in commercial business and advertising, combined with technological improvements, made a daily press inevitable' (Distad, 69). On the other hand, at mid-century, magazines, after a shaky start, were still struggling to survive. *Snow Drop*, which may be the only colonial 'children's' magazine so far noted, managed to last for six years, 1847–53. Notable among literary magazines was the *Literary Garland and North American Magazine, A Monthly Repository of Tales, Sketches, Poetry, Music, etc.* (1838–52), for it was the first one to achieve any longevity. It was also notable for several other features: it included lithographic illustrations and engraved musical scores; it paid its contributors; it produced sizeable amounts of original Canadian material; it was the first to include the names of several women writers among its contributors – Anna Jameson, Susanna Moodie, and Catharine Parr Traill; and its second editor was a woman, Mrs Eliza Lanesford Cushing (Distad, 76, 77).

Women's involvement with colonial periodicals appears to have been marginal until late in the century. Australia pioneered women's involvement in journalism. As early as 1857, Harriet Clisby became the first woman to edit an Australian periodical, the *Southern Phonographic Harmonica*, a promotional journal for Pitman's shorthand. In 1858–9, the *Spectator: Journal of Literature and Art* was edited by Cora Ann Weekes and owned by 'An Association of Ladies.' In 1861, the *Interpreter* was owned and edited by Caroline Dexter. During the 1850s and 1860s, the *Melbourne Review* was printing the work of Catherine Helen Spence, a novelist and political reformer. Frances Gillam Holden contributed to the *Sydney Quarterly Magazine* (1883–92), while Annie Bright was editor of *Cosmos, an Illustrated Australian Magazine*, and novelist Ethel Turner was in charge of its 'Women's Department.' From the 1880s onward, there were a number of journals intended for female readership.

Canada produced its first woman editor at mid-century in Mary Eliza Herbert, of Halifax, who edited the *Mayflower, or Ladies' Acadian Newspaper*, 1851–2. It printed pieces by a number of female writers. Canada's second woman editor was Mary Jane Lawson, who conducted the *Provincial: or Halifax Monthly Magazine* (1852–3). However, barriers to women as professional journalists in Canada were only seriously challenged in the 1880s, and even then male pseudonyms were often required. Acceptance of participation by women came even later in conservative Roman Catholic Quebec. A number of women were involved with journals, as writers, editors, or correspondents from the late 1880s on, but sadly, their work was confined mostly to social news or women's pages, with occasional pieces allowed on suffrage and temperance, subjects on which editors reluctantly conceded women might be competent.

In India, there is no evidence to suggest women's participation, nor do they appear to have participated in South Africa. There were some titles aimed at females, such as the *South African Lady's Companion* (1858) among others, but there is no record of female editors or writers. Although New Zealand gave women the vote in 1893, there is no mention of female writers or editors until very late in the century. In 1895–6, Louisa Adams became editor of *Daybreak*, an eight-page quarto publication, advertised as 'edited and carried out by the weaker sex,' and that appears to have been the first. A few journals contain 'Fashion Notes,' presumably aimed at women. It is possible, however, that some women may have been involved with periodicals through the missionary press, although the editors know of no research on this subject. In the colonies which made up the 'Outposts' of Empire, journalism was certainly a male bastion, with one lone exception. In Antigua, in the West Indies, *Carib: A West Indies Magazine*, published in St John's, was edited by a Miss F. Cassin. It contained poems, essays, and serialized fiction.

The reader is reminded of the quotation on page 4 of this Introduction: the editors and authors of this book offer the volume as an initial step toward understanding and analysing the 'unseen power' of the periodical press in the British Empire of the nineteenth century.

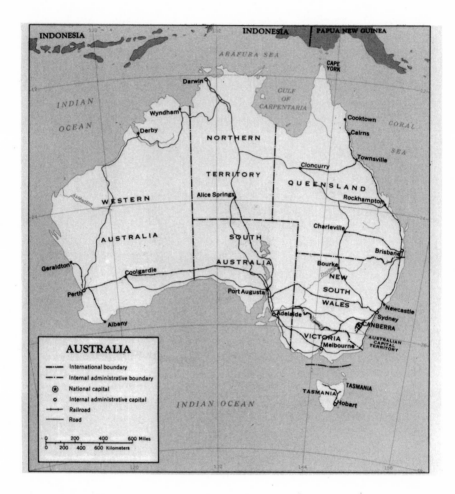

Central Intelligence Agency map, courtesy of the Map Collection, University of
Washington Libraries.

1

Australia

ELIZABETH WEBBY

Introduction

The first magazine to be published in Australia appeared in May 1821. It was a monthly called the *Australian Magazine*, edited in Sydney by a group of Methodist missionaries. One of the last new journals to attempt to find readers in nineteenth-century Australia was also a monthly called the *Australian Magazine*. It first appeared in March 1899, again in Sydney, and was edited by some of Australia's first professional literary men. It survived for six months; the 1821 version had lasted more than twice as long.

To trace the history of journals in nineteenth-century Australia is not, then, a matter of following a track which begins as faint wheel-marks but gradually widens into a six-lane highway. Instead, it is very much a thing of fits and starts, of byways which lead nowhere, of seemingly promising paths which peter out just round the corner, and the very occasional throughway. Probably over eight hundred journals were begun in Australia during the nineteenth century; only a handful of them survive today.[1] At least half, like the *Australian Magazine* of 1899, failed in their first year of operation. The reasons for these repeated failures are not hard to find: limited circulation, poor distribution, failure to attract advertising, high production costs. This series of interrelated factors, endemic to a large country with a small population, continues to work against smaller and more specialized journals today. During the nineteenth century there was also greater competition from overseas publications, particularly from Britain. Journals could be fairly rapidly and cheaply imported, often selling for less than their Australian imitators. They had the advantage of well-known contributors and could also draw on the nostalgia of a predominantly British migrant population.

Brief History

The continent of Australia and its associated islands, including the largest of them, Tasmania, have been populated for well over forty thousand years. The indigenous peoples had strong oral cultures but, being largely nomadic, did not develop writing. From the seventeenth century onwards, European navigators and sailors began bumping into the west coast of Australia, sometimes disastrously, and in 1770 Captain James Cook charted the east coast and took possession of eastern Australia in the name of King George III of England.

Various theories have been put forward to explain the decision some sixteen years later to establish an English colony in Australia. While it clearly was strategically important to the English to have a beach-head in the South Pacific, especially as the French were also interested in the new territory, most commentators agree that the main reason was the need for new penal settlements after the loss of the American colonies in the War of Independence. Early in 1788, Governor Arthur Phillip, with 756 convicts and about 450 civil and military personnel, landed in Botany Bay. On 26 January 1788, they transferred the settlement to Sydney Cove and established the penal colony of New South Wales.

This initial colony also included what are now the separate states of Tasmania, Victoria, and Queensland. In 1803 a new settlement was established in Tasmania, then called Van Diemen's Land, to prevent its being annexed by the French. In 1804, this party was joined by a group of convicts and others who had attempted unsuccessfully to establish a settlement at Port Phillip, near the present site of Melbourne. By 1825, Van Diemen's Land had grown sufficiently to be politically separated from New South Wales. The years before the gold discoveries of the 1850s brought great prosperity to the island with the growth of wheat and wool industries, and something of a plantation society was established, with the convicts providing the labour, and wealthy landowners building large mansions and having a cultured and gentlemanly life-style.

In 1828, a settlement was established at the Swan River in what is now Western Australia, again prompted in part by fear of French interest in the area. This was a free settlement where growth was hampered by lack of labour and poor organization; in 1850 convicts were introduced, though development remained slow until the discovery of gold in the 1890s. In contrast to the rather chaotic situation in the west, the colonization of South Australia was based on a planned migration scheme. The settlers who arrived in present-day Adelaide in 1836 had, for example, already established a literary society and a newspaper, and periodical publication began a few years later.

After the abortive official attempt in 1803, subsequent colonization of Victoria was carried out unofficially by settlers arriving overland from the north and across Bass Strait from Tasmania. An official settlement was established at Melbourne in 1836; the new town grew rapidly, with several newspapers and magazines printed in the 1840s, and Victoria was separated from New South Wales in 1851. The discovery of gold that same year heralded a period of enormous growth that saw Victoria become the largest and leading colony, and Melbourne the cultural and financial capital of Australia, for the rest of the century. In contrast, Queensland progressed much more slowly, initial settlement commencing in 1824 when a penal out-station was established for recalcitrant convicts at what is now Brisbane. Free settlers began arriving in the 1840s, but when Queensland was separated from New South Wales in 1859, the population was still barely twenty thousand. Growth of what is now the Northern Territory was even slower. A short-lived penal station was established in 1824, as a result of another scare over French intentions; another abortive attempt was made in 1839. By the 1870s gold had been discovered and a cattle industry begun, but there was little in the way of print culture until the twentieth century.

Beginnings of Newspaper Publishing

This brief history of the spread of white settlement in Australia will help to explain the different rates at which periodical publications developed in each of the present-day states, as summarized in table 2 (see p. 27). Publication of periodicals was, of course, in all cases preceded by publication of newspapers, with classification often being difficult to determine. Most early Australian newspapers began as weekly publications; most also included a great deal of general material, such as serialized novels and poetry.

Materials for printing had arrived in Australia with Governor Phillip's first fleet in 1788: 'an old wooden screen press, a small selection of used type and some paper and ink.'[2] Whoever had thought to include these goods in the cargo, however, had not taken the next step and included someone with printing experience. The press evidently lay idle until 1795, when a convict named George Hughes, who appears to have been self-taught, began working it. The earliest extant production is a government order, 'Instructions to the watchmen of the town division,' dated 18 November 1796.

In 1800 another convict, George Howe, arrived in Sydney and took over the press. He had been born in the West Indies in 1769 and learnt the printing trade from his father. In 1790 he went to London and worked on a number of newspapers, including *The Times*, but was convicted of shoplifting in 1799. After Howe's arrival in Sydney, government printing rapidly expanded, and the first Australian newspaper, the *Sydney Gazette and New South Wales Advertiser*, was issued on 5 March 1803. Initially, it included little more than the government orders Howe had been printing earlier, along with summaries of English news. But it soon expanded to include local news, the occasional original poem, and that staple of the nineteenth-century Australian newspaper, advertisements, especially for real estate.

It was, of course, the need for an advertising medium for land and other goods which ensured the rapid spread of newspapers throughout Australia once free settlement began to get properly underway from the 1820s. While local magazines always had to struggle against better-printed, more prestigious, and often cheaper English competitors, only a local press could provide advertisers with immediate and frequent access to potential buyers. It is significant that, apart from special-interest magazines such as those run by religious groups, the only three long-running nineteenth-century Australian magazines all began as weeklies, allowing them to tap in, at least in part, to advertising revenue. The much more sporadic publication of monthly and quarterly magazines made them less able to draw on this source of income, while their editors would, in many cases, have seen the carrying of advertising as aesthetically undesirable.

In 1803, a printing press also accompanied the party which attempted the first settlement in Victoria and then moved to Tasmania. Governor Collins apparently printed a little newspaper, called the 'Derwent Star,' while at Port Phillip, as well as government orders.[3] While government orders continued to be printed after the settlement's removal to Hobart, a new *Derwent Star and Van Diemen's Land Intelligencer* did not appear until 1810. It appeared only sporadically, with regular newspaper publication in Tasmania not established until 1816, and the appearance of the *Hobart Town Gazette and Southern Reporter*. Like the *Sydney Gazette*, it was edited and printed by a convict, Andrew Bent, who was also Government Printer. Like George Howe, Bent had worked as a printer in London before being convicted of burglary in 1810 and transported to Van Diemen's Land. Unlike Howe, Bent subsequently fell foul of the government in the 1820s when he printed material critical of official policies. He was dismissed as government printer and imprisoned, and his newspaper's title was taken over. The same decade saw the establishment of alternative newspapers in Sydney – the *Australian* (1824) and the *Sydney Monitor* (1826) – with further clashes there over freedom of the press, accompanied by imprisonment of editors.

By the 1830s, and the establishment of the still-surviving *Sydney Herald* (1831), the principle of freedom of the press was well established, and subsequent papers rose and fell according to commercial pressures alone. The *Western Australian Chronicle* had a brief run in 1831; it was followed by the *Perth Gazette* (1833–79). In South Australia, as noted above, the first issue of the *South Australian Gazette and Colonial Register* was printed in London in 1836. The first, handwritten, issue of the *Melbourne Advertiser* appeared on 1 January 1838; several copies were made and passed from hand to hand. In Brisbane, the *Moreton Bay Courier* began printing on 20 June 1846.

Overview of Journal Publication in Nineteenth-Century Australia

Only about 8 per cent of nineteenth-century Australian journals achieved runs of longer than twenty-five years. But, though their history is far from being one of unimpeded progress, there are some important differences between the *Australian Magazine*s of 1821 and 1899. While the earlier journal was edited by amateurs, the later was produced by professionals. Professional literary men were, for obvious reasons, not attracted to early Australia, though a few came without choice as convicts. Until mid-century, colonial literary culture was largely in the hands of professionals in other areas – a spare-time indulgence from more utilitarian duties for lawyers, medical officers, government officials, and clergymen. For the latter, indeed, given the close connection between religion and education at this period, and the even closer one between reading and education, it could be argued that the promotion of literary culture was a vital part of their duties. The Rev. Samuel Marsden appears to have been the first to attempt a lending library in Australia; the Wesleyans planned to set one up in Sydney in 1816 and succeeded in doing so in Hobart ten years later.

It is in this context, then, that we should view the establishment by the Rev. Ralph Mansfield and others of the 1821 *Australian Magazine*. The name of the pioneering Sydney editor and printer, George Howe, also appears on the first issue of the *Australian Magazine*, though he died before it was offered for sale. The remaining issues were printed by his son Robert, an ardent Methodist who was only too happy to assist in this educational and uplifting enterprise. So, unlike many later journal editors, Mansfield had no problems with his printers. Nor, it appears, was there any lack of readers and buyers. On 13 October 1821, Mansfield wrote to his brother Archibald that the *Magazine*'s 'sale is very good, and we hope it will be a means of intellectual, moral, and spiritual improvement.'[4]

The full title of Mansfield's journal was *The Australian Magazine; or, Compendium of Religious, Literary, and Miscellaneous Intelligence.* Its prospectus spoke of the 'progressive advancement in literary Taste and Genius' apparent in New South Wales since first settlement. This magazine was to ensure still further progress by providing information on important topics from the Mother Country, defending the vital principles of Christianity, and providing an outlet for local writers. Though later journals differed widely in their aims and intended audiences, most would have endorsed Mansfield's third aim to the full. Like most general magazines of the first half of the century, the *Australian Magazine* banned discussion of political and controversial questions, seen as too divisive in a colony where many other divisions already existed. Its main topics were to be biography, especially of eminent and pious men 'whose example may be safely exhibited for imitation,' theology, philosophy, particularly if it demonstrated the wisdom and grandeur of the Creator, miscellaneous, obituaries, religious intelligence, and poetry.

In the preface to the magazine's first volume, its proprietors were able to congratulate themselves on having carried out their initial aims to the letter, 'though some, we are aware, object to our Magazine, that it wears too grave and religious an aspect.' A glance through the first volume shows this complaint to have been well founded. In the first number alone one finds articles on 'Life of the Eminent Missionary Swartz,' 'The Truth, Importance and Design of Revelation,' and 'Sixteenth Anniversary of the British and Foreign Bible Society.' There was little of what would be called 'literature' in the modern sense of the term, apart from a few verses, an occasional review, and, in the issue for November 1821, a short story, 'A Tale of Vavoo.' Nearly all of the contents, with the exception of one poem and a few brief articles, were reprinted from overseas sources. In one of the exceptions, an article on 'Emigration' in the September 1821 issue, Mansfield spoke of the difficulties of producing a journal in a region so remote from 'the grand emporium of Literature, the British Capital,' especially at a time when shipping was irregular and voyages lengthy. Yet it was not lack of material, or subscribers, the usual reasons for the very high casualty rate of nineteenth-century Australian journals, which caused the *Australian Magazine* to close after fourteen issues. Despite its impeccable aims and highly serious content, the London Wesleyan Committee thought running a magazine not an appropriate missionary endeavour and ordered its closure.

Unlike the *Australian Magazine* of 1821, its 1899 namesake had no interest in theology or philosophy. It aimed to promote literature, in the narrower sense of that term, and art, and printed only original contributions by Australian authors and illustrators. Its editors were professional literary men, R.F. Irvine and Arthur Jose, who had varied careers as school and university teachers, journalists, and writers. Sidney Long, D.H. Souter, and George Lambert were equally professional art editors. Most of the magazine's seventy-two pages were devoted to original fiction, both short and serialized, poetry, literary articles, and lavishly illustrated accounts of local artists and exhibitions. The poet and academic Christopher Brennan contributed poetry and literary criticism; other literary contributors were Lillian Turner, Arthur Adams, and Roderic Quinn. There were also some less highbrow items such as 'Golf notes' and theatre reviews and gossip. As well as being much more original and, to a modern eye, much more lively and interesting than its 1821 namesake, the 1899 *Australian Magazine* was also considerably cheaper. It offered seventy-two pages of print and pictures for 9d. In 1821 readers had been charged 1s. 3d. for thirty-two illustrated pages. In July 1899 the price was lowered even further, to 6d., a fatal sign of a journal in difficulties. New, more popular features – 'Music notes,' 'Women's chat' – were introduced in the next number, besides another attempt to boost circulation with prize competitions. All to no avail; the magazine closed after the following number, its sixth. If like the 1821 *Australian Magazine* in nothing else, the 1899 version was like it in avoiding politics and in appealing to too narrow a section of the still limited Australian reading public. The 1821 *Australian Magazine* had been too serious and religious; the 1899 was too literary and arty.

Two important differences between the *Australian Magazine*s of 1821 and 1899 point to some of the major changes in Australian journalism in the course of the nineteenth century. Vast improvements in printing technology had not only made magazines much cheaper in 1899 than in 1821 but also allowed them, by the end of the century, to be lavishly illustrated. Another major difference was the replacement of reprinted material by original contributions. For Mansfield, and many other early editors, there was little choice; it was either reprint, or write most of the magazine's contents oneself. For some, however, it was an ideological matter. What was the best method of cultivating Australian 'taste and genius'? Was this best done by printing local contributions, even if they fell short of the standards prevailing in London? Or should one begin by reprinting the best material available, since, as William à Beckett, editor of the *Sydney Literary News* (1837–8), put it, 'a taste must be first established for the literary offspring of others, before genius can be aroused to the desire of creating for itself'?[5]

Such debates have been a continual part of Australian cultural life, with occasional changes in site but not in terms. As late as the 1940s, for example, Tyrone Guthrie argued that Australian drama could best be helped not by the establishment of a National Theatre but by importing more English companies and sending Australian actors to train in London.[6] Australian literary editors still sometimes reprint book reviews from English and American journals; syndicated material appears in most newspapers and magazines. But, by the end of the nineteenth century, it was accepted that most of the material printed in Australian journals would be original and local. 'Australian' now meant a magazine written by Australians as well as one intended to be read by them. Perhaps, in another hundred years, a similar change may have occurred in Australian television.

Broadly, then, during the nineteenth century, Australian journals changed in several ways: from amateurism to professionalism; from a high level of reprinted material to a high level of original; from an expensive, luxury product to a cheaper, everyday one; from unillustrated to illustrated. There was also a trend toward more frequent publication. In neither the 1820s nor the 1890s was monthly publication the most favoured form. Quarterly publication was slightly more favoured in the 1820s, no doubt because of shortages of paper and other materials and the expense and difficulty of printing in early Sydney and Hobart. By the end of the century, weekly journals were markedly more popular, as shown in table 1:1 below. The two *Australian Magazines*, both produced in Sydney, also do not reflect changes in place of publication. From the mid-century onwards (that is, after the gold rushes), Melbourne was very much the centre of Australian journalism. Despite Sydney's

TABLE 1:1
Frequency

	Daily	Weekly	Fortnightly	Monthly	Quarterly	Irregular
1820s	–	1	–	2	3	1
1830s	–	2	–	7	–	–
1840s	–	22	–	10	3	2
1850s	–	28	3	30	3	–
1860s	3	29	4	15	–	2
1870s	2	32	–	21	3	2
1880s	4	42	6	26	3	2
1890s	1	47	3	31	4	2
Totals	10	203	16	142	19	11

TABLE 1:2
Place of publication

	Sydney	Melbourne	Adelaide	Hobart	Perth	Brisbane	Other
1820s	11	–	–	2	–	–	–
1830s	9	–	–	7	–	–	–
1840s	29	3	7	4	2	–	1
1850s	24	34	4	3	1	–	4
1860s	9	29	10	4	2	1	3
1870s	18	23	15	3	–	2	1
1880s	31	45	4	–	2	5	5
1890s	24	50	6	2	2	5	5
Totals	155	184	46	25	9	13	19

Note: These two tables are based on lists in Lurline Stuart, *Nineteenth-Century Australian Periodicals* (1979).

head start with forty-nine pre-1850 publications to Melbourne's three, more nineteenth-century Australian journals were produced in Melbourne than in any other centre. There is a marked falling off after the two main cities, though Adelaide managed forty-six journals and Hobart twenty-five, more than half of them in the pre-1850 period, the time of Tasmania's cultural pre-eminence. The statistics are shown in table 1:2; note that the *Sun* (1888–1903) has been classed as a Melbourne publication because more issues were published there.

Classification of journals in terms of frequency and place of publication is relatively straightforward, though some changed from weekly to monthly publication or vice versa and one had a joint Sydney and Melbourne imprint. Other types of classification are more problematic. The one adopted here involves an initial distinction between whether a journal appears to be aiming for a general readership or appealing to a distinct section or group. Both the *Australian Magazine*s of 1821 and 1899 are, by this criterion, general magazines, even though, as mentioned earlier, they may now seem to have courted failure by appealing to too small a section of the population. Neither, however, made a direct appeal to a special-interest group, such as a sect or club, or concentrated on one particular activity, such as sport or drama. Most of the journals to appear in Australia before 1850 were of this general variety. As the century progressed, increasing numbers of specialized publications appeared, a tendency which has, of course, continued in this century. Now, general magazines are very much in the minority, their place in the entertainment and information sections of the media having been filled by television. Because of their relatively greater importance in the nineteenth century, however, this chapter will concentrate on general magazines.

Quarterlies

As already mentioned, most of the journals of the 1820s appeared quarterly. This frequency of publication, associated in Britain with highbrow reviews like the *Edinburgh* and the *Quarterly*, became increasingly rarer in later decades. Like the *Australian Magazine* of 1821, many of the early quarterlies were projected or produced by clergymen. In July 1826, Rev. John McGarvie recorded a meeting of various Wesleyan and Presbyterian ministers: 'At Rev. Mr Horton's, Wesleyan Mint. Mr Mansfield commenced a long oration on the utility of a Mag. or Review, proposed to commence it and offered the Editorship to Dr Lang when in fact they could do nothing.'[7] One of the reasons for this impotence was announced in a 'Notice' appended to Lang's collection of poems, *Aurora Australia* (1826), which informed the public of the delay in the publication of the *Australian Magazine or Quarterly Journal of Literature, Science, Philosophy, Agriculture, Morals, and Religion* 'from the want of Paper of the requisite size and quality.' Clearly, a large size would have been required to fit in the title. At much the same time, another quarterly, the *Australian Journal*, was advertised as about to appear 'under the superintendence of the Rev. W. Walker.' Prospectuses for other quarterlies had been issued in 1824 and 1825 but apparently did not attract sufficient subscribers.[8]

In 1827 a quarterly finally managed to attract the two hundred subscribers who seem to have been the minimum required to cover costs. This, the second Australian journal to appear, had an unusually brief, and modern-sounding, title, the *South-Asian Register*. It also seems not to have been edited by a clergyman. The editor was said to be Dr Roger Oldfield, but, according to the *Sydney Gazette* of 26 May 1828, this was a pseudonym. Though still predominantly serious, the *Register*'s articles were more local and original than the *Australian Magazine*'s. There were discussions of Aboriginal language and of theatre in Sydney, a historical account of 'New Holland,' and reviews of several recent local publications, besides selected items from English books and journals. A similar array of topics can be found in the single issue of the *Blossom* (1828), the first journal to have an Australian-born editor. John Walker Fulton was the son of the Rev. Henry Fulton, who had been transported for seditious practices. Perhaps for this reason, Fulton did not follow the usual gentlemanly practice of refraining from comment on local politics. Like the other editors, however, he saw literature as having a beneficial influence on the moral state of colonial society.

So, inevitably, did the Rev. C.P.N. Wilton, editor of the *Australian Quarterly Journal of Theology, Literature and Science* (1828). Again, to a modern eye, his journal is more notable for its theology and science than for its literary qualities. A reviewer in a contemporary Tasmanian publication, Murray's *Austral-Asian Review* for August 1828, succinctly summarized the *Quarterly Journal* as 'staid, didactic, and ... highly respectable.'

Very few general quarterlies were attempted in Australia during the remainder of the century. The *Australasian*, which ran for four issues in 1850–1, is best summed up by its lengthy subtitle, 'A quarterly reprint of articles selected from the periodicals of the United Kingdom; with original contributions chiefly on subjects of colonial interest.' There was no successor until 1876 and the commencement of the best-known nineteenth-century Australian quarterly, the *Melbourne Review*. The latter's opening address, 'To Our Readers,' blamed the failure of numerous monthly magazines attempted in Australia over the past fifty years on their over-concentration on fiction and lighter literature, which could be obtained better and cheaper from England, and on their 'practice of dealing too exclusively with local topics of no intrinsic interest.' Like its quarterly predecessors of the 1820s, the *Review* would instead concentrate on 'subjects of a more solid character and of more permanent interest,' such as philosophy, theology, science, and politics. Its proprietors were described as 'a group of literary gentlemen.'

Control of the higher reaches of Australian culture had now passed from the clergy to the businessman and academic. The banker and littérateur Henry Gyles Turner was one of the founders of the *Review* and remained an editor during the ten years of its existence. He had also been associated with several of the short-lived monthlies of the earlier decades such as the *Journal of Australia* (1856) and the *Australian Monthly Magazine* (1856–70). His extensive literary contacts, together with those of fellow editors like Alexander Sutherland and A.P. Martin, enabled the *Melbourne Review* to attract lengthy, erudite articles from many well-known writers and intellectuals. Regular contributors included the novelist and political reformer Catherine Helen Spence, the politician Charles Gavan Duffy, the scientist the Rev. Julian Tennison Woods, and the classicist Professor H.A. Strong. One finds reviews of Herbert Spencer's *The Principles of Sociology* (1877) and articles on 'Old Testament difficulties,' 'Money in its relation to the state,' and 'The morals of politics.' Local subjects were not neglected. Besides dealing with such perennial journal topics as Aboriginals, Australian history and literature, and the press, contributors discussed 'Political parties in Victoria,' 'The land question in New Zealand and in Australia,' and even 'Colonial beer.' There were, of course, also numerous reviews of local publications.

Some insights into the still largely unresearched area of the economics of journal and newspaper publication in nineteenth-century Australia are provided by an exchange of letters between Turner and George Robertson, the Melbourne bookseller who published the *Review* during its final seven years. On 6 October 1885, just after what was to be the final number of the *Review* had appeared, Turner wrote to Robertson about its future.[9] He began by correctly stating that the *Review* had maintained a high standard despite not paying contributors:

We feel however if it is to go on and progress towards being recognised as a high class medium of cultivated thought it wants some infusion of the business element of push that would necessarily be associated with it if it were worked from motives of profit. Personally I cannot undertake to do anything on those lines; it would be inconsistent with my official position, and as my income is more than sufficient for all my wants I lack the ordinary stimulant.

But while I am willing to continue the editorial duties from love of the work I desire its financial success for two reasons. Firstly I should like to be able to secure occasionally the co-operation of professional litterateurs whose articles would be worth paying for alike for their intrinsic value and from the collateral advantages of their press connection – and secondly I could secure the voluntary contributions of able men if I could assure them a wider publicity and a quad-rupled circulation.

If you consider it worth while to make the venture a business success I am certain that a good canvasser could work up a list of nearly 1000 subscribers and a dozen pages of advertisements. I will not quote the Victorian Review against it, because now that the support of the Henty's is withdrawn I expect to see that collapse – but 'Once a Month' which is largely made up of copied matter and English reprints has a sale of 5000 to 6000 and about 25 pages of advertisements. Even the Queensland Review, the same price and about the same size as the Melbourne but disgracefully printed and most carelessly edited, has 25 pages of advertisements and claims to have 2000 subscribers.

With the largely increased population of the colonies, and the general spread of culture and intelligence and wealth I believe we have not now as many subscribers as we had at its inception ten years ago. You may say perhaps that this is due to the falling away from the high standard we set up at starting but on looking through the columns I do not think we are answerable to the charges. It is true that in the early days I induced a number of prominent men to write for it who would now think it was hiding their light under a bushel to confide their thoughts to such a small if select circle of readers.

One particular point of interest here is the information on the circulation of rival journals and on the practice of canvassing for subscribers and advertisers. One assumes from Turner's letter that nothing of this sort had been attempted for the 'gentlemanly' and 'amateur' *Melbourne Review*. Nevertheless it had a much longer run than any of the other journals mentioned by Turner. The *Victorian Review* was, indeed, to end its run of just over seven years in February 1886; *Once a Month* lasted just two years, and only three issues of the *Queensland Review* were published. The other specially interesting piece of information is that most of the *Melbourne Review*'s contributors were unpaid. Turner ended his letter with the suggestion that one paid article be included in each future issue of the *Review*. Robertson's delightful letter in reply makes it clear that while the 'literary gentlemen' may have been listed as the *Review*'s proprietors, its financial backing was now coming from the publisher.

Since the receipt of yours of 6th inst. I have given its contents my most careful and deliberate consideration and I regret that I cannot see my way to any adequate return for the additional expenditure on the Melbourne Review that you advise. In the process of the suns all literary quarterlies must eventually die – they are out of harmony with the nineteenth century, and they will be impossible in the twentieth. Whither the 'Westminster' is going there also must go the 'Edinburgh' and the 'Quarterly' and if these things be done in the green tree of Britain, what can you expect in the dry (not to say burning) bush of Australia.

The loss on the publication is about £25 or £30 per ann. Perhaps I ought not to encounter this further, as I have a large family and no regular salary, but if you are willing to go on as hitherto, I, for my part, am willing for another year to sacrifice my family on the altar of 'littry enthoosm.' On the other hand, if the editors are weary in this sort of well doing, or if a more spirited publisher can be found let the review be discontinued or carried on just as they think best, without reference in either case to the lacerated feelings of Yours very truly Geo Robertson & Co.

Robertson's response to Turner's self-satisfied remarks about his income may have touched him on a sore spot – Turner and his wife were childless. At any rate, there were no more issues of the *Melbourne Review*.

Robertson's comment on generalist literary quarterlies like the *Westminster* as being 'out of harmony with the nineteenth century' is also of particular astuteness. Apart from the short-lived quarterlies of the 1820s and the *Melbourne Review*, only three other journals of this type were attempted in Australia. The *Austral Review* (1877–8) and the *Imperial Review* (1879–1919), both published in Melbourne, were edited, and largely written, by the same person. An editorial note in no. 2 (1879) 225 said, 'Some of our critics have rightly surmised that this periodical is a continuation of the Austral Review.' Turner dismissed the *Austral* as 'A worthless, scrappy, and generally inaccurate repository.'[10] Certainly, both it and the *Imperial* were very different from the *Melbourne Review*. Their articles were unsigned and generally short. Sixteen, for example, together with an 'Olio' collection of even shorter items, appeared in the 80 pages of the first issue of the *Imperial Review*. (By contrast, the *Melbourne Review* usually devoted 120 or more pages to eight or ten articles.) The range of material covered was also very wide. As well as such staple subjects as 'History of Victoria,' 'Our state,' and 'Aborigines,' the *Imperial* dealt with 'modern warfare,' 'Samoa,' and 'The Gas Act.' In many ways the shorter and more brightly written articles in the *Austral* and the *Imperial* are more to modern taste than the serious but heavier pieces in the *Melbourne Review*. The long run of the *Imperial* does, however, perhaps owe more to its unknown editor's financial independence than to his ability to attract subscribers. A brief editorial in the first issue advised

Contributors will be paid for, as much as they are worth, but we don't want any sent in. Our style will be to pick the writer, and give him his money, to turn out what we want. We are not in a hurry with this review, and need not stop for want of cash.

The progressive reductions in the price of the *Imperial*, from 2s. 6d. in 1879 to 9d in 1919, while in keeping with the general reduction in journal prices over this period, also argue for a proprietor who, unlike George Robertson, did not have to worry about a large and hungry family.

The only Sydney quarterly of this later period, the *Sydney Quarterly Magazine* (1883–92), managed a fairly respectable run of nine years. Like many earlier journals, it deplored the slow progress of literature in Australia and saw its chief purpose as the encouragement of a distinctively Australian literature:

It is our intention to leave upon record another attempt to arouse young Australians from their lethargic indifference, and to afford an opportunity for the display of any literary prowess which may be lying dormant or unrecognised in our midst.[11]

In style, its articles fell midway between the 'short and scrappy' *Austral* and *Imperial* reviews and the lengthy but ponderous *Melbourne*. Some poetry and fiction were included, as well as lighter essays like 'Human fossils' and sketches like 'A holiday ramble in Victoria.' Among the more prolific contributors was a woman, Frances Gillam Holden, who in 1888 was to be, along with Louisa Lawson, one of the founders of the 'Dawn' club, which agitated for female suffrage. She wrote on such topics as 'Body and soul,' 'Petticoat government in theory and practice,' and 'Institute reform.'

Early Monthly Magazines

If the 1820s were the only decade when generalist quarterlies were dominant in Australian journal production, the 1830s were the decade of the general monthly magazine. The 1821 *Australian Magazine* had, of course, appeared monthly, as had a Tasmanian periodical, Andrew Bent's *Colonial Advocate* (1828), actually a newspaper put out in magazine dress to subvert Governor Arthur's new newspaper licensing laws. The 1830s saw, however, one of the best Tasmanian magazines of the century, the *Hobart Town Magazine* (1833–4). Like many of this period, it was directed less at the undiscovered local genius than at friends and relatives at home. Its opening 'Address' announced an aspiration

to establish such a Miscellany, as shall not only prove highly acceptable to their fellow colonists but, at the same time, show their friends and well-wishers in 'Old England,' that Tasmania is not devoid of individuals who have the means, as well as the desire, of cultivating Literature as well as Land, and of devoting their best and liveliest energies to its interests and advancement.

If literature and other cultural pursuits were often seen at this time as a sort of moral cement, holding together the heterogeneous elements of colonial society, they were clearly also a form of display. Through their journals, their theatres, their schools of arts and debating societies, colonists could affirm their heritage of British civilization and demonstrate that it was not going to decline into barbarism at the antipodes.[12]

One of the major differences between quarterly and monthly general magazines was that the latter usually included some fiction while the former did not. The quantity and quality of this fiction would, particularly in later decades, be determined by the market at which a magazine was aimed. It would also often determine a magazine's success. Eighteen monthly issues of the *Hobart Town Magazine* were produced in 1833 and 1834. This may not seem like a long run, but it was one of the

longest achieved by a pre-1850 journal. The *Magazine* published a great
deal of original fiction, mostly of a much higher quality than usual at this
period. Most of it appears to have been written by one of the editors,
Thomas Richards.[13] If modern journal editors still have some of the problems of earlier ones, such as containing costs and attracting subscribers, at least they usually don't have to write most of their magazine's
material as well. As Marcus Clarke was later to complain in 'On the
Pleasures of Editorship':

> It began all right. The screw was drawn with refreshing regularity and the MSS
> were plentiful ... But by and by the contributors fell off. One went melancholy
> mad, and another took to the city missionary line of business. He said it paid him
> better than comic writing. I had to do all the MSS myself, and for some weeks
> used to write about five pages weekly of brilliant satire.
>
> The Proud Proprietor I believe thought that I had several thousand yards of
> that article coiled away inside me, and had only to pull thirty feet or so out, and
> cut it off.[14]

Something similar appears to have happened with the *Hobart Town Magazine*. As Richards was forced to write more and more of its material
himself, standards dropped and so, it seems, did subscribers.

The *Hobart Town Magazine* had been deliberately directed at all classes
of readers: 'from the very highest personage in the colony to the low-
liest,' to 'our fair and feminine readers,' and to 'the young of both sexes,'
to quote from its opening Address. It can therefore be considered as the
first of the 'family' journals which were to become prevalent after 1850.
The other Tasmanian monthly of the 1830s was more in the heavier,
quarterly mould. James Ross, editor of the four numbers of the *Van
Diemen's Land Monthly Magazine* published in the second half of 1835,
was one of the leading lights of the Hobart Town Mechanic's Institute,
and useful knowledge rather than family entertainment was the keynote
of his journal.

This was also true of the Rev. Ralph Mansfield's second attempt at a
magazine, the *New South Wales Magazine*, which ran for eight months.
Unlike his previous venture, the emphasis now was on local rather than
religious information, but the general effect was still, as the *Australian*
newspaper observed on 21 October 1833, decidedly inferior to the *Hobart Town Magazine*. Earlier in 1833, the explorer John Lhotsky had
proposed a Sunday newspaper to be called the *Australian Minerva*. He
decided instead to join forces with Mansfield, becoming editor of the

Natural History section of the *New South Wales Magazine*. After its failure, he brought out five numbers of his *Illustrations of the Present State and Future Prospects of the Colony of New South Wales by an Impartial Observer* (1835–6). It was distinguished by strongly political and polemical articles and was also apparently the first Australian journal to be illustrated, though both the *Hobart Town* and *New South Wales* magazines had had illustrated frontispieces. The two remaining Sydney monthlies of this decade, *Tegg's Monthly* (1836) and the *Australian Magazine* (1838), aimed to entertain as well as instruct. Each included, as contemporary reviewers acknowledged, a good variety of material. The *Australian Magazine*, like the *Blossom* before it, also made a particular appeal to local patriotism, stressing that 'the most arduous part ... was written by the *Sons of Australia*.' Nevertheless, both magazines survived only a few months.

Monthly Magazines of the 1840s

If quarterlies had given way to monthlies in the 1830s, the 1840s saw the rise of the weekly journal, which, apart from a slight hiccup in the 1850s, was to be the dominant form for the remainder of the century. Most of these new weeklies appeared in Sydney. Indeed, the 1840s saw a four-fold increase in the number of new journals begun in Sydney, a number that was not to be surpassed, and then only slightly, till the 1880s. This would appear to provide further support for George Nadel's theory that the 1840s were in many ways a parallel decade to the 1890s.[15] There was a flowering of literature and national feeling that was then swamped by the massive influx of new settlers following the discovery of gold in 1851. It would be another fifty years before Australia began to seem like home again to a majority of the population.

The 1840s are also notable for the spread in journal production away from the two earliest centres of Sydney and Hobart. Two general monthlies were published in Sydney, both in 1843 before the severe depression of this decade struck. *Arden's Sydney Magazine* ran for only two issues before succumbing to editorial fatigue – it had not been Arden's magazine in name only as Tegg's had been – and the effects of the depression. The latter also appears to have killed off the 1843 *New South Wales Magazine* after eleven issues. In comparison with its 1833 namesake, and earlier New South Wales magazines in general, it had been very well received, praised as 'a clever and well conducted miscellany, containing many useful and ably written articles.'[16]

The 1843 depression, perhaps, also shortened the life of Tasmania's one monthly of this decade, *The South Briton; or Tasmanian Literary Journal* (1843), which appeared only twice. It was edited by the playwright David Burn and, as its subtitle suggests, was more exclusively literary than any of the earlier journals. This degree of specialization may have been another factor in its rapid demise. If magazines needed some fiction to be truly popular, in early Australia they also seem to have needed some politics as well. Achieving the right balance was difficult and, as we have seen, few editors could sustain it for long.

The most successful at doing so for general monthlies of the 1840s were the editors of the *South Australian Magazine*, which ran from July 1841 to November 1843. South Australia, of course, prided itself on having a higher, more intellectual and cultured class of settler. As noted above, they had established a newspaper and a literary society before leaving England. These advantages were acknowledged in the *Magazine*'s opening address, which also, like most others in the earlier nineteenth century, commented on the special utility of literature for colonial societies:

Among the many advantages eagerly to be sought by a young and rising community like this, no one, perhaps, deserves to be ranked higher, than a steady pursuit of knowledge, or an ardent cultivation of true literary taste.

For the acquisition of these, no colony, perhaps, in the fourth year of its existence, ever before presented such facilities as South Australia, whether it be considered in reference to the amount of active literary talent which it possesses, or whether it be considered in reference to that rich and endless variety of materials upon which it is desirable to see that talent at once set to work.

For once, the high aims and principles of a magazine's opening address were borne out by its practice. Contemporary reviewers were unanimous in their praise of the *South Australian Magazine*, those from other colonies lamenting the absence of a similar journal there. William Duncan of the *Australian Chronicle*, a Sydney newspaper, wrote on 8 January 1842, of the first five numbers,

We opened this periodical with no slight feeling of shame at the reflection that a small community of yesterday should be enabled to send forth an elegant, monthly magazine, while this extensive colony, is to this hour all but a blank in the republic of letters ... The South Australian Magazine is in point of typography not inferior to any of the English monthlies, and many of the articles are extremely well written.

Despite its excellence, however, the *South Australian Magazine* could not sustain a paying circulation. The *Adelaide Magazine* of 1845, a much more exclusively literary monthly, managed only two issues. Wesleyan missionaries had the honour of founding the first magazine in Western Australia as well as in Australia. A religious monthly circulated briefly in 1842, the *Record, or Pastorals for Guildford*. Six issues of the *Western Australian Monthly Magazine* appeared from October 1843. As with the earlier Wesleyan *Australian Magazine*, there was a strong emphasis on religious matters, and nearly all material was reprinted from overseas journals. The two Victorian monthlies of the 1840s were much more interesting affairs, if not much longer lived, reflecting the amazingly rapid growth of literary culture in the new colony, even before the discovery of gold.[17] The four issues of the *Port Phillip Magazine*, founded in 1843, show the usual mix of original and select material, fiction and non-fiction, and the usual belief that local politics should be avoided. So do the two issues of the *Australia Felix Monthly Magazine* (1849), the first to appear from a provincial centre, being jointly published in Melbourne and Geelong.

Monthly Magazines of the 1850s

There was a strong surge of monthlies in the 1850s, with almost as many appearing as in the last decade of the century. Most of these were printed in Melbourne and were, of course, a consequence of the enormous increase in population produced by the gold rushes. Though several of the general 'literature-and-science-but-no-politics' monthlies from the earlier period continued to appear, one sees the beginnings of an appeal to different groups, an acknowledgment that gentlemen were not the only people who read monthly magazines. James Bonwick published eight numbers of his *Australian Gold-Diggers' Monthly Magazine* (1852–3), from a 'desire to interest and elevate the diggers as a class.'[18] As its subtitle, 'Colonial family visitor,' indicates, however, Bonwick also wished to appeal to the diggers' wives and children, and his was one of the first Australian magazines to run women's and children's sections. As their titles suggest, the wider, family readership was also the target of the *Australian Family Journal* (1855) and the *Australian Home Companion* (1856–7). Others specialized in selected overseas material, such as *Spirit of the Age* (1855–6) and *Crouch's Epitome of News* (1858–60), while the *Newsletter of Australia* (1856–62), subtitled 'A narrative of events, or a letter to send to friends,' did the reverse, summarizing local news and affairs, with a space left for personal messages. All, in their various ways, attempted to cater for the particular needs of the vast influx of new settlers.

Among the journals of the older style, and often with the old names, one finds another *Australian Magazine* (1859), begun in full awareness of the fates of its predecessors and having an even shorter life.[19] The *Melbourne Monthly Magazine* (1855) and *Victorian Monthly* (1859) fared little better, despite having such eminent contributors as David Blair, R.H. Horne, and William à Beckett. Nor did Adelaide's the *Wanderer* (1853) or Hobart's *Tasmanian Monthly* (1853). The *Tasmanian Athenaeum* (1853–4) was slightly more up-market, publishing no fiction and including reports of the meetings of learned societies and meteorological and astronomical tables. In the preface of their first, and only, volume, its editors bemoaned the technical difficulties they had encountered:

The deficient means of printers, the conflicting interests of publishers, exist here to an extent not to be conceived by authors at home. One sheet had to be struck off ere another was set up; hence a complete revisal of even a single number was impracticable. Neither could any illustrations deserving of the name be procured. This to scientific articles was an insurmountable difficulty. But the editors console themselves that the obstacles they met are by no means peculiar to their undertaking – they need not wonder at the absence of engravers in a colony which possesses not at the present time capacity sufficient to manufacture a simple flower-pot.

They also bemoan the apathy of the very class of readers they had hoped to attract and enlighten – those born in the colony – without stopping to wonder whether the latter had 2s. 6d. to spare each month for this worthy cause. All the more enterprising ones had probably left for Victoria.

The *Month*, a literary and critical journal printed in Sydney, also reported on the doings of local learned societies and, at least initially, did not print fiction. Yet it was one of the most successful general literary journals of this period, in terms of its run of eighteen months, its apparent high circulation and the standard of many of its articles, which still make interesting reading today. A feature of early numbers, edited by the visiting English writer Frank Fowler, was 'The World of Books,' a regular survey of contemporary literature that was probably not bettered until the *Bulletin*'s 'Red Page' of the 1890s.

Monthly Magazines of the 1860s

Only half as many new monthlies were attempted in the 1860s. Few, apart from the *Australasian Monthly Review* (1866) and the *Australian*

Monthly Magazine (1864–70), tried to be broadly representative in the style of past decades. That they had now decidedly moved away from the old days of journals edited by clergymen and lawyers for the moral and intellectual benefit of fellow colonists is clear from the *Australasian Monthly*'s opening editorial. Instead of the usual pious platitudes about the value of literature and of this new journal in particular, G.A. Walstab gave a forthright statement of the economics of magazine publishing:

No one in the nineteenth century would suspect another of such disinterestedness as would be evinced by the carrying on of non-paying speculation of any nature; and literature is quite as much a speculation as anything else. There is no special current coin among literary men. Butchers and bakers do not feed them; tailors and shoemakers do not clothe them, gratis. The proprietors of a magazine have, if they wish good writing, to pay good authors, and to pay them well; and the public if they want good reading, must not object to pay the proprietors. All that can be done will be done to make 'The Australasian Monthly Review' a production creditable to the country; but its continuance beyond a certain time must depend upon the public. It will be for the reading men of Australia to show that they can appreciate a 'good thing', even though it come out of Galilee, instead of being imported from home.

Unfortunately, the 'reading men of Australia' were clearly not yet ready to part with 2s. 6d. for seventy-six pages of local reading; the *Review* closed after two issues. The *Australian Monthly*, later the *Colonial Monthly*, was, at 1s., considerably cheaper and could also boast such clever and distinguished writers as Marcus Clarke, Adam Lindsay Gordon, Henry Kendall, James Smith, J.E. Neild, and J.J. Shillinglaw. Its much longer run suggests that the Australian reading public would support the local product if offered value for money. The *Australian Monthly* was one of the best literary magazines of nineteenth-century Australia and one of the longest lasting of those modelled on semi-popular English monthlies like the *Cornhill Magazine*. Most other general monthlies of this decade did not survive to a second issue.

Monthly Magazines of the 1870s and 1880s

The 1870s also saw one outstanding general monthly, the *Victorian Review* (1879–86), which had many contributors in common with the *Australian Monthly*, though its tone was more serious and its articles usually more weighty. Its 'Prefatory note' opened with the usual high-sounding sentiments:

It is felt by many of the leading men in Melbourne that there is wanting in Victoria a first-class Magazine which shall reflect its highest culture and express the opinions of the best thinkers of the day.

Elsewhere in this note, however, there are many signs of changes in attitudes toward the appropriate attributes and contents of a general monthly magazine. The *Victorian Review* 'shall be distinctively Australian in tone, while eclectic in character, patriotic in aim, and progressive in policy.' The old taboos against discussion of religion, politics, and any other controversial topics were also firmly renounced. It was to be allowed, 'provided such controversies are conducted with moderation and mutual courtesy, and a grateful consideration for the feelings and convictions of opponents.' Accordingly, the first issue of the *Review* printed Marcus Clarke's attack on conventional religion, 'Civilization without Delusion,' as well as several articles on local political issues. The *Victorian Review* also differed from earlier, more serious, journals by printing fiction. Unlike its articles, this was usually imported from England.

Many of the contributors to the *Victorian Review* also published in a Sydney journal, *Australian: A Monthly Magazine* (1878–81), which suggests that journals were now less parochial, finally deserving the continental title they had claimed for most of the century. The *Australian* was, however, more like its near-namesake the *Australian Monthly Magazine* than the *Victorian Review*, including fewer serious and controversial articles and much more original short and serialized fiction. The *Sydney Magazine* (1878) adopted a similar format, but was more of a 'one-man-band' type of journal and, lacking variety and well-known contributors, survived only the usual few months. The second *Sydney University Magazine* (1878–9) should perhaps also be included here, since, despite its name, it had no close ties with the university and was very much a general monthly in its mix of essays, fiction, and poetry.[20] Few journals were attempted in Tasmania after the 1860s, a sign of the island's general economic decline following the cessation of transportation and the gold rush exodus. One of the brave few had the unusual title *Quadrilateral: Moral, Social, Scientific and Artistic*, a foursome which, though not usually spelt out as here, had by this period tended to replace the older trio of 'Literature, science and art.' *Quadrilateral* offered the usual mix of non-fiction, fiction, and poetry and survived for ten numbers in 1874.

The 1880s saw something of a boom in monthly magazines, with the 1888 centenary of white settlement in particular inspiring several new ventures. These, however, soon went the way of their predecessors: the *Australian Argosy* (1888) lasted for one issue; the *Australian Century* (1888–9) produced two volumes, and the most ambitious of all, the *Centennial Magazine* (1888–90), survived just over two years. Even more than earlier journals, the *Centennial* attempted to break out of colonial boundaries, as signified by its joint Sydney/Melbourne imprint during 1889 (earlier issues had a Melbourne imprint; later ones were printed in Sydney). Its contributors included Louisa Meredith from Tasmania and South Australia's Catherine Helen Spence as well as many other leading writers of the 1870–1900 period: Melbourne's David Blair, James Smith, and Alexander Sutherland; Sydney's Rolf Boldrewood, G.B. Barton, and Arthur Jose. The *Centennial* was also, like most of the more expensive monthlies from the 1880s onwards, illustrated, in its case by the leading lights of the new Heidelberg School of Australian impressionists – Charles Conder, Frederick McCubbin, Tom Roberts, and Arthur Streeton.

Though the 1880s were the nadir of Hobart as a centre of journal publication and also saw a rapid decline in the number of new titles attempted in Adelaide, they marked the beginning of Brisbane as a literary centre. The *Queensland Review* (1885–6) deserved most of what H.G. Turner said of it (that it was 'disgracefully printed and most carelessly edited') and never managed to appear monthly, only three issues being published in just over twelve months. (This, however, seems to have been the fault of the printer rather than the editor. In no. 2 of the *Queensland Review*, dated September/October 1885 but not published until May 1886, the editor noted that the issue had been three months with the printer and even then was full of errors.) If the *Review*'s subtitle, 'A Literary and Political Monthly for Queensland and all the Colonies,' reflected the newer school of non-parochial and polemical monthlies, its motto was still very much of the old: 'A nation is known by its literature, and the energy of its sons.'

Monthly Magazines of the 1890s

While the number of new monthly magazines attempted each decade rose slowly during the century, there was also a progressive trend toward specialization. Only half a dozen of the twenty-six new titles begun in the 1890s could be described as general journals. The most interesting of these are the *Australasian Critic* (1890–1), *Cosmos* (1894–9), and *Review of Reviews for Australia* (1892–1934). One of their most notable features is their cheapness. Whereas monthlies and quarterlies of the 1820s and the 1830s had cost five shillings, those of the 1850s and 1860s two shillings, and those of the 1870s and 1880s one shilling, the standard price was now sixpence.

Demarcation disputes could again arise with the *Australasian Critic*, since, with two university professors as general editors and others as editors of specific departments, it was obviously aimed at a fairly specialized, highbrow readership. Yet it was still a general magazine in the amount of material it attempted to cover: not just literature but also science, art, music, and drama. Its proprietors began with a murderously ambitious list of aims. There were to be articles relating to all the journal's areas of interest, besides reviews of new books in each of these areas and of art exhibitions and musical and dramatic performances. 'News and notes will be a strong feature, and a record will be kept of what is being done in these departments throughout Australasia and of what Australians are doing in them abroad.' The Science Department, accordingly, proposed to provide:

1. Diary of Meetings for the ensuing month.
2. Monthly lists of papers read at the meetings of the scientific societies of Australasia.
3. A monthly record of the progress of scientific work in the Australasian colonies.

It was, alas, impossible for the editors to maintain this flow of information – far more than had ever been attempted before, or since – beyond a few issues. The *Australasian Critic* commenced publication in October 1890; by May 1891 there were hardly any news items being printed and there was nothing at all on music and drama. When the final number appeared in September 1891 – there had, inevitably, been insufficient subscribers to sustain it any longer – Literature and Science were the only departments left. Nevertheless, the *Australasian Critic* was rightly singled out by H.M. Green in his chapter on magazines of the 1850–90 period: 'there is academicism at somewhere near its best, and Australia has had no other magazine superior in its kind.'[21] Nor, given the ever-increasing specialization of both academics and magazines during the twentieth century, is it ever likely to.

The 'Literary Notes' published in the *Australasian Critic* often contain very useful information on contemporary journals. In November 1890, of a proposed revival of the *Melbourne Review*, it was observed that 'If the proprietors want the new series to be successful, they should lower the price to a shilling,' confirming a resistance by buyers to higher prices deducible from the general lowering of magazine prices in the 1890s.

The same issue notes that the *Centennial Magazine*, which 'died of bad business management, combined with unskilful editing,' will perhaps be replaced by an Australian edition of either *Harper's* or the *Century*:

the monthly numbers will be printed in Australia from stereos, sent out from America, and each will contain, in addition to the American matter, at least 24 pages, printed here, of specially written Australian matter by the best colonial writers.

Though this particular proposal was not carried out, a highly successful journal of this type, *Review of Reviews for Australia* (1892–1934) ran, under various titles, for over forty years.

Despite its title, *Cosmos, an Illustrated Australian Magazine* (1894–9) began with this period's typical stress on nationalism and original contributions:

Does Australia realize the fact that with nearly 5,000,000 inhabitants, a national feeling growing up in spite of provincial demarcations, a distinctive mode of life and ever-increasing patriotic love for a starry banner yet to be unfurled, that it has no living productions of its own in the realms of magazine literature, beyond that of which this is the first number? Does it realize that of the vast field of fictional opportunity, the bush, the settlement and the township offer, scarcely an acre has been taken up? And does it realize that of the writers it has bred scarcely one but has been forced from its shores in search of a market for their creations? Even of those who remain true to their country and cling to the soil that is to them their motherland, how many of them but are compelled to send all their choicest productions away to amuse, instruct and entertain the readers of other lands because there are no means of reaching their own people otherwise? [22]

Written at a time when the Sydney *Bulletin* is usually seen as being close to its peak, this could be read as a mere piece of self-promotion. Alternatively, it could lead us to think again about the position of Australian writers during the 1890s. What markets were open to them? What were they paid in Australia and overseas? Were many of them forced to become expatriates in order to sell their work?

Unlike many earlier editors and proprietors, those connected with *Cosmos* were not content with fine rhetoric and noble sentiments. They realized that, by the end of the century, a successful general magazine needed 'no policy save the entertainment of its readers and ... no cause save that of an ever-increasing circulation.' Accordingly, a very broad range of topics was covered. There were articles on famous Australians, much local fiction and poetry, news and notes on drama, music, art, and sport, as well as an extensive 'Women's Department,' initially conducted by novelist Ethel Turner. Nor were those favourite circulation boosters, 'novelty competitions,' ignored. But the circulation refused to increase. In 'Our First Year,' printed in the August 1896 issue, the then editor, Annie Bright, acknowledged that survival had partly depended on many contributors giving their work gratis. Beginning with high hopes of helping Australian writers, *Cosmos* was, at least for a time, saved by them.

Weeklies, 1850–1900

As has already been noted, weekly magazines were, from the 1840s onwards, more often attempted than quarterlies and monthlies. The most successful nineteenth-century Australian journals were also predominantly weekly publications. Of the thirty-nine journals which survived for longer than twenty-five years, twenty-seven began as weeklies.[23] The remaining twelve all had special features which helped their longevity. Apart from the already mentioned *Imperial Review* and *Review of Reviews for Australia*, which had the advantage of secure financial backing, they were directed at particular sections of the market: *Melbourne Church of England Messenger* (1850–1910), the *Victorian Miscellany and Wesleyan Chronicle* (1894–) and the *Catholic Magazine* (1888–1920) at church members; the *Harbinger of Light* (1850–1956) at spiritualists; the *Australian Home Journal* (1894–) at women, the *Melbourne Journal* (1894–1927) at readers of light fiction; *Walch's Literary Intelligencer and General Advertiser* (1859–1915) and *George Robertson's Monthly Book Circular* (1861–89) at booksellers and book-buyers; the *Brisbane Worker* (1890–1974) at union members; and *Australian News for Home Readers*, later the *Illustrated Australian News* (1862–96), at English readers. All apart from the highly specialized *Walch's* and the much later established *Worker* and *Australian Home Journal*, also came from Victoria, the most heavily populated colony of the second half of the century. Three other journals, which began as weeklies but later became monthlies or fortnightlies, were also able to survive because of specialized appeal. The *Illustrated Sydney News* (1864–94) had the advantage of pictures, the *Australian Journal* (1865–1962) concentrated on popular, mostly original, fiction, and the *Hummer*, later the *Australian Worker* (1891–), was targeted at union members.

Of the remaining twenty-four long-lasting weeklies, four more were directed at special audiences: the Roman Catholic *Freeman's Journal* (1850–1942) and its Melbourne equivalent, the *Advocate* (1868–), the labour weekly the *Tocsin* (1897–1961), and, for the man on the land, the *Sydney Stock and Station Journal* (1888–1972). The other twenty all succeeded by combining features of the newspaper and the magazine. Indeed, particularly in the first half of the century, when most Australian newspapers printed some poetry and fiction fairly regularly, it is often difficult to decide whether a weekly publication should be classed as a newspaper or a magazine. Many titles appear both in Lurline Stuart's *Nineteenth Century Australian Periodicals* (1979) and *Newspapers in Australian Libraries: A Union List* (fourth edition, 1984–5).

Newspaper Weeklies

Half of the remaining twenty most popular journals were, in fact, weeklies associated with leading metropolitan daily newspapers. They were particularly directed at country readers to whom a daily newspaper, received days late, was an unnecessary luxury. Their magazine features, however, also made them attractive to city readers. Though individual titles offered different emphases, and the mix also changed from decade to decade, by the end of the century these weeklies normally included a summary of the week's news, an illustrated section (greatly extended when reproduction of photographs became possible), rural news and affairs, sections on sport, drama, mining, and commercial matters, women's and also often children's pages, serialized and other fiction and poetry. Because of their wide circulation and the financial backing of their parent papers, they were a far more important source of income for local writers than monthlies like *Cosmos*.

The earliest, the *Melbourne Leader* (1856–1957), associated with the *Age* newspaper, published work by Marcus Clarke and James Smith, its first editor. Clarke also published in the rival *Australasian* (1864–1957), issued by the *Argus*, which Smith also edited at one time. The *Australasian* gave particular emphasis to literature, and many leading local writers published there, including Rolf Boldrewood, Catherine Spence, 'Tasma,' Ada Cambridge, Louisa Meredith, and J.E. Neild, the theatre critic. A third Melbourne weekly, the *Weekly Times* (1869–), was initially associated with the *Daily Telegraph*, later with the *Herald*. After the *Australasian*, the best-known weekly was the *Sydney Mail* (1860–1938), published by the *Sydney Morning Herald* group. Though its literary material was not of the same quality as the *Australasian*'s, the *Mail* can claim the honour of serializing Boldrewood's *Robbery Under Arms* after its first chapters had been rejected by both the *Australasian* and the *Australian Town and Country Journal* (1870–1919), associated with the *Sydney Evening News*. Louisa Atkinson and Boldrewood also published there, besides many other notable writers, including Louis Becke and Ethel Turner. Long-lasting weeklies of this type also appeared in Brisbane and Adelaide during this period. Leading writers and journalists connected with the *Queenslander* (1866–1939), the weekly companion of the *Brisbane Courier*, included Mary Hannay Foott, Ernest Favenc, and W.H. Traill. The *Week* (1876–1905) was associated with the Brisbane *Telegraph*. Several novels by Catherine Helen Spence were originally serialized in the *Adelaide Observer* (1843–1931), which began as an independent journal but later became the weekly associated with the *South Australian Register*. A later rival was the *Adelaide Advertiser*'s *South Australian Chronicle* (1858–1975). Readers in Tasmania and Western Australia also supported successful weeklies in the *Tasmanian Mail* (1877–1935) and the *Western Mail* (1885–1955).

It is difficult to overestimate the importance of these long-lasting and widely circulating weeklies to Australian writers and so to Australian literature and culture generally. During the nineteenth century it was virtually impossible for writers to publish novels in Australia unless they were willing and able to bear the costs of their publication. Given the small size of the local market and the competition from imported books, they were more likely to lose money than gain it by self-publication. Serialization, particularly in the most popular weeklies, was the only reliable source of local income. If an Australian novel had been successful serialized it was also more likely to be taken up by an English publisher. All the leading Australian novelists – those at least who chose to remain in Australia rather than follow the market to England – took the path of local serialization and subsequent volume publication in England: Marcus Clarke, Rolf Boldrewood, Ada Cambridge, Catherine Spence. So, of course, did many of the second and lower ranks. Since little indexing has so far been carried out for nineteenth-century Australian journals, particularly the newspaper weeklies, many early novels, besides stories, essays, and poems, remain to be uncovered.[24]

Illustrated Weeklies

The earliest illustrated weekly, Sydney's *Heads of the People* (1847–8), was, like many of the later ones, clearly based on its English namesake, *Heads of the People: or, Portraits of the English* (1840–1), and highlighted, as it did, a portrait and essay on a local luminary. The portraits especially have been a great boon to later historians, as have the illustrations found in later magazines.

The *Illustrated Australian Magazine* (1850–2) appeared eight years after the first *Illustrated London News*. There were many later copies, the two most successful having already been discussed. Of the many copies of *Punch*, the first and most successful was *Melbourne Punch* (1855–1925). Thanks to Sydney's then smaller population, *Sydney Punch* (1864–88) took longer to get established, with two unsuccessful attempts in 1856 and 1857, and appears to have been killed off by the rise of the *Bulletin*. Local versions of *Punch* also appeared in Adelaide (1868–84), Queensland (1878–85), Tasmania (1866–8), and even, briefly, Ballarat (1867–70).[25]

Many other *Punch*-type weekly journals, featuring topical and local, especially political, satire and cartoons, along with more general humorous articles, jokes, and illustrations, appeared in Australia during the nineteenth century. Some of the more important were Marcus Clarke's *Humbug* (1869–70), *Touchstone* (1869–70), also from Melbourne and edited for a time by the poet Henry Kendall, and the longer-running Adelaide *Lantern* (1874–90). While some, like *Laughing Jackass* (1867–8) and the Sydney *Boomerang* (1877), adopted local names, they rarely attempted to disguise their parentage. *Boomerang*'s cover, for example, featured an Aborigine with Mr Punch features. It should be noted that there were three other nineteenth-century Australian journals with this title, published in Melbourne (1861), Brisbane (1887–92), and Melbourne (1894).

The Sydney *Bulletin*, Its Imitators and Predecessors

Though the American influence on Australia's most famous nineteenth-century journal, the Sydney *Bulletin* (1880–), should not be discounted, it is important to realize that the *Bulletin* carried on many of the features of earlier Australian journals. It combined topical news items and political comment with, at least initially, a heavy emphasis on sport, the theatre, and local gossip. Regular early columns were headed 'Dramatic and Musical Review,' 'Stage Gossip,' 'Sporting Notes,' 'Fun and Fancy,' 'The News in a Nutshell,' 'Personal Items,' and 'Brief Mention.' None of them was, in itself, new; the novelty was in the combination and in the verve with which the early *Bulletin* was conducted.[26]

The rapid success of the *Bulletin* is clearly indicated by the growth in its advertising pages. Begun as an eight-page folio on 31 January 1880, three months later it had about three of these pages devoted to ads. Regular features had to be omitted, so its size was increased to twelve pages. On 26 June, the editors announced that circulation had doubled, from five to ten thousand, and advertising support increased fourfold. By September 1880, the *Bulletin* had doubled its size to sixteen pages, about half of them given over to advertisements. All of this, it should be noted, happened in the first six months, without the features for which the *Bulletin* of the 1890s is renowned – the local fiction and poetry of Henry Lawson and A.B. 'Banjo' Paterson, the cartoons of 'Hop' and Phil May, the criticism of A.G. Stephens and the 'Red Page.'

The amazing success of the *Bulletin* naturally soon produced its imitators. The most obvious of these was the *Melbourne Bulletin* (1880–6) which, in its first issue for 15 October, outlined what it saw as the *Bulletin* formula:

This paper has been started with the object of supplying news in a condensed form for those who do not care, or have not the time, for heavy reading. Life is short, and so are our paragraphs. Crystallised information of every sort will fill out our columns. A few comments on current topics will occupy our first page, and we shall devote a large space to items for ladies, for at the present moment there is not a paper in Melbourne in which a woman can take any interest. The Church, Stage, Sport, fashionable and personal Topics will be well represented, and we shall eschew politics as far as possible. They are hammered out thin enough by our contemporaries. Our motto is 'brevity.'

The main differences between the Sydney *Bulletin* and the Melbourne one were, then, that the latter avoided politics and from the beginning included special features for women. The *Melbourne Bulletin* also attempted to cover a wider range of areas: the fourteen of its sixteen pages not devoted to advertisements were divided into nineteen different sections. On 22 October it printed extracts from the more favourable reviews it had received. Several papers noted the American influence, the *Daily Telegraph* commenting that it will be 'very acceptable to people who find newspapers generally rather heavy reading, and would prefer something more in the way of those pithy personal items, which are a prominent feature of the newspaper literature of the States.' There was, however, less agreement as to how far the *Melbourne Bulletin* had been influenced by, and resembled, the Sydney one. The *Bendigo Independent*, for example, congratulated the *Melbourne Bulletin* because it had 'about it none of the smart vulgarity of its Sydney brother and consequently may be read without anyone's sensibilities being shocked.'

Smartness and the ability to shock were, however, two of the things which, distinguishing the Sydney *Bulletin* from other weeklies of its day, clearly led to its success. This was recognized by other imitators such as Brisbane's *Street* (1897–8), which, like the *Bulletin*, was a folio with pink covers. Its subtitle was 'Verve, originality, modernity,' and some of its departments were headed 'Lies and libels' (on local affairs), 'Sports, swindles, etc.,' 'Giddy Gold,' and 'Mammon.' More successful journals in the *Bulletin* mode were Adelaide's *Critic* (1897–1924) and *Quiz: A Satirical, Social and Sporting Journal* (1889–1930). Both, as *Quiz*'s subtitle implies, followed the American, and early *Bulletin*, pattern of short paragraphs of news and comment, with a particular emphasis on politics, sport, the theatre, and local affairs. As its full title makes clear, this was also the pattern adopted by *Queensland Figaro: Titbits of Everyday about Everybody and Everything with a Peep at Society, Sport, and the Drama* (1883–1936). The *Tit-bits* formula alone was, however, not a recipe for success, as the three attempts at an *Australian Tit-bits*, Melbourne (1884–91), Melbourne (1887–94), and Sydney (1899–1900), demonstrate. (In 1886, the title of the first Melbourne publication became *Life, Fun, Fact and Fiction.*)

Clearly Australian audiences demanded rather more bite and scandal, offered by other successful weeklies like Melbourne's *Hawk* (1892–1931), with its Byronic motto to 'sketch the world exactly as it goes,' and, most notorious of all, Sydney's *Truth* (1890–1958). This was one of the first Australian journals to be published on Sundays, and, particularly under its second editor, John Norton, it had a heyday exposing the sexual, criminal, and political scandals of Sydney. Again, sensationalism alone did not make for a successful journal. An earlier Sydney *Truth* (1879–80), subtitled 'A fearless exposer of folly, vice and crime,' survived for only a few months. An even shorter career appears to have been the lot of another Sydney sensation sheet, the *Scorpion: Stinging, Spicy, Sensational* (1895). The only surviving issue featured articles on 'The Oscar Wildes of Sydney,' the Dean murder case, and 'Cronk betting shops,' together with stories entitled 'Married to his mother-in-law' and 'The parson and the widow.' This type of journal has a long history but one which suppression and censorship have made difficult to trace. The earliest Australian example appears to have been another Sydney weekly, the *Satirist and Sporting Chronicle* (1843).

Sporting Journals

As the last example indicates, sensation and sport usually went hand in hand in nineteenth-century journalism, forming, with politics and the theatre, the four most popular topics. Sporting newspapers and magazines also date from the Sydney of the 1840s, beginning with weeklies such as *Bell's Life in Sydney* (1845–70). This, like later *Bell's Life*s in Victoria (1857–68), Adelaide (1861–2), Tasmania (1859), and Western Australia (1896), was modelled on *Bell's Life in London and Sporting Chronicle* (1822–86). Though these journals gave detailed coverage of local sporting events, they also included much political and other local satire, humorous articles, cartoons, and theatrical reviews and gossip. There were also early attempts to establish sporting monthlies, such as the *New South Wales Sporting Magazine* (1848–9) and the *Australasian Sporting Magazine* (1850–1), but, lacking topicality, they could not survive. The longest-running nineteenth-century Australian sporting journal gloried in a number of unusual titles. Begun as *Dead Bird: A Journal Devoted to Sport and the Drama* (1889–91), it successively became *Bird of Freedom* (1891–6), and *Arrow: Sport and Play* (1896–1912) before finishing, more prosaically, as the *Saturday Referee and Arrow* (1912–16).

Women's Magazines

Though journals for women began to appear in Australia from the 1880s onwards, only the already mentioned *Australian Home Journal* continued for more than twenty-five years. The first woman to edit an Australian journal appears to have been Harriet Clisby, who from January to June 1857 edited a promotional journal for Pitman's shorthand, the *Southern Phonographic Harmonica*. Clisby is better known for the monthly magazine the *Interpreter* (1861) she later ran with Caroline Dexter. This is usually claimed to be the first Australian journal to be edited and owned by women. The earlier *Spectator: Journal of Literature and Art* (1858–9) was, however, edited by Cora Anna Weekes and owned by 'An association of ladies.' Neither of these journals was specifically directed at women readers, though both carried articles and features of special interest to them. The best known of the more specialized women's magazines which began appearing in the 1880s was Louisa Lawson's monthly the *Dawn: A Journal for Australian Women* (1888–1905). It had the distinction of employing women to produce the magazine as well as write and edit it, besides lasting much longer than earlier attempts run and edited by men, such as the *Australian Women's Magazine* (1882–4) and *Women's World* (1886–7).

Other Weekly Magazines

Of the nine long-lasting weeklies which were neither specialist nor associated with newspapers, only one attempted a specific appeal, as its subtitle indicated, to both men and women. This was Melbourne's *Table Talk* (1885–1939), the most successful of a line of more general weeklies which dates back to Sydney's *Literary News* (1837–8) and *Colonial Literary Journal* (1844–5). Many later excellent weeklies of this type were published in Melbourne, including *My Note Book* (1856–9), the *Examiner* (1857–64), and the *Literary News* (1882–3).

Another very significant magazine, the *Australian Journal* (1865–1962), began as a weekly, clearly copying the popular cheap fiction magazine the *London Journal*, imitating its layout and only slightly modifying its subtitle, 'A Weekly Source of Literature, Science and Art,' by substituting 'the Arts' for 'Art.' In 1869 it became a monthly magazine, continuing successfully until the introduction of television into Australia in 1956 killed off its market for thrilling narratives. The *Australian Journal* is now best known for its serialization of the original version of Marcus Clarke's classic novel of the convict period, *His Natural Life*, in 1870–2. It did, however, publish much other original Australian fiction, including some of the earliest detective fiction by women. Ellen Davitt's *Force and Fraud* (reprinted by Mullini Press, Canberra, 1993) was the lead serial in the first issue of the magazine. Mary Helena Fortune was an even more prolific producer of detective stories, her 'Detective's Album' continuing as a regular feature well into this century.

The rapid rise to popularity of the *Australian Journal* can be seen from G.B. Barton's comment in *Literature in New South Wales* (1866) that its circulation averaged about 5,500 copies weekly, including 1,750 in New South Wales (p. 88). This later figure may be compared with ones Barton gives for the monthly circulation of English periodicals in New South Wales in this period. The *Australian Journal's* circulation was equalled only by *Good Words*, followed by the *London Journal* with 1,500 copies and the *Family Herald* with 900 (pp. 8–9). Like the *Australian Journal*, these were cheap publications which emphasized fiction.

Religious, Spiritual, and Temperance Journals

As noted above, the earliest *Australian Magazine* (1821) was in a sense a religious magazine, since it was conducted by Methodist missionaries, though it aimed at a more general audience. Many other earlier magazines were also conducted by clergymen, who were among the few educated people in Australia before the 1840s. After that date, specialist newspapers advocating specific religious beliefs including temperance began appearing – the *Australasian*, later the *Monthly*, and then the *Sydney Chronicle* (1839–48), a Roman Catholic paper; the *Temperance Advocate*, later *Teetotallers' and General Advertiser* (1840–3); and the

Southern Queen (1845), a Church of England paper, to list just a few from Sydney.

The first specifically religious journal, the *Sydney Protestant Magazine*, ran from 1840 to 1841, followed by the *True Catholic or Tasmanian Evangelical Miscellany* (1843). Subsequent long-running journals of this type include the *Freeman's Journal* (1850; incorporated in *Catholic Weekly* from 1942), an influential Roman Catholic paper published in Sydney; the *Melbourne Church of England Messenger* (1850–1910); the *Advocate: A Weekly Catholic Journal* (1868–), still being published in Melbourne; the *Wesleyan Chronicle and Victorian Miscellany* (1857–1977). A significant later temperance periodical was the *Australian Band of Hope Review and Children's Friend* (1856–61), a Sydney fortnightly continued under various titles.

From the 1860s onwards a number of spiritualist magazines were published, the longest lasting being the *Harbinger of Light* (1870–1956), a Melbourne monthly. The *Austral Theosophist* (1894–5) was also a Melbourne monthly. Journals for free-thinkers abounded in the 1880s, the most successful being the *Liberator: A Weekly Radical and Free Thought Paper* (1884–1904), published in Melbourne. Sydney saw three such shorter-lived ventures, the weekly *Freethinker and New South Wales Reformer* (1886) and two monthlies, *Free Thought* (1880) and *Freedom: An Advocate of Social, Political and Religious Liberty* (1889–90).

Political Journals

As their subtitles indicate, a number of free-thought journals also advocated political reform, and in one sense all the newspapers and magazines discussed in this chapter were political journals. The press began in Australia as an instrument of government, and each subsequent publication advocated a particular political position, whether consciously or not. Journals specifically directed at the working man date from the 1840s and include the *Star and Working Man's Guardian* (1844–6), a Sydney weekly, and another Sydney paper, the *Citizen: A Weekly Paper of Politics, Literature, Science and the Arts* (1846–7).

In the 1880s and 1890s the development of the union movement and labour political parties saw several influential workers' journals established. While no less than four nineteenth-century Australian magazines rejoiced in the indigenous title of *Boomerang*, the most famous was a radical weekly published in Brisbane between 1887 and 1892. It was initially edited by William Lane and included Henry Lawson and A.G. Stephens among its contributors. In 1890, Lane became editor of another

Brisbane paper, the *Worker*, the organ of the Australian Labor Federation, initially published monthly, then fortnightly, and finally weekly until well past 1900. The *Australian Workman* (1890–9), published in Sydney, was the official organ of the Trades and Labor Council of New South Wales. The *Hummer*, a weekly, later fortnightly, established in Wagga Wagga in southern New South Wales in 1891, was initially the organ of the Amalgamated Shearers' Union. In 1893 it moved to Sydney, where as the *Australian Worker* it continues as the official publication of the Australian Workers' Union. *Tocsin: The People's Penny Paper*, a labour weekly published in Melbourne, ran from 1897 to 1961, under various titles.

Guides to Research

LIBRARY HOLDINGS

The main repositories are the Mitchell Library of the State Library of New South Wales, Sydney, and the National Library of Australia, Canberra. State libraries and government archives in other capital cities also have considerable holdings of local newspapers and magazines. The British Library's newspaper section at Colindale includes many Australian titles. In the past twenty-five years many newspaper titles have been microfilmed and so are more readily accessible. Less microfilming has been carried out for magazines.

BIBLIOGRAPHIES

The basic bibliography is Lurline Stuart, *Nineteenth Century Australian Periodicals, An Annotated Bibliography* (Sydney: Hale and Iremonger 1979). This lists 449 periodicals, confining itself to those with more literary interest. Listings include, where possible, place of publication, proprietor, editor, frequency of publication, dates of publication, size, number of pages, price, and main locations, together with a brief description of contents and names of any significant contributors. A second edition is in progress.

Alfred Pong's *Checklist of Nineteenth Century Australian Periodicals* (La Trobe University Publication 29, 1985) lists nearly eight hundred titles, but provides much less information than Stuart, giving dates, place, and frequency of publication only.

Part 2 of *Newspapers in Australian Libraries: A Union List*, fourth edition (National Library of Australia 1984–5) lists Australian newspapers by place of publication giving dates, frequency, and location of holdings.

HISTORIES OF AUSTRALIAN LITERATURE AND COMPANIONS

Andrews, B.G., and W.H. Wilde. *Australian Literature to 1900. A Guide to Information Sources*. Michigan: Gale Research Company 1980. Section 5 deals with nineteenth-century journals, including an annotated list of some of the more significant newspapers and periodicals.

Green, H.M. *A History of Australian Literature*. 2 vols, Sydney: Angus and Robertson 1961. Revised Dorothy Green, 1984. Provides much information on earlier writers and includes chapters on magazines and newspapers for each of its four periods: 1789–1850, 1850–90, 1890–1923, 1923–50.

Hergenhan, L., gen. ed. *The Penguin New Literary History of Australia*. Ringwood: Penguin Books 1988. The most recent literary history; includes 'Writers, Printers, Readers: the Production of Australian Literature before 1855' by Elizabeth Webby, and 'Journalism and the World of the Writer: The Production of Australian Literature, 1855–1915' by Ken Stewart.

Webby, Elizabeth. *Early Australian Poetry: An Annotated Bibliography*. Sydney: Hale and Iremonger 1982. An annotated listing of all original poetry published in Australian newspapers and magazines before 1850.

Wilde, W.H., J. Hooton, and B. Andrews. *The Oxford Companion to Australian Literature*. Melbourne: Oxford University Press 1985; rev. ed. 1994. Includes brief articles on some of the more significant newspapers and periodicals.

HISTORIES OF NEWSPAPERS AND MAGAZINES

Some pioneering studies of Australian newspapers and magazines include:

Bonwick, James. *Early Struggles of the Australian Press*. London: Gordon and Gotch 1890. Now rather outdated but still worth reading.

Cryle, Dennis. *The Press in Colonial Queensland: A Social and Political History, 1845–1875*. St Lucia: University of Queensland Press 1989. A very detailed study of the development of newspapers in this colony.

Ferguson, J.A., *et al. The Howes and Their Press*. Sydney: Sunnybrook Press 1936. Concentrates on beginnings of printing and newspapers in Sydney.

Greenop, F.S. *History of Magazine Publishing in Australia.* Sydney: K.G. Murray 1947. So far the only general history of periodical publication; a useful guide.

Mayer, Henry. *The Press in Australia.* Melbourne: Landsdowne 1964. A useful general history, including social and political analysis.

Miller, E. Morris. *Pressmen and Governors: Australian Editors and Writers in Early Tasmania.* Sydney: Angus and Robertson 1952. Facsimile edition, Sydney University Press, 1973. By far the most detailed and useful of these histories of early printing. Much information on early Tasmanian magazines and their writers and editors.

Pitt, G.H. *The Press in South Australia, 1836–1850.* Adelaide: Wakefield Press 1946. Looks at the beginnings of printing and newspaper publication in Adelaide.

Walker, R.B. *The Newspaper Press in New South Wales, 1803–1920.* Sydney: Sydney University Press 1976. A scholarly history giving detailed information on editors, circulation, readership, etc. Volume 2, published in 1980, covers the period 1920–45.

SPECIALIZED STUDIES

The only nineteenth-century Australian periodical to have received much detailed study is the Sydney *Bulletin,* 1880–.

Bennett, Bruce, ed. *Cross Currents: Magazines and Newspapers in Australian Literature.* Melbourne: Longman Cheshire 1981. Includes an essay by Elizabeth Webby, 'Before the *Bulletin*: Nineteenth Century Literary Journalism,' discussing literary periodicals published in Australia before 1880, and a transcript of the diary A.G. Stephens, literary editor of the *Bulletin* 1894–1906, kept between 1896 and 1932, edited by Leon Cantrell.

Rolfe, Patricia. *The Journalistic Javelin: An Illustrated History of the Bulletin.* Sydney: Wildcat Press 1979. An in-house history published for the magazine's centenary.

Lawson, Sylvia. *The Archibald Paradox: A Strange Case of Authorship.* Ringwood, Vic.: Allen Lane 1913. A ground-breaking study of the first twenty or so years of the *Bulletin* and of its first editor, J.F. Archibald.

THESES

Union List of Higher Degree Theses in Australian University Libraries: Cumulative Edition to 1965. Hobart: University of Tasmania Library 1967. With five supplements from 1966 to 1975, and annually

thereafter. Theses are arranged by subject, with an index of authors.
See also two significant recent PhD dissertations on the nineteenth-century press:

Blair, Sandy. 'Newspapers and Their Readers: The *Sydney Gazette* and Its Contemporaries.' University of New South Wales 1991.

Morrison, Elizabeth. 'The Contribution of the Country Press to the Making of Victoria, 1840–1890.' Monash University 1991.

INDEXES

Little systematic indexing of nineteenth-century Australian magazines had been carried out before the 1980s because of the general lack of interest in nineteenth-century Australian literature. Much indexing is now underway, and attempts are being made to co-ordinate projects to avoid overlap. In June 1991, the Australian Literature Research Group at La Trobe University, Melbourne, began a Periodicals Indexing Project but has not yet published any results.

The English Department, University of Sydney, holds card indexes to literary material in the *Australasian* (1880–1900), the *Sydney Mail* (1860–1900), and the *Australian Journal* (1865–1900), as well as to several more minor magazines.

Card indexes to some of the shorter magazines are also held at the University of Queensland, English Department, where a project is currently underway to index the *Queenslander* (1866–1939). Indexing of the *Bulletin* (1880–), is underway at University College, Australian Defence Force Academy, Canberra, and of the *Dawn* (1888–1905) at the Barr Smith Library, University of Adelaide.

FURTHER RESEARCH

Most areas relating to nineteenth-century Australian periodicals require further investigation, particularly for the period after 1850. While some journals are finally being indexed, there is need for better co-ordination, especially to ensure compatibility of indexing procedures and databases.

Apart from studies of the *Sydney Gazette*, the *Bulletin*, and the *Sydney Morning Herald*, there has been little detailed work on even the more major journals: their editors, circulation, readership, advertising, the economics of publishing in general. Nor has there been much study of the technologies of printing and illustration, let alone of ink and paper manufacture.

Notes

An earlier version of this essay appeared as chapter 3 of *The Book in Australia: Essays towards a Cultural and Social History*, edited by D.H. Borchardt and W. Kirsop (Melbourne: Australian Reference Publications 1988).

1 Nearly eight hundred titles are listed in Alfred Pong, *Checklist of Nineteenth Century Australian Periodicals* (Bundoora, Vic.: Borchardt Library 1985). To keep this chapter within manageable limits, however, I have concentrated on the 449 more general journals listed in Lurline Stuart, *Nineteenth Century Australian Periodicals* (Sydney: Hale and Iremonger 1979).
2 D.H. Borchardt, 'Printing Comes to Australia,' in D.H. Borchardt and W. Kirsop, eds., *The Book in Australia: Essays towards a Cultural and Social History* (Melbourne: ARP 1988), 2.
3 Ibid., 11.
4 From the original, now in the Ralph Mansfield Papers held by the National Library, Canberra.
5 'Australia and Her Prospects,' *Literary News*, 7 Oct. 1837.
6 'The State of the Theatre in the Late 1940s,' in Harold Love, ed., *The Australian Stage: A Documentary History* (Kensington, NSW: University of New South Wales Press 1984), 233–4.
7 Entry in John McGarvie's Diary, 17 July 1826, from the original now in the Mitchell Library, Sydney.
8 See Elizabeth Webby, 'Literature and the Reading Public in Australia: 1800–1849,' PhD thesis, University of Sydney, vol. 1, 1971, 175–80.
9 ALS George Robertson to H.G. Turner, 15 Oct. 1885. Copies of both this letter and Turner's letter to Robertson are now in the H.G. Turner Papers, La Trobe Library, Melbourne.
10 'A Final Batch of Victorian Magazines,' *Library Record of Australia* 1 (1901), 135.
11 'Introduction,' *Sydney Quarterly Magazine* 1 (1883), 4.
12 For further discussion of this point see George Nadel, *Australia's Colonial Culture* (Cambridge, Mass.: Harvard University Press 1957); Terry Sturm, 'Drama,' in L. Kramer, ed., *The Oxford History of Australian Literature* (Melbourne: Oxford University Press 1981); G.A. Wilkes, *The Stockyard and the Croquet Lawn* (Melbourne: Edward Arnold 1981); Robert Dixon, *The Course of Empire* (Melbourne: Oxford University Press 1986).
13 See E. Morris Miller, *Pressmen and Governors* (Sydney: Angus and Robertson 1952), 93–117, for a further discussion of Thomas Richards and the *Hobart Town Magazine*.
14 From *Humbug*, 5 Jan. 1870.
15 Nadel, *Australia's Colonial Culture*, 96–9.
16 In the *Port Phillip Patriot*, 20 Nov. 1843.

17 In the 1840s, for example, more books were advertised for sale in Victoria than in Tasmania. See Elizabeth Webby, 'Literature and the Reading Public,' 2:165.
18 'The Farewell,' *Australian Gold-Diggers' Monthly Magazine*, May 1853.
19 'Ourselves,' *Australian Magazine*, Oct. 1859.
20 G.D. Ailwood Keel, 'Sheridan Moore and the *Sydney University Magazine*, 1878–79,' *Southerly* 38 (1978), 91–110.
21 *A History of Australian Literature* (Sydney: Angus and Robertson 1961), 1:289.
22 'The Month,' *Cosmos*, Sept. 1894.
23 Based on the journals listed by Lurline Stuart.
24 On this point see Elizabeth Morrison, 'Bibliographical Revisionism: The Novels of Ada Cambridge,' in Forum on Australian Colonial Library History, Monash University, 1984, *Books, Libraries and Readers in Colonial Australia* (Clayton, Vic.: Graduate School of Librarianship, Monash University 1985), 67–75.
25 For further information see Marguerite Mahood, *The Loaded Line: Australian Political Caricature, 1788–1901* (Carlton, Vic.: Melbourne University Press 1973).
26 For an excellent account of the early *Bulletin*, see Sylvia Lawson, *The Archibald Paradox* (Melbourne: Allen Lane 1983). This is so far the only detailed study of a major nineteenth-century Australian journal.

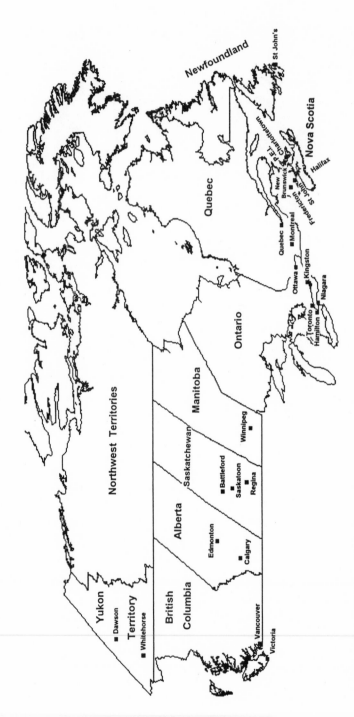

Canada. Map courtesy of Jerry Kowalyk.

2

Canada

N. MERRILL DISTAD
with the assistance of
LINDA M. DISTAD

Historical Introduction: Canada to 1900

Canada is a confederation of ten provinces and two territories. From east to west these consist of the four 'Atlantic' provinces of Newfoundland, Nova Scotia, New Brunswick, and Prince Edward Island; the two 'central' provinces of Quebec and Ontario; the three 'prairie' provinces of Manitoba, Saskatchewan, and Alberta; the 'Pacific' province of British Columbia; and, north of the ten provinces, the Northwest and Yukon Territories. This vast territory, exceeded in size only by the Russian Republic, had a population of 2.4 million in 1851, 3.3 million in 1867, and 5.4 million in 1900 (versus 27.3 million in 1991).

Canada as a modern nation traces its origins, in part, to the French colonies of New France and Acadia. The part of Acadia which became Nova Scotia was ceded to Britain by the Treaty of Utrecht in 1713. British victories in two subsequent wars led to the surrender of virtually all remaining French claims by 1763. Under the terms of the Quebec Act of 1774, Britain's Parliament established civilian rule under an appointed governor and council, and conceded to Roman Catholics both civil rights and retention of the French code of civil law. In the wake of the American Revolutionary War (1775–83), large numbers of United Empire Loyalists, who maintained their allegiance to the British Crown, fled the thirteen American colonies and settled in Britain's remaining colonies to the north and northeast. This migration prompted the creation of New Brunswick as a separate colony in 1784, and the passage of the Constitutional (also known as the Canada) Act in 1791, under which Quebec was divided to create Upper Canada (later known as Ontario) and Lower Canada (later known as Quebec).

After internal political pressures led to armed rebellions in both the Canadas in 1837, Lord Durham's celebrated *Report* (1839) recommended union of the Canadas, a goal long sought by Montreal's English merchant community. In 1840 an Act of Union united Upper and Lower Canada – known thereafter as 'Canada West' and 'Canada East' – into the Province of Canada under a single legislative assembly. Durham's *Report* also pointed the way to union of all British North American colonies. However, nothing happened until political deadlock in the Canadas, a vision of Canadian westward expansion, and some fear of American expansionism in that direction, once Americans stopped fighting each other, led to a series of meetings at Charlottetown, Prince Edward Island, in September, 1864. These culminated in the British North America Act of 1867, which united Canada (Ontario and Quebec) with New Brunswick and Nova Scotia, and granted autonomous government. The British North America Act placed Canada halfway on the road to full independence, a process only completed by passage of the Statute of Westminster in 1931. In 1869 the government of the newly created Dominion of Canada negotiated the purchase of Rupert's Land from the Hudson's Bay Company. From this vast territory, stretching from Labrador to the Rocky Mountains, the new Province of Manitoba was carved, and joined in confederation in 1870. The following year, the Pacific coastal colony of British Columbia joined the union, after receiving promises of a transcontinental railway link. Prince Edward Island followed suit in 1873. In 1880, Britain ceded title to the Arctic Islands to Canada. In 1905, the prairie provinces of Alberta and Saskatchewan were created from the southern extension of the Northwest Territories. The last province, Newfoundland, voted for confederation in two referenda held in 1948, and became part of Canada in 1949.

The process by which these scattered territories were welded into a modern nation was long and complex. The development of a periodical press played a significant role, for periodicals served as political tools: in the creation of representative government in the provinces; in the establishment of a press free of political censorship; in the creation of a unified nation '*a mari usque ad mare*'; in the creation of distinct cultures, both local and national; and in the promotion of innumerable other religious, commercial, and special-interest causes. Canada's cultural and social heterogeneity, combined with the British imperial connection and the dominating presence of the American 'colossus' to the south, have led generations of Canadian scholars and intellectuals to agonize over the alleged absence of a distinct Canadian national identity. Frequently that is attributed to the suffocating influence and domination of British or American culture. While some feel this perennial debate has grown tiresome, it is obviously relevant to the history of Canada's periodical press, which was the first medium of national mass-communication. The local nature of Canadian newspapers helped ensure their viability, but Canadian magazines, forced to compete with high-quality, foreign imports, were – and remain – a risky financial undertaking.[1]

Scope of Chapter

Other authors have chosen to treat the history of the Canadian newspaper press and Canadian magazine publishing separately, for the very good reason that any attempt to do comprehensive justice to both would involve prodigious labour and result in a massive work. Clearly, given the common origins of the two forms, and their custom of sharing subject matter, social roles, audience, contributors, and personnel, this exclusionary approach owes more to convenience than to logic. Moreover, the history of Canadian magazines before 1901 is largely a story of attrition and failure, while the newspaper press, though not without its many casualties, grew to unprecedented size and power by adapting more successfully to the economic necessities of mass sales and distribution. Generally speaking, Canadian magazine publishers only made this transition after 1900, although the trial-and-error process, as well as the first few successes, occurred in the nineteenth century.

Neither newspapers nor magazines have attracted the amount of scholarly attention in Canada that their importance warrants. Indeed, only two authors have attempted book-length, general studies of magazines, and the results were more successful in the treatment of the twentieth-century portion of the story; Canada's newspaper press, however, has been somewhat better served.[2] A major impediment to scholarship has been the lack of a definitive, centralized, national collection. Canada's National Library was founded as late as 1953, while the National Archives began as a branch of the Department of Agriculture (1872–1912). Canadian periodicals are scattered about the country in provincial and university libraries and archives. Only in recent years have microfilming projects, such as those of the Canadian Institute for Historical Microreproductions (CIHM) begun to broaden access to early Canadian periodicals.

While obviously too short to offer a complete enumeration of Canadian periodical titles, this chapter is an attempt to survey both newspapers and magazines through the era in which they evolved into separate media. Precise definition of the two media is elusive, for prior to the development of national and mass-market magazines, newspapers often performed the functions of both. This was particularly true in rural and frontier regions. Also, throughout the nineteenth century the publishers of Canada's magazines and newspapers were often one and the same. Later, newspaper proprietors, in search of still larger circulation, resorted to crossing format boundaries again with their enormously successful weekly magazine supplements.

Although Canada, like the other 'white dominions,' is a nation of immigrants in which many languages are spoken, very little space is devoted here to the 'ethnic-language' or 'allophone' press, which was very small in the nineteenth century. Similarly, the interesting and colourful aboriginal-language press of Canada's Native people (or First Nations as they now prefer to be called) lies almost wholly in the twentieth century. As for French, Canada's other official language, this chapter traces the early development of French-language periodical publishing. Despite some early effort at bilingual publication, English- and French- language publishing have developed in parallel paths, with bilingual publication now largely confined to the realm of government or corporate publications.[3]

While bibliographers of English-Canadian publications have done yeoman service in both enumerating and describing titles well into the nineteenth century, much work remains to be done at many levels, from tracking down fugitive copies of one- or two-issue 'orphan' titles, to producing detailed studies, and ultimately to producing the Canadian equivalent of Frank Luther Mott's multi-volume *A History of Magazines in America*. French-language periodicals bearing Quebec imprints, however, are subject to a degree of bibliographic control which scholars working on their English-language counterparts can only envy.

On the Character of the Canadian Periodical Press

One characteristic of the Canadian periodical press, both past and present, is the existence of numerous obstacles to commercial success. Among those obstacles may be numbered an extremely small population base, whether contrasted with the British motherland or, even more significantly, with the United States; the geographic distribution of that population from coast to coast; the linguistic fragmentation between anglophones and francophones; the historically lower literacy levels among francophones; and foreign (particularly American) competition for readership, advertising revenue, and editorial talent. Inadequate copyright protection was another obstacle. It should be noted, however, that this also enabled Canadian publishers to pirate and plagiarize American works freely throughout much of this period.[4]

Foreign periodicals have always found a ready audience in Canada. Major British periodicals, particularly the 'quarterlies,' were popular with Canada's elite readers, but it was beyond the capacity of a small colonial society to offer more than pale domestic imitations. The ability of American publishers to produce 'split-runs' of their titles – in which extra copies containing Canadian advertisements, with or without additional Canadian content, are run off at very low unit costs – enabled them to export their publications to Canada on highly competitive terms. Indeed, Canadians could offer scarcely any competition that depended upon price, when, for example, American publications entered Canada duty-free directly through the post, whereas the same publications were subject to duty when imported by Canadian newsagents and booksellers. Moreover, throughout this period, Canadian publishers and printers were forced to pay a duty of 25 per cent on paper stock and printing equipment. The Canadian government did not act to ease postage rates for magazines until 1880, when a second-class rate was created for all domestic periodicals. This was again lowered from four cents to one cent per pound in 1900. Characteristically, the government justified this reduction, not on the basis of promoting literacy or an informed electorate, but instead on promoting 'a national consciousness.' One authority has suggested the elusive growth of a Canadian 'national consciousness' was already reflected in the increase in Canadian monthly magazines from 41 in 1874 to 202 in 1900. Resisting pleas for further assistance to Canadian publishers, however, the government refused to remove the duty on paper and printing equipment.[5]

Another characteristic of Canadian periodicals was lack of longevity. Precious few survived more than three years; yet despite this high attrition rate, new titles proliferated. As well, these periodicals tended to be largely derivative in both format and content from American and British models. This lack of originality can be explained on two grounds. First, because Canada's early printers and publishers were themselves immigrants, they transplanted foreign models in the process of creating a Canadian periodical press. Second, the need to compete with foreign imports encouraged imitation at the expense of innovation. Thus, in a sample of twenty-five Canadian humour publications, four incorporated 'Punch' in their titles. This reputation for mimicry transferred itself from the format and appearance of Canadian periodicals to their content, and saddled much of Canada's nineteenth-century literary heritage with a reputation for imitation and mediocrity that, because it was not unfounded, is likely never to be entirely dispelled.

A further characteristic was that Canadian periodicals remained essentially local until developments such as the building of the railways made possible the production and much wider distribution of truly national publications. Whereas the power to influence public opinion was confined originally to publishers in major centres such as Montreal, Toronto, Ottawa, or Halifax, by the end of this era, geographic proximity to the centres of population and power was less important, as the example of the *Manitoba Free Press* (1872–) subsequently demonstrated.[6] In 1931 the title was changed to *Winnipeg Free Press*.

Origins of the Canadian Periodical Press

Canadian periodicals began modestly with the establishment of the *Halifax Gazette* (1752–66) by John Bushell (1715–61) of Boston. Bushell was succeeded by his partner, Anthony Henry (né Anthon Heinrich, 1734–1800), who published the *Gazette* until his death. For a brief period in the 1760s he operated without official government patronage – the first printer in Canada to do so. Later publishers kept the *Gazette* going, as an official government organ, until 1867.

Under the French regime New France lacked any printing establishments. The civil and religious authorities need not, however, have worried about the potential of printers to spread sedition or heresy, for virtually all the elements needed to sustain a publishing industry were absent. There were fewer than fifty thousand *habitants* in New France and most were scattered in rural or semi-rural settlements, were illiterate, lived close to subsistence in an economy perennially short of cash, and were without regular postal service, or, before 1730, any roads to augment the transportation and distribution of people and goods by water. Many of these conditions still prevailed long after the transfer of sovereignty to the English.[7] Nonetheless, in 1764, two other American printers, William Brown (1738–89) and Thomas Gilmore (d.1773), established the bilingual *Quebec Gazette* (1764–1934). The first *Montreal Gazette* (1778–) followed under the proprietorship of Fleury Mesplet (1735?–94), a printer from France and protégé of Benjamin Franklin.

In 1793 Lieutenant-Governor John Graves Simcoe (1752–1806) established the *Upper Canada Gazette, or American Oracle* (1793–1849) at Newark [Niagara-on-the-Lake]. Initially Simcoe employed a Québécois printer, Louis Roy (1771–99), but Roy was succeeded the following year by an American, Gideon Tiffany (1774–1854), whose older brother Silvester (1758–1811) joined him as assistant printer in 1796. The Tiffany brothers went on to found Upper Canada's second and third papers, the short-lived *Canada Constellation* (Niagara, 1799–1800) and *Niagara Herald* (1801–2).

The use of 'gazette' in many of the early titles indicates an emphasis on public affairs, and indeed these early publications were dependent upon government contracts and patronage for their very survival. However, these political ties characterized the Canadian press long after it had achieved economic independence. The Loyalist sentiments of many of the early printer-proprietors were also a factor in their tendency to act as government mouthpieces. For example, before his appointment in 1784 as the first King's Printer and deputy Postmaster-General of the new Colony of New Brunswick, Christopher Sower III (1754–99) of Pennsylvania had served the British as a spy in the American Revolutionary War. In some cases, however, the American roots of these men showed when they crossed verbal and legal swords with a governing establishment determined to control the press as thoroughly as it controlled the legislature and the courts. Hence the struggle to establish a press free of government interference lasted into the 1830s.[8]

The Loyalist printer-proprietors established papers on the Anglo-American model in the newer colonies. In Nova Scotia, the Bostonian John Howe (1754–1835) established the *Halifax Journal* (1781–1870), which soon had to compete with the *Halifax Chronicle* (1786–1837) established by William Minns (c.1763–1827), Howe's brother-in-law and former assistant. John Ryan (1761?–1847) of Rhode Island established the first publication in what became New Brunswick, the *Royal Saint John's Gazette and Nova Scotia Intelligencer* (1783–1807; in 1785 renamed the *Saint John Gazette and Weekly Advertiser*). Ryan's son Michael produced the *Fredericton Telegraph* (1806–7), but abandoned it to accompany his father to Newfoundland, where they founded the *Royal Gazette and Newfoundland Advertiser* at St John's (1807–1924). Christopher Sower III established New Brunswick's second paper, the weekly *Royal Gazette and New Brunswick Advertiser* (1784–1977) at Saint John. After Sower's death in 1799 it was taken over by Ryan, who remained with it until 1832. It survived in various forms for another 145 years.

Scots-born James Robertson (1747–1816), late of New York, began the *Royal American Gazette and Weekly Intelligencer* (1787–8) at Charlottetown, Island of Saint John (known as Prince Edward Island after 1799). Robertson's apprentice, Virginia-born William Alexander Rind, produced the Island's second periodical, the fortnightly *Royal Gazette and Miscellany of the Island of Saint John* (1791–4), before returning to Virginia in 1798. Rind's brother-in-law and apprentice, James Bagnall (1783–1855), accompanied him to Virginia, but returned to the Island in 1804, and the following year began publishing the *Royal Herald* (1805–6?).

Well into the nineteenth century, printers continued to cross the border seeking opportunities. Nahum Mower (1779?–1830), of Worcester, Massachusetts, immigrated to Montreal, where he founded and edited the *Canadian Courant and Montreal Advertiser* (1807–34). Mower's apprentice, Stephen Miles (1789–1870) of Royalton, Vermont, accompanied him to Montreal, and then moved to Kingston in 1810, where he set up the first press and produced the *Kingston Gazette* (1810–18). Afterwards he worked as printer of the *Upper Canada Herald* from 1819 to 1828, and publisher of the short-lived *Kingston Gazette and Religious Advocate* (1828–30), before becoming a Wesleyan Methodist circuit preacher. Scots-born George Brown (1818–80) relocated to Toronto in 1843 after a sojourn in New York. Brown's Irish contemporary Thomas D'Arcy McGee (1825–68) moved from New York to Montreal as late as 1857.[9]

SPREAD OF NEWSPAPERS

After the turn of the nineteenth century, newspapers began to proliferate, for in that era it was still relatively cheap and easy to found one. The more successful and long-lived included the *Quebec Mercury* (1805–1903), founded by Thomas Cary (1751–1823), and *Le Canadien* (1806–10, revived 1817–19, 1820–5, 1831–1909), founded by editor and politician Pierre-Stanislas Bédard (1762–1829) and physician François-Xavier Blanchet (1776–1830). Although the slow hand-presses kept circulation small, proprietors even then showed an inclination to appeal to specialized audiences and to practise an early form of 'class journalism.' Thus, the *Quebec Mercury*, as well as the *Canadian Courant* and the Montreal *Herald* (1811–1926), represented the interests of Lower Canada's anglophone merchant class, while *Le Canadien* and later *La Minerve* (1826–99) guarded francophone professional interests and campaigned for government reform. In the Atlantic colonies, Halifax's *The Novascotian, or Colonial Herald* (1824–92?) and *Acadian Recorder* (1813–1930), New Brunswick's *Saint John Courier* (1811–65), Prince Edward Island's *Charlottetown Examiner* (1847–1922), and Newfoundland's *Saint John's Times and General Commercial Gazette* (1832–95) all enjoyed long runs, as did Upper Canada's outstanding example of such longevity, George Brown's *Globe* (1844–).

Though at least half their number died within three years, the proliferation of newspapers meant that Upper and Lower Canada together enjoyed twenty by 1824 (all but two with circulations under four hundred), and fifty by 1836, while the distinctive semantic connotations of their titles – Advertiser, Gazette, Herald, and Mercury – had blurred beyond recognition, as the press became more and more commercialized. An increase in commercial business and advertising, combined with technological improvements, made a daily press inevitable by mid-century. Before the advent of steamships or the telegraph, editors had plundered other newspapers for the bulk of their regional, national, and international coverage. Increased speed in the transmission of news impelled more frequent publication, which faster presses made possible. Canada's first daily, the *Daily Advertiser* of Montreal (1833), was a financial failure, as was the *British Standard* in Toronto (1836). In the 1840s the Montreal *Herald* and *Gazette* each published daily during the busy summer months when traffic on the St Lawrence River was heavy. Regular daily publication was adopted by the Toronto *Globe* in 1853. Within twenty years the new nation boasted forty-seven daily newspapers. During the 1860s the circulation of individual dailies approached, but rarely exceeded, 5,000 copies. In 1876 the combined circulation of daily papers in nine urban centres across Canada totalled 113,000. Seven years later that figure had more than doubled. By 1900 the number of Canadian dailies stood at 112 and the larger urban markets supported multiple dailies. In 1872, Halifax, Saint John, and Toronto each had four dailies; Hamilton, London, and Ottawa each had three; and Montreal had four English-language and three French-language dailies. Over the remainder of the century, twenty-three other dailies were founded in Montreal alone, and twenty-five folded. One authority has calculated that over the years 3,500 different newspapers have been published in Ontario alone, while Quebec has been home to roughly 3,000.[10]

The newspaper press had spread meanwhile to the vast lands of the Canadian West. In 1858, three papers were founded at Fort Victoria on Vancouver Island. The first, *Le Courrier de la Nouvelle Caledonie, journal politique et littéraire, organ des populations françaises dans les possessions anglaises*, was edited by Paul de Garro, a French aristocrat exiled after Louis Napoleon's 1851 coup d'état, and printed on a press supplied to Mgr Modeste Demers (1809–71), first Roman Catholic Bishop of Victoria, by La Société de la propagation de la foi de Paris. It lasted only two issues. Next came the *Victoria Gazette* (1858–60), founded by two Americans, and finally the *British Colonist* (1858–1980), the most successful of the trio. Meanwhile, at Fort Garry [Winnipeg], two journalist-entrepreneurs, William Coldwell (1834–1907) and William Buckingham (1832–1915), began publication of the *Nor'-Wester* (1859–69) on a second-hand screw press hauled by ox-cart on an eventful journey from St Paul in the state of Minnesota.

In 1869–70 when the francophone Métis population of the Red River Valley resisted the transfer of power in Rupert's Land from the Hudson's Bay Company to the Canadian federal government, the result was the Red River Resistance, or first North-West Rebellion. The forces of Métis leader Louis Riel (1844–85) seized Fort Garry, and in December 1869 stopped publication of both the *Nor'-Wester* and the *Red River Pioneer*, a new journal that had yet to produce its first issue. The Riel forces bought out the proprietor of the *Pioneer* with a settlement of £550, and began their own newspaper, *New Nation* (1870). The first issue is a curiosity, for it combined the first two pages of the abortive first issue of the *Pioneer* with two pages entitled *New Nation*. In August 1870, following Riel's departure to exile in the United States, the original proprietor of the *Pioneer* reacquired his press and the *New Nation*, and changed its title the following year to the *Manitoban* (Fort Garry, 1871–2).

Le Métis (St-Boniface, 1871–81), Manitoba's first francophone paper, was founded by Joseph Royal (1837–1902), an experienced Montreal journalist and lawyer. Joseph Dubuc (1840–1914), another Québécois journalist who, like Royal, wrote for *La Minerve*, served as his 'collaborateur.' Both men had been persuaded to relocate in the West by none other than Louis Riel. After Royal was elected to Canada's House of Commons in 1879, under his successor, Alphonse-Alexandre-Clément Larivière (1842–1925), *Le Métis* was retitled *Le Manitoba* (1881–1925). Riel's rebellion had been a failure: however, the new francophone press, although Conservative politically, served to promote the causes of the Métis, including encouragement of francophone immigration into the new province of Manitoba. Its hold on its readership is reflected in the following decades, when James-Émile-Pierre Prendergast (1858–1945) and Joseph-Ernest Cyr (1854–1929) founded three short-lived, Liberal, francophone weeklies: *Le Trappeur* (St-Boniface, 1887), *Le Courrier du Nord-Ouest* (Winnipeg, 1888), and *L'Ouest Canadien* (St-Boniface, 1889). These efforts nonetheless earned their principals patronage appointments under Laurier's Liberal government (1896–1911). *L'Agriculteur* (St-Boniface, 1889–91), a politically neutral semi-monthly aimed at farmers, fared little better.

The promotion of francophone immigration was also the expressed aim of *L'Ouest canadien* (Edmonton, 1898–1900), Alberta's first French-language newspaper, which was launched by the Société de la colonisation d'Edmonton. The following year the enterprise was incorporated as The Edmonton Printing Company, Ltd. However, the size of its audience and concomitantly small advertising and job-printing revenues brought it to a halt early in 1900, and it was another five years before a successor appeared in Alberta, *Le Courrier de l'Ouest* (Edmonton, 1905–16).[11]

In 1878 Patrick Gammie Laurie (1833–1903), a witness of the first Métis uprising, as well as a veteran of newspapers in the United States and at least five Ontario towns, set off from Fort Garry by ox cart with a second-hand press bound for Battleford, then the capital of the Northwest Territories. There he founded the *Saskatchewan Herald* (1878–1938), and his luck held, despite flood, fire, and being at a focal point of the second North-West Rebellion in 1885, led as before by Louis Riel. In 1880, another ox cart left Fort Garry bearing a second-hand press and type, purchased this time from the *Manitoba Free Press* by Frank Oliver (né Bowsfield, 1853–1933), who established the long-lived Fort Edmonton *Bulletin* (1880–1951), the first newspaper in what became the province of Alberta. Shortly thereafter the *Calgary [Weekly] Herald, [Mining and Ranch Advocate]* (1883–) and Regina *Leader* (1883–) were established. Numerous other papers appeared over the years, until every town of any consequence could boast of at least one paper, if not necessarily a daily or even a weekly. When the lure of gold in the Klondike created a rush to the far north, the newspaper press followed. Between 1897 and 1900 twelve newspapers were established in the Yukon Territory, but only four survived more than a year: *Dawson News* (1899–1954), *Klondike Nugget* (1898–1903), *Yukon [Midnight] Sun* (1898–1904), and *Whitehorse Star* (1900–).[12]

EVOLUTION OF NEWSPAPERS INTO MAGAZINES: THE 'PIONEER' ERA

Despite the aptness of its name (from the Arabic verb kh-za-na, 'to store things away'), few tangible objects are as elusive of precise definition as the periodical magazine. Definitions which go beyond 'regular publication issued less often than daily' founder on the shoals of numerous exceptions. While magazines and newspapers often mirror each other's content and function, the former began to differentiate themselves in eighteenth-century England by focusing narrowly on the literary – *Spectator* (1711–14) – or the political – *Craftsman* (1726–50) – to the exclusion of 'news' and commerce. *Gentleman's Magazine* (1731–1907) established the modern paradigm. For much of the 'pioneer' era, however, Canada had no publishers or publishing houses in the modern sense. Books consisted virtually exclusively of imports from Europe or the United States. Indeed, British copyright law long forbade the reprinting of British books in the colonies, and any domestic publication, whether of a journal or an entire volume, emanated from the printing shops of newspapers or job-printers (usually one and the same), who generally were under-capitalized. The wonder, therefore, is that so many found the courage to hazard their money on such risky ventures as magazines. Not surprisingly, pre-paid subscriptions were required for almost all periodicals.

The precise identity of Canada's first magazine is moot, for when Fleury Mesplet first attempted to publish his weekly *Gazette de commerce et littéraire* in 1778–9, it was bereft of news, though it contained enough criticism of the authorities to land Mesplet and his editor, Valentin Jautard (1738?–87), in jail. However, there is no question that Canada's first English-language magazine was published in Halifax by *Halifax Journal* publisher John Howe: *Nova Scotia Magazine and Comprehensive Review of Literature, Politics, and News* (1789–92). This ambitious and expensive eighty-page monthly was, despite two hundred subscribers, a steady money-loser, which reductions in both the size and price could not change. The same year that Howe terminated the *Nova Scotia Magazine*, Samuel Neilson (1771–93), nephew of the printer William Brown, launched the *Magazine de Québec, ou receuil utile et amusant de littéraire, histoire, politique, etc., particulièrement adapté à l'usage de l'Amérique brittanique* (later *Quebec Magazine/Le Magazine de Québec*, 1792–4), edited by Scots-born Rev. Mr Alexander Spark (1762–1819). Upon Samuel Neilson's death in 1793, the bilingual monthly passed, with the printing business, to his younger brother, John (1776–1848), who wound up publication the following year. A decade later John, in partnership with Pierre-Édouard Desbarats (1764–1828), issued a sixteen-page weekly entitled the *British-American Register* during the first eight months of 1803. Desbarats struck again with the short-lived *Le Vrai canadien* (1810–11), which, despite its title, printed little native material.

Publishing periodicals was hazardous in ways beyond the merely financial, as Pierre-Stanislas Bédard and his colleagues discovered when the contents of their mildly nationalistic *Le Canadien* landed them in jail, and caused a mob to wreck the printing office. However, Bédard's star later rose as far as an appointment to the judicial bench. Other publishers and editors were less fortunate. Henry David Winton (1793–1855), the editor of the St John's *Public Ledger* (1820–82) in Newfoundland, was attacked by ruffians in 1835 and had one ear sliced off and two pieces cut out of the other. Five years later one of his associates was mutilated similarly.[13] Samuel Hull Wilcocke (also known as 'Lewis Luke MacCulloh, Esq.,' 1766?–1833) was another dauntless periodical publisher. Like his English contemporary and countryman Richard Carlisle, he edited and produced a magazine – *Scribbler: A Series of Weekly Essays on Literary, Critical, Satirical, Moral, and Local Subjects, Interspersed with Pieces of Poetry* (Montreal, 1822–7) – from a prison cell, where he was held on a forgery charge by his former employers, the North West Company (trading rival of the Hudson's Bay Company). Upon his release, he moved first to Vermont, then to New York, where he continued publishing his journal, full of lampoons and scandalous accusations against prominent Montrealers, particularly those connected with the North West Company. While this is apparently unique among nineteenth-century Canadian periodicals, it closely resembled the 'bon ton' scandal sheets then produced in London, and may even be said to have anticipated the tabloid 'gutter-press' which flourishes in present-day Montreal.

Despite such varied risks, other early English-language literary efforts appeared in Montreal, Canada's largest city throughout this period, such as *Literary Miscellany* (1822–3); *Canadian Magazine and Literary Repository* (1823–5), edited by David Chisholme (1796?–1842) and printed by newspaper proprietor Nahum Mower for Joseph Nickless's bookshop; and its rival, the *Canadian Review and Literary and Historical Journal* (later, *Canadian Review and Magazine*, 1824–6), published by bookseller H.H. Cunningham, who lured Chisholme away from Mower to become his editor. On the French side, one of the most protean figures of the 'pioneer' era of periodical publication in Quebec was her first native-born historian, Michel Bibaud (1782–1857). After some editorial experience with the newspaper *Le Spectateur* (1813–29), Bibaud sought to promote literature and science by founding and editing a number of periodicals, including *L'Aurore des Canadas, journal politique, littéraire, et anecdotique* (1816–19), *Le Courrier du Bas-Canada* (1819), *La bibliothèque canadienne; ou, miscellanés historiques, scientifiques, et littéraires* (1825–30), *L'Observateur* (later *Le Magazine du Bas-Canada, journal littéraire et scientifique*, 1831–2), and *L'Encyclopédie canadienne, journal littéraire et scientifique* (1842–3).

In the Maritimes, more than three decades passed between Howe's publication and the area's second magazine: *Acadian Monthly or Literary Mirror, Consisting of Original and Selected Matter on Literary and Other Subjects* (1826–8). Publisher Jacob Sparling Cunnabell (1803–c.85) provided a forty-page forum for local authors, the intellectual significance of which was out of all proportion to its brief life. Undeterred by the commercial failure of the *Acadian Monthly*, Cunnabell rallied with a second literary journal, the *Halifax Monthly Magazine* (1830–3), which featured an important innovation, paid advertising, though it was discreetly confined to a supplement. The indefatigable Cunnabell tried one more time, with *Colonial Pearl: A Volume Devoted to Polite Literature, Science, and Religion* (1837–40). The field of Maritime magazines was also joined by the *British North American Magazine and Colonial*

Journal, whose publisher, Edmund Ward (1787–1853) of Halifax, appears to have lost his nerve after the appearance of a single ninety-six-page issue in 1831. In Pictou, Nova Scotia, the prolific printer James Dawson (1789–1862) enjoyed some success with *Bee: A Weekly Journal Devoted to News, Politics, Literature, Agriculture, etc.* (1835–8). Mrs Mary Jane Lawson (née Katzmann, 1828–90) became Canada's second woman editor, with her *Provincial, or Halifax Monthly Magazine* (1852–3). In neighbouring New Brunswick, Alexander M'Leod of Saint John produced a short-lived but quality weekly entitled the *New Brunswick Religious and Literary Journal* (1829–30). The notion of literary 'blossoms' being sown and gathered perhaps explains the titles of some literary journals such as *Amaranth* (Saint John, 1841–3) edited by Robert Shives (1815–79) and the *Mayflower, or Ladies Acadian Newspaper* (Halifax, 1851–2), edited by Mary Eliza Herbert (1829–72), to whom goes the honour of being Canada's first woman editor. Although the genteel and literary *Mayflower* lasted only nine issues, it featured the work of a number of women writers, and its young editor continued to write poems, essays, and tales for newspaper publication.[14]

The nineteenth century was well advanced before Upper Canada spawned its first magazine to last more than a few issues. The *Christian Recorder* (1819–21) was produced by Anglican Archdeacon (later Bishop) John Strachan (1778–1867) at York [Toronto] for an elite audience. Advertised as 'a passing map of the religious world,' it dwelled upon church issues, including education. The first organ of the Dissenting denominations was a newspaper, Stephen Miles's *Kingston Gazette and Religious Advocate*, which was put out of business by the rival Wesleyan Methodist *Christian Guardian* (1829–1925), edited by the Rev. Mr Egerton Ryerson (1803–82). Ryerson first came to prominence as a polemicist who equalled his principal opponent, Bishop Strachan. Under Ryerson's able editorship (1829–40), the *Christian Guardian* became one of the most widely circulated and influential publications in Upper Canada. Indeed, it was a principal vehicle to promote moral values and political positions, and it elevated Ryerson to a position of influence rivalled or equalled by few other journalists in the pre-Confederation era. In 1830 he wrote that the principal aim of the *Guardian* was 'to promote and support religious and civil rights,' as well as 'practical Christianity – to teach men how to live and how to die.' In addition to the general litany of obstacles, in the 1820s Canadian magazine publishers faced such an uphill struggle to compete with the newspaper press, then enjoying a period of rapid expansion, that more years passed before the appearance of another Upper Canadian magazine: *Canadian Casket* (1831–2), produced at Hamilton and 'devoted exclusively to polite literature.' Over the course of the next decade thirteen more such titles appeared, primarily literary or religious, or a mixture, and all of them lived only a year or two.[15]

MID-CENTURY MAGAZINES: STRUGGLING TO SURVIVE

As the nineteenth century advanced, magazines evolved into a number of increasingly specialized strains. The literary journal was the first specialized genre to appear, and it played a major role in creation of a Canadian cultural consciousness. Quebec was richly supplied with periodicals in both English and French, and particularly with journals devoted to *belles lettres*. In a culture in which books were both expensive and scarce, and the literacy rate was quite low, the development of its literature depended on periodicals to an extent that is remarkable even in what is widely acknowledged today to have been the 'golden age' of the periodical as the primary instrument and medium of public discourse. Moreover, the powerful influence of the Catholic church in Quebec provided an additional cross for nineteenth-century Québécois writers, editors, and publishers to bear. Journals of purely literary content, however, generally avoided controversy and censure by the Church.

Michel Bibaud's numerous publications had a number of contemporary rivals, most of them also short-lived. *L'Abeille canadienne: journal de littérature et de science*, edited by Henri-Antoine de Mézières (1771–c.1819), appeared in Montreal (1818–19). Its title was echoed in the weekly published later at Quebec, *L'Abeille canadienne; publication de littérature* (1833–4), edited by François-Xavier Garneau (1809–66), nineteenth-century Quebec's pre-eminent author and historian, and in still another weekly, *L'Abeille* (1848–81), published intermittently at Quebec. Equally persistent was the Montreal monthly *L'Album littéraire et musical de la revue canadienne* (later *L'Album littéraire et musical de la Minerve*), a magazine supplement of musical scores, which began in 1846 and survived, off and on, until 1874.[16]

The founding of the *Mouvement littéraire de Québec* in 1852, by a coterie of habitués of Octave Crémazie's Quebec City bookshop, led to the founding of two literary journals – the very popular monthly *Les Soirées canadiennes: recueil de littérature nationale* (1861–5) and *Le Foyer canadien: recueil littéraire et historique* (1863–6) – to promote the publication of works on Canadian literary and historical themes. *Le Foyer* proved so popular that over two thousand copies were distributed to readers as far afield as Detroit. Considered by some to have been nineteenth-century Canada's most outstanding literary magazine, *Le Foyer* was established as a result of a schism within the original *Mouvement littéraire*, which left Dr Joseph-Charles Taché (1820–94) in sole editorial control of *Les Soirées*, a title his nephew, Louis-J.-C.-Hyppolite Taché (1859–1927), revived as *Nouvelles soirées canadiennes* (1882–8).

The elder Taché, trained as a physician and surgeon, was a man of enormous and varied talents. In a series of articles in *Le Courrier du Canada* (reprinted as *Des Provinces de l'Amérique du Nord et d'une union fédérale*, Quebec, 1858), he urged intercolonial union as the means of securing a transcontinental nation that would include the great expanses that lay north and west of Canada. With equal skill Taché could shift from such a serious topic to writing witty satire lampooning the work of Émile Chevalier (1828–79), a novelist who was also founder and editor of the journal *La Ruche littéraire* (Montreal, 1853–9). While francophone Canadian authors pursued the goal of a *patriote*, or national, literature, reflecting French-Canadian history and themes, literary developments in Europe were not ignored. Indeed, the Montreal monthly *L'Écho de France: revue étrangère de science et littéraire* (1865–9) was devoted to reporting on them. Despite the popularity and prestige of several of these French-language journals, they were condemned to commercial failure, if only because their potential audience was too small. At least 40 per cent of Canada's nineteenth-century francophone population was illiterate, and precious few of the literate remainder were inclined to purchase and read literary magazines. While the margin for success among French-language journals was undoubtedly thin, it was not beyond reach, as demonstrated by the success of the somewhat less specialized, if no less highbrow, Montreal monthly *La Revue canadienne: philosophie, histoire, droit, littérature, économie sociale* (1863–1922).[17]

In 1838 Montreal printer John Lovell (1810–93), with his brother-in-law John Gibson (d.1850) as editor, launched Canada's first English-language literary magazine to achieve anything like longevity: *Literary Garland and British North American Magazine: A Monthly Repository of Tales, Sketches, Poetry, Music, Etc.* (1838–52). An innovative publication that featured lithographic illustrations and engraved musical scores, *Literary Garland* also paid its contributors, who included such important Canadian writers as Anna Jameson (1794–1860), Susanna Moodie (1803–85), Charles Sangster (1822–93), and Catharine Parr Traill (1802–99). Moodie, whose best-known work, *Roughing It in the Bush* (1852), first appeared as sketches in *Literary Garland*, was the most frequent contributor. Lovell's payments were not sufficiently large, however, to discourage her from a brief collaboration with Belleville printer Joseph Wilson (c.1806–80) to produce *Victoria Magazine: A Cheap Periodical for the Canadian People* (1847–8). The *Literary Garland* is also noteworthy for the large amount of original Canadian material that appeared in its pages, alongside imports from American and British authors, as well as translations of French and German works. Gibson's successor as editor of the *Garland*, Mrs Eliza Lanesford Cushing (née Foster, 1794–1886), was also a prolific contributor to magazines. In 1847 she and her sister, Mrs Harriet Cheney (1796–?), created Canada's first purely children's magazine, *Snow Drop; or, Juvenile Magazine* (Montreal, 1847–53), also published by Lovell and Gibson. With typical Victorian rhetoric, it was outspokenly devoted to 'progress and improvement' as well as 'amusement and instruction.' Its relatively long run may be attributed to its handsome appearance, considerable appeal to young girls, and absence of temperance rhetoric.

While *Literary Garland* played a significant role in the development and promotion of Canadian letters, other literary magazines survived too briefly to enjoy much impact. They included: *Barker's Canadian Monthly Magazine* (Kingston, 1846–7), published by Edward John Barker (1799–1884), proprietor of the Kingston *British Whig* (merged with the *Daily Standard* [1908–26] to become the *Whig-Standard* [1926–]); *Canadian Gem and Family Visitor: A Literary and Religious Magazine* (Cobourg, 1848–9); *Anglo-American Magazine and Canadian Journal* (Toronto, 1852–5); *British Colonial Magazine* (Toronto, 1852–3); *British American Magazine: Devoted to Literature, Science, and Art* (Toronto, 1863–4); and *British American Review* (1865–7). Although several of these journals made an attempt to reach a national audience, the conditions necessary for such ventures to succeed really only coalesced after Confederation in 1867.[18]

Changing Technology and Markets

Paralleling Canada's confederation and development into a country, which created a national market for publishers, merchants, and advertisers, were advances in printing technology, including the reproduction and use of illustrations, and the rise of a recognizably modern advertising industry. All of these were crucial to the evolution and development of the periodical press. The earliest Canadian periodicals were printed in small formats on wooden hand-presses that had changed little over three centuries, and which were replaced by iron hand-presses only in the second decade of the nineteenth century. Such presses were manufactured in Toronto by the 1830s. However, the innovations which permitted mass production were the introduction of rotary presses and the application of steam power to run them. Such presses had to be imported from manufacturers such as Richard Hoe and Company of New York, but as these presses grew in size and complexity, they enabled proprietors to produce large-format newspapers on a daily basis. In 1851 the Rev. Mr Anson Green (1801–79) introduced the first steam-powered newspaper press to Canada to produce the *Christian Guardian*. When George Brown of Toronto introduced a daily edition of the *Globe* in 1853, he imported a new American press. In 1860, the daily edition of the *Globe* began running on two Taylor double-cylinder presses. Each of these produced three thousand sheets an hour, which were fed into a new, American-built folding machine. In 1867, in search of greater production capacity, Brown added a Hoe 'Lightning' press at a cost of $15,000, an enormous sum of money then. The *Globe* also appeared in weekly and tri-weekly editions for distribution outside Toronto. Combined circulations ran to 30,000 and more, at a time when Toronto's population was a mere 40,000, and that of Canada West only about 1,250,000. While presses were automated, type continued to be hand-set, a time-consuming process, until the 1880s, when Mergenthaler's Linotype brought typesetting closer to the speed of the power presses. Large dailies required many of these high-speed type-casting machines, while a single machine would suffice to provide the smaller weeklies with all the local news they required.[19]

As the city dailies upgraded their printing plants with larger, faster, and inevitably more expensive machines, their old presses, however obsolete, were eagerly purchased by would-be proprietors of small-town and rural weeklies, for whom miscellaneous job-printing would be a necessary sideline. For example, a Washington-style screw press built by Hoe served the Kingston *Daily British Whig* until 1881, then passed to a succession of increasingly smaller papers, beginning with the Whitby *Gazette* and the Pickering *News*, before finally becoming a working exhibit at Upper Canada Village in 1964.[20]

ILLUSTRATION AND ILLUSTRATORS

Experiments with illustration in Canadian periodicals began early. In 1777 the first printed Canadian picture, a view of Halifax, graced Anthony Henry's *Nova-Scotia Calender, or, an Almanac*. In 1792 the *Quebec Gazette* published Canada's first two engraved landscapes, while the *Quebec Magazine/Magazine de Québec* issued the first known engraved portrait. George Gurnett (1792?–1861), successful Toronto newspaper proprietor, included a lithographic portrait in each issue of Upper Canada's fourth magazine, his *Canadian Literary Magazine* (1833), making it the first title to be illustrated regularly. John Allanson (1800–59), a student of the great English wood engraver Thomas Bewick (1753–1828), included wood-engraved views of Hamilton, Kingston, and Toronto in his *Anglo-American Magazine and Canadian Journal.*

By mid-century publishers were seeking new ways to use illustrations to break up the unrelieved columns of letterpress text that characterized both newspapers and magazines. Between 1832 and 1843 two lithographers had set up shop in Toronto. Over the next few decades a proliferation of engraving firms prompted increased use of illustrations in both magazines and the daily press. The Toronto Engraving Company (later Brigden's) made a specialty of catalogue, newspaper, and periodical work. The work of 'artist-reporters' began to grace the pages of newspapers such as the Toronto *Globe*, which collaborated with the Toronto Lithographing Company to produce the *Canadian War News*, a weekly special that reported on the North-West Rebellion of 1885.

Photographic Portfolio: A Monthly View of Canadian Scenes and Scenery (1858–60) was an impressive, if somewhat short-lived, production by Samuel McLaughlin (1826–1914), an Irish-born watchmaker who, in 1861, became Canada's first official photographer. *Portfolio* featured actual mounted photographs of views in and around Quebec City. At that early date, however, the mass production of photographic prints suffered from obvious technical and cost limitations that led to the invention and exploitation of photo-engraving, both of which first occurred in Canada. The *Canadian Illustrated News* (Hamilton, then Toronto, 1862–4) was the brain-child of a retired Scots soldier, Alexander Somerville (1811–85), who had arrived in Canada in 1858. It featured five engravings per issue, and local artists and photographers were commissioned to provide the pictures from which the engravers worked. This was, of course, an expensive undertaking, and Canada had nothing like the population enjoyed by the publishers of such archetypes as the British *Illustrated London News* (1842–) or the American *Harper's Weekly: A Journal of Civilization* (1857–1916), so it ceased publication after fifteen months.

In 1865 William Leggo (1830–1915) of Montreal patented the 'Leggotype,' the world's first true photo-engraving process. It was employed to produce the first half-tone magazine engravings when Georges Édouard Desbarats (1838–93) launched his very successful *Canadian Illustrated News* (1869–83); its success was due in part to this new technology. A French-language co-publication, *L'Opinion publique illustré* (1870–83), shared illustrations. These, in turn, inspired similar illustrated efforts, such as *Dominion Illustrated News* (1888–95) and *[Toronto] Saturday Night* (1887–). Zinc engraving ('zincography'), another photo-engraving technology, was pioneered in Toronto in the 1880s by the Grip Printing and Publishing Company.[21]

EVOLUTION OF MODERN ADVERTISING

While advertisements had appeared in Canadian periodicals as early as 1752 in the *Halifax Gazette,* and 1764 in the *Quebec Gazette,* advertising was then only in its infancy as a business activity. Although the need for a firm financial underpinning based upon paid advertising was obvious as a way to free printer-publishers from complete dependence upon government contracts and patronage as well as readers' subscriptions, the essentially local nature of periodicals was a handicap. Some useful guidance toward national advertising was provided in 1858 with the publication of William Meikle's *Canadian Newspaper Directory, or Advertiser's Guide,* which classified 207 newspapers located in the Districts of Canada East and Canada West by publication schedule as well as political or religious affiliation.

In 1889 Anson McKim (1855–1917) founded the first national advertising agency in Canada, initially to assist Montreal merchants in placing advertisements in Ontario publications. McKim's company, which pioneered the strategy of the national advertising campaign, flourished, despite some early resistance by newspaper proprietors to paying an agency commission to a third party. By 1892 publication of *The Canadian Newspaper Directory* (later *McKim's Directory of Canadian Publications*) began, in part, to deflate the circulation claims of numerous publishers in the era prior to the auditing of circulation figures.[22] These innovations in the technology of printing and illustrating – along with the rise of modern commercial advertising – transformed the physical appearance of newspapers and magazines into recognizably modern formats. They also facilitated the emergence of mass-market publications that depended on advertising revenues – and ever-increasing circulation figures – rather than on cash subsidies from political parties and government printing contracts. Without these developments an independent and 'free' press would scarcely have been possible. Similarly, the technological revolution that yielded railways, telegraphs, and copious supplies of cheap paper was a necessary prerequisite to the emergence of communication media that were both mass-produced and nationally distributed.

The People behind the Periodical Press

The rise and development of Canada's periodical press was, naturally, a function of the people who served it, and it is mirrored in their evolving roles and professional differentiation. In the pioneering days of the job-printing proprietor, often his sole capital was his hand-press, fonts of type, and skill as a printer. The evolution of the Canadian press from a highly politicized and 'sectarian' orientation to one more attuned to a businesslike appeal to a mass audience served by several distinct and professional groups is perhaps best illustrated by a brief survey and categorization of some archetypes. Because these same people produced some of Canada's most successful and historically significant periodicals, this approach also highlights many of these important titles.

POLITICS AND THE 'SECTARIAN' PRESS

Canada's early printer-proprietors had been, of necessity, the clients, and in most cases even the direct hirelings, of government authorities. With the emergence of legislative bodies and political factions, however, it was inevitable that periodicals would be pressed into service as a vehicle for opposition as well as for defence of the establishment. Thus the proliferation of newspapers was fuelled further by the adoption of partisan roles. While the first generation or two of Canadian periodical publishers were primarily job-printers, for whom producing gazettes and almanacs was a sideline, frequently they were succeeded by politicians who established publications mainly to promote their political agendas and careers. It has been said that it was practically impossible for nineteenth-century editors not to be (or to become) politicians. Practically speaking, however, the emergence of politicians from the world of journalism, as well as the emergence of the modern professional journalist, whether editor or reporter, required the separation of editing and writing for a living from proprietorship. Only proprietors enjoyed the leisure to aspire to full-time political careers.

The most celebrated and colourful of the proprietors who ranged themselves in opposition to government by oligarchy was a transplanted Scot named William Lyon Mackenzie (1795–1861). In the pages of his *Colonial Advocate* (1824–34) and *The Constitution* (1836–7), he attacked Upper Canada's ruling clique in language so sulphurous and virulent that, in 1826, his press office was destroyed by a mob. Undeterred, Mackenzie brought suit against the sheriff who had led the mob, won a substantial cash settlement, and was soon back in business with a better press and other new equipment. In 1828, he was elected to the House of Assembly of Upper Canada, in which he served as a leader and focus of the opposition.

Mackenzie's was not a lonely voice in the wilderness, for several other Upper Canadian weeklies embraced the cause of moderate reform, including the *Upper Canada Herald* (Kingston, 1819–51), *Brockville Recorder* (1821–1922), *Cobourg Reformer* (1832–7), *Hamilton Free Press* (1831–7?), *Kingston Spectator* (1833–40?), *British Colonial Argus* (St Catharines, 1833–1918), and *St Thomas Liberal* (1832–7). Arrayed on the establishment side were such papers as the *Cobourg Star* (1831–80), Hamilton *Western Mercury* (1831–5?), *Kingston Chronicle* (1819–33), Sandwich [Windsor] *Canadian Emigrant and Western District ... Advertiser* (1834–7?), and the Toronto-based semi-weeklies *Courier of Upper Canada* (1829–37) and *Patriot* (1828–52). Of all the early Upper Canada newspapers, the *Upper Canada Herald* was declared to be 'perhaps the most consistent, temperate, and useful periodical work in the Province,' by no less an authority than William Lyon Mackenzie. Indeed, the proprietor and editor of the *Herald*, Hugh C. Thomson (1791–1834), who served from 1824 in the Legislative Assembly, was as moderate and fair-minded a man as Mackenzie was intemperate and brash. Although not nearly as well known today as Mackenzie, 'Reforming Thomson' earned the respect of his contemporaries, and during his brief career made several lasting contributions both as publisher and parliamentarian.[23]

Meanwhile, in Lower Canada, opposition leader Louis-Joseph Papineau (1786–1871) enjoyed the support of *Le Canadien* under the brilliant editorship of Étienne Parent (1802–74), as well as the somewhat more extreme *La Minerve* under the editorship of Joseph-Ludger Duvernay (1799–1852) and Augustin-Norbert Morin (1803–65), and *Le Fantasque* (St Roch, 1837–49), a magazine devoted to political satire, founded and edited by the Swiss-born Napoléon Aubin (1812–90). On the other side of the political fence, such firmly Tory papers as the Montreal *Courant*, *Gazette*, and *Herald* and the Quebec City *Mercury* and *Morning Telegraph* supported the unreformed political establishment. In 1837 the political conflicts in the two Canadas boiled over, when both Mackenzie and Papineau led their supporters in armed rebellion. When the uprisings collapsed, Mackenzie, Papineau, and Duvernay fled to the United States to avoid arrest, Morin went into hiding, and Aubin and Parent were both jailed, despite the latter's having denounced the rebellion and dissociated himself from the *patriote* extremists.

During his lengthy exile, Mackenzie issued two émigré journals. *Mackenzie's British, Irish, and Canadian Gazette* (1838–40, first issued from New York City, then from Rochester, New York) printed Mackenzie's own account of the late rebellion, as well as the characteristic invective he hurled at British authorities. From June 1839 until April 1840, the *Gazette* was edited from Mackenzie's prison cell, while he served part of an eighteen-month sentence for violating American neutrality laws. During his incarceration he also began attacking American authorities. He amused himself by varying the banners of the *Gazette*: 'Monroe County Jail, Rochester,' 'the American Bastile [sic],' 'Sheriff Perrin's Bastile,' and finally 'Van Buren and Victoria's Bastile.' When it expired for lack of funds in December 1840, the *Gazette's* banner read *Mackenzie's Last Gazette*, but it was not his last publication. In April 1841 he launched the *Volunteer* (Rochester, 1841–2) with appeals for financial support and more invective against British authorities in Canada and London. It died the following spring after only nineteen issues.[24]

In Lower Canada, after Aubin and Parent were released from jail, they returned to the helms of their respective publications. In 1841 both Parent and Morin were elected to the Legislative Assembly of the newly unified province of Canada, and Morin ended his career as a judge. Napoléon Aubin was, in many ways, a francophone version of Mackenzie: a fierce opponent of authority and privilege; a dedicated (Quebec) nationalist who favoured independence, or, failing that, annexation by the United States; and an indefatigible journalist, who founded and conducted at least six periodicals and contributed regularly to at least four others. Although he concealed his Swiss-Protestant background, it no doubt coloured his hostility toward the Roman Catholic church, but where Mackenzie's prose was all bludgeoning bombast and invective, Aubin was a skilled satirist and poet who earned an honoured place in the canon of French-Canadian literature. *Le Fantasque* sold out as fast as it could be printed, and inspired many imitators, but was never equalled.[25]

Arthur Buies (born Joseph-Marie-Arthur Buie, 1840–1901) was perhaps Aubin's nearest rival as a stylist, wit, satirist, polemicist, nationalist, foe of clericalism, and progenitor of periodicals. As well as becoming Quebec's most prominent columnist, through his contributions to a variety of newspapers, Buies founded and edited several journals, including two satirical titles. In *La Lanterne canadienne* (1868–9, modelled on *La Lanterne* in Paris), and *Le Réveil* (1876) Buies waged a weekly war of words against Ultramontanism and the other excesses of the Roman

Catholic church in Quebec, particularly its stranglehold on the educational system. The Church hierarchy declared both journals anathema, thus sealing their fate, though Buies persisted with *La Lanterne* for twenty-seven weeks, and moved *Le Réveil* from Quebec City to Montreal in a futile attempt to salvage it. These were only early rounds in the struggle by elements of the Québécois press for complete intellectual freedom.[26]

The failed rebellion of 1837 temporarily blunted the edge of French-Canadian nationalism, but journalism continued to flourish there after the union of the two Canadas in 1840. Parent was succeeded as editor of *Le Canadien* by Joseph Édouard Cauchon (1816–85), who also founded *Journal de Québec* (1842–9). In 1844 he, too, turned to a political career, and was elected to the Legislative Assembly of Canada. He later served in the Dominion cabinet and as Lieutenant-Governor of Manitoba, and supported the movement for confederation in an influential book addressed to French Canadians. *Le Canadien* lost the pre-eminence it had enjoyed under Parent, but Cauchon's *Journal de Québec* and *La Minerve* under the revived editorship of Duvernay continued to serve as the leading French-language organs of reform-liberalism. Extreme nationalism died hard, however, and by 1847 it had found renewed expression in both the *parti rouge* and an extremely influential publication, *L'Avenir* (Montreal, 1847–57), under the editorship of Jean-Baptiste-Eric Dorion (1826–66). Opposition to such views was provided by both moderate and extreme conservatives and by the Roman Catholic church, whose Montreal diocesan paper, *Mélanges religieux* (1840–52), under the editorship of Hector Langevin (1826–1906), became a widely influential voice for pro-clerical or Ultramontane ('Ultra') views.

The Ultramontanist cause was also served by journalists of considerable flamboyance. François-Xavier-Anselme Trudel (1838–90) began his career while still a seminary student, working for the controversial Liberal paper *Le Pays* (Montreal, 1852–71). Although he switched from the priesthood to law, he was a committed 'Ultra,' believed in militant Catholic activism, and was generally regarded as the lay leader of the 'Castors,' or extreme 'Ultras,' whose views he promoted in his newspaper *L'Étendard* (Montreal, 1883–93). At the same time, Trudel served in Canada's federal Parliament as both member and speaker of the House of Commons. Still more extreme was Jules-Paul Tardivel (1851–1905). Born in Kentucky of European immigrant parents, he was educated in Quebec, where he chose to make his home. After working for such Conservative party papers as *Le Courrier de Saint Hyacinthe, La Minerve*

(Montreal), and *Le Canadien* (Quebec City), he borrowed money to found *La Verité* (Montreal, 1881–1923), which he modelled on *L'Univers* in Paris. He sought to keep it financially independent of all political parties. In it he promoted uncompromising Catholicism and French-Canadian separatism, and attacked everyone – Liberals, Conservatives, and Roman Catholic bishops for being too liberal, and Radicals for their anticlericalism – although he was frequently in agreement with Trudel and his *L'Étendard.* Tardivel's feuds even with the 'Ultra' bishops caused Archbishop Louis-Nazaire Bégin (1840–1925) to despair of his inflexibility, while his novel *Pour la patrie* (1895), in which he celebrated his vision of an independent French-Catholic nation, was said to have shocked even conservative 'Ultras.' While *La Verité* was a prime example of 'sectarian' journalism, and in its best years achieved a circulation of no more than three thousand, it was progressive in the narrow sense of eschewing, along with the new 'mass-market, populist' press, any direct financial dependency upon political parties.[27]

In the face of a militantly Roman Catholic brand of 'sectarian' journalism, it should be no surprise to find another variety which was militantly Protestant. John Dougall (1808–86), an enterprising Scot and editor (1835–45) of the *Canadian Temperance Advocate,* developed a flourishing printing and publishing business. It produced the fiercely Protestant *Witness* (1846–1938), the first Canadian paper to employ newsboys to hawk it in the streets, and *Canadian Messenger* (Montreal, 1866–75, continued by *Northern Messenger,* 1876–1935), a twice-monthly temperance paper. In the year of Confederation, he launched the *New Dominion Monthly* (1867–79), a self-proclaimed 'high class literary magazine' aimed at a national audience. At its peak, circulation of the *New Dominion* reached eight thousand, and it quickly evolved into a handsome, general-interest magazine with subject departments calculated to appeal to many readers. Nonetheless, it depended too heavily upon subscription revenues, and Dougall neglected to capitalize on its advertising potential, perhaps because of his religious scruples.[28]

Although Quebec was the centre of the most politicized and 'sectarian' journalism, it also throve in Atlantic Canada. An outstanding example was Joseph Howe (1804–73) of Halifax, son of Loyalist printer and publisher John Howe (who had produced Canada's first English-language magazine). Joseph was apprenticed in the printing trade, but he devoted the bulk of his energies and career to politics. In 1828 he sold his interest in *Acadian Recorder* (formerly, *Weekly Chronicle*), and purchased the four-year-old *Novascotian,* which he turned into a reform organ.

Although much less flamboyant and more cautious than Mackenzie, Howe was charged with libel in 1835, for publishing a letter critical of the Nova Scotia magistracy. Howe was acquitted following a six-hour oration in his own defence, and his case was a milestone in the establishment of a free press in Canada. Thereafter, except for one interlude when he returned to the editorship of the *Novascotian* (1843–8), Howe pursued reform from within the halls of government. In 1847 Nova Scotia became the first province to achieve fully representative government, in large measure because of the efforts of Howe and the *Novascotian*.[29]

Irish immigrant Timothy Warren Anglin (1822–96), like Joseph Howe an opponent of confederation, also mixed a career in politics with one in journalism. Anglin arrived in Saint John, New Brunswick, in 1849, and lost no time in establishing the *Freeman* (1849–84), first as a weekly, then as a daily newspaper representing the views and interests of Irish Catholics. Eventually reconciled to the reality of confederation, he served in the federal House of Commons as both member and speaker. The *Freeman* typified the third distinct strain of militant 'sectarian' journalism, the Irish-Catholic.[30]

A young Nova Scotian named William Alexander Smith (1825–97), a disciple of Howe's, arrived on Vancouver Island by way of the California gold rush. Taking the name 'Amor De Cosmos' for more than a mere nom de plume, he established the *British Colonist* at Victoria in 1858 and set about attacking the colonial government. By the time he sold the paper in 1863, it had evolved into a daily with a circulation of several thousand. It had also served its purpose of launching him on a political career, which led to the premiership of a united province of British Columbia within the Canadian confederation.[31]

In Canada West, the new, post-rebellion generation of journalists was typified by George Brown, who, if less colourful than Mackenzie, was considerably more influential. Indeed, in that respect, his principal rivals were Ryerson of *Christian Guardian* and Duvernay of *La Minerve*. Perhaps Brown is the best example of the publisher as politician manqué and arch-manipulator. After a brief spell in New York, where Brown and his father published the *British Chronicle* for British immigrants, they moved to Toronto in 1843, and began publication of a Presbyterian paper, *Banner* (1843–8). The following year the younger Brown founded the *Globe*, progenitor of today's *Globe and Mail* ('Canada's National Newspaper'). While its descendant is somewhat stuffily conservative, Brown's *Globe* was a reform journal, instrumental in the formation of Canada's Liberal party. Brown entered the provincial House of Assembly in 1851 and pursued the Reformers' political agenda there, as well as in the pages of his increasingly influential newspaper. The status of the *Globe* as the voice of the opposition was solidified in 1855, when it absorbed two other reform journals, James Lesslie's (1800–85) *Toronto Examiner* (1838–55) and William McDougall's (1822–1905) *North American* (1850–5). Although he was a supporter of confederation, Brown's aggressive and domineering personality made co-operation with Sir John A. Macdonald and the Conservatives a trial for all concerned. Employees of the *Globe* fared little better, and one, who had been given the sack, invaded his office with a revolver, and extracted a lethal revenge.[32]

Coincidentally, a similar fate awaited Thomas D'Arcy McGee, one of Brown's contemporaries and counterparts in Montreal. After a long career as journalist and editor in Ireland and the United States, he moved to Montreal in 1857, where he founded a newspaper, *New Era* (1857–8), before entering the Legislative Assembly the following year. McGee became a powerful advocate, not merely of confederation, but also of Canadian culture and nationalism. He argued the need to develop a Canadian consciousness through a new, national literature, and repented his youthful anglophobia. His new-found Loyalist sentiments led him to criticize the Irish nationalist Fenian Society, which had mounted an ill-fated invasion of Canada West from across the American border in 1866. In reprisal McGee was later shot down in the street in Ottawa by a Fenian assassin.[33]

Two final examples of political, or 'sectarian,' journalists are worthy of mention, both of them mavericks who were viewed with disdain by many as mercenaries, or at least as opportunists. Edward 'Ned' Farrer (c.1846–1916) was an Irish immigrant, who, as editor of the Toronto *Mail* (1872–95; afterward merged to form the *Mail and Empire*, 1896–1936; still later the *Globe and Mail*, 1936–) in the 1880s, took an extreme Anglo-Protestant stance, attacked the Roman Catholic church, broke with Macdonald's government, denounced the British connection, and promoted 'annexationism,' that is, union with the United States. Farrer was equally celebrated for his gift of friendship, even with obvious political opponents. Like Farrer, Nicholas Flood Davin (1840–1901) hailed from Ireland, and, also like Farrer, he freely embroidered or invented his early biography. After pursuing a career in journalism and law in Toronto, and failing in his first attempt to win a seat in Parliament, Davin moved west in 1882, and the following year founded the conservative Regina *Leader*. In 1887 he at last won a seat in the Commons, but was frustrated in his pursuit of cabinet office. This disappointment and his weakness for drink are generally held to have led to his suicide.[34]

EDITOR-PUBLISHERS AS BUSINESS MAGNATES

In the second half of the nineteenth century a new breed of proprietor began to emerge, the publisher as businessman. If not devoid of political interests or objectives, he was at least content to pursue them through the influence of the press, rather than seek office to participate personally in governing. The emergence of editors and publishers who were primarily devoted to the business of editing and publishing coincided, as Rutherford has observed, with the decline of the overtly 'sectarian' press in Canada, and its replacement by the 'popular' or 'mass-market' press, and what was called the 'new journalism,' a trend also discernible in Britain and the United States.

Georges Édouard Desbarats succeeded his father Georges Paschal Desbarats (1808–64) in the role of Queen's Printer in 1865, but after a disastrous fire destroyed his Ottawa printing plant, he focused his business in Montreal. He saw the commercial possibilities of William Leggo's 'Leggotypes,' and launched *Canadian Illustrated News*, which featured the world's first published photo-engravings. It was an instant success. The following year it was joined by *L'Opinion publique illustré*, and for the next decade and a half they chronicled Canadian events in words and pictures. Desbarats quickly capitalized upon his successes. In 1871–2 he founded several new publications, including *L'Étendard publique*, yet another version of *Illustrated News*, for export to francophones in the United States. He also purchased the *Hearthstone* (1870–2), a weekly fiction magazine which he renamed the *Favourite: An Illustrated Journal of Amusing and Useful Reading* (1873). However, his ambitious invasion of the New York City newspaper market with the *New York Daily Graphic* (1873–80) – the world's first illustrated daily paper and the first daily to use photographic half-tones – led to bankruptcy. Desbarats was down, but undeterred. Following the demise (in others' hands) of *Illustrated News*, he founded *Dominion Illustrated News [Monthly]*, which carried on the tradition for a few more years, though now on glossy stock and with the finest half-tones. *L'Opinion publique illustré* also had a successor, *Le Monde illustré* (1884–1900), published by Trefflé Berthiaume (1848–1915), a seasoned Québécois journalist, who in 1889 purchased the Montreal daily *La Presse* (1884–), a paper that revolutionized Quebec journalism by introducing the sensationalist approach pioneered in the United States by Joseph Pulitzer (1847–1911).[35]

John Ross Robertson (1841–1918), another magnate, began his publishing career while still in high school. In 1857 he produced the first school newspaper in Canada, the *College Times*, on a hand-press at

Upper Canada College in Toronto. When his journalism fell afoul of school authorities, production briefly went underground, and the title changed to the *Boy's Times* and the *Monthly Times*, but the paper survived. He repeated the formula with *Young Canada* (1859–60) while attending the Model Grammar School, and as a young entrepreneur established Canada's first sports periodical, *Sporting Life* (Toronto, 1863–?), as well as the country's first regularly published railway guides (*Robertson's Railway Guide*, 1860–? and the *International Railway Guide*, 1864–?). Robertson's next major venture was to found the Toronto *Daily Telegraph* (1866–72), but he lost control of it. After a stint working for George Brown at the *Globe*, Robertson borrowed enough money to found the Toronto *Evening Telegram* (1876–1971), which brought him both fame and riches. From his office in the *Telegram* building he devoted much of the rest of his long life to philanthropy and to composing a multivolume history of Toronto.[36]

John Wilson Bengough (1851–1923) was yet another editor whose efforts led to the creation of a major business. He apprenticed as a printer on the *Whitby Gazette* (1862–1941) in Ontario, and later worked as a reporter for Brown's *Globe*, though his heart and destiny lay in cartooning. He idolized Thomas Nast (1840–1902), the American whose crusading political cartoons adorned the pages of *Harper's Weekly*. While exploring the use of lithography to reproduce cartoons, Bengough turned his cartoonist's pen to creating *Grip* (1873–94), Canada's most celebrated magazine of political satire. Fate soon smiled on him in the form of the 'Pacific Scandal,' in which contractors building the Canadian Pacific Railway were forced to make campaign contributions to the Conservative party. The ensuing uproar led to the fall of Sir John A. Macdonald's first government and his party's defeat in the election of 1873. Bengough's caricatures of Macdonald not only helped the circulation figures of *Grip* burgeon, they were a staple in the magazine until Macdonald's death in office in 1891. In addition to its social and political significance, Bengough's satirical magazine also served as a place to experiment with the printing of illustrations, including 'zincography.' In partnership with his brothers, Bengough founded Grip Printing and Publishing Company, which flourished for many years as a major book- and job-printing firm and publisher of numerous books and journals.[37]

Edmund Ernest Sheppard (1855–1924) went to the United States to pursue his education, as well as adventure, which he found working as a cowboy in Texas. Back in Canada by 1878, he worked for a succession of newspapers, including the Toronto *News* (1881–1919), where he was editor-in-chief and proprietor (1883–7). He was forced to sell that newspaper by a disastrous libel judgment, but fresh success beckoned in the form of a new publishing venture. In 1887 he launched a weekly 'non-political' magazine, *Toronto Saturday Night* (after 1889, *Saturday Night*). Notable today as the only continuously published popular magazine from Canada's Victorian past, *Saturday Night* was an immediate success. Handsomely produced with fine illustrations, it featured departments of commerce, drama, music, society, and sport. One key to its popularity may have been the considerable attention it paid to women and women's issues. Writing as 'Don,' Sheppard found an editorial platform that brought him national prominence, and, despite a failed attempt in 1893 to create a separate western edition in Winnipeg, the magazine flourished. By 1900 it had achieved a national circulation of fifteen thousand.[38]

Colonel (of Militia) John Bayne Maclean (1862–1950) apprenticed as a reporter for several Toronto newspapers, including the *Mail*, where in 1884 he was made assistant commercial-financial-marine editor. The assignment did little to alleviate Maclean's perennial innocence about finance, but it did bring him the acquaintance of the city's business elite, and soon inspired him to publish his first trade journal, *Canadian Grocer and General Storekeeper* (1887–93, continued as *Canadian Grocer*, 1894–), with three thousand dollars in capital. Such a specialized publication could give the business community the detailed information that the general newspapers of the day could not, and its success soon led to the appearance of *Hardware: The Organ of Wrought, Cast, Stamped, Sheet, and Spun Metal Trades* (1888–), *Canadian Dry Goods Review* (1891–1901, continued as *Dry Goods Review*, 1902–), *Printer and Publisher* (1892–), and *Books and Notions* (1894–5, continued as *Bookseller and Stationer*, 1896–1910). Thus began a magazine publishing empire based upon the profitability of upwards of eighty trade journals, but that is only half of the story.

In 1893 Maclean's old friends at the *Mail* commissioned him to produce a premium supplement entitled *Art Weekly*, that could be sold in bulk to other newspapers. Maclean left his trade journals in the capable hands of his brother, Hugh, and moved to New York City to organize production of the supplement. There he met the American publishing giants William Randolph Hearst (1863–1951), S.S. McClure (1857–1949), and Frank Andrew Munsey (1854–1925). Maclean's lifelong friendship with Munsey influenced him greatly, and helped inspire him to branch out into publication of high-quality general-interest and women's magazines. The other great passion of Maclean's life, the Canadian Militia in which he served for over twenty years, inspired him in 1896 to purchase the *Canadian Military Gazette* (Montreal, 1892–1948; renamed *Canadian Military Gazette and Gentlemen's Magazine* in 1900; sold in 1906). Maclean's colleague (and later, partner) Horace T. Hunter (1881–1961) was a shrewd money manager, whose skills perfectly complemented Maclean's expansive manner and inattention to financial details. By mastering the art of mass-market journal publishing, Maclean-Hunter Limited elevated its founder to a position of national prominence and influence, and in the next century the firm became the largest private publisher in Canada. Maclean defined a successful formula for periodical publication in Canada. In addition, his policy of staffing his publications with university graduates, such as Hunter, was a watershed in the professionalization of Canadian journalism and publishing. Political ambition was rapidly declining as a motive for entering these fields.[39]

EMERGENCE OF PROFESSIONAL EDITORS AND JOURNALISTS

While editors, as distinct from printers and publishers, had been involved in the production of Canadian periodicals almost from the beginning, the role of editor was primarily a sideline for gentlemen or well-educated professionals, clergymen, and the like, who harboured literary interests and could spare the time. The emergence of full-time professionals who were paid to gather, write, and edit was essential to the development of modern periodicals as we know them. Before considering a few archetypal figures, however, one prominent and prolific writer must be mentioned – Goldwin Smith – who really fits none of these categories because of his unwillingness to assume the mantle of proprietor or editor.

Goldwin Smith (1823–1910) resigned the Professorship of Modern History at Oxford and, after a brief tenure at Cornell, settled in Toronto in 1871. Already a man of independent means, he married a wealthy Toronto widow, and thus obtained further resources to support publications and political causes with cash subsidies as well as his copious writings. As 'A Bystander,' he was a frequent contributor to *Canadian Monthly* (1872–8), although he declined the editorship. As a leader of the patriotic Canada First movement, which sought to promote Canadian nationalism, he founded the *Nation* (1874–6) as its chief organ, and contributed up to three leaders a week. In 1874 Smith also provided backing for the short-lived paper the *Liberal* (1875), produced by politician Edward Blake (1833–1912) during his brief flirtation with Canada First. In 1876 Smith loaned John Ross Robertson the capital to found his long-running Toronto *Telegram*. In 1880 Smith founded another journal of opinion, the *Bystander* (1880–1 monthly; 1883 quarterly; 1889–90 monthly), which he wrote virtually in its entirety. In 1883, wearying of the labour of writing the *Bystander*, he helped found yet another organ of public debate, the *Week: An Independent Journal of Literature, Politics, and Criticism* (1883–96), for which he produced weekly articles. Under the editorship of Charles G.D. Roberts (1860–1943), the *Week* achieved lasting literary significance by publishing work by Canada's leading authors and poets. Despite the stimulus it provided to writers, the Canada First movement succumbed to conflicting agendas, and Goldwin Smith alienated many former colleagues at the *Week* when his advocacy of a North American commercial union led him to speculate about the inevitability of political union with the United States. The mere suggestion of that was tantamount to treason in the eyes of many, but Smith would not be stilled. From 1893 he was a regular contributor to *Canadian Magazine*, and in 1896 he purchased the faltering *Farmer's Sun* (London, Ont., 1892–6) and christened it *Weekly Sun* (1896–1934). In his weekly contributions for the next thirteen years he promoted the interests of farmers, advocated his brand of 'continentalism,' and pronounced upon society's ills, including the tendency of the press and journalists to become the pawns of big business and the marketplace at the expense of their independence and integrity.[40]

Graeme Mercer Adam (1839–1912), who emigrated from Scotland in 1858, began as a proprietor. In 1863 he married Joan, the widow of John Gibson, co-publisher of *Literary Garland*, whose business he thus acquired. He founded *British-America Magazine* (1865–6); *Canadian Bookseller and Miscellany* (1865–7), an early trade journal; and *Canadian Monthly and National Review* (1872–7). Goldwin Smith declined the editorship, but was a frequent contributor to this high-quality review. When Adam, Stevenson, and Company went bankrupt in 1876, Adam departed for the United States to pursue new opportunities. He was reduced to hired editor, but he remained a prolific writer throughout his life. *Canadian Monthly*, after a long financial struggle, was acquired by Charles Belford (1837–80), who, with his two brothers as partners, had begun *Belford's Monthly Magazine: A Magazine of Literature and Art* in 1876. The following year, *Canadian Monthly* and *Belford's Monthly* were merged to form *Rose-Belford's Canadian Monthly and National Review* (1878–82). The rechristened magazine was edited by George Stewart (1848–1906), former proprietor and editor of *Stewart's Literary Quarterly Magazine* (1867–72). When he left to edit the Quebec *Chronicle* (1847–1934), he was succeeded by Graeme Mercer Adam, who had returned to Toronto and founded yet another magazine, *Canadian Edu-*

cational Monthly (1879–84). After the demise of *Rose-Belford's Canadian Monthly*, Adam went to work for Goldwin Smith, and served as business manager of the *Bystander*. Adam returned to the United States in 1891, and spent the remainder of his life engaged in various editorial and publishing jobs.[41]

James Gordon Mowat (1851–1906) was both proprietor and editor of the Galt, Ontario, *Reformer* (1874–81) while still in his twenties. Later he joined the staff of the Toronto *Globe*. In 1893, with a group of fellow Liberals, he founded *Canadian Magazine of Politics, Science, Art, and Literature* (1893–1939), and he became the first editor. Patterned on such high-quality American titles as *Atlantic*, *Harper's*, and *Scribner's*, the new journal was priced aggressively at twenty-five cents per issue, each of which ran to approximately 150 pages. It was illustrated with photo half-tones, a third of which might contain advertisements, although these were segregated, as was the practice, at the front and rear of the text. John Alexander Cooper (1868–1956) replaced Mowat, who returned to the *Globe* in 1895, and under Cooper's aegis the editorial tone of *Canadian Magazine* shifted markedly to the right. It absorbed *Massey's Illustrated* (Toronto, 1882–95), and by the end of the decade *Canadian Magazine* ranked alongside the *Week* as one of Canada's most outstanding national magazines. Later, however, *Canadian Magazine* evolved into a bland, mass-circulation, family magazine, which may just explain its forty-six-year run.[42]

Sir John Stephen Willison (1856–1927) earned his living at a succession of storekeeping jobs before finding work in 1881 as a reporter for the London *Advertiser* (1863–1936), the leading Liberal paper in western Ontario. When the founding publisher of the *Advertiser*, John Cameron (1843–1908), moved to Toronto in 1883 to assume the post of editor and general manager of the *Globe*, he took young Willison with him. Willison gained journalistic stature as the Ottawa parliamentary correspondent of the *Globe*. In 1890 he succeeded Cameron as its editor, a post he held for the next twelve years. Willison became one of the most famous and influential journalists in English Canada.[43]

Henri d'Hellencourt (1862–1940) came from a very different background. He gave up his commission in the French army for the love of a divorced woman, with whom he immigrated in 1891 to Ste-Anne-des-Chênes, Manitoba, where they soon took up a homestead. Farming failed to engage his considerable intellect, however, so late in 1897 they moved to nearby Winnipeg, where in January 1898, d'Hellencourt became editor of a new Liberal weekly journal, *L'Écho de Manitoba* (1898–1905, after November 1903, *L'Écho du Manitoba*). In 1905 d'Hellencourt collected on his Liberal loyalty and went east as an editor, first to *Le Temps* (Ottawa, 1894–1916) in 1905–6, then to *Le Soleil* (Quebec, 1880–), and finally to *La Presse*, from 1920 to 1928. He retired to France in ill-health in 1929.[44]

John Wesley Dafoe (1866–1944) served a nearly twenty-year apprenticeship. From novice reporter in 1883 for *Family Herald and Weekly Star* (Montreal, 1869–1968), he was promoted in 1884 to serve as the Ottawa correspondent of the *Star*. In 1885 he served briefly on the Ottawa *Evening Journal*. After considering a move to the United States, he went west instead, and spent five years working for the *Manitoba Free Press* under the editorship of its founder, William F. Luxton (1844–1907). The political Liberalism of the *Free Press* was a refreshing change for Dafoe, after the Conservatism of his Ottawa employers, but he was lured back to Montreal by an editorial appointment. In 1897 the *Free Press* was acquired by Sir Clifford Sifton (1861–1929), then federal minister of the interior and a leader of the Manitoba Liberals. In the process of reorganizing the *Free Press*, Sifton sought a sound Liberal to fill the editor's chair. Dafoe was a happy choice, and over the next forty-five years he turned the *Free Press* into a newspaper of national importance, while he himself became arguably the most politically influential and respected newspaper editor in Canadian history.[45]

Joseph E. Atkinson (1865–1948), like Willison and Dafoe, came from a rural Ontario background. He served a four-year apprenticeship on the Port Hope, Ontario, *Times* (1862–1926), but in 1888 he left for a job with the Toronto *World* (1880–1921) after being refused a one-dollar-a-week raise. Recruited for the *Globe* by its new editor, J.S. Willison, Atkinson, at the age of twenty-three, was covering the Ontario Legislature, while showing his special talent for writing human interest stories. From 1891 to 1896 he served as the Ottawa parliamentary correspondent of the *Globe*, before becoming managing editor of the Montreal *Herald* in 1897, which was a Liberal paper under its new owner, J.S. Brierley (1858–1935). In 1899 Atkinson was offered a similar post at the Montreal *Star*, then the largest, richest, and most staunchly Conservative daily in Canada. As he agonized over the prospect of compromising his Liberal principles, he was at first urged to accept by his mentor, Willison, who next suggested Atkinson might wish to take the editor's chair at the foundering Toronto *Evening Star*, which had been founded by striking printers in 1892 as an organ of the trade unions. Toronto supporters of Sir Wilfrid Laurier's Liberal government considered the *Evening Star* a good evening complement to the morning *Globe*, so the purchase of the *Evening Star* by Liberal interests was arranged. Atkinson then turned down the offer from the more prestigious Montreal *Star*, and accepted the editorship of the Toronto *Star*, but only after insisting upon the right to maintain editorial independence and discretion. Thus began another long and distinguished editorial reign, as Atkinson – later owner as well as editor – used his personal, human-interest style of journalism to build the Toronto *Star* into Canada's largest and most profitable newspaper.[46]

From 1863 to 1876 (Clement-)Arthur Dansereau (1844–1918) had been editor-in-chief and co-proprietor of *La Minerve*. Known as 'Le Boss' when he was editor at *La Presse*, he played a key role in building *La Presse* into the premier French-language daily in Montreal. Like so many Québécois editors, Dansereau played an active role in politics, although the main hiatus in his career as a journalist was his appointment as Director of Posts for Montreal (1891–9). Upon his death he was hailed not just by *La Presse* but also by the Toronto *Mail and Empire* as 'one of the master journalists of his time.'[47]

Godfroy Langlois (1866–1928) has not been well served by either popular memory or memorials, despite a long career in journalism and politics during which, from 1897 to 1915, he edited, in succession, three major Montreal Liberal dailies – *La Patrie* (1879–), *Le Canada* (1903–54), and *La Pays* (1910–21) – and served in Quebec's provincial legislature. Langlois described himself as an extreme *rouge* in the tradition of Papineau, and his anticlericalism was reminiscent of Aubin and Buies. Langlois began his career as a journalist with savage attacks on the Church in the pages of *Le Clairon* (1889–90), which he also helped found. These attacks, as much as his ongoing, progressive crusades for educational and government reform, not only prompted the Church hierarchy to label him 'Lucifer's direct representative,' but in the end led to a break with Laurier and the more conservative elements which dominated the Liberal party in Quebec, and forced him and other progressives into political wilderness.[48]

Finally, no survey of archetypal Canadian professional editors and journalists would be complete without including (Thomas) Phillips Thompson (1844–1933), lawyer, humorist, journalist, socialist theorist, and author. Writing as 'Jimuel Briggs, D[ead] B[eat], of Coboconk University,' Thompson contributed satirical pieces to newspapers in St Catharines and Toronto, as well as to Bengough's *Grip*. In addition to a short-lived Toronto daily, Thompson founded a series of increasingly radical publications as platforms to advocate the redress of working-class grievances through unionization under the aegis of the American-based Knights of Labor, as well as a socialism that evolved from utopian to guild to Marxist. Over the years, Thompson's rhetoric grew more strident, and his vision more pessimistic, as he called not merely for social justice but for the overhaul of the entire social system, and anticipated violent social revolution. Thompson founded the *National* (1874–80) as a journal of political commentary, which at first supported the principles of the Canada First movement, although he broke with it over its intolerance of trade unions. After a sojourn in the United States, where he worked for the Boston *Courier* and *American Punch*, Thompson became a regular columnist – 'Enjolras' after a character in Hugo's *Les Misérables* – in the *Palladium of Labour* (Hamilton, 1883–6), the most outstanding example of the growing crop of labour publications in Canada addressed to the working class. Thompson's last project was to found the *Labour Advocate* (Toronto, 1890–1), the voice of the labour movement's radical socialist fringe. Its commercial failure, however, did not stop his tireless writing and organizing on behalf of socialism. He initiated much of that debate in the labour and establishment political press. As the leading student of the labour press has observed, Thompson's contribution to social reform in Canada can scarcely be overestimated. He also set the highest standards for labour journalism over the course of a long and colourful career.[49]

WOMEN AS JOURNALISTS

Mary Eliza Herbert and Mary Jane Lawson were Canada's first two women editors, and numerous women writers were at least occasional contributors to periodicals. However, the barriers to women earning their living as professional journalists were challenged only in the 1880s, and progress was slow, despite some few success stories. Male pseudonyms were still too often required in order for the few women who reported 'hard news' to be taken seriously by readers.

The first woman known to serve as the principal editor of a Canadian newspaper was the Black teacher and abolitionist Mary Ann Camberton Cary (née Shadd, 1823–93). Born in Delaware, the daughter of freemen and prominent abolitionists, she pursued a teaching career in the northern United States. In 1851 she moved to Windsor, Ontario, to work among the many American Blacks who took refuge in Canada following passage of the U.S. Fugitive Slave Act of 1850. After publishing pamphlets urging Black migration to and integration in Canada, she helped found *Provincial Freeman* (Windsor, 1853–4; Toronto, 1854–5; continued as *Provincial Freeman and Weekly Advertiser*, Chatham, 1855–9), and served as its actual, though not titular, editor. Over the next decade she served as the driving editorial force behind the financially troubled newspaper, married a local Black businessman, and bore two children. In 1863 she returned to the United States to work recruiting Black volunteers to serve in the Union Army. In 1865, at war's end, she elected to remain in the United States, where she devoted the rest of her life to the education and assimilation of her people. Mary Shadd Cary's situation was perhaps unique in the annals of Canadian journalism. The marginal status of the 'ethnic' press provided wide editorial scope for her leadership, though still camouflaged behind the names of figurehead male editors. On the other hand, her executive role in producing the *Provincial Freeman* meant that Mary Shadd Cary was not forced to choose between her work and marriage and family.[50]

Kate Eva Westlake (1856–1906) carried on the St Thomas, Ontario, *Evening Journal* (1876–1909?) for more than a decade after the sudden death of her brother in 1881. She often signed her contributions with pseudonyms, including 'Aunt Polly Wogg.' In 1893 she was hired by E.E. Sheppard (of *Saturday Night*) to become his assistant editor to produce *Canadian Fireside Weekly*, his newly acquired digest of fiction. She also contributed numerous articles, both signed and unsigned, to *Saturday Night* and *Canadian Magazine*.[51]

In 1886 Sara Jeannette Duncan (1862–1922) returned to her native Ontario, after working for the *Washington Post* and *Memphis Appeal*, to become the first woman writer to be employed full-time by the Toronto *Globe*. There she employed the pseudonym 'Garth Grafton.' In 1888 she was appointed Ottawa parliamentary correspondent of the Montreal *Star*.[52]

Equally well remembered as a pioneer Canadian woman journalist is Kathleen 'Kit' Coleman (née Watkins, 1854–1915). In 1889 she was hired by the Toronto *Mail* to edit Canada's first women's page, a post she held for more than twenty years. In addition to writing a weekly column that included Canada's first 'advice to the lovelorn' department, she gained fame through her special assignments. She covered such events as the 1893 Chicago World's Fair, Queen Victoria's second Jubilee in 1897, the great San Francisco earthquake and fire of 1906, and the sensational 1907 trial of Harry Thaw for the murder of New York architect Stanford White. With her coverage of the Spanish-American War in 1898, she became the world's first accredited woman war correspondent. When she at last parted company with the *Mail and Empire* (as it had become) in 1911, she continued writing as Canada's first syndicated columnist.[53]

(Ella) Cora Hind (1861–1942) was turned down in 1882 when she first applied for work at the Winnipeg *Free Press*. Ironically, at the end of the century the same newspaper appointed her its agricultural editor for, as Canada's leading authority on farming and marketing, she had won the acceptance and trust of farmers and stockmen, while her uncanny ability to forecast crop yields had gained her the devoted admiration of grain buyers and speculators. In a nation that was still primarily agricultural, she became Canada's 'best known newspaperman.'[54]

Admission of women to the journalism profession came even later in Quebec than it did in English Canada. Anne-Marie Huguenin (1875–1943), writing as 'Myrto,' began contributing to Berthiaume's *Le Monde illustré* in 1897, and later founded and edited two magazines of her own. Robertine Barry (1866–1910), writing as 'Françoise,' worked at *La Patrie* in Montreal in the 1890s. She left at the end of the century to found her own bi-monthly review, *Le Journal de Françoise*.[55]

Because the work of most women journalists was confined to the ghetto of the women's pages or society columns, they either went to the United States in search of wider opportunities, like Eve Brodlique, Ottawa correspondent for the London *Advertiser*, or remained in Canada and made the most of the opportunities, however limited. Many of them devoted their free time to such causes as temperance and women's suffrage. For some a successful journalistic career did not rule out other, more traditional, possibilities. Elmina Elliott (1867–1931) became the society editor of *Saturday Night*, and in 1888 succeeded Sara Duncan at the *Globe*, where her women's page column appeared under the name 'Madge Merton.' Later, as Mrs Joseph Atkinson, she enjoyed a long career as one of the 'powers behind the editor' at the Toronto *Star*.[56]

Survey and Summary by Genre

Early periodicals in Canada generally adopted a broad scope, if only because the road to financially viable circulation lay in trying to offer all things to all readers. This, in turn, often led to the use of pretentiously sweeping titles or subtitles, which not infrequently promised the reader more than the contents routinely delivered. However, the need to find and please a sufficiently large readership to achieve and sustain profitable publication generally did little to dilute the characteristic moral earnestness which coloured both contents and editorial tone. Favourite Victorian phrases, such as 'to amuse and instruct,' occur repeatedly in ornately decorated banners, mastheads, subtitles, and editorial policy statements.

Several principal subjects emerged early: horology (in the form of calendars and almanacs), politics, religion, and literature. As the nineteenth century progressed, especially during the second half, subject specialization increased, while newspapers and magazines evolved into more sharply differentiated media. This increasing specialization led to what was often called 'class periodicals' and 'class journalism.' In this context, that means the 'classification' of audience into special status or interest groups, which could reflect age, gender, occupation, recreation, or other affiliations. Two genres – political and literary – have already been discussed in some detail, so most of those titles need not be reiterated here. While any one of the other subject genres might repay further study, at least one – the labour press – already has yielded a substantial monograph.

Although a complete enumeration of Canadian periodicals prior to 1901 is not possible within the confines of this chapter, some enumerative analysis is both appropriate and feasible by using the largest extant list of pre-1901 Canadian serials. Ms Linda M. Jones, the compiler of this list, of necessity relied on library catalogues, databases, and various published bibliographies. While many institutional locations are given, Jones was unable to examine the publications, and she notes that the reliability of her sources was uneven, although overlapping institutional holdings permitted some corroboration. Predictable difficulties were encountered in distinguishing newspapers from magazines, and the list reflects an obvious bent toward what librarians and archivists have seen fit to preserve, with a consequent loss of the overly ephemeral and the excessively vulgar.[57]

A somewhat arbitrary scheme of single-category assignment was employed on the 1,944 titles in the primary sample. This distribution revealed that almost half of the magazine titles in the sample fall into the categories listed in table 2:1 under the general heading of 'Home and Farm.' These include: family, women's domestic, and children's magazines; the numerous agricultural publications which also addressed rural home life; those titles which catered for people's religious, fraternal, and educational affiliations; and journals addressed to recreational pursuits.

Those titles shown in table 2:2, which were addressed to the numerous 'Trades and Professions' in the rapidly expanding non-agricultural sector of the Canadian economy, account for more than 20 per cent of the sample.

Finally, the categories aggregated in table 2:3 as 'Improvement Literature' include a wide variety of genres, which have in common the aim of informing, enlightening, educating, and – at least in the case of the temperance publications – perhaps also reforming their readers.

TABLE 2:1
Home and Farm

	Number of Titles	Percentage of Sample
Family	50	2.6
Domestic/Women's	48	2.5
Children's	48	2.5
Agricultural	100	5.1
Religious	422	21.0
Fraternal (Lodges & Clubs)	47	2.4
School/Student	82	4.2
Hobbyist	98	5.0
Sporting	27	1.4
Total	922	47.4

TABLE 2:2
Trades and Professions

	Number of Titles	Percentage of Sample
Business/Trade/Industrial	262	13.5
Professional	156	8.0
Military	14	0.7
Labour	12	0.6
Total	444	22.8

TABLE 2:3
Improvement Literature

	Number of Titles	Percentage of Sample
General Interest	160	8.2
Literary/Cultural/Art/Music	167	8.6
Literary/Cultural (Regional)	73	3.8
University/Scholarly/Learned	26	1.3
Politics/Commentary	45	2.3
Humour/Satire	25	1.3
Ethnic/Native	27	1.4
Temperance	39	2
Total	562	28.9

HOME AND FARM

Almanacs

Almanacs deserve at least brief mention, both because they were among the first periodical publications in Canada, and because of their ubiquity in the early Canadian home, where they probably ranked second only to the Bible. Designed to lay out the astronomical calendar year, and to inform the farmer 'when to plant and when to pray,' they originally appeared in Canada, as elsewhere, in single-sheet format, akin to the modern wall calendar. The first in Canada, the *Almanac de cabinet*, was produced by the American printers Brown and Gilmore in 1765, the year after they established the *Quebec Gazette*. The *Nova-Scotia Calendar*, the first Canadian almanac in the more familiar pamphlet format, appeared in 1769. Others followed in New Brunswick (1786), Upper Canada (1800), and Prince Edward Island (1829). In addition to serving as agricultural and religious calendars, almanacs were usually filled with 'useful information,' ranging from weather forecasts, shipping rates, and directories of civil government, to tide tables in versions published in coastal cities. Throughout the nineteenth century, almanacs proliferated – Jones lists 427 of them – and, as an increasingly popular advertising medium, many were issued under the sponsorship of commercial institutions.[58]

Family/Domestic/Women's

These portmanteau categories may be joined with the titles classed as 'Agriculture/Farm Home,' for many of the latter included domestic material to appeal to farmers' wives, and some of these are among the earliest of domestic periodicals. As with all Canadian periodicals, the attrition rate for domestic and women's titles was very high, and many such efforts proved to be one- or two-issue phenomena. Some were published under institutional sponsorship, such as *Calliopean* (Hamilton, 1847–8) from the Burlington Ladies' Academy, although the majority appear to have been commercial ventures, albeit mostly unsuccessful ones.[59]

Somewhat more successful were *Gazette des familles [canadiennes et acadiennes]* (Ottawa, 1869–77); *Franc-parleur: journal à tous, journal pour tous* (Montreal, 1870–8); *Foyer domestique* (Ottawa, 1876–80, continued as *Album des familles*, 1880–4); John Dougall's *Household Journal* (Montreal, 1878–88); *Ladies' Journal: Devoted to Literature, Fashion, Domestic Matters &c.* (Toronto, 1880–1903); *Family Journal* (1882–1972), an English transplant which succeeded despite its stodginess in resisting design changes for its cover or advertising; *Ladies'*

Bazar [sic]: *A Journal of Fashion, Instruction, and Domestic Economy* (Toronto, 1887–90); *Modes françaises illustrées* (1887–92); *Home Circle Leader* (Guelph, 1889–1909); *Ladies' Home Monthly* (Toronto, 1889–93); *Ladies' Pictorial Weekly* (later *Monthly*) (Toronto, 1890–3); *Canadian Queen: A Magazine of Fashion, Art, Literature &c.* (Toronto, 1890–2), a failure despite being based on a highly successful English model; *Pacific Harbour Light* (Victoria, 1891, continued as *Victoria Home Journal*, 1891–4, *British Columbia Home Journal*, 1894–5); *Our Home: A Monthly Family Magazine* (Montreal, 1892–7, continued as *Home and Youth*, 1897–8); *Coin du feu: revue féminine* (Montreal, 1893–6); and, finally, *Le Cyclorama universel* (Montreal, 1895–7), which offered weekly dollops of arts, science, fashion, travel, and sports, and was the editorial handiwork of Jules Helbronner (1852–1921), better known as an editor of *La Presse*.

While it is outclassed in longevity by some of the agriculture and farm home periodicals such as *Family Herald and Weekly Star*, which lasted for about a century, the title in this genre most notable for survival is *Canadian Home Journal* (Toronto, 1895–1958), which persisted for more than sixty years before being absorbed by *Chatelaine*. While nineteenth-century improvements in the printing of illustrations had significant impact upon women's magazines, particularly in illustrating fashion and advertising new consumer products, nonetheless, the enormous success of this genre, especially for French-language magazines, came only in the twentieth century.

Children's

The low esteem into which religion lately has fallen is reflected in the frequency with which scholars overlook or dismiss the importance that our forbears placed on it. Thus, *Snow Drop; or, Juvenile Magazine*, and its rival, *Maple Leaf: A Juvenile Monthly Magazine* (Montreal, 1852–3, continued by *Illustrated Maple Leaf: A Canadian Magazine*, 1853–4), are cited routinely as the first periodicals for children in Canada.[60] Earlier examples of Canadian magazines for children appeared, but were suffused with the religiosity so characteristic of the period, and all were – also characteristically – short-lived. Among the earlier titles was the *Youth's Instructor* (1823–5), produced by Henry Chubb (1787–1855), printer at Saint John, New Brunswick, thus anticipating by more than a decade the similarly titled *Youth's Monitor and Monthly Magazine* (Toronto, 1836), by Samuel Read (d.1869), who issued only six numbers. Read declared his intention 'to instruct and generally improve ... to help the intellect – to pour light into the understanding – to inform the judgement – to improve the morals and correct the taste,' but this noble effort succeeded in attracting only twenty-three paid subscribers.[61] This rhetoric of moral uplift, standard for the period, may be overlooked by children's literature specialists either because of its religious agenda, or because it was addressed to the post-pubescent.

The *Child's Bible Expositor, or, Lessons and Records of the Sunday School* (Toronto, 1841–2), published by Henry Rowsell (1807–90), was no more successful than John Dougall's similar effort more than a decade later on behalf of the Canadian Sunday School Union: *Children's Missionary and Sabbath School Record* (Montreal, 1844–5). Similar magazines sponsored by particular denominations had more staying power – for example, *Juvenile Presbyterian: A Missionary Record and Sabbath Scholar's Newspaper* (Montreal, 1856–63) and *Children's Record: A Monthly Missionary Magazine for the Children of the Presbyterian Church in Canada* (New Glasgow, N.S., and Montreal, 1886–96), although the Anglican *Young Churchman: A Literary Magazine* (Toronto, 1851) appears to have foundered after a single issue. The *Life Boat: A Juvenile Temperance Magazine* (Montreal, 1852–3) stayed afloat somewhat longer. Foreign-language juveniles also failed to find a successful formula, as is suggested by *Deutsche Jugend-Zeitung* (Elmira, Ont., 1875–7?); *Christliche Kinderwelt* (Listowel, Ont., 1885); *Kindergarten* (Toronto, 1885); and *Young Highland Visitor/An Gartear Og Gaelach* (Antigonish, N.S., 1851).

Late in the century a few titles specializing in fiction found favour with Canadian youth, such as *Young Canada: Illustrated Annual for Boys* (Toronto, 1880–?), *Écho des jeunes: revue littéraire* (Ste Cunégond, Que., 1891–5), and Canadian editions of the British *Boy's Own Paper* and *Girl's Own Paper* (Toronto, 1880–1907?). During much of this period Canadian children and adolescents were supplied with imported titles, or made do without periodicals.

Agricultural

The importance of agriculture in Canada is reflected in the number of agricultural journals produced in this period – one hundred in Jones's *Preliminary Checklist* – as well as in the titles of some early Canadian weeklies: *Farmer's Gazette* (Markham, Ont., 1826–7), *Farmer's Journal and Welland Canal Intelligencer* (St Catharines, 1826–34), *Farmer's and Mechanic's Journal and Eastern Township Gazette* (1834–8), and *Bytown Independent and Farmers' Advocate* (1836). These weekly newspapers catered for a rural, agrarian readership with features and columns; agriculture, however, was not their principal focus. The first journal to focus primarily, but not exclusively, on agriculture was *Glaneur, journal littéraire et d'industrie* (St Charles, Que., 1836–7). The following year William Evans (1786–1857), an immigrant agricultural reformer from Ireland, published two issues of *Canadian Quarterly Agricultural and Industrial Magazine* (Montreal, 1838). Undeterred by this failure, he tried again in 1844 with *Canadian Agricultural Journal*, for which he later secured the backing of the Agricultural Society of Lower Canada, and which was issued in parallel English- and French-language editions for many years. Evans remained editor until his death.[62]

Meanwhile, in Canada West, an Agricultural Society was formed in 1846, a government Board of Agriculture followed in 1850, and the Board and Society merged in 1851. The Society's first secretary, William Graham Edmundson (c.1815–52), was the founder of a journal which, under a number of titles, proved to be very long-lived. His *British-American Cultivator* (Toronto, 1842–8) was absorbed by *Canada Farmer* (1847–9), and continued as *Canadian Agriculturist*. It passed through the ownership of the Board of Agriculture before being sold to George Brown of the Toronto *Globe*, who retitled it *Canada Farmer* (1864–9). It was the first of these journals to use extensive illustrations, and was soon selling twenty thousand copies fortnightly. Finally, Brown merged it with the weekly edition of his *Globe*, and it became the weekly *Globe and Canada Farmer* (1869–76).[63]

Farther west, William Weld (1824–91) established the long-running *Farmer's Advocate [and Home Magazine]* (London, Ont., 1866–1951), which later produced a 'Manitoba and western' edition (Winnipeg, 1890–1924). Earlier, the Winnipeg *Free Press* had begun the *Free Press Prairie Farmer* (1872–1965). At about the same time, the Montreal *Star* undertook publication of its enormously successful *Family Herald and Weekly Star* – 'Canada's National Farm Journal' – which enjoyed a ninety-nine-year run, and included a Boston edition. A similarly impressive run was displayed by the influential *Nor'West Farmer and Manitoba Miller* (Winnipeg, 1882–1936).[64]

These publications were a valuable way to advertise farm-oriented products, so it is not surprising that some of those advertisers entered the field with publications of their own, such as *Massey's Illustrated: A Journal of News and Literature for Rural Homes*, founded by Walter Massey (1864–1901) of the agricultural implement manufacturing family, or *Farmer's Advance* (Toronto, 1900–?), published by the McCormick Harvester Machine Company. Even that irrepressible crusading journalist, Goldwin Smith, entered the field when he purchased the foundering *Farmer's Sun* in 1896. Retitled the *Weekly Sun*, it served as his editorial platform for the remainder of his life, and became the most frequently quoted paper in the province.[65]

Despite these success stories, this genre, too, was filled with failures in both English and French. The most successful of these journals succeeded precisely because they adopted the 'something for the whole farm family' formula, which made them precursors of the general family, domestic, and women's magazines. Thus, *Family Herald and Weekly Star* was particularly well regarded for its offerings of high-grade fiction. This was no doubt an inevitable result of the substitution of commercial publishers for the agricultural societies and boards which had often provided the sponsorship needed to launch and sustain such publications. As these farm journals became more commercial and general in scope and content, there naturally arose a wave of more specialized titles devoted to practical applications or to more abstract, scientific research. The publishers of the latter were generally associations of growers and breeders, or learned societies or universities.[66]

Religious

That religion and religious concerns permeated nearly every aspect of nineteenth-century life is reflected in the plethora of religious periodicals that were produced. Even after newspapers are excluded, Jones enumerated 422 examples, or more than 20 per cent of her sample. Some of this quantity is attributable to the urge to present devoutly religious alternatives to the increasingly secular publications of the day. *Écho du cabinet de lecture paroissial* (Montreal, 1859–75), for example, was produced by a literary circle of Sulpician priests to report news and to present religion, philosophy, science, and literature from a devoutly Roman Catholic viewpoint. The Abbé Thomas-Aimé Chandonnet (1834–81) attempted to offer a general-interest magazine in the same spirit with his *Revue de Montréal* (1877–81), a project which died with its founder. The same need to interpret the world through the filter of religion was no less evident among the Protestant faithful in Canada, whose sectarian fragmentation only multiplied the number of titles required to do the job. Among the first of these was Egerton Ryerson's Wesleyan Methodist *Christian Guardian*, published by the Methodist Book Room, which evolved into the Methodist Book and Publishing House (known after 1919 as Ryerson Press). After 1879, under the stewardship of William Briggs (1836–1922), it became one of Canada's most important publishers. The *Christian Guardian* was joined later by the *British North American Wesleyan Magazine* (Saint John, N.B., 1840–7), edited by James Hogg (1800–66) for the 'New Connection' Methodists, and the *[Cana-*

dian] Methodist Magazine [and Review] (Toronto, 1875–1906), edited by W.H. Withrow (1839–1908), and 'devoted to religion, literature, and social progress.' Withrow's journal, a general magazine of commentary, promoted social reform and pioneered the use of illustrations in this genre.

In addition to sectarian differentiation, churchmen in Canada were not immune to that peculiarly nineteenth-century disease which drove its many victims constantly to found new periodicals. A fair example was the Rev. Mr Robert Jackson MacGeorge (1811?–84), known as 'the Solomon of Streetsville,' where he held the Anglican living. In addition to his own *Canadian Christian Offering* (Toronto, 1848), *Streetsville Review* (1848–58), and *Anglo-American Magazine* (Toronto, 1852–5), MacGeorge also edited and contributed to the Anglican church's periodical, *Church* (Cobourg, 1837–56; later Toronto, *Canadian Churchman, Dominion Churchman,* etc., 1871–). More specialized titles reported on the work of the missionary societies attached to each confession. *Foreign Missionary Tidings* (Toronto, 1884–1914) represented the Women's Foreign Mission Society of the Presbyterian Church in Canada, while *Canadian Church Magazine and Mission News* (Hamilton, 1886–1902?) performed the same function for the Domestic and Foreign Mission Society of the Church of England in Canada. Nor was the work of the domestic or 'inland' missionaries bereft of periodicals as tools. Two early titles, *Canada Christian Advocate* (Hamilton, 1845–84) and *Canada Evangelist: A Religious Periodical Devoted to the Exhibition of the Gospel in its Fulness, Fitness, and Freeness to All* (Montreal/Hamilton, 1851–60), specifically targeted the working class. The catalogue of religious titles was compounded further by the proliferation of local publications, as well as by the numerous titles aimed at the young. Some rationalization was achieved in 1875, when four titles were amalgamated under the editorship of James Croil (1821–1916) to form *Presbyterian Record* (Toronto, 1875–), which became that denomination's official periodical. More amalgamation occurred when the creation of the United Church of Canada led to the merger of Ryerson's *Christian Guardian* with *Presbyterian Witness* (1845–1925) and *Canadian Congregationalist* (1853?–1925).[67]

Fragmentation among Protestants had its positive aspects, such as freedom from the monolithic and occasionally censorious Roman Catholic church in Quebec, which could be the bane of some French-Canadian writers, editors, and publishers. During the episcopal reign of Bishop Ignace Bourget (1799–1885) of Montreal, a strong Ultramontane movement flourished in Quebec, which was opposed to the principle of secular government, and sought to strengthen the authority of the Church. Purely literary publications were not harassed, but some of the intellectuals who produced and consumed them grew restive under restraint. The power of the Church was demonstrated at mid-century, when Narcisse Cyr's *Le Semeur canadien* (Napierville, Que., 1851–2), a journal of discussion and commentary aimed at Protestant francophones, was branded as heretical. The same treatment killed off Arthur Buies's satirical journals *La Lanterne* and *Le Réveil* after only a few issues. The tension between the Church and its critics again broke into open, print warfare in 1891, when the monthly *Le Canada-artistique: musique, théâtre, beaux-arts, littérature* (Montreal, 1890) was revamped in January 1891 into the politically contentious weekly *Le Canada-Revue: politique, littérature, théâtre, beaux-arts* (1891–4), which immediately launched an attack on the Church for alleged abuses. The retaliation – condemnation and addition to the *Index* of publications prohibited to Roman Catholics – caused circulation and revenue to drop dramatically. This, in turn, prompted the proprietors of the journal to sue Archbishop Fabre (1827–96) of Montreal in civil court for damages. The suit attracted considerable public attention, as well as support for the plaintiffs. While the court found for the archbishop, who acted within the rights of his ecclesiastical jurisdiction, the trial cast the Church and its leader in the worst possible light, especially since the court urged that the law be amended to limit the power of the Church to use censorship as a tool for economic reprisal. *Le Canada-Revue* continued publication, and, retitled *Le Réveil* (1894–1901), survived into the next century. That lawsuit, though unsuccessful, was nonetheless a watershed in the struggle for literary and press freedom in Quebec. At the end of the century the quarterly reviewing organ *Le Courrier du livre: revue mensuelle de bibliophile et de bibliographie* (Quebec, 1896–1901), in what was perhaps a sly blow aimed at censorship, printed the entire *Index Librorum et Prohibitorum* of the Church, by then bloated to more than twenty thousand titles by more than eight thousand authors, which filled over four hundred pages.[68]

Because the audience addressed by anglophone Roman Catholic periodicals was overwhelmingly Irish, these journals might as easily be classified with the 'ethnic' as with the 'religious' press. Toronto's large population of Irish Catholics was catered for by rival titles in the later nineteenth century: the *Irish Canadian* (Toronto, 1863–92, known as *Evening Canadian* in 1882–3) emphasized political issues such as Home Rule for Ireland, while *Canadian Freeman* (Toronto, 1858–73, a continuation of *Catholic Citizen*, 1854–8), and its successors, *Toronto Tribune and*

Catholic Vindicator (1873–87) and *Catholic Weekly Review* (1887–92), emphasized the religious bond among readers over secular issues, and thus enjoyed the patronage of both J.J. Lynch (1816–88), the first Roman Catholic Archbishop of Toronto, and his successor, Archbishop John Walsh (1830–98). The *Irish Canadian* and the *Canadian Freeman* and its descendants maintained a spirited rivalry for decades, until economic pressures led to their merger in 1893, to create *Catholic Register* (Toronto, 1893–1941?). Farther east, Irish Catholic publications in English were less numerous; Saint John and Quebec City were home to two each, and Montreal had four, although all but one of these – *Irish Vindicator* (Montreal, 1828–37) – were short-lived.[69]

Although the first Jewish settlers arrived in Canada with General Jeffery Amherst in 1760, later Jewish immigration was slow. The 1851 census recorded only 451 Jews, but by 1901 there were about 17,000, largely through immigration. Thus, with sufficient numbers to support periodical publications, a Canadian Jewish press was off to a belated, but ultimately flourishing start. The *Jewish Times* (Montreal, 1897–1976), founded in part to combat the anti-Semitism of J.-P. Tardivel's *La Verité*, was only the first of a number of Jewish newspapers and magazines published primarily in English and Yiddish.[70]

Before closing the book on the religious periodical press, it should be noted that, for all their earnestness about the faith, many of these publications sought to broaden their appeal and circulation base by catering for the public thirst for entertaining reading by providing poetry, essays, and even serial fiction.

Fraternal

'All the fraternal organizations – Free Masons, Odd Fellows and the like – all had their arcanely insular journals,' declares Sutherland. If this were true, then 'arcane' is the correct word, and subscribers must have done their part in helping to maintain the mysteries of their respective lodges and clubs by carefully destroying their copies. Jones's *Preliminary Checklist* turned up only forty-seven of them – 2.4 per cent of her sample – and most of these were short-lived. Even had they all succeeded they would have left many lodges and much of the country unrepresented. For the record, the Masonic titles win in terms of both number (thirteen) and longevity, with *[Canadian] Craftsman and [British-American] Masonic Record* (Hamilton, 1866–1909) taking the prize for durability. The Odd Fellows are represented by eight titles, including the earliest in this genre, *Odd Fellows Record* (Montreal, 1846–7); the Good Templars by five; the International Order of Foresters and the Knights of Pythias by four each; the Sons of England by three; while the Chosen Friends, Eagle Knights, Orange Order, Select Knights, and Woodmen are represented in the sample by one title each.[71]

Hobbyist

The general category of 'hobbyist' embraces a total of ninety-eight titles in Jones's *Preliminary Checklist* (5 per cent of the sample). Of these, an astonishing eighty-two are philatelic titles. Stamp collecting began in the early Victorian period among ladies, who would clip and save the recently introduced, pre-paid, adhesive postage stamps. By the late nineteenth century this had developed into a serious hobby and a very large business. Nonetheless, it would appear to have claimed a disproportionate number of titles, even if many were short-lived. The temptation is to assume that the majority were merely dealers' catalogues and advertising circulars, particularly since only seventeen of them are cited as sources for articles in the standard bibliography of Canadian philately. However, the happy circumstance that the majority of these short-lived titles were filmed by CIHM meant that it was possible to examine sixty (73 per cent) of them.[72] Articles predominated over advertisements in thirty-four (56.6 per cent) of these titles. Advertisements predominated in twenty (33.3 per cent) other titles, but the sources of these advertisements, like those in the first group, were diverse. Five (8.3 per cent) further titles began with a predominance of advertisements, all stemming from the journal proprietor's own company, but these five soon began accepting advertisements from other sources.

The *Stamp Collector's Record* appeared in Montreal in February 1864 and declared that as the first and only publication in Canada devoted to philately, 'we boldly take our stand in the ranks of the Journals of Canada, and we would respectfully state ... that our influence may not be purchased either through fear, favour, affection, or hope of reward.' A second, and apparently final, issue appeared in March of that year; ironically, both numbers are now rarer than the stamps they described. Of the sample available on CIHM microfiche, thirty-three (55 per cent) of the titles died after publishing between one and six issues, while eighteen others (30 per cent) produced more than twelve issues. Although more than half of the philatelic publications lasted less than a year, some of their publishers remained undiscouraged, and returned to try again. A few titles continued for three to five years, while *Dominion Philatelist* (Belleville, Ont., 1889–97) and *Canadian Philatelic Magazine* (Halifax, 1893–1901) each survived the better part of a decade.[73]

Apart from two philatelic journals which declared coins to be within their purview, only a single numismatic journal appears in the sample. This, however, was of major importance. The *Canadian Antiquarian and Numismatic Journal* (Montreal, 1876–86, 1889–94, 1898–1916, 1930– 3) was published by the Antiquarian and Numismatic Society of Montreal, and its long- serving first editor, Robert Wallace McLachlan (1845– 1926), was the foremost authority on, and leading collector of, coins in Canada.

Jones's *Preliminary Checklist* enumerates four Toronto titles devoted to photography. However, three of these – *Canadian Journal of Photography* (1869–71, 1875), *Canadian Photographic Journal* (1871), and *Canadian Photographic Standard* (1893) – were merely trade catalogues masquerading as journals. To Jones's list could be added another, also entitled *Canadian Journal of Photography* (1864–?), five issues of which were produced by Maclear and Company, the Toronto stationers and booksellers. The first true journal of photography, which concentrated upon techniques and processes, and not merely the selling of photographic equipment and supplies, was George Gilson and H.C. Tugwell's *Canadian Photographic Journal Illustrated* (Toronto, 1892–7), which was absorbed and continued by its American offspring, *Professional Photographer* (Buffalo, N.Y.), when Canadian subscribers proved too few in number to justify a separate publication.[74]

When the Victorian bicycling craze swept Canada, as it did so many parts of the world, it generated only two specialized publications in Jones's *Preliminary Checklist* – *Canadian Wheelman* (London, Ont., 1883–99?) and *Cycling* (Toronto, 1891–9?). The former did double duty, by serving as the official organ of both the Canadian Wheelman's Association and the Cyclists' Touring Club in Canada. Of the remaining 'hobbyist' titles in the sample, three are devoted to dog breeding (including the Toronto Kennel Club's *Canadian Kennel Gazette* [1898–191–?] and long-running *Canadian Kennel Club Stud Book* [1891–1958]), two titles are devoted to other kinds of pets, one to chess and checkers, and one each to the amateur genealogist, journalist, and naturalist.

Sporting

Although the world of sport was long confined to the leisured classes, as well as being restricted generally to such pastimes as the turf and the hunting field, it began to open up socially during the latter half of the nineteenth century in response to the growing popularity of athletic competitions and team sports. This created the classic dichotomy between 'gentlemen' and 'players,' which distinguished between those of independent means and their social inferiors who accepted money for their participation. Growth in urban population and literacy brought together a natural audience to consume eagerly both newspapers and magazines devoted to sport. However, this unexplored territory awaiting its academic Columbus may well go uncharted because the medium is ephemeral and the surviving backfiles scant. The biographer of John Ross Robertson said his *Sporting Life* was the first such publication in Canada. Jones's *Preliminary Checklist* records twenty-seven titles – 1.4 per cent of the sample – none of which antedates that work. These figures suggest a poor rate of preservation, corroborated by the sparseness of recorded holdings and the number of known but unlocated titles, which may be a consequence of the disdain librarians and archivists feel for this genre.

Field sports were covered, as were athletics, by titles such as the monthly *Fin, Fur, and Feather: The Sportsman's Pocket Journal* (Amherst, N.S., 1894–?), *Rod and Gun in Canada [and Other Diversions]* (Woodstock, Ont., 1899–1906), and *Canadian Sportsman and Naturalist* (Montreal, 1881–3). The weekly *Sporting Times and Canadian Gentleman's Journal* (Toronto, 1871–, later *Canadian Gentleman's Journal and Sporting Times*, *Canadian Sportsman and Live Stock Journal*, and *Canadian Sportsman*), the longest lived of them, eventually dropped its claim to gentility. French-language titles in this genre were few and short-lived, though *Montréal: sports, littérature, théâtre* (Montreal, 1899) promised broad subject coverage, as did a similarly titled weekly effort in the West, *Sporting and Dramatic Review* (Winnipeg, 1899).

TRADES AND PROFESSIONS

Business/Trade/Industrial

During the last two decades of the nineteenth century the general explosion in the production of periodicals overtook virtually every trade and industry in Canada. There are 262 titles in this classification in Jones's *Preliminary Checklist* – 13.5 per cent of the primary sample; these figures are second only to the religious periodicals. The proliferation of so many trade- and product-specific titles merely reflects the suitability of periodicals as an advertising medium, which allowed manufacturers and wholesalers to target their trade audiences. Indeed, this level of periodical, confined to 'the trades,' presaged the rise of the modern consumer-oriented magazine, in which advertising targets the domestic consumer with the aim of generating more consumer demand, and thus larger product markets and market share.

Mention has been made of the Maclean family of trade journals – beginning with *Canadian Grocer, Hardware, Canadian Dry Goods Re-*

view, Printer and Publisher, and *Bookseller and Stationer* – which were archetypes, and the most successful of a very large genre. Dionne and Jones both list a *Mercantile Journal* (Quebec) for as early as 1816, although no copies appear to have survived. Toronto publishers turned out a stream of similarly titled productions: *Merchantman* (1873–4?), *Merchant and Manufacturer and Miller's Gazette* (1880–9?), and *Merchant and General Store Keeper* (1885–93?). Most successful among them was *Canadian Monetary Times and Insurance Chronicle* (1867–1970). Nor was the primary producer ignored, for *Canadian Manufacturer and Industrial World* (1882–1908), an early title in the field, was joined by the even longer running *Industrial Canada* (1900–73), the organ of the Canadian Manufacturers' Association. An overwhelming number of these publications were in English, though a noteworthy exception was *Le Moniteur du commerce: revue des marchés, de la finance, de l'industrie et des assurances* (Montreal, 1881–1929), a successful attempt to promote French-Canadian commercial and industrial activity.[75]

The banking and insurance industries also had specialized publications, such as *Journal of the Canadian Bankers' Association* (1893–1936), *Budget* [later *Bulletin*]: *An Insurance Journal* (Toronto, 1881–1950), and *Insurance Society and Fireman's Review* (Montreal, 1881–1965). The various skilled trades elicited their share of titles, including *Canadian Architect and Builder* (Toronto, 1888–1908), *Canadian Baker and Confectioner* (Toronto, 1888–1922), *Canadian Engineer* (Toronto/Montreal, 1893–1939), *Printer's Miscellany* (Saint John, 1876–82), and *Canadian Upholstery Journal and Undertaker's Gazette* (Toronto, 1894–9?). Before the century ended, even hired office workers were being catered for in the pages of *Canadian Stenographer* (Toronto, 1899–1900?).

Professional
The 'learned professions' of law and medicine are both based, to an extreme degree, upon case histories and precedents. Recording and disseminating these requires voluminous publications, so not surprisingly both types of specialized publication began relatively early in Canada. The first medical title antedates the first legal journal by almost twenty years. Rather than a shortage of lawyers, this suggests the legal profession's long contentment with the official publication of statutes and cases, while for the medical profession no such official substitute existed to communicate and record information. Adding education and dentistry titles brings the total number of pre-1901 journals in the 'professional' category to 156 (8.02 per cent of Jones's primary sample).

The first medical journal in Canada, *Quebec Medical Journal/Journal de médecine de Québec* (Quebec, 1826–7), was a bilingual effort, with distinct, not merely translated, contents in each language. The editor, F.-Xavier Tessier (1799–1835), solicited original contributions and plundered major foreign journals for material to reprint. A review section covered recent medical publications from abroad, while another section was devoted to recent medical discoveries and case histories. Altogether, it was an impressive and important effort. *Montreal Medical Gazette: Being a Monthly Journal of Medicine and the Collateral Sciences* (Montreal, 1844–5), the second medical journal in Canada, was founded by editors Francis Badgley (1807–63) and William Sutherland (1814–74), partly to give editorial vent to their feud with the medical faculty at McGill University. (Badgley and Sutherland were among a group of physicians who, after they were excluded by McGill, founded a rival Montreal School of Medicine and Surgery in 1843.) The contributors to the new journal were mainly local. The McGill faculty found their voice in *British American Journal of Medical and Physical Science* (Montreal, 1845–52, continued as *British American Medical and Physical Journal*), founded by Archibald Hall (1813–68). Although his rechristened journal failed, the irascible Dr Hall was not finished as an editor; his *British American Journal Devoted to the Advancement of Medical and Physical Sciences in the British-American Provinces* (Montreal, 1860–2) returned him to the fray. Meanwhile, *Lancette canadienne: journal médico-chirurgical* (Montreal, 1847), consisting of reprinted foreign material, came and went. It is of interest primarily for being the first of several to incorporate the word 'lancet,' after its more famous British counterpart.

Upper Canada failed to produce a serious medical journal until mid-century – *Upper Canada Journal of Medical, Surgical, and Physical Science* (Toronto, 1851–4) – while the country as a whole waited

TABLE 2:4
Professional Journals

Field	Number of Titles	Percentage of Professional Category	Percentage of Total Primary Sample
Medicine	59	37.8	3.0
Law	49	31.4	2.5
Education	50	32.0	2.6
Dentistry	2	1.3	0.1

decades for titles with any longevity to appear: *Canada Lancet: A Monthly Journal of Medical and Surgical Science* (Toronto, 1870–1922), *Canada Medical Record* (Montreal, 1872–1904), and *L'Union médicale du Canada* (Montreal, 1872–). Moderately successful titles were established thereafter in various parts of the country, such as *Manitoba, Northwest and British Columbia Lancet* (Winnipeg, 1887–99) and *Maritime Medical News* (Halifax, 1888–1910), although the attrition rate, as in other subject categories, remained high.[76]

In contrast with the numerous attempts to publish medical and surgical journals, dentistry, a profession only recently liberated from the purview of the barber's shop, made do with only two journals founded before the turn of the century: *Canada Journal of Dental Science* (Montreal, 1868–79) and *Dominion Dental Journal* (Toronto, 1889–1934).

The legal profession in Canada was long content with only domestic statutes and law reports, supplemented by British legal imports. The first law journal in Canada, *Revue de législation et de jurisprudence et collections de décisions des divers tribunaux du Bas-Canada* (Montreal, 1845–8), held the field alone until other titles followed in the 1850s, including *Upper Canada Law Journal and Local Courts' Gazette* (Toronto, 1855–64, continued as *Canada Law Journal*, 1865–1922), *Lower Canada Jurist/Collections de décisions du Bas-Canada* (Montreal, 1856–91), and the *Canadian Law Times* (Toronto, 1881–1922). There was even an attempt to provide the profession with its own humour organ – *Canadian Green Bag: An Entertaining Magazine for Lawyers* (Montreal, 1895), which borrowed its name from the barristers' ubiquitous tote bags and theatrical icon for lawyers – but only one issue was produced.[77]

Canadian pedagogic serials may have begun with the weekly *Instructor* (Montreal, 1835–6), which apparently died after fifty-one issues. The first certain publication in this genre, however, was *Journal of Education for Upper Canada* (Toronto, 1848–66), founded and edited by Egerton Ryerson, the father of Ontario's public school system. It was continued, still under Ryerson's editorship, as *Journal of Education for Ontario* (1867–77), by then officially sponsored by that province's Department of Education. Indeed, this kind of officially sponsored publishing characterized all of the other early, successful, and long-running educational journals, such as *Journal of Education [and Agriculture] for [the Province of] Nova Scotia* (Halifax, 1851–60), published by the Nova Scotia Council of Public Instruction, and later revived as *Journal of Education (Nova Scotia)* (1866–). Similarly, the Quebec Department of Education/Instruction Publique issued parallel editions of its journal in English and French

– *Journal of Education for Lower Canada* (Montreal, 1857–67, continued as *Journal of Education for the Province of Quebec*, Quebec, 1867–79), and *Journal de l'instruction publique de Bas-Canada* (Montreal, 1857–66, continued as *Journal de l'instruction publique*, Quebec, 1867–79).

As the century progressed, replete with the usual proportion of short-lived attempts at publication, non-official journals began to appear, some sponsored by teachers' associations, notably *Educational Review* (Saint John, 1887–, later the *New Brunswick Journal of Education*), as well as by independent publishers. Thus, in 1887 *Canada School Journal [and Weekly Review]* (Toronto, 1877–87) was merged with the Grip Printing and Publishing Company's *Educational Weekly* (Toronto, 1885–7) to form *Educational Journal [and Practical Teacher]* (Toronto, 1887–97). It appeared under the imprint of the 'Educational Publishing Company,' which continued it as *Canadian Teacher* (Toronto, 1897–).[78]

Military

Despite Canadians' preference for thinking of themselves as an 'un-military people,' for more than three centuries our history has been steeped in conquest, invasion, rebellion, and war. However, while under the protective wing of Great Britain, and thus until the present century, Canada had no need of a separate navy or of land forces other than militia units. This lack of regular forces may help to explain a paucity of military periodicals. Even the broadly drawn scope of the weekly *Canadian Military Gazette: Sporting and Literary Chronicle* (Ottawa, 1857), the first military title in Jones's sample, did not ensure success. A variety of titles in both English and French, aimed at volunteer forces, made brief appearances over the years, such as *Militia and Volunteer Service Gazette* (Quebec, 1862), *Organe de la milice: journal militaire, littéraire, et national* (Quebec, 1865–6), and *Volunteer Review and Military and Naval Gazette* (Ottawa, 1867–76). *Canadian Military Review* (Ottawa, 1877) should not be confused with the Dominion Artillery Association's *Canadian Military Review*, which was also issued with a French-language supplement, *Partie française de la revue militaire canadienne* (Kingston, 1880–1). The most significant title was the *Canadian Militia Gazette* (Ottawa, 1885–92), a weekly-cum-fortnightly continued as the semi-weekly *Canadian Military Gazette*. Maclean turned it into an instrument to criticize and force reform of the military while he owned it.[79]

Labour

From the earliest days of the printing trade in the fifteenth century, printers earned a reputation for political activism, even radicalism, perhaps because they were perceived as a literate elite, among all the manual trades. It was therefore natural that they were in the vanguard of the nineteenth-century labour movement in Canada, formed a typographical union as early as 1832, and provided the workers with published voices. For this genre Jones's *Preliminary Checklist*, which lists only twelve titles (0.6 per cent of the primary sample), is clearly misleading. This is probably the result of classifying many labour movement titles as newspapers, and thus excluding them. Weinrich's bibliography, *Social Protest*, identifies fifty Canadian periodicals in this genre that appeared between 1870 and 1900, and would, with an earlier starting date, have listed still more. The first surviving example of a Canadian labour journal, *People's Magazine and Workingman's Guardian*, appeared in Quebec in March, 1842. It was the handiwork of R.M. Moore, and was apparently inspired by the example of the British radical and 'unstamped' press. It was an instant failure, but Moore tried again the following November with *Standard*, which experienced no greater success. Two other false starts are recorded: *Le Peuple travailleur* (Montreal, c.1850) and *Journal of Industry* (London, Ont., 1850s).

Workingman's Journal (Hamilton, 1864–7?) was produced by Hamilton dry-goods wholesaler, politician, and Board of Trade president Isaac Buchanan (d.1883), to promote both his political career and his notion of an 'alliance of manufacturers and mechanics' in order to encourage industrial harmony and prosperity. Hamilton, at the western end of Lake Ontario, was already home to a growing iron and steel industry, but implementation of Sir John A. Macdonald's National Policy of 1879, a nationalistic program of high tariff barriers, led to wide-scale industrialization, and the rapid growth of an urban, industrial working class, which fuelled development of both the labour movement and the labour press. James Samuel Williams's (1838–1929) *Ontario Workman* (Toronto, 1872–5) spearheaded the movement for a nine-hour work day, and served as the organ of the Trades Assembly in Toronto. (Williams was jailed for helping organize the Toronto printers' strike in 1872.) Elsewhere, former Halifax journalist Robert Drummond (d.1925) established the reformist weekly *Trades Journal* (Stellerton, N.S., 1880–91, later *Journal and Pictou News*) on behalf of the Provincial Miner's (later Workman's) Association, and soon was circulating two thousand copies.

From the mid-1870s the American Knights of Labor, founded in Philadelphia in 1869, began organizing Canadian workers under its banner of 'one big union.' The most prominent labour publications of the 1880s served as platforms for the Knights' movement, although their internecine feuding, which culminated in the 'press-war' of 1886–7, contributed to the demise of several of them. The first Knights' paper was *Trades Union Advocate* (Toronto, 1882–3, later *Wage-Worker*), edited by Toronto printer Eugene Donovan. Its stated mission to 'agitate, educate, and organize' proved a brief one. W.H. Rowe's *Palladium of Labour* proved the genre's most outstanding example, both editorially and (though too briefly) financially. With a then-astounding 40 per cent of its space devoted to paid advertising, it reached peak circulations of five to seven thousand copies, and spawned short-lived Toronto (1885–6) and daily (1886) editions. Distinguished by the flamboyant columns of Phillips Thompson, the *Palladium* campaigned for an eight-hour work day, old age pensions, compulsory school attendance, and – notably for this genre – working women's right to equal pay for equal work. Alexander Whyte Wright's (1845–1919) *Canadian Labour Reformer* (Toronto, 1886–8, 1889) grew out of the failed Toronto edition of the *Palladium*, and survived all rivals in the 'press war.' Yet, even Phillips Thompson's touch failed to revive it more than briefly in 1889.

Other notable titles include *Echo* (Montreal, 1890–1), edited by printer David Taylor, which began as a strike paper when the typographers of the Montreal *Herald* walked out; sheetmetal worker Joseph Marks's *Industrial Banner* (London, Ont., 1891–1922); *People's Voice* (Winnipeg, 1894–1918), edited by Arthur W. Puttee (1868–1957), a one-time Winnipeg *Free Press* journeyman printer and sometime Member of Parliament (1900–4); and George Wrigley's (1847–1907) *Citizen and Country: A Journal of Social, Moral, and Economic Reform* (Toronto, 1898–1918, 1921–5, later moved to Vancouver and renamed *Canadian Socialist* and then *Western Socialist*), which became the official organ of the Canadian Socialist League.[80]

IMPROVEMENT LITERATURE

Literary/Cultural/Art/Music

In their pursuit of a tenable subscription base, early Canadian periodicals cast their editorial nets very wide, and in that sense a huge percentage of them might, with some justice, be described as 'general interest' publications. Indeed, it was standard practice for publishers and editors not merely to promise the news of the day or practical advice on farming, but to throw in claims to edify, instruct, and amuse the reader in literature, art, music, science, and kindred cultural realms. An impressive number of publications, both national and regional, did, in fact, focus considerable attention on cultural themes, hence the section title of 'Improvement Literature.' Magazines of this type account for 167 titles in Jones's *Preliminary Checklist* (8.6 per cent of the primary sample), and if one blends in the seventy-three strictly regional or local titles (3.8 per cent), the total rises to 240 (12.4 per cent of Jones's primary sample).

French-language examples are numerous. The 'pioneer' era literary titles have been cited already, but some later representative examples may be considered chronologically. *Le Moniteur canadien: journal du peuple* (1849–55) covered politics, literature, science, commerce, agriculture, and industry. Lawyer Louis Ricard (1827–94), the proprietor-editor of *L'Écho de la France: revue étrangère de science et de littérature* (Montreal, 1865–70), sought to educate his readers in European (particularly French) literature, science, history, and politics. *Musée canadien* (St Roch, 1875) was a first attempt at a scientific and literary journal by J.-Ferdinand Morissette (c.1858–1901), a classical scholar, who founded six literary journals and revues between 1875 and 1896, all of them ephemeral. His second attempt was the revival of *Musée canadien* in 1880 as a humour magazine. *Le Journal du dimanche: revue littéraire, artistique et de modes* (Montreal, 1883–5) was an eclectic weekly featuring Québécois poetry and prose, while the fortnightly *Le Chercheur* (Quebec, 1888–9) featured literature, science, beaux-arts, and general bibliography from French sources. *Lyre d'or: revue mensuelle de littérature, d'histoire, d'archéologie, biographie, légendes, &c.* (Ottawa, 1888–9) was also known as *Soirées en famille. Le Glaneur: revue mensuelle* (Lévis, later Montreal, 1890–2) absorbed *Le Recueil littéraire* (1889–92), and continued as *L'Écrin littéraire: journal du foyer* (1893). *Revue de l'art: littérature, esthétique, peinture, sculpture, architecture, etc.* (Montreal, 1895) was a one-issue effort. *Le Courrier du livre* (1896–1901), a bilingual illustrated monthly conducted by Joseph-Eugène Raoul Renault (1869?–193?), was devoted to covering Canadian history and letters, especially those of Quebec. *Le Revue des deux Frances: revue franco-canadienne* (Paris, Quebec, Montreal, 1897–9) was a monthly effort, with offices in France, Canada, and the United States.

On the English-language side, in addition to the literary titles cited earlier, some titles should be cited here. *Montreal Museum, or Journal of Literature and Arts* (Montreal, 1832–4) was edited by Mrs Mary Gosselin (née Graddon), later associate editor of *Literary Garland*, and featured short stories, articles, poetry, fashion news, and musical scores. *People's Magazine* (Montreal, 1846, continued as *People's Magazine and Weekly Review: Comprising Information on the Arts and Sciences, Interesting Histories and Biographies, Etc.*, 1846–7), was published by John Dougall and edited by R.D. Wadsworth, perhaps in conscious imitation of M. Bibaud's style. *Saturday Reader* (Montreal, 1865–6, continued as *Illustrated Saturday Reader*, 1866–7) mixed Canadian stories and poems with political commentary. Titles of the monthly *Canadian Literary Journal: Devoted to Select Original Literature and the Interests of Canadian Literary Societies* (Toronto, 1870–1, continued by *Canadian Magazine*, 1871–2) and *Canadian Eclectic Magazine of Foreign Literature, Science, and Art* (Toronto, 1871–2) encapsulate the inclusiveness typical of the period. The monthly *Arion: A Canadian Journal of Art, Devoted to Music, Arts, Literature, and the Drama* (Toronto, 1880–1) set a precedent by reviewing local Canadian artists and their exhibitions. *Arcadia: A Semi-Monthly Journal Devoted Exclusively to Music, Art, and Literature* (Montreal, 1892–3) and *Our Monthly: A Magazine of Canadian Literature, Science, and Art* (Toronto, 1896) are also short-lived examples. Finally, there was *Massey's Magazine* (1896–7), something of a reincarnation of *Massey's Illustrated*, under editor Frank Vipond (1866–c.1941), who assembled the best Canadian authors and artists (including J.W. Bengough) in an attempt to produce a magazine of high quality. Alas, with little advertising revenue, *Massey's Magazine* proved too expensive to maintain, so it was merged with *Canadian Magazine*.[81]

A.-N. Morin's *La Minerve* was the first newspaper to publish any music in Canada. The *Montreal Museum* did so only infrequently. Lovell and Gibson's *Literary Garland* was the first periodical to publish sheet music as a regular feature. Marc-Aurèle Plamondon's *Le Ménestrel: journal littéraire et musical* (1844–5) copied this practice, with a regular four-page sheet music section. This was imitated by Louis-Octave LeTourneau, whose *La Revue canadienne* (1845–8) began issuing a monthly supplement of musical scores entitled *Album littéraire et musical de la revue canadienne* (1846–7). When *La Revue canadienne* ceased publication in February, 1848, LeTourneau sold the music supplement to Ludger Duvernay, who continued it until December, then retitled it *Album littéraire et musical de la Minerve* (1849–51), and issued it with his own paper, *La Minerve*.[82]

Other musical titles came and went quickly, such as the monthly *Canadian Musical Review* (Toronto, 1856), for which one issue has been located; *L'Artiste* (Montreal, 1860), for which two issues are known; and the monthly *New Brunswick Minstrel: A Collection of Standard and Popular Vocal and Pianoforte Music* (Saint John, 1863), for which only two issues have been located. Musician Adélard Boucher (1835–1912, of Boucher and Manseau, Music Dealers) founded *Beaux-arts* (Montreal, 1863–4), which included a separate sheet music supplement under its own title, *Album des Beaux-Arts*. Two years later Boucher founded *Le*

Canada musical: revue artistique et littéraire (Montreal, 1866–7, continued by *Le Journal musical*, 1875–81) to raise musical tastes, publish
biographical information on musicians, and make available music suitable for church use. *Album musical* (Montreal, 1882–4) was founded by
Aristide Filiatreault (1851–1913) to promote a national music and to
record the history of Canadian music and musicians. Later Filiatreault
revived it as *Le Canada-artistique* (1890), which he revamped into the
politically contentious and 'heretical' *Le Canada-Revue*.

Periodicals containing music scores and criticism were eventually
joined by such titles as *[Canadian] Musician* (Toronto, 1889–1906?)
and *Canadian Music and Trade Journal* (1900–30?), which might just
as easily be listed in the 'trades' category. As for the others, their inclusion of sheet music accessible to the amateur performer was a major
sales device. Kallmann notes that while they published a good deal of
original Canadian music (with the complete exception of folk music),
and despite their high-flown claims to the contrary, they did more to
cater for popular taste than to elevate it. Though their numbers were
small – Kallmann's list tallies thirty-four musical journals by the end of
the nineteenth century – the music they published helped enliven many
a Canadian home and public hall, and made at least that much of a
contribution to Canadian culture.[83]

Literary/Cultural (Regional)

This subcategory of seventy-three titles in Jones's *Preliminary Checklist*
covers a wide variety of papers and magazines that made a point of
focusing upon local urban or regional matters, instead of seeking a national audience. Their scope varied from reviews of live arts and sporting events, to domestic issues that might also place them in the Family/
Domestic/Women's category. Although the *Montreal Tattler* (1844) may
be mistaken for a short-lived (six issues) forerunner, this genre did not
reach its peak until near the end of the century, with Toronto's *Town
Talk* (1884–6, continued as *Town Talk About Toronto*, 1886–?), and *Observer* (1891). Montreal produced its own *Town Topics* (1896). Winnipeg
was particularly well endowed, with the *Mirror* (1890–1902?), *Star* (1890),
Town Talk (1890–1), a western edition of *Saturday Night* (1892–4), *Winnipeg Town Topics* (1898–1913?), and *Sporting and Dramatic Review*
(1899), as well as the regional *Western Home Monthly* (Winnipeg, 1889–
1932) and *Great West Magazine* (1891–1908). Farther west, the *Pacific
Harbour Light* (Victoria, 1891, continued as *Victoria Home Journal: A
Journal Devoted to Social, Political, Literary, Musical, and Dramatic
Gossip*, 1891–4), was founded by D.M. Carley and devoted to local
exposés.

Early Canadian magazines had, perforce, been focused locally. However, long after national magazines had become the norm, the closing years of the century witnessed the establishment of yet another wave of magazines targeted at residents of particular provinces. This trend in local publishing yielded the *Manitoban: A Monthly Magazine and Review of Current Events* (Winnipeg, 1891–3); *New Brunswick Magazine* (Saint John, 1898–9, 1904–6), initially a general magazine founded by local journalist and author William Kilbey Reynolds (1848–1902); *Prince Edward Island Magazine* (Charlottetown, 1899–1905), under Archibald Irwin; *Nova Scotia Illustrated* (1895), conducted by J.H. Bradford; and *British Columbia Magazine: With Illustrations* (Victoria, 1899).

University/Scholarly/Learned/Student

This category numbers only twenty-six titles in Jones's primary sample (1.3 per cent of the total), which appears to be numerically insignificant. However, because many early scientific or scholarly periodicals were issued under the aegis of various societies, in their annual reports, transactions, and proceedings, Jones's primary sample (Part A, *Preliminary Checklist*), does not give a very complete picture for this genre. Such titles are to be found scattered between 'Part A: Periodicals' and 'Part C: Annual Reports, Transactions, Proceedings, Etc.' While such titles are nonetheless few in number, they carry an intellectual importance out of all proportion to their quantity, for these were Canada's most serious journals, of both academic research and critical discussion.

Clearly based upon European prototypes, the first serious periodical of this kind in Canada was *Canadian Journal: A Repertory of Industry, Science, and Art* (Toronto, 1852–78; retitled *Journal of Science, Literature, and History* in 1856), established by the Royal Canadian Institute, whose proceedings it recorded. Henry Youle Hind (1823–1908), the geologist and explorer, was placed in charge as editor. The Natural History Society of Montreal soon followed suit with its *Canadian Naturalist and Geologist* (Montreal, 1856–68; continued as *Canadian Naturalist and Quarterly Journal of Science*, 1869–83; *Canadian Record of Natural History and Geology* ... , 1884; and finally, *Canadian Record of Science*, 1884–1916). *Canadian Entomologist* (Ottawa, 1868–) began its long and successful run in the same year as the French-language *Naturaliste canadien* (Quebec, 1868–). Other science journals were less successful. Both *Astronomy and Meteorology* (Montreal, 1887) and the *Biological Review of Ontario* (Toronto, 1894) failed within a year.

Historical publications fared comparatively well. Quebec's Société des études historiques launched its *Bulletin des recherches historiques* (Lévis, 1895–), which was followed a year later by *Review of Historical Publi-*

cations Related to Canada (Toronto, 1896–1919), the direct predecessor of *Canadian Historical Review* (1920–). In contrast, *Canadian Historical Quarterly* (Toronto, 1899) proved a quick casualty, as did *North American Notes and Queries* (Quebec, 1900–1), another noble effort on the part of J.-E. Raoul Renault, but one which could not compete with its British and American counterparts.

The university magazines were of great intellectual significance, for they came to play a role in Canada akin to that of Britain's 'great quarterlies' such as *Edinburgh Review, Quarterly Review,* and *Blackwood's Edinburgh Magazine,* and influenced the affairs of society beyond the campuses where they were produced, while drawing upon the intellectual and creative resources of the universities. In Canada it was in the pages of university magazines that public and academic issues were discussed, debated, and shared among the nation's educated elite. The first such magazine in English was *King's College University Magazine* (Halifax, 1871), while almost two decades passed before the appearance of the French-language quarterly, *Canada-français: revue publiée sous la direction d'un comité de professeurs de l'université de Laval, religion, philosophie, histoire, beaux-arts* (Quebec, 1888–91; n.s. 1918–46; continued as *Revue de l'université de Laval,* 1946–). In a statement of purpose that ran to five pages in the first issue, the editors of *Canada-français* declared their intention to cover religion, science, literature, and economic issues for all of North American francophonie. Five years later, George Monro Grant (1825–1902), principal of Queen's University, founded *Queen's Quarterly* (1893–) as a non-partisan, non-sectarian publication under the ownership of a joint-stock company of academics at Queen's. *Queen's Quarterly* stood pre-eminent in this genre thanks to its felicitous balance of contemporary comment and abstract thought. The *University of Toronto Quarterly* was founded in 1895, but died a year later, only to be revived, with great success, in the twentieth century. *Revue littéraire de l'université d'Ottawa* (1900–) appeared a few years later. Finally, worthy of mention though it appeared only at century's end, the *McGill University Magazine* (1901–20) achieved great literary distinction under the editorship of Sir Andrew Macphail (1864–1938).

College and university journalism by Canadian students also produced a notable crop of publications. *Students' Monthly,* published at Bishop's University in Lennoxville, Quebec (1867), was succeeded by the *Lennoxville Magazine* (1868). The *Dalhousie College Gazette* (Halifax, 1869–), the oldest extant Canadian student paper, began as a monthly magazine, and continues as a weekly newspaper. *Queen's College Journal* (Kingston, 1873–93) first saw light in the same year as the *McGill University*

Gazette (Montreal, 1873–82). The following year *Athenaeum* (Wolfville, N.S., 1874–) appeared at Acadia University, and two months later came the birth of *Eurhetorian Argosy* (later *Argosy*, Sackville, N.B., 1874–) at Mount Allison. *Acta Victoriana* (Toronto, 1876–), from Victoria College at the University of Toronto, was joined by *Rouge et Noir* (Toronto, 1880–7, continued by *Trinity University Review*, 1888–1975) from Trinity College. The *Varsity* (Toronto, 1880–) continues to serve the entire University of Toronto. Indeed, of the ten university student periodicals published in 1880, seven are extant. By 1890 at least twenty student periodicals emanated from Canadian campuses. In 1888 the editor of the *Varsity* in Toronto proposed creation of a Canadian intercollegiate press association. Although his proposal was premature, it is instructive that the proponent estimated that the sixteen student periodicals probably employed 150 to 200 students, and enjoyed combined monthly circulations of at least ten thousand. This class of periodicals, then as now, served as the training ground for many Canadian writers and journalists.[84]

Politics/Commentary

For much of the nineteenth century, newspapers in Canada, like those elsewhere, served more as vehicles for politics, opinion, and partisanship than for news. With hundreds of daily and weekly newspapers offering such a diet, the public might easily have been surfeited. It may therefore come as little surprise that there are only forty-five magazines specializing in politics and commentary in Jones's *Preliminary Checklist* (2.3 per cent of the primary sample). Some of these titles are important ones that have already been cited. *Canadian Magazine* and Goldwin Smith's *Week* emerged as the most important English-language organs of opinion and political commentary during the last decade of the century. *La Revue canadienne* played a similar role among francophone readers. The *Bystander*, virtually all of it written by Goldwin Smith, was also disproportionately influential. Like Smith, Joseph-Demers Chartrand (1852–1905) showed a penchant for political issues in the pages of his ostensibly general-interest *Revue nationale: magazine mensuel illustré* (Montreal, 1895–6). The role of *Le Canada-Revue* in leading the attack on the Roman Catholic hierarchy has already been cited. Desbarats's *Canadian Illustrated News* is also included in this category, along with its French-language twin, *L'Opinion publique illustré*. Its circulation, by century's end, was ten thousand copies a week.[85]

The rest of the titles in this genre consist of parliamentary reviews and guides, political party propaganda sheets, single-issue advocacy screeds, and digests of the press, such as the presciently titled *Newsweek*

(Toronto, 1883–96), *Press Siftings* (Toronto, 1889–93), *Semaine: revue de la presse* (Quebec, 1895), and the colourfully forthright *City Life: A Weekly Periodical Devoted to the Censure and Criticism of the Follies of the Day* (Montreal, 1879). The titles devoted to advocacy were also usually forthright, to wit: *Antivaccinateur canadien-français* (Montreal, 1885–6); *Anti-usury Advocate and Social Reformer* (Montreal, 1859; prospectus only); *Monthly Review Devoted to Canadian Emancipation and Commercial Union with the United States* and its French twin, *Emancipation coloniale et l'union douanière avec les États-Unis* (Montreal, 1880); *Patriot: An Anti-Confederation Journal* (Saint John, N.B., 1865); and *Single Tax Advocate* (New Westminster, B.C., 1889).

Humour/Satire

Although many of the politically oriented journals were unintentionally humorous, this section is restricted to those titles which were self-consciously so. They constitute twenty-five titles in Jones's *Preliminary Checklist* (1.3 per cent of the primary sample), with a virtually even division of English- and French-language titles. Napoléon Aubin's weekly, *Le Fantasque*, the satirical organ of the Papineau or *patriote* faction, has been cited already. At its peak in 1840 it circulated 1,200 copies, and two attempts were later made to revive it – in 1857–8 by O. Coté, and in 1879 by Alphonse Trépanier. Britain's famous humour magazine *Punch* was imitated in Canada no fewer than four times. James Jamieson's *Montreal Punch* (1846) folded after a single issue, and neither William Hicks's *Canadian Punch* (Montreal, 1868) nor the Associated Mashers' *Punch* (Montreal, 1878) fared much better. Even the more successful *Punch in Canada* (Montreal, 1849–50), published by Thomas Blades de Walden, lasted fewer than eighteen months, although it featured notable woodcuts, and was the first Canadian periodical to publish political cartoons regularly.

A host of similarly short-lived magazines featuring political cartoons included *Flysheet* (Toronto, fl.1857); George Burden's *Diogenes* (Montreal, 1868–70); *Grinchuckle* (Montreal, 1869–79), which featured cartoons by John Henry Walker (1831–99), who had contributed to *Punch in Canada*; and *Grumbler* (Toronto, 1858–65, 1869), a semi-libellous sheet founded by Erastus Wiman (1834–1904), which was published anonymously in 1862–4 by John Ross Robertson. G.-E. Desbarats had some limited success with *Jester: A Comical Satirical Record of the Times* (Montreal, 1878–9), which lasted for three volumes. Meanwhile, in the Maritimes, George W. Day, 'a persistent launcher of newspapers and other periodicals,' founded the *True Humorist* (Saint John, N.B., 1864–7, continued as *New Dominion and True Humorist*, 1867–78, and *New Dominion*, 1878–9), which was followed by the long-running *Gripsack: Facts, Figures, and Fancies* (Saint John, 1888–1902), produced by local journalist and author William Kilbey Reynolds (1848–1902). The greatest success in this field, however, was reserved for *Grip*, immortalized by the cartoons of J.W. Bengough. Ferdinand Poirier (1858–c.1910) founded *Le Samedi* (Montreal, 1888–1963) as a gentle magazine of humour, but over the course of its seventy-five-year run it became a general-interest periodical. By the end of the nineteenth century, it ranked with *Le Monde illustré* as one of the two most important magazines in French Canada.[86]

Ethnic/Native

In Canada, a nation of immigrants, current use of the term 'ethnic' tends to provoke controversy. Here, it means publications by or for those whose ethnicity or 'race' was neither English nor French, but not necessarily published in languages other than English or French. 'Native' refers to publications by or about aboriginal people in Canada. Because Jones's *Preliminary Checklist* excluded newspapers, it records a mere twenty ethnic titles (1.0 per cent of the sample) and seven Native ones (0.4 per cent). Other bibliographic sources are clearly more useful in coping with this category of material, most especially Ruth Bogusis's *Checklist of Canadian Ethnic Serials*.[87]

Scottish and Irish settlement in Atlantic Canada began early, stamped those provinces indelibly with Celtic culture, and continues to supply the rest of Canada with Celtic transplants. The first periodical result of this was *Irish Vindicator*, a Reformist paper published by immigrant Irish physician and journalist Dr Daniel Tracy (1795–1832), whose career was cut short by cholera. In the following decade Patrick 'Paddy' Bennett's *Weekly True Liberator* (Saint John, 1847–50) provided printed aid and comfort to new and old arrivals alike. Mention has already been made of Timothy Anglin's *Freeman*. The *Harp: An Illustrated Journal of General Literature* (Montreal and Hamilton, 1874–81), a proper magazine addressed to an Irish-Canadian audience, appeared somewhat later, and mixed Irish literature and biography with Roman Catholicism and serial fiction.

Germans began arriving in the mid-eighteenth century, when several thousand Hanoverian subjects of George II were settled in Nova Scotia as a buffer against the as-yet-unconquered French. Anthony Henry – partner of Halifax printer John Bushell, who began publishing the *Halifax Gazette*, Canada's first 'newspaper,' in 1752 – was an Alsatian German who issued a German-language almanac in 1788 and projected a weekly newspaper to be titled *Die Welt, und die Neuschottländische Corres-pondenz*. Later, German immigration to Upper Canada led to the publi-cation of *Canada Museum und Allgemeine Zeitung* in 1835 at, appropri-ately, Berlin [Kitchener], Ontario. Many other German titles followed before the end of the century.[88]

Blacks have been present in Canada since 1628, although large-scale immigration only began with the Loyalist migration after the American Revolutionary War, which created Black settlements in what became Nova Scotia, New Brunswick, and Upper Canada. This population, aug-mented by a steady influx of Black freed and runaway slaves from the United States prior to emancipation, produced a number of publications. Robin Winks, eminent historian of Blacks in Canada, has written that in addition to the usual handicaps faced by Canadian periodical publishers, including competition from American publications (in this case, Black titles), Canadian Black journals had no specific mercantile community from which to draw advertising revenue, while non-Black advertisers naturally gave their trade to publications with greater circulations. Also, Black editors addressed an audience really too small to support such publications: the literacy rate, while rising, was still very low; they had to compete with the non-Black press; and Blacks could generally only be united in support of one issue, namely, the abolition of slavery and other racial discrimination. Canadian Black editors did promote abolitionism, but this was too small an editorial base to lead to commercial success.

British American (Toronto, 1845), the first periodical in Canada aimed at Blacks, was published for less than a month. However, five more Black publications appeared prior to 1901. *Provincial Freeman*, which Winks calls 'as good as any weekly paper in Canada West,' promoted tem-perance as well as abolitionism. The original proprietor and nominal editor, Samuel Ringgold Ward (1817–c.66), was actually a 'front' for the real editor, Mary Shadd Cary. Shadd Cary used the *Freeman* to promote racial integration, assimilation, and adoption of British culture by the American fugitive slave community in Canada West, at a time when they were encouraged to think of themselves as temporary exiles by other Black editors, such as Henry Walton Bibb (1815–54), of the rival *Voice of the Fugitive* (Windsor, 1851–3). These two titles were the most success-ful. Two other papers aimed at Blacks in Canada West were more ephem-eral. *Voice of the Bondsman* (Stratford, 1856) was produced by the Scots Presbyterian abolitionist J.J.E. Linton (1804–69). Another well-meaning clergyman, A.R. Green, of the British Methodist Episcopal church, pro-duced ten numbers of the *True Royalist and Weekly Intelligencer* (Wind-sor, 1860–1) before he left for the United States. Green stressed loyalty to the Crown rather than racial issues.

The return of many American Blacks to the United States after the Civil War reduced the audience for Black publications in Canada still further. No further Black titles appeared until Charles A. Johnson's sporadically issued monthly, *British Lion* (Hamilton, 1881–92), which Winks describes as merely an organ of the Conservative party aimed at Blacks in Hamilton. Abraham Beverley Walker (1851–1909), a Canadian-born and American-educated Black lawyer, produced a short-lived yet highly distinguished monthly magazine, *Neith* (Saint John, N.B., 1903–4), but it falls just outside our chronological scope.[89]

The earliest periodicals created by or for aboriginal people in Canada were produced through their co-operation with various missionary groups. Indeed, the 'Cree syllabic' alphabet still used to print both Native Indian and Inuit ('Eskimo') languages was invented by a Methodist missionary, the Rev. Mr James Evans (1801–46), who employed it to print gospel texts and hymns. Various missionary endeavours produced a small crop of Native periodicals before 1901. *Petaubun, Peep of the Day* (Sarnia, 1861–2), a monthly conducted by the Rev. Mr Thomas Hurlburt (1808–73, former missionary in residence and printer of the Rossville Mission Press in Rupert's Land at the head of Lake Winnipeg), was printed mostly in Ojibway with some English text. *Algoma Quarterly* (Sault Ste Marie, Ont., 1874–1956) had a relatively long run. The *Indian: Devoted to the Interests of the Aborigines of North America* (Hagersville, Ont., 1885–6) was printed partly in Ojibway and focused on acculturation. *Toestloes-Nahwoelnoek, or, Carrier Review* (Stuart's Lake, B.C., 1891–4) was printed entirely in Déné syllabics. *Kamloops Wawa* (Kamloops, B.C., 1892) was divided equally between English and Chinook text. *Indian Magazine* (Ohsweken, Ont., 1893–7, continued as *Brant Agriculturist and Indian Magazine*, 1897–?) was produced on the Six Nations Reserve. *Onkweonwe* (Ottawa, 1900–?) was a semi-weekly newspaper printed entirely in Iroquois. Reference has already been made to short-lived Métis publications during the North-West Rebellions. The Métis also produced a more successful French-language, weekly newspaper, *Le Métis* (continued as *Le Manitoba*).[90]

Canada's Inuit people in the North were the object of missionary efforts that began in Labrador with the Moravians in the eighteenth century. In addition to annual journal records of their missions (*Nachrichten*, 1819–) and other German-language texts, the Moravians published religious texts in the vernacular of the Inuit throughout the nineteenth century. However, these were all printed abroad. In 1900, Inuit-language publishing began at the mission at Nain (established in 1771), the northernmost community on the Labrador coast. This included the very first Inuit newspaper, *Aglait Illunainortut* (1900–7?).[91] These nineteenth-century efforts represent the beginning of a flourishing modern Native periodical press.

Temperance

Although people have been prey to drunkenness since time immemorial, the industrialization and urbanization movements so exacerbated the problem that by the fourth decade of the nineteenth century there arose in England, and very soon thereafter in Canada, a large and pervasive social reform movement. Under the banner of the Temperance movement marched a variety of formal organizations, which originally espoused everything from mere moderation to personal abstinence ('teetotalism') to outright prohibition of all alcoholic beverages. Although endorsed from many a church pulpit, and pursued by some with an evangelical fervour usually reserved for religion, Temperance was an essentially secular reform movement. Since no self-respecting Victorian cause lacked either organizations or periodicals, Verzuh notes that, by the mid-1860s, 'there were dozens of temperance publications circulating through Upper Canada homes.' Thus the relatively low number of Temperance titles enumerated in Jones's *Preliminary Checklist* (a scant thirty-nine, or 2 per cent of the primary sample) requires some explanation. There is a twofold solution to this apparent problem. First, and most obvious, is Jones's exclusion of 'newspapers.' Second, the ephemerality of format, combined with the disdain of those charged with the custody of institutional collections, has probably condemned many backfiles, and even entire titles, to wholesale extinction, as with sports periodicals.

Some Temperance titles have already been cited in other sections – 'Religious' (for the religious press often took up the cause) and 'Children's' (for example, *Life Boat: A Juvenile Temperance Magazine*). *Christian Reporter and Temperance Advocate* (Saint John, 1833–41) was the first Temperance journal in New Brunswick. *Canadian Temperance Advocate* (Montreal, 1835–54?), organ of the Montreal Temperance Society, was edited by publishing magnate John Dougall. He also published *Montreal Witness*, [N.Y.] *Daily Witness* (1871–8), a strong Temperance paper for the American market, and *Canadian Messenger: Devoted to Temperance, Science, Education, and Agriculture*, a handsomely illustrated semi-monthly magazine addressed to families, and edited by three generations of Dougalls.

Temperance was yet another subject that crossed periodical genre lines. The enthusiasm of some of the religious press has been noted. Thus, Egerton Ryerson campaigned for Temperance in his *Christian Guardian*, and in 1830 he helped found an early Temperance Society at

York [Toronto]. Halifax printer Clement Horton Belcher (1801–67) issued a *Nova-Scotia Temperance Almanac* (Halifax, 1835–7). Of course
children were at risk, so they were provided with additional 'lifeboats'
such as the titles named for the Temperance movement's children's auxiliary, *Canadian Band of Hope*, monthly versions of which appeared in
Montreal (1862–5), London, Ont. (1878–?), and no doubt elsewhere in
Canada. Where so much periodical publication occurred, there were
bound to be failures, as Henry Winton Jr of Newfoundland discovered
with his short-lived fortnightly, *Banner of Temperance* (St John's, 1851).[92]

Conclusion

TRIUMPH OF THE POPULAR DAILY PRESS

Early newspapers in Canada were primitive affairs of no more than four
pages, printed on hand-presses, and distributed within a small area in
editions of a few hundred copies. Their proprietors were job-printers,
whose incomes were precarious and often dependent upon government
contracts. By mid-century, with the advent of new, industrial technology,
papers could circulate thousands of copies daily, and their proprietors
and editors often evolved into men of substance and considerable political influence. Some newspapers became mere organs of, and apologists
for, specific political parties. The increasingly exclusive focus of the
urban newspaper press upon politics, with particular attention to the
business community's need for commercial information, reduced the ability of newspaper editors to offer a broader range of subject coverage,
and may well have promoted the growth of more specialized periodicals,
such as the agricultural and farm press, as well as magazines of all types.

Until the advent of the popular or mass-audience 'new journalism'
after about 1880, Canadian newspapers were filled mainly with political
reportage and editorializing, often with no shortage of 'sectarian' invective. When newspaper editors were either politicians themselves, or the
hired tools of political parties, and depended on political patronage for
at least some of their revenue, few among them may have imagined that
newspapers might exist to serve any but political ends, and thus the
news they served up was often quite secondary, and much of it was
cribbed from distant and foreign sources. With the emergence of the
'people's press' – *Evening Telegram*, *News*, and *Star* (1892–) in Toronto;
Star (1869–1979) and *La Presse* in Montreal; and *Journal* (1885–) in
Ottawa, among others – came the recognizably modern, urban, daily
newspaper, with its focus on local as well as national and foreign events;

its human-interest stories; its detailed, sometimes lurid, coverage of crime and disaster; its campaigns, crusades, and contests; its increasing use of illustrations; and, above all, its dependence upon advertising and the concomitant relentless pursuit of increased circulation to satisfy major advertisers and increase the revenue which they provided. At its best, this new, popular press was free of direct control by political factions, and its values and biases were those which it shared with a majority of its readers. As Rutherford has observed, however, these 'people's papers' were eventually absorbed into the social and political establishment, and their formerly maverick, crusading editors and publishers were elevated to the Canadian equivalent of British press lords.[93]

EMERGENCE OF SUCCESSFUL MASS-MARKET MAGAZINES

From the somewhat pretentiously titled general magazines of the earlier period, with their promises to cover every conceivable subject, evolved both the later, popular, general-interest magazines more familiar to modern readers, and magazines aimed at a specialized audience. Thus, as the nineteenth century wore on, more and more titles appeared that targeted particular interests, whether of class, trade, profession, or hobby. At the same time, technological advances in the making of paper, in printing, and especially in the reproduction of illustrations combined with the rise of a recognizably modern advertising industry to transform the appearance of both newspapers and magazines. When one is leafing through periodicals from the end of the nineteenth century, the most obvious clue that differentiates them from their descendants is the dated nature of the fashions and the technology shown in the illustrations and advertisements. Another clue is the lingering reluctance of many magazine proprietors to integrate advertisements with pages of text, a fetish which lasted well into the current century.

French-language magazines in Canada appear to have maintained the tendency to unspecialized, even encyclopedic, scope far longer than their English-language counterparts. This was perhaps a function of their smaller share of population, with its considerably lower level of literacy. Thus, to succeed commercially, French-language magazines had to appeal to the widest possible audience. At the same time, a contrary tendency was acceptance of a greater degree of editorial intellectualism, and often of a self-conscious didacticism, aimed at erecting bulwarks to defend French culture from hostile, assimilating influences. While purely literary publications generally escaped the displeasure and censure of the Church, those which challenged its teachings or authority could be quickly brought to heel. Although Ultramontanism enjoyed its periodical spokesmen at one extreme, some of the more daring and outspoken of the intellectuals who produced French-language periodicals of an opposite viewpoint sought to challenge, without concern for reprisals, the moral authority or intellectual integrity of the Roman Catholic hierarchy in Quebec. That victory took several more generations to achieve.

The irrepressible urge to set down opinions in print underlies nearly all publication; however, it was nowhere more apparent than in the nineteenth-century explosion of periodical publications. The multiplication of their numbers continued despite abundant evidence that competition from cheaper foreign imports, combined with high overheads, low circulations, economic fluctuations, and other hazards, laid a curse upon the majority of new periodicals; the same hazards brought the lives of many older titles to an abrupt, and often ignominious, end. While the proprietors of the newspaper press learned earlier the lesson of mass appeal, at no time were they truly dependent upon the acquisition of a national audience. Thus, while Canadian newspapers grew and prospered with the burgeoning growth and urbanization of the new nation, the publishers of magazines continued to struggle against, and often appeared to ignore, hard demographic and economic realities. Apart from some few religious titles, nineteenth-century Canadian magazine circulations were pathetically small. The remarkably popular *Saturday Night* and *Le Samedi* were quite exceptional in achieving weekly circulations in the ten to fifteen thousand range. Thus, almost no magazine proprietor or editor ever attained the audience, and the perceived concomitant power to influence public opinion, that had become commonplace for their counterparts at the larger daily newspapers. A select few, however, beginning with Colonel J.B. Maclean, found a formula for success in the magazine business. Many others tried, and continue to try, with mixed success, to duplicate that formula, and one must applaud their efforts, for Canada's domestic periodicals owe their existence, then as now, to their proprietors' venturesome spirit.

Notes

ACKNOWLEDGMENTS

For their invaluable assistance with this project we should like to thank, in no particular order, Ms Sandra Alston, Mr Graham Bradshaw, Dr Jennifer Connor, Ms Anne Dondertman, Professors Patricia Fleming and Paul Rutherford all of the University of Toronto; Ms Mary Bentley,

Executive Editor of the *Dictionary of Canadian Biography* in Toronto; Professor Tom Vincent of Canada's Royal Military College, Kingston; Dr Mary Jane Edwards, Carleton University; Professor Bertrum MacDonald of Dalhousie University; Professor Ron Love of the University of Saskatchewan; Dr Joyce Banks, formerly of the Rare Books Division and her colleague Ms Mary Collis of the Children's Services Division, National Library of Canada; Dr Carl Spadoni of McMaster University; Professors Anna Altmann, David Hall, and Doug Owram, Ms Alexis Gibb, Mr Ernie Ingles, Jerry Kowalyk, Ms Lillian MacPherson, Dr Bruce Peel, Ms Wanda Quoika-Stanka, Ms Elaine Simpson, Ms Lea Starr, and Ms Lynn Thompson, all of the University of Alberta; and last, though scarcely least, our old friends as well as long-suffering and patient editors, Professors Rosemary VanArsdel and J. Don Vann.

ABOUT GEOGRAPHIC NAMES

Throughout this chapter we have followed the convention of using the term 'Canada,' even though such a national entity did not exist before 1867, and, strictly speaking, was not complete until the addition of Newfoundland in 1949. When referring to specific provinces, which had the legal status of colonies until Confederation, we have attempted to avoid anachronism. For specific information on dates and names see section 1 above, Historical Introduction: Canada to 1900.

ABOUT TITLES

It can be stated categorically that most newspaper titles and many magazine titles vary over the life-span of their publications. To avoid repetition, we have dispensed with the phrase 'title varies,' and have tried to give dates of publication that reflect all changes of title and successor publications, while detailing those successors in only a limited number of cases; for example, to show when the Toronto *Globe*, *Mail*, and *Empire* became the *Globe and Mail*.

ABBREVIATIONS

CanEncyc	*Canadian Encyclopedia*
CHR	*Canadian Historical Review*
CIHM	Canadian Institute for Historical Microreproductions
DalRev	*Dalhousie Review*

DCB   *Dictionary of Canadian Biography*
Klinck 1965   *Literary History of Canada* 1st ed.
Klinck 1976   *Literary History of Canada* 2nd ed.
Papers BSC/Cahiers SBC *Papers of the Bibliographical Society of*
                       Canada/Cahiers de la société biblio-
                       graphique du Canada
TRSC   *Transactions of the Royal Society of*
                       Canada

1 The literature of the Canadian national identity debate is vast. Prominent
   among modern scholars who have studied the question from the perspective
   of newspapers, magazines, and other 'mass-media' are Paul Rutherford,
   whose books – *A Victorian Authority* (1982) on the daily press and *The
   Making of the Canadian Media* (1978) – are indispensable to the serious
   student, and Mary Vipond, who has focused mainly on the twentieth century
   – *The Mass Media in Canada* (1989), *Listening In: The First Decade of
   Canadian Broadcasting, 1922–1932* (1992), and 'National Consciousness in
   English-Speaking Canada in the 1920s' (Ph.D. thesis, Toronto, 1974).
      For Canadian attitudes toward the United States, see Reginald C. Stuart,
   United States Expansionism and British North America, 1775–1871
   (1988); Donald F. Warner, *The Idea of Continental Union: Agitation for the
   Annexation of Canada to the United States, 1849–1893* (1960); and H.F.
   Angus, ed., *Canada and Her great Neighbour: Sociological Surveys of
   Opinions and Attitudes in Canada concerning the United States*, in The
   Relations of Canada and the United States Series (1938; repr. 1970). The last
   includes extensive sections on attitudes – both editorial and corporate – in
   the Canadian book, newspaper, and magazine publishing industries.
2 Despite such limitations as excluding French- and allophone-language
   magazines, Sutherland, *Monthly Epic*, is the best book on the subject. Its
   only rival, Barbour, *Amazing People*, does include the French side of the
   story, but on the whole must be used with extreme caution, for its accuracy
   is variable. The newspaper press in Canada has been better served with
   recent general histories: Fetherling, *Rise of the Canadian Newspaper*;
   Rutherford, *Victorian Authority*; Bonville, *La presse québécoise*; Godin,
   La lutte pour l'information; Galarneau, 'La presse périodique au Québec';
   and the somewhat idiosyncratic works of J.-P. de Lagrave.
3 Sutherland, *Monthly Epic*, 8. The volume of government publication in
   Canada accounts for 60–70 per cent of the national total. For more on the
   interconnections between English- and French-language publishing see
   Whiteman, *Lasting Impressions*; Hare and Wallot, 'Le livre au Québec';
   Buono, 'Imprimerie et diffusion'; and David Ruddell, *Quebec City, 1765–
   1832: The Evolution of a Colonial Town* (Ottawa 1987), 149–53.
4 Publishing in the colonies operated under two layers of copyright legislation,
   imperial and colonial. Lower Canada enacted local copyright protection as
   early as 1832 (2 Wm IV, cap. 53), followed by Nova Scotia in 1839 (2 Victoria,

cap. 36). After union of the Canadas, a statute was passed in 1841 to protect resident authors whose works were produced in the province (4 & 5 Victoria, cap. 61). Imperial legislation, such as that passed in 1842 (5 & 6 Victoria, cap. 45), to revise the original 1709 copyright act (8 Anne, cap. 19), governed the importing and exporting of publications. Here the interest of mother country and colonists were at cross purposes; British authors sought protection from cheap pirated reprints in colonial markets, while Canadians sought cheap books, particularly from American or domestic sources. In 1847 a temporary 'compromise' was reached with the passage of Britain's Foreign Reprints Act (10 & 11 Victoria, cap. 95), and its colonial analogues, which allowed the importation of cheap foreign (i.e. American) piracies, provided a special duty was collected to compensate British authors and publishers. In practice, very little of this duty was ever collected. This fact and numerous unaddressed issues led to further lobbying and legislation. This complicated topic and its impact on publishing and the book trade are handled admirably in Parker, *Beginnings of the Book Trade*, esp. chs. 3, 5, 6, and appendix D; and idem, 'Publishing in Nineteenth-Century Canada.' See also Kesterton, *Law and Press in Canada*, ch. 8, 'Copyright'; H.G. Fox, *The Canadian Law of Copyright and Industrial Designs*, 2nd ed. (Toronto 1967); and Gundy, 'Literary Publishing,' 197–9.

5 On the growing pains of publishing and bookselling see Parker, *Beginnings of the Book Trade*, and idem, 'Publishing in Nineteenth-Century Canada.' As early as 1844 the postage rate for newspapers was reduced in the Canadas, whereas in the Atlantic colonies newspapers went post-free to subscribers. Free posting became the rule across the country from 1854 until the imposition of a uniform second-class rate for all periodicals in 1880. The 'free-ride' through the mails was a factor in the proliferation of newspapers in that period. Fetherling, *Rise of the Canadian Newspaper*, 34; Sutherland, *Monthly Epic*, 27–8; and Barbour, *Amazing People*, 79. See also Rutherford, *Making of the Media*, 45–8; and idem, *Victorian Authority*, ch. 1, 'The Prerequisites of Mass Communication'; cf. Bonville, *La presse québécoise*, esp. ch. 1, 2, and 6. For a description of the colonial book trade in Canada and its vicissitudes with copyright and other legislated regulation see Parker, 'The British North American Book Trade,' 82–99; and idem, *Beginnings of the Book Trade*, chs. 3, 5, and 6. For the dissemination of books and periodicals, see Wiseman, 'Silent Companions.' The flood of foreign periodicals continued to be one of the 'facts of life' faced by Canadian publishers. By the 1920s an estimated fifty million copies of American magazines were being sold annually in Canada. See J.A. Stevenson, 'The Campaign of Canadian Publishers for Protection,' in Angus, ed., *Canada and Her Great Neighbour*, 154.

6 For the debate over the need for a Canadian national literature, which began in the columns of nineteenth-century periodicals, and some insight into the role those periodicals played in the early development of Canadian literature, see the admirable collection assembled by Ballstadt, *Search for Eng-*

lish Canadian Literature. See also Gundy, 'Literary Publishing'; MacDonald, 'English and French-Language Periodicals,' 221–7; idem, *Literature and Society*; and Parker, *Beginnings of the Book Trade*, ch. 2.

Based upon content analysis of commercial and economic news in various Canadian newspapers, urban geographer Peter Goheen argues that the rapidly growing urban 'communications networks' in Canada developed first along international lines – principally British and American – prior to more localized, regional development. P.G. Goheen, 'Communications and Urban Systems in Mid-Nineteenth Century Canada,' *Urban History Review/Revue d'histoire urbaine* 14:3 (1986), 235–45; idem, 'Canadian Communications circa 1845,' *Geographical Review* 77 (1987), 35–51; idem, 'The Changing Bias of Inter-Urban Communications in Nineteenth-Century Canada,' *Historical Geography* 16:2 (1990), 177–96; and for a summary in cartographic form, idem, 'An Emerging Urban System, 1845, 1885,' in *Historical Atlas of Canada*, 2:175 and plate 45.

7 Felteau, 'Aspects de l'histoire de la presse'; Neatby, *Quebec*, 240–5; cf. Lagrave, *Liberté d'expression.* Using the ability to sign one's own name as a test of literacy, fewer than one person in four (23.3 per cent) in New France outside of Quebec City at the time of the Conquest was literate. Within the city that number almost doubled. The figures for literacy in Quebec (apart from Montreal) then went into decline until about 1810. As late as 1890 one-quarter of the rural population of Quebec was illiterate. Michel Verrette, 'L'Alphabétisation au Québec, 1660–1900' (Ph.D. thesis, Laval, 1989); idem, 'L'Alphabétisation de la population de la ville de Québec de 1750–1849,' *Revue d'histoire de l'Amérique française* 39:1 (été 1985), 51–76; and Allan Greer, 'The Pattern of Literacy in Quebec, 1745–1899,' *Histoire sociale/ Social History* 11:22 (Nov. 1978), 295–335.

8 The current management of the Montreal *Gazette* trace the paper's lineage back to Mesplet's first efforts in Montreal (1778–9, resumed 1785), even though several other Montreal proprietors appropriated the title *Gazette* following his death in 1794. On developing press freedom see Kesterton, *Law and Press in Canada*, passim; idem, *History of Journalism*, 8–9, 19–23, 56–61; Gundy, 'Liberty and License,' 71–92; and Rutherford, *Making of the Media*, 5–6. For the *Halifax Gazette*, see Vincent, *Nova Scotia Newspapers*, 19. On the Tiffany brothers see Wallace, 'First Journalists'; Tobin, *'Upper Canada Gazette' and Its Printers*; Benn, 'Upper Canadian Press'; and Gundy, *Early Printers.*

9 Bagnall was equally prolific in starting newspapers. In 1808 he went to Halifax and founded the *Novator and Nova Scotia Literary Gazette* (1808–9), then returned to Charlottetown, where his third effort was the *Weekly Recorder of Prince Edward Island* (1810–14, continued as the *Prince Edward Island Gazette*, 1814, 1817–22). Thereafter, he produced the *Royal Gazette and Prince Edward Island Recorder* (1826–7), and *Phenix* (1828), his last production, which represented the first attempt by a consortium of citizens on the Island to sponsor a paper. See *DCB*, 8:35–7. From 1813 to

1815 Miles's press at Kingston was the only one functioning in Upper
Canada, for those at Newark [Niagara-on-the-Lake] and York [Toronto] had
been seized by invading American forces. Gundy, *Early Printers*, 22–30.

10 Fetherling, *Rise of the Canadian Newspaper*, 25–6, 31. On the expansion
and significance of the Maritime press see Martell, 'Press of the Maritime
Provinces,' 109–34; and Harvey, 'Newspapers of Nova Scotia,' 135–56. For
Quebec see Felteau, 'Aspects de l'histoire de la presse.' For Ontario see
Talman, 'Newspaper Press in Canada West'; idem, 'Newspapers of Upper
Canada'; and idem, 'Pioneer Press in Western Ontario.'

11 The Métis are the descendants of French-Canadian fur-trading company
employees and the Native women whom they took as wives. See Marcel
Giraud, *Le Métis canadien* (Paris 1945); and idem, *The Métis in the Canadian West*, English ed., 2 vols. (Edmonton 1986). See Peel, *Early Printing
in the Red River Settlement*. With the establishment of 'peace, order, and
good government,' Winnipeg became a competitive hotbed and national
microcosm of Canadian newspaper and, on a still smaller scale, magazine
publishing in English and French, as well as 'ethnic' languages, although the
first of these in Manitoba, the Icelandic *Framfari* (1877), was published in
Riverton [Lundi]. In 1890 fifty-two different newspapers were published in
the province, and five had died by year's end. Figures from Loveridge, *Manitoba Newspapers*, 7–8, et passim; Aubry, 'Presse francophone'; Pénisson,
Henri d'Hellencourt; idem, 'Un hebdomadaire libéral'; and *Manitoba Newspaper Checklist*. Cf. Fetherling, *Rise of the Canadian Newspaper*, 45–8,
who oversimplifies the complicated bibliographic story of the Red River
Resistance and its aftermath. See also Landry, 'Franco-Albertan Newspapers.'
Two massive indexes, *Index du Journal Le Métis* and *Index du Journal Le
Manitoba*, were published by the Centre d'études franco-canadiennes de
l'ouest at the Collège universitaire de Saint-Boniface in 1981 and 1982
respectively. For more on the early Western press see *The Story of the Press*
(Battleford 1928); Dafoe, 'Presses on the Prairies,' which is a revised and
illustrated reprint of idem, 'Early Winnipeg Newspapers'; Drake, 'Pioneer
Journalism in Saskatchewan'; Davis, 'Pinafored Printer'; Waddell, 'Frank
Oliver'; Steele, *Prairie Editor*; Lamb, 'Notes on Early Vancouver Newspapers';
and Rutherford, 'Western Press and Regionalism.'

12 Fetherling, *Rise of the Canadian Newspaper*, 1–3, 12, 31, 42–57, 58–72,
et passim; Waddell, 'Frank Oliver'; and Wearmouth, *Yukon Newspapers*.
R.A. Bankson, *The Klondike Nugget* (Caldwell, Idaho 1935), is a charming
history and anthology. On the 'pioneer' era of the Canadian press see also
Kesterton, *History of Journalism*; Walkom, 'Newspapers,' *CanEncyc*;
A. Fauteau, *The Introduction of Printing into Canada: A Brief History*
(Montreal 1930); Sutherland, *Monthly Epic*; Barbour, *Amazing People*; and
Rutherford, *Making of the Media*. For a cartographic summary of the spread
of newspapers etc. see J.H. Wadland and M. Hobbs, 'The Printed Word,' in
Historical Atlas of Canada, 2:179–80 and plate 51.

13 'Jautard,' *DCB*, 4:390; S. Martin, 'Magazines,' *CanEncyc*; Sutherland, *Monthly Epic*, 18–19; and Barbour, *Amazing People*, 1–12. Winton's *Public Ledger and Newfoundland General Advertiser* was the fourth newspaper in St John's. His hostility to Catholicism, the Island's majority religion, led to his unpopularity. After the attack, a doggerel ballad of 'Croppy Winton' made the rounds. *DCB*, 8:947–51. For a long litany of outrages against the press, see Kesterton, *History of Journalism*, 19–21. For a description and index of John Howe's pioneering journal, see Vincent and LaBrash, *'Nova Scotia Magazine.'*

14 Miss Herbert was a Temperance advocate, and the *Mayflower* was printed at the Halifax Athenaeum, a Temperance press. *DCB*, 10:348. Mary Shadd Cary, the pioneering editor of a Black, abolitionist newspaper (1853–9), is dealt with below, in the sections 'Women as Journalists' and 'Ethnic/Native Press.' For the fullest treatment of Maritime Canada's literary culture and the role of literary magazines, see Davies, 'Belles and the Backwoods'; and idem, 'Literary Study of Selected Periodicals from Maritime Canada.' See also Jack, 'Acadian Magazines,' *TRSC*; Talman, 'First Prince Edward Island Literary Journal'; Fraser, 'Two Nova Scotian Literary Periodicals'; Martin, 'Magazines,' *CanEncyc*; M.G. Flitton, 'Literary Magazines in English,' *CanEncyc*; 'Literary Magazines,' in Story, *Oxford Companion*; W. Francis, 'Literary Magazines in English: I. The 18th and 19th Centuries,' in Toye, *Oxford Companion*, 1983; Sutherland, *Monthly Epic*, 19; and Barbour, *Amazing People*, 13–23. On S.H. Wilcocke, see Klinck, 'Samuel Hull Wilcocke.' The *Nova-Scotia Magazine* (1789–92), *Canadian Magazine* (1823–5), *Acadian* (1826–8), *Provincial* (1852–3), and *Amaranth* (1841–3) have been described and indexed in a series of 'Occasional Publications' by Vincent and LaBrash. For the prose and poetry content of early Quebec journals, see Camille Roy, 'Étude sur l'histoire de la littérature canadienne, 1800–1820,' *Mémoires de la Société royale au Canada* XI, sec. 1 (mai 1905), 89–133. See also Benjamin Sulte, 'The Historical and Miscellaneous Literature of Quebec, 1764–1830,' *TRSC* III, sec. 2 (May 1897), 269–78.

15 Ryerson quoted in *DCB*, 11:783–95. See also Clara Thomas, *Ryerson of Upper Canada* (Toronto 1969). The next thirteen Upper Canadian titles are, in chronological order: *Canadian Garland* (1832–3), *Canadian Literary Magazine* (1833), *Canadian Magazine* (1833), *Roseharp* (1835), *Mirror of Literature* (1835–6), *Upper Canada Baptist Missionary Magazine* (1836), *Youth's Monitor and Monthly Magazine* (1836), *Canadian Christian Examiner and Presbyterian Review* (1837–40), *Cabinet of Literature* (1838–9), *Canadian Mirror of Parliament* (1841), *Monthly Review* (1841), *Wilson's Border Tales* (1841), and *The Child's Bible Expositor* (1841–2). All are described in great detail in Fleming, *Upper Canadian Imprints*. Sandra Alston of the University of Toronto has been at work for some years upon a further enumeration of pre-Confederation Upper Canadian magazines. At the time of writing she had identified 127 separate titles. These include the

apparently short-lived *Bee* (1812), of which no copies have been located, and the *Evangelical Herald* (1819).

16 The *Album*, an early example of music publishing, was sold on the demise of *La Revue canadienne* (1845–8) to fiercely nationalistic publisher Ludger Duvernay, who retitled it, and issued it as a supplement to his *La Minerve*, the main organ of *patriote* sentiment. Duvernay founded the *patriote* Saint Jean Baptiste Society, and is credited with first suggesting the maple leaf as a national symbol. Calderisi, *Music Publishing*, 27–8. For Duvernay, see Monière, *Ludger Duvernay*.

17 For the elder Taché, see Bossé, *Joseph-Charles Taché*. Although anglophones never accounted for more than 22 per cent of the population of Quebec, English-language periodicals were 58 per cent of the total number published in that province between 1764 and 1859. This reflects both higher literacy and a greater degree of urbanization among anglophones. For an analysis of the growth of Quebec periodicals by number, language, longevity, frequency of publication, and editors, see Galarneau, 'La presse périodique au Québec.' On the question of literacy, see note 7 (above). Gauvin, 'Literary Periodicals in French' and Sarfati, 'Magazines in French,' *CanEncyc*; Story, 'Literary Magazines in French,' in Story, *Oxford Companion*, 460–1; Gauvin, 'Literary Magazines in Quebec'; Hayne, '*Foyer canadien*,' and idem, '*Soirées canadiennes*,' in Toye, *Oxford Companion*, 1983; Barbour, *Amazing People*, 21–3, 39–41; Robidoux, 'Les *Soirées canadiennes* et le *Foyer canadien*'; and Hayne, '*Nouvelles soirées canadiennes*.'

18 For Lovell see *DCB*, 12:569–74. Mrs Cushing claimed that the *Garland* was a victim of a hopeless competition with American publications, *DCB*, 11:321–2; C. Gerson, 'The *Snow Drop* and the *Maple Leaf*: Canada's First Periodicals for Children,' *Canadian Children's Literature* 18/19 (1980), 10–23; J. Weller, 'Canadian English-Language Juvenile Periodicals: An Historical Overview, 1847–1990,' *Canadian Children's Literature* 59 (1990), 38–69; Calderisi, *Music Publishing*, 24; Martin, 'Magazines' and Flitton, 'Literary Magazines in English,' *CanEncyc*; Story, 'Literary Magazines'; MacDonald, *Literature and Society*; Sutherland, *Monthly Epic*, 20–1; Barbour, *Amazing People*, 29–31; and Fetherling, 'E.J. Baker.' On *Victoria Magazine* see William H. New's 'Introduction' to the four-volume facsimile reprint edition (Vancouver 1968), 1:vii–x.

19 For Anson Green see *DCB*, 10:316–18. Extra copy could readily be secured for small rural papers from 'co-operative' or 'auxiliary' publishers, a trade engendered by labour shortages in the United States during their Civil War, and carried on in Canada by the Auxiliary Publishing Company of Toronto and D.R. Dewey of Hamilton. In 1889 the former claimed 121 subscribing Canadian newspapers, the latter 49. By contrast, the Kellogg Newspaper Company of Chicago, the largest such firm, enrolled about 1,400 subscribers in 1886. Originally these firms supplied rural publishers with sheets printed on one side only; the subscribing proprietor would then print local material on the blank sides. These 'patent insides' or 'ready print' sheets evolved into

full-scale printed inserts, as well as the magazine supplements and syndicated features still widely used today. See Hulse, 'Newspapers Printed on the Co-operative Plan'; Wiseman, 'Silent Companions,' n. 113; Elmo Scott Watson, *History of Auxiliary Newspaper Service in the United States* (Champaign, Ill. 1923); idem, *History of Newspaper Syndicates in the United States, 1865–1935* (Chicago 1936).

20 Fetherling, *Rise of the Canadian Newspaper*, 12, 28–30, 35, cf. 49, 65; Careless, *Brown of the 'Globe,'* 2:5; Rutherford, *Victorian Authority*, chs. 1 and 2; Kesterton, *History of Journalism*, 23–5, et passim; and Moran, *Printing Presses*. For still more remarkable provenances of particular presses, see Parker, *Beginnings of the Book Trade*, 269, n.105.

21 R. Stacey, 'Graphic Art and Design' and 'Illustration, Art,' *CanEncyc*; T. Kōdar, 'Northern Lights: Canadian Photography Journals Past and Present,' in McKenzie and Williamson, eds., *Art and Pictorial Press*, 54; Spadoni, *'Grip'*; and Sutherland, *Monthly Epic*, 20, 47–58, 69–79. For the significance of the commercial art work of Frederick Brigden (1814–1917) and the Toronto Engraving Co., see Davis, 'Art and Work.'

22 Meikle, *Canadian Newspaper Directory*; *McKim's Directory* (1892); J. Goodis, 'Advertising,' *CanEncyc*; Stephenson and McNaught, *Story of Advertising*; Fetherling, *Rise of the Canadian Newspaper*, 32–3, 75–6, et passim; Rutherford, *Victorian Authority*; and Bonville, *La presse québécoise*, 115–17, 317, et passim. Cf. R.M. Hower, *History of an Advertising Agency: N.W. Ayer and Son at Work, 1869–1949* (Cambridge, Mass. 1949). Other press directories of the era which covered Canada include Rowell, *American Newspaper Directory*, which was published at least annually (and in some years quarterly); *Canadian Newspaper Directory* (Montreal 1876); *Butcher's Canadian Newspaper Directory*; and Central Press Agency, *Directory of Canadian Newspapers*. These directories are an invaluable source of information on such things as advertising rates and circulation figures, though the latter must still be viewed with caution.
    National unification, so obviously essential for creating a viable market, not least for periodicals, was itself no preordained conclusion, but a process in which periodicals themselves were involved. For their role in the debate see Waite, *Life and Times of Confederation*; idem, 'Halifax Newspapers and the Federal Principle, 1864–65,' *DalRev* 37:1 (Spring 1957), 72–84; idem, *'Le Courrier du Canada* and the Quebec Resolutions, 1864–65,' *CHR* 40:4 (Dec. 1959), 294–303; and J.P. Heisler, 'The Attitude of the Halifax Press toward Union of the British North American Provinces,' *DalRev* 30:2 (July 1950), 188–95.

23 Gundy, 'Hugh C. Thomson.' Mackenzie's remark is quoted on p. 203.

24 Mackenzie returned to Canada following passage of the Amnesty Act of 1849, and from January, 1853, until mid-September, 1860, continued his quarrelsome ways in the pages of *Mackenzie's Toronto Weekly Message*. Lindsey, *Life and Times of William Lyon Mackenzie*; Kilbourn, *The Firebrand*; Gates, *After the Rebellion*; idem, 'Mackenzie's *Gazette'*; *DCB*,

9:496–510; Raible and Luno, 'Life after the Rebellion'; and Talman, 'Printing Presses of William Lyon Mackenzie. For Parent, see *DCB*, 10:579–86. For Duvernay, see Monière, *Ludger Duvernay*; and *DCB*, 8:258–63. See also Fetherling, *Rise of the Canadian Newspaper*, 11–24, 27–8; Craig, *Upper Canada*, 200; and Careless, *Union of the Canadas*, 32–3, 121–2, 158–9. For the role of the periodical press in *patriote* circles after the 1837 rebellions, see Monet, *Last Cannon Shot*. For English-Canadian press reaction to the *patriotes*, as typified by one (very) conservative newspaper, see Lefebvre, 'La Montréal *Gazette*.'

25 Aubin was responsible for founding and/or editing *Le Télégraphe* (Quebec, 1837); *Le Fantasque* (Quebec, 1837–49); *Le Castor* (Quebec, 1843–5); *Le Canadien* (Quebec, 1847–9); *Le Canadien indépendant* (Quebec, 1849); *Le Sentinelle du peuple/People's Sentinel* (Quebec, 1850); *La Tribune* (Quebec, 1863–4); and *Les Veillés du Père Bon Sens* (Montreal, 1865–6, 1873). He was also a regular contributor to *L'Ami du peuple, de l'ordre, et des lois* (Montreal, 1832–40), *La Minerve*, and *La Revue canadienne*. After moving from Quebec to Montreal in 1866 he also wrote for *Le Pays*. In 1845 *Le Fantasque* was halted by two disastrous fires that destroyed much of the St Roch quarter of Quebec City. It was revived on an irregular basis between 1846 and 1849, a 'new series' was conducted by other hands in 1857–9, and there were later appropriations of the title. Aubin's *Le Castor* was only the first of at least eight 'Castors,' including *Le Castor national* (Quebec, 1878) and *Le Castor rouge* (Montreal, 1898) – of which no copies can be located – but *not* counting the Hudson Bay Company's *Beaver* (Winnipeg, 1920–). The *Standard* (Quebec, 1842) was an English-language newspaper printed at Aubin's press for R.M. Moore. Beaulieu and Hamelin credit the editing of the *Standard* to Aubin and W.H. Rowen. That same year Moore produced Canada's first periodical addressed to workingmen, *People's Magazine and Workingman's Guardian* (Quebec, 1842), which Serge Gagnon in his *DCB* entry attributes to Aubin, something not corroborated by either Tremblay or Verzuh. See *DCB*, 11:34–7; Tremblay, 'Un journaliste satirique'; idem, *Napoléon Aubin*; and Felteau, 'Aspects de l'histoire de la presse.'

26 *DCB*, 13:126–31; Lamontagne, *Arthur Buies*; and Gagnon, *Le ciel et l'enfer*.

27 For Trudel, see *DCB*, 11:891–5. For Tardivel, see *DCB*, 13:1009–13.

28 *DCB*, 11:270–1; Rutherford, *Victorian Authority*, 48–51; Sutherland, *Monthly Epic*, 38–45; and Barbour, *Amazing People*, 37–8.

29 Beck, *Joseph Howe*, esp. I, ch. 9; *DCB*, 10:362–70; Kesterton, *History of Journalism*, 62–3; and Fetherling, *Rise of the Canadian Newspaper*, 21–2.

30 Baker, *Timothy Warren Anglin*; and *DCB*, 12:23–8.

31 Wild, *Amor De Cosmos*; Woodcock, *Amor De Cosmos*; *DCB*, 12:237–43; Fetherling, *Rise of the Canadian Newspaper*, 43–5.

32 Careless, *Brown of the 'Globe'*; *DCB*, 10:91–103; and Fetherling, *Rise of the Canadian Newspaper*, 25–8, 38, 40.

33 J. Phelan, *Ardent Exile: The Life and Times of Thomas D'Arcy McGee* (Toronto 1951); *DCB*, 9:489–94; and Fetherling, *Rise of the Canadian Newspaper*, 39–40.

34 For Farrer, see Cumming, *Secret Craft*. For Davin, see Koester, *Mr Davin*, *M.P.*; and *DCB*, 13:248–53.

35 *DCB*, 12:246–50; Rutherford, *Victorian Authority*, 65–71, et passim; Sutherland, *Monthly Epic*, 46–58; and Barbour, *Amazing People*, 55–7. See celebratory volume: Desbarats, *'Canadian Illustrated News.'*

36 Poulton, *Paper Tyrant*; and Rutherford, *Victorian Authority*, 53–4. Later editors of the *College Times* included such literary heavyweights as Stephen Leacock (1869–1944) and Robertson Davies (1913–96).

37 Spadoni, *'Grip'*; Sutherland, *Monthly Epic*, 69–79; and Barbour, *Amazing People*, 56–7. Bengough promoted the economic reform theories of Henry George in *Grip*, which is described and analysed in Cook, *The Regenerators*; see esp. ch. 8.

38 Sutherland, *Monthly Epic*, 80–95; and Barbour, *Amazing People*, 55–7. See also Hann, 'Brainworkers'; and Colquhoun, 'The Journalistic Field of 1887.' At a time when women were often discouraged in their attempts to find employment as journalists and editors, Sheppard displayed both a singular disposition to hire them and a sharp eye for talent. As befits one of the most important publications of its day, *Saturday Night* has been provided with a thorough, modern index. See Heggie and Adshead, *Index to 'Saturday Night.'*

39 Chalmers, *Gentleman of the Press*; Sutherland, *Monthly Epic*, 129–63, et passim; and Barbour, *Amazing People*, 73–6. In 1905 Maclean acquired a five-year-old periodical entitled *Business: The Businessman's Magazine*, which he revamped as *Business: The Busy Man's Magazine*, then simply as *Busy Man's Magazine*. Finally, in 1911, it was retitled *Maclean's*, a general-interest magazine along the lines of *Munsey's*. Over the years it went through several transformations as a general-interest and family magazine, surviving today as a weekly news magazine, Canada's answer to *Time*, *Newsweek*, and *U.S. News*. It is for the publication of popular titles such as *Maclean's* (1911–, French-language ed., 1961–), the *Financial Post* (1907–), *Mayfair* (1927–, sold 1955), *Canadian Homes and Gardens* (1925–, sold 1962), and *Chatelaine* (1928–, French-language ed., 1960–), and not for its scores of trade journals, that Maclean-Hunter is best known. The professionalization of journalism and publishing by university graduates, beginning with the industrial trade journals, is a principal theme of Levene, 'Machinery for Everybody.' See also Michael Bliss, *Northern Enterprise: Five Centuries of Canadian Business* (Toronto 1987), 341–2.

40 Wallace, *Goldwin Smith*, esp. 122–5; *DCB*, 13:968–74; Sutherland, *Monthly Epic*, 28–32 ; Barbour, *Amazing People*, 49–50; and Cook, *The Regenerators*. On the *Week's* literary importance see Bissell, 'Literary Taste.'

41 Sutherland, *Monthly Epic*, 59–68; and Wallace, *Goldwin Smith*, 72ff. See also Gundy, 'Literary Publishing.' Jones, *Preliminary Checklist*, maintains that *Canada Bookseller: A Chronicle of Current Literature* (1865–7) continued *Geikie's Literary News Letter* (Toronto, c.1856), and was revived as *Canada Bookseller: A Quarterly Record of British, American, and Native Literature, for the Use of the Trade and Book Buyers* (1870–1), continued as *Canada Bookseller, Miscellany, and Advertiser* (1872).

42 Cooper left in 1906 to edit *Canadian Courier* (1906–20), which was an ultimately unsuccessful attempt to challenge the primacy of the American *Saturday Evening Post* in the five-cent, family-magazine market. Sutherland, *Monthly Epic*, 96–111; and Barbour, *Amazing People*, 63–7, 71–2.

43 Willison, *Reminiscences*; Rutherford, *Victorian Authority*, 72, et passim; idem, *Making of the Media*, 51; Colquhoun, *Press, Politics, and People*; and Clippingdale, 'J.S. Willison.'

44 Pénisson, *Henri d'Hellencourt*; idem, 'Un hebdomadaire libéral'; Aubrey, 'Presse francophone au Manitoba'; and Felteau, *Histoire de 'La Presse,'* 1:374.

45 Cook, *Politics of John W. Dafoe*; Donnelly, *Dafoe and the 'Free Press'*; Ferguson, *John W. Dafoe*; and Hall, *Clifford Sifton*, 1:209–29, 2:20–2.

46 Harkness, *Atkinson of the 'Star.'* In 1895 E.E. Sheppard (*Saturday Night*) purchased the *Star* from W.J. Gage, the school-text publisher, and became titular editor. This sale was financed by F.B. Nicholls, president of Canadian General Electric, and publisher of *Canadian Manufacturer and Industrial World* (1882–1908). The *Star* thus shifted from Labour to Conservative to Liberal within its first decade. Sutherland, *Monthly Epic*, 87.

47 Felteau, *Histoire de 'La Presse,'* 1:316–17, et passim; Bonville, *La presse québécoise*; cf. Rutherford, *Victorian Authority*.

48. Dutil, *Devil's Advocate*.

49 Verzuh, *Radical Rag*, 52–7, 63–4, 71–81; Watt, 'Literature of Protest'; Watt, 'Growth of Proletarian Literature'; Hann, 'Brainworkers'; Sutherland, *Monthly Epic*, 76; Rutherford, *Victorian Authority*, 20–1; and Cook, *The Regenerators*. For an archetypal Victorian journalist who failed to achieve fame, fortune, or even much distinction, see Talman, 'George Sheppard.'

50 Bearden and Butler, *Shadd*; *DCB*, 12:960–1.

51 'In the 1880s, along with Sara Jeannette Duncan, Elmina Elliott, ... and others she spearheaded the entrance of women into the ranks of professional journalism in Canada' (*DCB*, 13:1084). *Canadian Fireside: An Entertaining Magazine for the Leisure Hour* (Montreal, 1888–93?), continued as *Canadian Fireside Weekly* (Toronto, 1893?–?).

52 Dean, *Different Point of View*; and Fowler, *Redney*. Duncan met her future husband while on an around-the-world tour. They settled in India, where over the following quarter-century she wrote more than twenty novels and travel books.

53 Freeman, *Kit's Kingdom*; and Ferguson, *Kit Coleman*. Ferguson's book is part biography, part anthology of Coleman's writings.

54 Haig, *Brave Harvest*; and Hacker, *E. Cora Hind*.

55 Huguenin founded *La Revue moderne* (1918–60, merged with the French edition of *Chatelaine*) and edited it for eight years, then founded *La Vie canadienne* (1928–9, merged with *La Revue moderne*). *La Revue moderne* developed a strong following among francophone women in Canada, which the otherwise successful family magazine *La Revue populaire* (1907–63) never quite achieved. Barry's *Journal de Françoise* (1901–10) was a much

more personal effort, which died with its editor. Sarfati, 'Magazines in French,' *CanEncyc*.

Barthiaume's daily, *La Presse* (Montreal, 1884–), was so successful through the early adoption of modern technology (Linotype, colour printing) and the importation of the sensationalist methods of the 'new journalism' (known in America as 'yellow journalism'), that it left other Montreal dailies scrambling to catch up. *La Presse* hired its first full-time woman writer in 1903. Once hired as the society editor, however, Édouardina Lesage ('Colette,' 1875–1961) stayed at *La Presse* for fifty-three years. Rutherford, *Victorian Authority*, 64–5, 68–71, 80–1; and Felteau, *Histoire de 'La Presse,'* 1:358.

56 After her marriage to Atkinson, Elliott edited the women's page of the Montreal *Herald*, where he was editor. Harkness, *Atkinson of the 'Star'*; and Sutherland, *Monthly Epic*, 87. Outside the large cities, at the smaller weeklies, women and girls appear to have enjoyed employment opportunities as typesetters, proofreaders, and binders. For a memoir of one who worked on Davin's Regina *Leader* between 1886 and 1890, see Davis, 'Pinafored Printer.'

57 Jones, *Preliminary Checklist*. This work lists, usually with locations, 2,204 different periodical titles in part A, 427 almanacs in part B, and approximately 1,000 annual reports etc. in part C. Of the 2,204 periodicals, 260 are unclassifiable without examination. Although many statistical questions might readily be posed beyond the simple classification offered here in tables 2:1, 2:2, and 2:3, the current state of the data is too imprecise and incomplete to yield meaningful answers.

In distinguishing between newspapers and magazines, the rule adopted was: 'to follow the guidelines of the National Library [of Canada] and to exclude publications printed and distributed on a daily, semi-weekly, weekly, or similar short interval which consist of news, editorials, features, advertising, etc. and which are not solely devoted to a specific subject. Suspect titles were routinely checked against the *Union List of Canadian Newspapers* (*ULCN*) and when found in the list, excluded. ... Because the *ULCN* is not comprehensive there are many titles of dubious status.' Jones, *Preliminary Checklist*, iii.

58 Donnelly, 'January hath 31 Days'; Dondertman, 'Anthony Henry'; and Jones, *Preliminary Checklist, Part B: Almanacs*. That almanacs were a lucrative publishing genre may be inferred from the appearance of many familiar printers' names, as well as the longevity of some titles. Patricia Fleming (with Donnelly and Dondertman) is preparing a bibliography of Canadian almanacs, 1765–1900 – based upon research initiated by Dorothy Ryder – which will provide both publishing histories and locations.

59 *Calliopean* was produced by young ladies enrolled at the Burlington Ladies' Academy, and therefore could be considered the earliest example of a student periodical, a full decade ahead of John Ross Robertson's *College Times* (1857). One published analysis of the *Calliopean* places it in the context of the Academy's highly literary curriculum, and characterizes it as a student

literary magazine. Sonser, 'Literary Ladies and *The Calliopean*.' However, the contents of its twenty-three issues reveal it was more of a prototypical women's magazine, with articles ranging from world affairs to self-improvement. We have therefore classified it in this section. A sampling of the meteoric failures: *Charivari* (Hamilton, 1857) a moralistic women's monthly quite dissimilar from the Parisian satirical journal whose title it appropriated; *Canadian Family Herald* (Toronto, 1851–2); *Cottager's Friend and Guide of the Young* (Toronto, 1854–5); *Metropolitan Fashions* (Toronto, 1860); *Home Journal* (Toronto, 1861); *Protestant Home Journal* (Saint John, 1864–5, continued as *Home Journal*, 1866); *Household Journal* (Montreal, 1866); *Album de la Minerve: journal de la famille* (Montreal, 1872–4); *Ladies' Monthly Review* (Welland, 1879); *Household Life* (Toronto, 1884); *Home Cheer* (Vancouver, 1888); *Wives and Daughters* (London, Ont., 1890); *Mère et l'enfant* (Montreal, 1890–1); *Ladies' Companion* (Toronto, 1893); *Ladies at Home* (Toronto, 1893); *Psyché: revue mensuelle de nouveautés de mode* (Montreal, 1894); *Women's Realm* (Montreal, 1896); *Home Companion* (Montreal, 1898); *House Companion* (Montreal, 1898); and finally two which were obviously devoted to match-making, the weekly *Barter and Swap and Matrimonial Gazette* (Montreal, 1879), and the monthly *Anglo-American Matrimonial Journal* (Toronto, 1886). All dates in parentheses represent years for which issues have been recorded. Scholarly studies of women's periodicals are not numerous, and – like Cynthia White's *Women's Magazines, 1693–1968* (London 1970) – tend to focus on British and American titles. Much work remains to be done in this area. See Sutherland, *Monthly Epic*, 3–12, 153–63, 243–55.

60 Gerson, 'The *Snow Drop* and the *Maple Leaf*,' contains a detailed publishing history of these two excellent magazines; Weller, 'Canadian English-Language Juvenile Periodicals' captures the flavour of the contents of *Snow Drop*, but her survey ignores its predecessors as well as later devotional titles. This kind of scholarly omission appears true not only for English Canada, but also for French Canada, where the first widely acknowledged French-Canadian children's magazine, *L'Oiseaux bleu: revue mensuelle illustrée pour la jeunesse*, did not appear until 1920. See Louise Lemieux, *Pleins feux sur la littérature de jeunesse au Canada français* (Montreal 1972), 23–5, and Marie-Louise d'Auteuil, 'A l'origine de *L'Oiseaux bleu*,' *L'Oiseaux bleu* 16:6 (janvier 1936), 131–2.

61 Quoted in Fleming, *Upper Canadian Imprints*, 452.

62 *Farmer's Journal and Welland Canal Intelligencer* merged with the *British Colonial Argus* to form the *British American Journal* (1834–5, continued as the *Farmer's Journal*, daily after 1859). *Farmer's and Mechanic's Journal* continued after 1838 as the *Sherbrooke Gazette and Eastern Township Advertiser*. The *Bytown Independent* was sold the same year, and renamed the *Bytown Gazette and Ottawa and Rideau Advertiser*. *Canadian Agricultural Journal* (Montreal, 1844–7) was continued as *Agricultural Journal and Transactions of the Lower Canada Agricultural Society*

+ French edition, 1848–53; continued as *Farmer's Journal and Transactions of the Lower Canada Board of Agriculture* + French edition, 1853–61; continued as *Lower Canada Agriculturist* + French edition, 1861–7; continued by *Canadian Agriculturist, 'Official Series of the Agriculture Board and Societies'* + French edition, 1867–9?. This section on agriculture owes much to Duke's work, 'Agricultural Periodicals,' as well as to the pioneering work of Landon, 'Agricultural Journals of Upper Canada.' Duke, 'Agricultural Periodicals,' 6–7, 19–25. Cf. Jones, *Preliminary Checklist*; and Sutherland, *Monthly Epic*, 19.

63 *British American Cultivator* (1–2, 1842–4; n.s. 1–3, 1845–7); merged with *Canadian Farmer: A Family Journal Devoted to Agriculture, Internal Improvement, Literature, Science, and General Intelligence* (Toronto, 1847); and continued as *Agriculturist and Canadian Journal: Devoted to Agriculture, Literature, Education, Useful Improvements, Science, and General News* (1848); continued by *Canadian Agriculturist: A Monthly Journal of Agriculture, Horticulture, Mechanics & General Science, Domestic Economy &c.* (1849–63); continued as *Canada Farmer: A Fortnightly Journal of Agriculture, Horticulture, and Rural Affairs* (1864–8); merged with *Globe Weekly* edition to become *Globe and Canada Farmer* (1869–76).

The Board of Agriculture of Upper Canada issued its *Transactions* from 1855 until around 1868. The Rev. Mr W.F. Clarke (1824–1902) edited Brown's *Canada Farmer* for five years, then left in 1869 to found the *Ontario Farmer* (1869–71). Landon notes the generally imitative nature of the early Ontario journals; in both titles and content they aped the already popular American journals. Duke, 'Agricultural Periodicals,' 25–30; Landon, 'Agricultural Journals of Upper Canada,' 167–70, 173–4 and n. 8; Rutherford, 'Making of the Media,' 10; Sutherland, *Monthly Epic*, 23.

64 *Nor'West Farmer and Manitoba Miller* (Winnipeg, 1882–9, monthly); continued by *Nor'West Farmer and Miller* (1889–92); continued by *Nor'West Farmer* (1893–1931); continued by *Nor'West Farmer and Farm and Home* (1931–6); merged with *Country Guide [and Grain Grower's Guide]* (Winnipeg, 1908–36) to become *Country Guide and Nor'West Farmer* (1936–42). Duke, 'Agricultural Periodicals,' 33–4; Sutherland, *Monthly Epic*, 24; and Fetherling, *Rise of the Canadian Newspaper*, 56–7.

65 Wallace, *Goldwin Smith*, 122–9; and Sutherland, *Monthly Epic*, 32.

66 Sutherland, *Monthly Epic*, 24. Examples of the journals of practical applications include: *Canadian Poultry Review* (1877–1975), *Canadian Horticulturist* (1878–1914), *Canadian Stock Raiser's Journal* (1881–4; title varies on successors which lasted until 1934), and *Canadian Bee Journal* (1885–1913), most of which underwent the usual series of mergers, amalgamations, and title changes. Among the second type were *Canadian Naturalist and Quarterly Journal of Science* (1856–83), *Canadian Entomologist*, and *Naturaliste canadien*. The last title was somewhat unusual, for it did not originate with a learned society, but instead, later, found a home at Laval

University. Duke, 'Agricultural Periodicals,' passim. Cf. Jones, *Preliminary Checklist.*

67 This merger of titles occurred in 1925, and resulted in the United Church's *New Outlook and Observer* (1925–). The new United Church did not include all Presbyterian congregations, and so some independent Presbyterian publications continued to be published. For MacGeorge, see Talman, 'Three Scottish-Canadian Newspaper Editor Poets'; and *DCB*, 11:557–8.

68 Story s.v. 'Buies'; *La Grande cause eccelésiastique: le Canada-Revue vs. Mgr E.C. Fabre; procédure, pleuve, pièces du dossier, plaidoyers des avocats, reproduction des textes originaux et des notes sténographique officielles* (Montreal 1894); Bonville, 'La liberté de presse'; Chassay, 'Une attitude critique'; and Barbour, *Amazing People,* 33–4, 39–41, 59–61. For Fabre, see *DCB*, 12:300–5.

The more moderate editorial line in *Le Réveil* lasted only until 1896, when the editors resumed their attacks on the Roman Catholic clergy. In 1898 they declared themselves rededicated to the spirit of *Le Canada-Revue.* However, after three further years of publishing little other than religious, political, and educational polemics, and incurring the ban not only of the Church but also of the Liberal party, *Le Réveil* expired in 1901. Chassay, 'Une attitude critique,' 31.

69 Stortz, 'Irish Catholic Press'; Doherty, 'Analysis of Social and Political Thought'; O'Flynn, 'An Irishman, a Catholic, and an Editor'; and Bogusis, *Checklist of Canadian Ethnic Serials,* 172–4.

70 We have chosen to categorize Jewish periodicals here in the 'religious' instead of the 'ethnic' section. Cukier records a still earlier Jewish title, *Di Zeit* (Montreal, 1887), of which only a single issue, lithographed from manuscript, is said to have been published by A. Harkavy. Cukier, *Canadian Jewish Periodicals,* 7; Bogusis, *Checklist of Canadian Ethnic Serials*; Beaulieu and Hamelin, *La presse québécoise,* 4:46–8; and Levendel, *Canadian Jewish Press.*

71 Sutherland, *Monthly Epic,* 25; and Jones, *Preliminary Checklist.*

72 The first adhesive postage stamps were issued by Britain in 1840; for New Brunswick, Nova Scotia, and the Canadas in 1851; for Newfoundland in 1857; for British Columbia in 1860; for Prince Edward Island in 1861, and for Vancouver Island in 1865. Dominion of Canada issues (1868–) superseded colonial issues as each province joined in the confederation. C. Morin, *Canadian Philately, Bibliography and Index, 1864–1973/Philatélie canadienne, bibliographie et index* (Ottawa 1979).

73 While these titles were no doubt perused by young as well as older collectors, there was one pointedly juvenile example: *Boy's Own Philatelist* (Berlin [Kitchener], 1897–9), continued as *Canadian Philatelic Weekly* (1898–9). The *Stamp Collector's Monthly Gazette* (Saint John, 1865–7) was the youthful production of journalist George Stewart (1848–1906), who even in his teens was a prodigious writer and editor. He went on to publish *Stewart's Literary Quarterly* (1867–72), and in later years was successively

editor of *Rose-Belford's Canadian Monthly and National Review* and of the
Quebec *Daily Chronicle.* Sutherland, *Monthly Epic,* 63–4. For *Stewart's Literary Quarterly,* which 'began in protest against American influence and soon became the literary voice of the new Confederation,' see Davies, 'Literary Study,' vii, et passim; and idem, 'Belles and the Backwoods,' 53–4.

74 Kôdar, 'Northern Lights.' McLaughlin's *Photographic Portfolio* (1858–80) may qualify as the first 'photographic journal' in Canada, based on the technicality that it was illustrated with mounted prints of photographs.

75 Bliss, *Northern Enterprise,* 341. The role of commercial advertising in all its aspects is the subject of Levene, 'Machinery for Everybody.'

76 The *Unfettered Canadian* (Brockville, later Toronto, 1849), eight numbers of which were produced by the Rev. Mr Robert Dick (1814–90; see *DCB,* 11:259–61), is sometimes cited as the first medical journal in Canada West. Jennifer J. Connor has analysed this title – which promoted both social and medical reforms, particularly the botanical remedies of the American Samuel Thomson (1769–1843) – in 'Thomsonian Medical Literature and Reformist Discourse in Upper Canada,' *Canadian Literature/Litterature canadienne* 131 (Winter, 1991), 140–55.

For extended discussions of Canadian medical periodicals see also J.J. Connor, 'Medical Journals and L'Histoire du Livre,' *AB Bookman's Weekly* 94:1 (4 July, 1994), 5–12, and idem, 'To Advocate to Diffuse, and to Elevate.' See also Roland and Potter, *Bibliography of Canadian Medical Periodicals,* 3–4, 39, 45–50, 52–3, 59. This section on medical journals owes much to this excellent bibliography and to the advice of Dr Connor.

77 The number of domestic professional periodicals was directly related to the numbers of practioners, which in fields like medicine, law, and teaching, was growing rapidly at mid-century. See R.D. Gidney and W.P.J. Miller, *Professional Gentlemen: The Professions in Nineteenth-Century Ontario* (Toronto 1994), esp. 76–7, 85, 212, 232–3ff. For law journals, see C.R. Brown, et al., *A Legal Bibliography of the British Commonwealth of Nations, Volume 3: Canadian and British-American Colonial Law* (London 1957), 11, et passim. For 'green bags,' see John Cordy Jeaffreson, *A Book about Lawyers* (London and New York 1867), 187–9ff.

78 See Spadoni, *'Grip,'* 22.

79 Arthur S. Woodburn, founder and joint publisher of the *Ottawa Journal,* founded the first *Canadian Military Review* (Ottawa, 1877), to plead for military reform. It died after a single issue. Chalmers, *Gentleman of the Press,* 71–7, 94, 207–8; Sutherland, *Monthly Epic,* 132, 138; Smith, *'Journal' Men,* 16–17; and Desmond Morton, *Ministers and Generals: Politics and the Canadian Militia, 1868–1904* (Toronto 1970), 54, et passim. Cf. G.F.G. Stanley, *Canada's Soldiers: The Military History of an Unmilitary People,* rev. 2nd ed. (Toronto 1960); and Stephen J. Harris, *Canadian Brass: The Making of a Professional Army, 1860–1939* (Toronto 1988).

80 By contrast, Elliott, 'Study of the Canadian Labour Press,' lists only ten titles for the period 1867–1900. Although the labour press promoted many pro-

gressive causes, there was ambivalence about the role of working women, and uniform opposition to the immigration of Chinese labourers, which led first to the infamous 'head tax' levied on Chinese immigrants and later to their total exclusion. This section owes a great debt to Verzuh's excellent *Radical Rag*, as well as to Watt, 'Growth of Proletarian Literature'; Watt, 'Literature of Protest'; and Weinrich, *Social Protest*. See also Hann, 'Brainworkers'; and Zerker, *Rise and Fall of the Toronto Typographical Union*.

81 See Karen McKenzie, 'The Nineteenth and Twentieth Centuries,' in McKenzie and Williamson, eds., *Art and Pictorial Press*, 25–33; J. Toupin, 'The Quebec Art Press, 1792–1945,' in *Art and Pictorial Press*, 34–9; A. Davis, 'Art Writing and Criticism,' *CanEncyc*; and Barbour, *Amazing People*, 71–2. McKenzie notes that outside of Quebec, only *Saturday Night* and *Canadian Magazine* demonstrated any staying power. In the same vein, Toupin calculates that of forty nineteenth-century periodicals produced in Quebec which mentioned 'art' in their subtitles, only five survived into the twentieth century, to wit: *La Revue canadienne, Canadian Antiquarian and Numismatic Journal, Le Monde illustré, Le Canada français,* and *Le Samedi.* Is it sheer coincidence that all seven long-lived titles cited by McKenzie and Toupin have been classified and dealt with in this chapter under primary headings *other* than 'Literary/Cultural'?

82 Calderisi, *Music Publishing*, ch. 3; Kallmann, 'Century of Musical Periodicals'; and idem, 'Periodicals.'

83 Kallmann, 'Periodicals'; and idem, 'Century of Musical Periodicals,' 41.

84 Sutherland, *Monthly Epic*, 32–5; and Vincent, 'College Journalism.' Thirty-five years passed before the *University of Toronto Quarterly* (1931–) was revived and achieved considerable prestige.

85 Rutherford, 'People's Press'; Story, 'Literary Magazines'; and Sarfati, 'Magazines in French,' *CanEncyc*.

86 Sutherland, *Monthly Epic*, 26, et passim; Petti, 'Horses of Instruction'; and Spadoni, *'Grip.'*

87 Jones, *Preliminary Checklist*, identifies nine German titles, six Scandinavian (mainly Icelandic), and two Gaelic (exclusive of newspapers). Cf. Bogusis, *Checklist of Canadian Ethnic Serials*, which identifies seventy-one German titles. Kalbfleisch, *Pioneer German Language Press*, enumerates more than thirty German newspapers prior to 1901 in Ontario alone. See also Turek, *Polish Language Press*; and *Multilingual Press in Manitoba*.

88 Kalbfleisch, *Pioneer German Language Press*, 13–14, 18, et passim; and H. Boeschenstein, 'Das Studium der deutschkanadischen Presse: Ein fruchtbares Arbeitsfeld,' *German-Canadian Yearbook* (1973), 41–6. For Henry's work, see Dondertman, 'Anthony Henry'; and *DCB*, 4:342.

89 For this section we are indebted to Robin Winks's admirable *The Blacks in Canada: A History* (Montreal and New Haven 1971), and to Bogusis, *Checklist of Canadian Ethnic Serials*. For a description and discussion of the early Black press, see Winks, 390–8. For Mary Shadd Cary, see Bearden

and Butler, *Shadd*, and *DCB*, 12:960–1. For S.R. Ward, see *DCB*, 9:820–1. For
H.W. Bibb, see *DCB*, 8:89–90. For A.B. Walker and a description of *Neith:
A Magazine of Literature, Science, Art, Philosophy, Jurisprudence,
Criticism, History, Reform, Economics* (Saint John, 1903–4), see Winks,
398–402.

90 Bruce Peel, *The Rossville Mission Press: The Invention of the Cree Syllabic
    Characters and the First Printing in Rupert's Land* (Montreal 1974); Joyce
    M. Banks, 'The Church Missionary Society and the Rossville Mission Press,'
    Papers BSC/Cahiers SBC 32:1 (Spring 1994), 31–44; idem, 'The Printing of
    the Cree Bible,' *Papers BSC/Cahiers SBC* 22 (1983), 12–24; and Danky and
    Hady, *Native American Periodicals.*
91 L. Lande, *The Moravian Missions to the Eskimos of Labrador: A Checklist
    of Manuscripts and Printed Material from 1715 to 1967* (Montreal 1973),
    31, no. 123. No copies of the first number of *Aglait Illunainortut* are known
    to survive, but later issues to no. 31, January 1907, themselves exceedingly
    rare, exist in the Lande Collection in the McGill University Library. See also
    R. McGrath, *Canadian Inuit Literature: The Development of a Tradition,*
    Canadian Ethnology Service Paper no. 94 (Ottawa 1984), 130–1.
92 Verzuh, *Radical Rag*, 15.
93 Brian Beaven has argued persuasively that patronage contracts for advertis-
    ing and printing, or even direct subsidies to newspapers, did not secure the
    slavish adherence of newspaper proprietors and editors to the will of
    political patrons, for the economics and market pressures in the newspaper
    industry were very complicated. Beaven, 'Partnership, Patronage, and the
    Press.' Cf. Walkom, 'Daily Newspaper Industry'; Sotiron, 'From Politics to
    Profit'; Rutherford, 'People's Press'; idem, *Victorian Authority*; and Hann,
    'Brainworkers.'

Bibliographic Essay

INTRODUCTION

While this bibliography cannot lay claim to comprehensiveness, it contains a wide range of the modern literature on Canadian periodicals and
the Canadian press to 1900, in the form of works consulted in the preparation of this chapter. We have avoided citing general histories of the
Canadian provinces and territories. Readers seeking more historical background should consult the excellent Canadian Centenary Series published over the last three decades by McClelland and Stewart of Toronto,
the eight most pertinent volumes of which are cited in section 1, below.
In the case of biographies, rather than seeking exhaustiveness, we have
tried to cite the best available modern, scholarly works. These, along

with the more general reference works cited, such as the *Canadian Encyclopedia, Dictionary of Canadian Biography,* or *Historical Atlas of Canada,* are easily available in Canada, and should also be accessible in any moderately large library outside of Canada.

PRESERVING AND LOCATING CANADIAN PERIODICALS

On the Preservation of Canadian Periodicals: Newspapers
Concern for the preservation of Canada's printed heritage has, over the last few decades, produced some noteworthy achievements. Planning began for a newspaper micropreservation project as early as 1942. In 1947 the newly formed Canadian Library Association obtained a fifteen-thousand-dollar capital grant from the Rockefeller Foundation to purchase a microfilm camera and began filming early Canadian newspapers. By 1957 more than 100 titles, representing over 1,000 years of newspaper backfiles, had been filmed. In 1958 the Canada Council provided a ten-thousand-dollar grant-in-aid to speed up the filming, and in 1959 a further ten-thousand-dollars to cover the cost of filming specific New Brunswick papers. By 1961 more than 150 titles had been filmed. The final count ran to over 200 titles In addition, five papers produced by Canadians and for Canadians abroad – one in the United Kingdom, three in the United States, and the *Maple Leaf* (1944–6) produced in Europe by the Canadian Forces – were filmed.[1]

TABLE 2:5
Newspapers Filmed

Province	Number of titles
Alberta	4
British Columbia	5
Manitoba	6
New Brunswick	28
Newfoundland	11
Nova Scotia	17
Ontario	65
Prince Edward Island	16
Quebec	46
Saskatchewan	6
Yukon	4
Total	208

Meanwhile, commercial firms also entered the field of preservation microfilming, and the encouragement of the National Library of Canada prompted efforts in every province to produce a census and union list of local holdings of newspapers (and occasionally other kinds of periodicals). Records of the fruits of these labours are listed in the second part of this bibliography.

On the Preservation of Canadian Periodicals: Magazines

During the 1970s the *Report of the Commission on Canadian Studies*, chaired by Professor Thomas Symons, recommended the strengthening of Canadiana research collections, while the *Report of the Consultative Group of University Research Libraries* urged immediate action to deal with problems of collection deterioration and access. As a result, the Canadian Institute for Historical Microreproductions (CIHM) was created and funded by a large grant from the Canada Council (which then included the Social Sciences and Humanities Research Council of Canada). Its mandate is to film early Canadian publications systematically and exhaustively, with the regrettable exception, initially, of omitting obviously important titles like *Canadian Illustrated News* and *Grip*, to avoid the appearance of using government funding to compete with private publishers. Despite these lacunae, the task of preserving on film some of the more obscure, and therefore harder to locate, titles is one that most scholars will applaud. CIHM devoted its first decade to filming more than 62,000 Canadian monographs published prior to 1901. In 1988 CIHM began the second phase of its mandate – filming annuals and periodicals. Complete backfiles were assembled for filming, often from several different libraries if a complete run does not exist in any single location. Some notion of the scope of the CIHM project may be conveyed from production statistics. By late 1994 CIHM had filmed 1,285 different periodical titles, which represented 57,500 separate issues, now preserved on 60,000 individual microfiche.[2]

On Locating Copies of Canadian Periodicals

The various bibliographies and union lists in the second part of this bibliography are essential to identifying Canadian periodicals and to obtaining bibliographic details. Some also contain information on library locations where specific titles may be found. In this age of highly automated library catalogues, the researcher who has access to the Internet is advised to begin the search for locations at the keyboard. Because some of these databases do not offer free, public access, collaborating with a local reference librarian may be necessary. For any Canadian title, regardless of subject, first resort should be made to the National Library of Canada's AMICUS database, which contains not merely the holdings of the National Library, but also union holdings of libraries across Canada. For scientific titles the next approach should be to the CISTISER database of the Canadian Institute for Scientific and Technical Information (CISTI), the scientific twin of the National Library of Canada, which is accessible as part of the CAN-OLE database.

The next step in any thorough search is to consult the databases of major cataloguing utilities, including OCLC in the State of Ohio, a database with over sixty million library records, and the Information Management Systems (IMS) REFCATSS database located in Winnipeg, Manitoba, which also contains a staggering number of records. However, OCLC's serials records are preferable, because – unlike those of IMS REFCATSS – they contain full records of volumes held. Failure to find holdings of a title in one of these databases is a guarantee of scarcity. Consult the printed source of the reference again to verify that it was copied out correctly, and hope that the same source may also record the existence of a backfile on the shelves of some as-yet-unautomated library. In addition to AMICUS, CISTISER, CAN-OLE, and IMS REFCATTS, other on-line searching tools in Canada that may prove useful include CISTI-2000 and ROMULUS. In the United States, in addition to OCLC, consult 1st Search, CARL UNCOVER, Center for Research Libraries, and Commercial Document Delivery Service. Once the title has been located, the next stop will be the office of either Inter-Library Loan or your travel agent. It is worth noting here that many libraries have loaded full catalogue records of their CIHM microreprint holdings, which are thus easily traced, and because they are so compact, they are a great boon to interlibrary lending.

NOTES

1 Canadian Library Association/Association canadienne des bibliothèques, Newspaper Microfilming Project Catalogue microfilms de journaux; idem, Catalogue of New Brunswick Newspapers on Microfilm (1961).
2 Bentley, 'Micro-Preservation'; CIHM, Catalogue of Periodicals (June 1994); and Pam Bjornson, 'Canadian Serials to 1900: CIHM's Micropreservation Project, Phase II,' unpublished background paper from Invitational Conference on National Library Collection Preservation Strategies, held at the National Library of Canada, Ottawa, 31 October and 1 November 1994. Still another microfilming project, sponsored by the Hannah Institute for the History of Medicine in Toronto, has reproduced all traceable Canadian medical journals down to 1910, based on the Rolland and Potter bibliography. Microfilm copies of these titles will soon be available for purchase from CIHM in Ottawa.

ANNOTATED BIBLIOGRAPHY

Anthologies, Articles, Biographies, Dissertations, and Monographs
Arnason, David. 'Canadian Literary Periodicals of the Nineteenth Century.' *Journal of Canadian Fiction* 2:3 (Special issue/Summer 1973), 125–8.

Aubry, Jean-Paul. 'Presse francophone au Manitoba.' *Vie française* 26 (1972), 115–36.

Baker, William M. *Timothy Warren Anglin 1822–96: Irish-Catholic Canadian*. Toronto 1977. [Biography of prominent Irish-Catholic journalist and politician.]

Ballstadt, Carl, ed. *The Search for English-Canadian Literature: An Anthology of Critical Articles from the Nineteenth and Early Twentieth Centuries*. Toronto 1975. See especially 'Introduction,' pp. xi–xlv. [Useful collection of original sources on role of a Canadian national literature.]

Barbour, Noel Robert. *Those Amazing People: The Story of the Canadian Magazine Industry, 1778–1967*. Toronto 1982. [Covers both French- and English-language magazines, but must be used with caution.]

Bearden, Jim, and Linda Jean Butler. *Shadd: The Life and Times of Mary Shadd Cary*. Toronto 1977. [Life of pioneering Black newspaper editor and teacher.]

Beaven, Brian P.N. 'Partnership, Patronage and the Press in Ontario, 1880–1914: Myths and Realities.' *CHR* 64:3 (Sept. 1983), 317–51.

Beck, J. Murray. *Joseph Howe, I: Conservative Reformer, 1804–1848; II: The Briton Becomes Canadian, 1848–1873*. 2 vols. Montreal 1983.

Bengough, John Wilson. *A Caricature History of Canadian Politics, Selected from the Original*. Ed. and with new introduction by Douglas Fetherling. Toronto 1974. [Choice example of Bengough's skill as cartoonist.]

Benn, Carl. 'The Upper Canadian Press, 1773–1815.' *Ontario History* 70 (1978), 91–114.

Bentley, David M.R. 'The Micro-Preservation of Canada's Early Periodicals.' *Victorian Periodicals Review* 25:3 (Fall 1992), 127–8. [On work of the Canadian Institute for Historical Microreproductions.]

Bissell, Claude T. 'Literary Taste in Central Canada during the Late Nineteenth Century.' *CHR* 31:2 (Sept. 1950) 237–51. Reprint. In McMullen, 24–40. [Focuses on the *Week*.]

Blyth, Jack A. 'The Development of the Paper Industry in Old Ontario, 1824–1867.' *Ontario History* 62:2 (June 1970), 119–33. [Technical and social historical approach to paper mills.]

Bone, John R., Joseph T. Clark, A.H.U. Colquhoun, and John F. MacKay. *A History of Canadian Journalism in the Several Portions of the Dominion with a Sketch of the Canadian Press Association, 1859–1908.* Toronto 1908. Reprint. New York 1976. [Primarily a history of the CPA – an association of newspaper editors and proprietors and sometime lobby group – and its annual excursions.]

Bonville, Jean de. 'La liberté de presse à la fin du 19e siècle: le cas de *Canada-Revue.*' *Revue d'histoire de l'Amérique française* 31 (1978), 501–23. [Most detailed account of the battles provoked by A. Filiatreault's *Le Canada-Revue* (later *Le Réveil*) in the 1890s. See also Chassay (below).]

– *La presse québécoise de 1884 à 1914: genèse d'un média de masse.* Quebec 1988. [Quebec equivalent of Rutherford's *Victorian Authority.*]

Bossé, Éveline. *Joseph-Charles Taché (1820–1894): un grand représentant de l'élite canadienne-française.* Quebec 1971.

Brown, Robert Craig. 'Canadian Nationalism in Western Newspapers.' *Alberta Historical Review* 10:3 (Spring 1962), 1–7. Reprint. In *Historical Essays on the Prairie Provinces,* ed. by D. Swainson. Carleton Library no. 53. Toronto 1970.

Brown, Robert Craig, and G. Ramsay Cook. *Canada, 1896–1921: A Nation Transformed.* Canadian Centenary Series, vol. 14. Toronto 1974.

Bruce, Charles. *News and the Southams.* Toronto 1968. [Account of the family which, after 1877, built Canada's largest chain of newspapers.]

Buono, Yolande. 'Imprimerie et diffusion de l'imprimé à Montréal, de 1776 à 1820.' MA thesis, Université de Montréal, 1980.

Calderisi, Maria. *Music Publishing in the Canadas, 1800–1867/L'Édition musicale au Canada, 1800–1867.* Ottawa 1981. See especially ch. 3, 'Newspaper and Periodical Publishers'/'Éditeurs de journaux et de périodiques.'

Canadian Institute for Historical Microreproductions/Institut canadien de microreproductions historiques. 'Towards a National Preservation Policy Statement: A Draft Report of the Working Group Advising on the Preservation Microfilming of Periodicals/Vers un énoncé de politique nationale de conservation: Document de travail à l'usage du groupe de travail consultatif sur la conservation des periodiques sur microfilms.' *FACSIMILE: A Publication of the Canadian Institute for Historical Microreproductions/FAC-SIMILÉ: Bulletin de l'institut canadien de microreproductions historiques,* no. 5 (May 1988/mai 1988).

Careless, J.M.S. 'The Toronto *Globe* and Agrarian Radicalism, 1850–1867.' *CHR* 29:1 (March 1948), 14–39.

– 'Mid-Victorian Liberalism in Central Canadian Newspapers, 1850–67.' *CHR* 31:3 (Sept. 1950), 221–36.

- *Brown of the 'Globe,' I: The Voice of Upper Canada, 1818–1859; II: Statesman of Confederation, 1860–1880.* 2 vols. Toronto 1959–63.
- *The Union of the Canadas: The Growth of Canadian Institutions, 1841–1857.* Canadian Centenary Series, vol. 10. Toronto 1967.

Chalmers, Floyd S. *A Gentleman of the Press.* Toronto 1969. [Authorized biography of magazine magnate Col. John B. Maclean by a colleague.]

Chassay, Jean-François. 'Une attitude critique: *Le Canada-Revue* et *Le Réveil.' Revue d'histoire littéraire du Québec et du Canada français* 6 (été–automne 1983), 27–31. [See also Bonville, 'La liberté de presse' (above).]

Clippingdale, Richard Thomas George. 'J.S. Willison, Political Journalist: From Liberalism to Independence, 1881–1905.' Ph.D. thesis, University of Toronto, 1970.

Colquhoun, Arthur H.U. 'A Century of Canadian Magazines.' *Canadian Magazine* 17:2 (June 1901), 141–9. [Includes illustrations of people and title pages; list of titles excludes religious, medical, educational, scientific, sporting, juvenile, college and class publications, and literary weeklies, yet includes: Ontario – 19 titles; Quebec English – 9; Quebec French – 15; Maritimes – 11; and Manitoba – 2.]

- 'After Twenty-One Years.' *Canadian Magazine* 42:4 (Feb. 1914), 362–4. [On early magazines in general plus insider's information on *Canadian Magazine.*]
- 'The Journalistic Field of 1887: Memoirs of the Background from which *Saturday Night* Sprang.' *Saturday Night* 43 (10 Dec. 1927), 2, 5.
- *Press, Politics, and People: The Life and Letters of Sir John Willison, Journalist and Correspondent of the 'Times.'* Toronto 1935. [See also Clippingdale's 'J.S. Willison' (above) and Willison's *Reminiscences* (below).]

Connor, Jennifer J. 'To Advocate, to Diffuse, and the Elevate: The Culture and Context of Medical Publishing in Canada, 1630 to 1920.' Ph.D. thesis, University of Western Ontario, 1992.

Cook, G. Ramsay. *The Politics of John W. Dafoe and the 'Free Press.'* Toronto 1963.

- *The Regenerators: Social Criticism in Late Victorian English Canada.* Toronto 1985. [Important study of J.W. Bengough, Goldwin Smith, T. Phillips Thompson, et al.]

Craig, Gerald M. *Upper Canada: The Formative Years, 1784–1841.* Canadian Centenary Series, vol. 7. Toronto 1963.

Cumming, Carman. *Secret Craft: The Journalism of Edward Farrer.* Toronto 1992. [Biography of the maverick editor of Toronto's *Daily Mail.*]

Dafoe, John W. 'Early Winnipeg Newspapers.' *Papers of the Historical and Scientific Society of Manitoba*, series III, no. 3 (1947), 14–24. Reprint, with illustrations. 'Presses on the Prairies: Memoirs of a Pioneer Editor.' *Beaver* 67:6 (Dec. 1987–Jan. 1988), 19–29. [Charming lecture delivered to Manitoba Historical Society in 1930.]

Davies, Gwendolyn. 'Belles and the Backwoods: A Study of Fiction in Nineteenth-Century Maritime Periodicals.' *Atlantic Provinces Literature Colloquium Papers/Communication du colloque sur la littérature des provinces atlantiques* (1977), 40–55.

– 'A Literary Study of Selected Periodicals from Maritime Canada: 1789–1872.' Ph.D. thesis, York University, 1979. [Analyses the content and social role of six titles: *Nova-Scotia Magazine* (1789–92), *Acadian Magazine* (1826–8), *Amaranth* (1841–3), *Mayflower* (1851–2), *Provincial, or Halifax Monthly Magazine* (1852–3), and *Stewart's Literary Quarterly* (1867–72). See also Fraser, 'Two Nova Scotian Literary Periodicals' (below).]

Davis, Angela E. 'Art and Work: Frederick Brigden and the History of the Canadian Illustrated Press.' *Journal of Canadian Studies/La Revue d'études canadiennes* 27:2 (Summer/été 1992), 22–36.

Davis, May. 'A Pinafored Printer.' *Saskatchewan History* 9:2 (Spring 1956), 63–9. [Author set type etc. for Regina *Leader* as a teenager.]

Dean, Misao. *A Different Point of View: Sara Jeannette Duncan*. Montreal/Kingston 1991. [First woman staff-writer on Toronto *Globe*; complements Fowler (below).]

Desbarats, Peter, ed. *'Canadian Illustrated News,' 1869–1883: Canada's First National Magazine*. Toronto [1970].

Doherty, Edward J. 'An Analysis of Social and Political Thought in the Irish Catholic Press in Upper Canada, 1858–1867,' MA thesis, University of Waterloo, 1976.

Dondertman, Anne. 'Anthony Henry, "Lilius," and the *Nova-Scotia Calendar.*' *Papers BSC/Cahiers SBC* 29:2 (Fall/automne 1991), 32–50.

Donnelly, Judy. 'January hath 31 Days: Early Canadian Almanacs as Primary Research Materials.' *Papers BSC/Cahiers SBC* 29:2 (Fall/automne 1991), 7–31.

Donnelly, Murray. *Dafoe and the 'Free Press.'* Toronto 1968.

Drake, Earl G. 'Pioneer Journalism in Saskatchewan, 1878–1887.' *Saskatchewan History* 5:1 (1952), 17–27; V:2, 41–54. [Part 1: 'The Founding of the Territorial Press'; 2: 'Some Characteristics of the Territorial Press.']

Dutil, Patrice. *Devil's Advocate: Godfroy Langlois and the Politics of Liberal Progressivism in Laurier's Quebec*. Montreal 1994. [Editor of *La Patrie, Le Canada*, and *La Pays* and his fight for reform.]

Elliott, Robbins Leonard. 'A Study of the Canadian Labour Press, 1867–1947.' MA thesis, University of Toronto, 1947. [Use with caution.]

Felteau, Cyrille. *Histoire de 'La Presse,' I: Le livre du peuple, 1884–1916; II: Le plus grand quotidien français d'Amérique.* 2 vols. Montreal 1983–4. [Detailed house history.]

– 'Aspects de l'histoire de la presse canadienne de langue française au 18e et au 19e siècles.' *Ecrits du Canada français* 47 (1983), 89–105; 48 (1983), 111–29. [Analysis of the necessary preconditions for periodical publication in eighteenth-century Quebec.]

Ferguson, George Victor. *John W. Dafoe.* Toronto 1948.

Ferguson, Ted. *Kit Coleman: Queen of Hearts.* Toronto 1978. [Part anthology of pioneer woman journalist's work and part biography. See also Freeman (below).]

Fetherling, Douglas. *The Rise of the Canadian Newspaper.* Perspectives on Canadian Culture series. Toronto 1990. [Impressive and useful survey despite occasional errors.]

– 'E.J. Baker and the *British Whig* of Kingston.' *Devil's Artisan* 29 (1991), 3–32. [The founder of the *British Whig* and its early years.]

– *A Little Bit of Thunder: The Strange Inner Life of the 'Kingston Whig-Standard.'* Toronto 1993. [Splendidly written history of one of Canada's more eccentric dailies. A substantial portion is devoted to the period 1834–1914.]

Flitton, Marilyn G. 'The *Canadian Monthly,* 1872–1882.' MA thesis, Simon Fraser University, 1974.

Ford, Arthur Rutherford. *As the World Wags On.* Toronto 1950. [Memoir of the London *Free Press* editor-in-chief; contains anecdotes on nineteenth-century journalists.]

Fowler, Marian. *Redney: A Life of Sara Jeannette Duncan.* Toronto 1983. [See also Dean (above).]

Fraser, Nancy. 'Two Nova Scotian Literary Periodicals of the 1830s: The *Halifax Monthly* and the *Pearl.*' MA thesis, Dalhousie University, 1977. [See also Davies, 'Literary Study' (above).]

Freeman, Barbara. *Kit's Kingdom: The Journalism of Kathleen Blake Coleman.* Ottawa 1989. [See also Ted Ferguson (above).]

Gagnon, Marcel-A. *Le ciel et l'enfer d'Arthur Buies.* Collection Vie des lettres canadiennes. Quebec 1965. [Liberal satirist, editor, columnist. See also Lamontagne (below).]

Galarneau, Claude. 'La presse périodique au Québec de 1764 à 1859.' *Mémoires de la Société royale au Canada,* 4e série, 22 (1984), 143–66. [Detailed and useful analysis based on numbers, rather than a mere enumeration of titles; important. See also Hare and Wallot, 'Les Imprimés au Québec' (below).]

Gates, Lillian F. 'Mackenzie's *Gazette*: An Aspect of W.L. Mackenzie's American Years.' *CHR* 46:4 (Dec. 1965), 323–45. Reprint. *Papers BSC/ Cahiers SBC* 25 (1986), 116–38.

– *After the Rebellion: The Later Years of William Lyon Mackenzie.* Toronto 1988.

Godin, Pierre. *L'Information-opium. Une histoire politique du journal 'La Presse.'* Collections ASPECTS no. 19. Montreal 1973. [A far less sympathetic view than Felteau (above).]

– *La lutte pour l'information: histoire de la presse écrite au Québec.* Montreal 1981. [Chapters 1 and 2 cover the pre-1914 era, but are mostly derivative, especially from the early work of Bonville.]

Gundy, H. Pearson. *Early Printers and Printing in the Canadas.* Toronto 1957; 2nd ed. 1964.

– 'Literary Publishing.' In Klinck 1965, 174–88; 1976, 1:188–202.

– 'Liberty and License of the Press in Upper Canada.' In *His Own Man: Essays in Honour of A.R.M. Lower*, ed. by W.H. Heick and R. Graham. Montreal 1974.

– 'Hugh C. Thomson: Editor, Publisher, and Politician, 1791–1834.' In *To Preserve and Defend: Essays on Kingston in the Nineteenth Century*, ed. Gerald Tulchinsky. Montreal 1976.

Hacker, Carlotta. *E. Cora Hind.* The Canadians Series. Toronto 1979.

Haig, Kennethe Macmahon. *Brave Harvest: The Life Story of E. Cora Hind.* Toronto 1945.

Hall, David J. *Clifford Sifton, I: The Young Napoleon, 1861–1900; II: A Lonely Eminence, 1901–1929.* 2 vols. Vancouver 1981–5. See especially vol. 1, ch. 9: 'A Party Organ: Sifton and the *Manitoba Free Press.*'

Ham, George H. *Reminiscences of a Raconteur between the 40s and the 20s.* Toronto 1921. [Memoirs of a Winnipeg journalist in the 1870s and 1880s, with data on the eastern Canadian press.]

Hann, Russell. 'Brainworkers and the Knights of Labour: E.E. Sheppard, Phillips Thompson, and the *Toronto News*, 1883–1887.' In *Essays in Canadian Working Class History*, ed. G.S. Kealey and P. Warrian. Toronto 1976.

Hare, John, and Jean-Pierre Wallot. 'Les Imprimés au Québec (1760–1820).' In *L'Imprimé au Québec: aspects historiques (18e–20e siècles)*, ed. Y. Lamonde. Collection 'Culture savante' no 2. Quebec 1983. [A survey of, and program for, research on Québécois imprints which emphasizes 1810–20; some content analysis and useful appendices, especially appendix 2, 'Périodiques,' pp. 95–8. See Galarneau, 'La presse périodique' (above) for related work by a collaborator.]

- 'Le livre au Québec et la librairie Neilson, au tournant du XIXe siècle.' In *Livre et lecture au Québec 1800–1850*, ed. Claude Galarneau and Maurice Lemire. Quebec 1988.

Harkness, Ross. *J.E. Atkinson of the 'Star.'* Toronto 1963. [House biography.]

Harvey, Daniel Cobb. 'Newspapers of Nova Scotia, 1840–1867.' *CHR* 26:3 (Sept. 1945), 279–301. Reprint. *Papers BSC/Cahiers SBC* 26 (1987), 135–56. [Includes chronological lists.]

Haworth, E. *Imprint of a Nation*. Toronto 1969. [Brief survey of Canadian printing history.]

Hayne, David. *'Nouvelles soirées canadiennes* (1882–83).' *Revue d'histoire littéraire du Québec et du Canada français* 6 (été/automne 1983), 17–25.

Hill, Robert Andrew. 'A Note on Newspaper Patronage in Canada during the late 1850s and early 1860s.' *CHR* 49:1 (March 1968), 44–59. [Exclusively Anglo titles; how they survived financially – or didn't.]

- *Pioneer Journalism in the Chateauguay Valley*. Howick, Quebec 1975. [Detailed histories of a dozen Eastern Townships newspapers, with three useful background chapters.]

Hulse, Elizabeth. 'Newspapers Printed on the Co-operative Plan.' *Papers BSC/Cahiers SBC* 22 (1983), 89–102. [Describes Canadian firms which syndicated 'auxiliary' news sheets and features to rural newspapers.]

Jack, D.R. 'Acadian Magazines.' *TRSC* series 2, 9, sec. 2 (May 1903), 173–203. ['Most comprehensive history of Maritime literary journals,' Talman *TRSC* 1949.]

Kalbfleisch, Herbert Karl. *The History of the Pioneer German Language Press of Ontario, 1835–1918*. Toronto 1968.

Kesterton, W.H. *A History of Journalism in Canada*. The Carleton Library no. 36. Toronto 1967. [Excellent survey includes much publishing history.]

- *The Law and the Press in Canada*. The Carleton Library no. 100. Toronto 1976. [Includes many legal case histories.]

Kilbourn, William. *The Firebrand: William Lyon Mackenzie and the Rebellion in Upper Canada*. Toronto 1956.

Klinck, Carl F. 'Samuel Hull Wilcocke.' *Journal of Canadian Fiction* 2:3 (Special issue, Summer 1973), 13–21. [Biography and information on his magazine, *Scribbler*.]

Klinck, Carl F., et al., eds. *Literary History of Canada: Canadian Literature in English*. Toronto 1st ed. 1965; 2nd ed., 4 vols., 1976–90. [The standard survey history.]

Koester, Charles B. *Mr Davin, M.P.: A Biography of Nicholas Flood Davin*. Saskatoon 1980. [Biography of Tory journalist, author, and founder of the Regina *Leader*.]

Lagrave, Jean Paul de. *La liberté d'expression en Nouvelle-France (1608–1760)*. Collections liberté. Montreal 1975. [An idiosyncratic, semi-scholarly, self-published work in five volumes (see below).]
– *Les origines de la presse au Québec, 1760–1791*. Collections liberté. Montreal 1975.
– *Les journalistes-démocrates au Bas-Canada (1791–1840)*. Collections liberté. Montreal 1975.
– *Le combat des idées au Québec-Uni, 1840–1867*. Collections liberté. Montreal 1976.
– *Liberté et servitude de l'information au Québec confédéré, 1867–1967*. Collections liberté. Ottawa 1978.
– *Histoire de l'information au Québec*. Montreal 1980. [A condensation of the author's earlier volumes.]
Lamb, Bessie. 'From *Tickler* to *Telegram*: Notes on Early Vancouver Newspapers.' *British Columbia Historical Quarterly* 9:3 (July 1945), 174–99. [Covers newspapers 1878–98.]
Lamonde, Yvan. *La librairie et l'édition à Montréal, 1776–1920*. Montreal 1991. [Study of the Montreal publishing and bookselling trades, with lists.]
Lamontagne, Léopold. *Arthur Buies: homme de lettres*. Quebec 1957. [Liberal satirist, editor, and columnist. See also Gagnon (above).]
Landon, Fred. 'The Agricultural Journals of Upper Canada (Ontario).' *Agricultural History* 9:4 (Oct. 1935), 167–75.
Lechasseur, Antonio, and Yvan Morin, eds. 'La presse périodique dans le Bas-Saint-Laurent: aspects historiques.' *Revue d'histoire du Bas-Saint-Laurent* 10:2–3 (1985), 35–149. [Significant study of newspapers of eastern Quebec, 1867–1983; a refreshing exception to the usually exclusive focus of attention on metropolitan Montreal and Quebec City.]
Lefebvre, André. *La 'Montreal Gazette' et le nationalisme canadien, 1835–1842*. Montreal 1970. [Extensive extracts in English reflect the *Gazette*'s hostile reaction to French-Canadian nationalism.]
Lennon, Wayne. 'Striking the Balance: The Labour Press and the National Question in Ontario and the Maritimes, 1872–1913.' MA thesis, Carleton University, 1981.
Levendel, Lewis. *A Century of the Canadian Jewish Press: 1880s–1980s*. Ottawa 1990.
Levene, Mark A. 'Machinery for Everybody: Advertising in Canadian Industrial Trade Papers, 1900–1911.' MA thesis, Carleton University, 1992.
Lindsay, Charles. *The Life and Times of William Lyon Mackenzie: With an Account of the Canadian Rebellion of 1837, and the Subsequent*

Frontier Disturbances, Chiefly from Unpublished Documents. 2 vols. Toronto 1862. Reprint. Toronto 1971. [The principal primary source; sympathetic work by Mackenzie's son-in-law.]

MacDonald, Mary Lu. 'Some Notes on the Montreal Literary Scene in the Mid-1820s.' *Canadian Poetry* 5 (Fall/Winter 1979), 29–40. [*Canadian Magazine* and *Canadian Review*.]

– *Literature and Society in the Canadas, 1817–1850*. Lewiston, NY 1992. [Contains much valuable information about both the English- and French-language literary periodicals and their contributors.]

– 'English and French-Language Periodicals and the Development of Literary Culture in Early Victorian Canada.' *Victorian Periodicals Review* 26:4 (Winter 1993), 221–7.

McDougall, Robert Law. 'A Study of Canadian Periodical Literature of the Nineteenth Century.' Ph.D. thesis, University of Toronto, 1950. [Covers only five titles: *Literary Garland, Canadian Journal, Anglo-American Magazine, British American Magazine,* and *Canadian Monthly and National Review*.]

McKenzie, Karen, and Mary F. Williamson, eds. *The Art and Pictorial Press in Canada: Two Centuries of Art Magazines*. Toronto 1979. [Eight useful articles.]

McLean, Mary. 'Early Parliamentary Reporting in Upper Canada.' *CHR* 20:4 (Dec. 1939), 378–91. [Covers 1820s to 1831.]

McMullen, Lorraine, ed. *Twentieth Century Essays on Confederation Literature*. Ottawa 1976.

MacNutt, W. Stewart. *The Atlantic Provinces: The Emergence of Colonial Society, 1712–1857*. Canadian Centenary Series, vol. 9. Toronto 1965.

MacPherson, Ian. 'The *Liberal* of St Thomas, Ontario, 1832–1833.' *Western Ontario Historical Notes* 21:2 (Sept. 1965), 10–29. [Thorough.]

Mahaffy, R.U. 'Ottawa Journalism, 1860 to 1870.' *Ontario History* 42:4 (Oct. 1950), 205–11. [Effect of technology and society on newspaper publishing; lists extant files.]

March, William. *Red Line: The 'Chronicle-Herald' and the 'Mail-Star,' 1875–1954*. Halifax 1986.

Martell, James Stuart. 'The Press of the Maritime Provinces in the 1830s.' *CHR* 19:1 (March 1938), 24–49. Reprint. *Papers BSC/Cahiers SBC* 26 (1987): 109–36. [On political and social origins of the press.]

– 'Some Editorial Opinions from the Newspapers of the Maritime Provinces in the 1830s.' *CHR* 19:1 (March 1938), 50–56.

– 'Early Parliamentary Reporting in Nova Scotia, 1817–1837.' *CHR* 21:4 (Dec. 1940), 384–93.

Miller, H. Orlo. 'The History of the Newspaper Press in London, 1830–1875.' *Ontario Historical Society Papers and Records* 32 (1937), 114–39. ['Essay' format on twenty-five titles.]

– *A Century of Western Ontario: The Story of London, The 'Free Press,' and Western Ontario, 1849–1949.* Toronto 1949. [House history.]

Monet, Jacques. *The Last Cannon Shot: A Study in French Canadian Nationalism.* Toronto 1969. [Formative role of periodical press, 1837–50.]

Monière, Denis. *Ludger Duvernay et la révolution intellectuelle au Bas-Canada.* Montreal 1987. [Influential editor of *La Minerve.*]

Moran, James. *Printing Presses: History and Development from the Fifteenth Century to Modern Times.* London 1973. [Beautifully illustrates the nineteenth-century revolution in printing technology.]

Morton, William Lewis. *The Critical Years: The Union of British North America, 1857–1873.* Canadian Centenary Series, vol. 12. Toronto 1964.

The Multilingual Press in Manitoba/La Presse multilingue au Manitoba. Winnipeg 1974. [Title-by-title anecdotal histories; some nineteenth-century content.]

Neatby, Hilda. *Quebec: The Revolutionary Age, 1760–1791.* Canadian Centenary Series, vol. 6. Toronto 1966.

O'Flynn, Philomena. 'An Irishman, a Catholic and an Editor: Irish Catholic Editors in Nineteenth-Century Canada.' MA thesis, Laurentian University, 1984.

Ouellet, Fernand. *Lower Canada, 1791–1840: Social Change and Nationalism.* Trans. and adapted by Patricia Claxton. Canadian Centenary Series, vol. 8. Toronto 1980.

Parker, George L. 'The British North American Book Trade in the 1840s: The First Crisis.' *Papers BSC/Cahiers SBC* 12 (1973), 82–99.

– 'Literary Journalism before Confederation.' *Canadian Literature* 68–9 (Spring–Summer 1976), 88–100. [Covers many magazine titles and their content.]

– *The Beginnings of the Book Trade in Canada.* Toronto 1985.

– 'Publishing in Nineteenth-Century Canada: Copyright and the Market for Books.' In *Questions of Funding, Publishing and Distribution/ Questions d'édition et de diffusion,* ed. I.S. MacLaren and C. Potvin. Proceedings of a Conference: Towards a History of the Literary Institution in Canada 2/Vers une histoire de l'institution littéraire au Canada 2. Edmonton 1989.

Peel, Bruce. *Early Printing in the Red River Settlement, 1859–1870, and Its Effect upon the Riel Rebellion.* Winnipeg 1974.

Pénisson, Bernard. 'Un hebdomadaire libéral: *L'Écho du Manitoba* (1898–1905).' *Revue d'histoire de l'Amérique français* 28:3 (déc. 1974), 367–84.
- *Henri d'Hellencourt: un journaliste français au Manitoba, 1898–1905*. St-Boniface 1986.
Petti, Anthony G. 'Horses of Instruction: Beasts in Canadian Political Cartoons of the Victorian Era.' *Victorian Periodicals Review* 16:3–4 (Fall/Winter 1983), 109–25. [Focuses on Bengough's *Grip* and other humour magazines.]
Poulton, Ron. *The Paper Tyrant: John Ross Robertson of the Toronto 'Telegram.'* Toronto 1971.
Raible, Chris, and Nancy Luno. 'Life after the Rebellion: William Lyon Mackenzie as Printer after 1837.' *Devil's Artisan* 27 (1990), 5–27.
Robidoux, Réjean. '*Les Soirées canadiennes* et *Le Foyer canadien* ou le répertoire littéraire d'une époque.' *Revue d'histoire littéraire du Québec et du Canada français* 6 (été–automne 1983), 11–6.
Ross, Philip Dansken. *Retrospects of a Newspaper Person.* 1931. [Reminiscences of long-time Ottawa *Journal* editor; see also Smith, '*Journal* Men' (below).]
Rutherford, Paul. 'The Western Press and Regionalism, 1870–1896.' *CHR* 52:3 (Sept. 1971), 287–305.
- 'The People's Press: The Emergence of the New Journalism in Canada, 1869–99.' *CHR* 56:2 (June 1975), 169–91.
- *The Making of the Canadian Media.* Toronto 1978. [Insightful survey.]
- *A Victorian Authority: The Daily Press in Late Nineteenth-Century Canada.* Toronto 1982. [Outstanding analytical history.]
Smith, Irving Norman. *The 'Journal' Men. Three Great Canadian Newspapermen and the Tradition They Created.* Toronto 1974. [Sketches of P.D. Ross, E. Norman Smith, and Grattan O'Leary, of the Ottawa *Journal*; Ross began his career in 1879. See also Ross, *Retrospects* (above).]
Sonser, Anna. 'Literary Ladies and *The Calliopean*: English Studies at the Burlington Ladies' Academy (1846–1851).' *University of Toronto Quarterly* 64:3 (Summer 1995), 368–80.
Sotiron, Minko Michael. 'From Politics to Profit: The Commercialization of Canadian English-Language Daily Newspapers, 1890–1920.' Ph.D. thesis, Concordia University, 1990.
Spadoni, Carl. '*Grip* and the Bengoughs as Publishers and Printers.' *Papers BSC/Cahiers SBC* 27 (1988), 12–37.
Steele, Charles Frank. *Prairie Editor: The Life and Times of Buchanan of Lethbridge.* Toronto 1961. See ch. 6, pp. 33–40, on frontier press.

Stephenson, Harry Edward, and Carlton McNaught. *The Story of Advertising in Canada: A Chronicle of the Years.* Toronto 1940. [A good survey, if necessarily brief on the early years.]

Stewart, George. 'The History of a Magazine.' *Dominion Illustrated Monthly* 1:7 (August 1892), 400–8.

Stewart, Walter, ed. *Canadian Newspapers: The Inside Story.* Edmonton 1980. [Popular work which treats origins briefly.]

Story of the Press: Chapters in the North-West History Prior to 1890, Related by Oldtimers. Battleford, Sask. 1928. [Reminiscences with photos; an important primary source. Includes: *Nor'-Wester* (1859), Saskatchewan *Herald* (1878), Prince Albert *Times* (1882), MacLeod *Gazette* (1882), Calgary *Herald* (1883), Regina *Leader* (1883), Medicine Hat *Times* (1884), Lethbridge *News* (1885). A second part, to include more on the Saskatchewan *Herald*, plus the Marquette *Review*, Edmonton *Bulletin*, Moosomin *Courier*, Moose Jaw *News*, *Vidette*, and *Progress*, was announced, but apparently never published.]

Stortz, Gerald J. 'The Irish Catholic Press in Toronto, 1887–1892.' *Canadian Journal of Communication* 10:3 (1984), 27–46.

Sutherland, Fraser. *The Monthly Epic: A History of Canadian Magazines.* Toronto 1989. [Best survey, but largely excludes French-language titles.]

Talman, James John. 'The Printing Presses of William Lyon Mackenzie Prior to 1837.' *CHR* 18:4 (Dec. 1937), 414–18.

– 'The Newspapers of Upper Canada a Century Ago.' *CHR* 19:1 (March 1938), 9–23. [Primarily 1830–7; no lists.]

– 'The Newspaper Press in Canada West, 1850–1860.' *TRSC*, series 3, 33, sec. 2 (May 1939), 149–74.

– 'Three Scottish-Canadian Newspaper Editor Poets.' *CHR* 38:2 (June 1947), 166–77. [George Menzies, Robert Jackson MacGeorge, and Thomas Macqueen.]

– 'The Pioneer Press in Western Ontario.' *Western Ontario Historical Notes* 5:2 (1947), 43–8.

– 'The First Prince Edward Island Literary Journal.' *TRSC*, series 3, 43, sec. 2 (June 1949), 153–6. [*Progress Magazine*, 1867; corrective to Jack, 1902.]

– 'George Sheppard, Journalist, 1819–1912.' *TRSC*, series 3, 44, sec. 2 (June 1950), 119–34.

Tobin, Brian. *The Upper Canada Gazette and Its Printers, 1793–1849.* Toronto 1993.

Tousignant, Pierre. 'La *Gazette* de Montréal de 1791–1896.' MA thesis, Université de Montréal, 1960.

Tremblay, Jean-Paul. 'Un journaliste satirique du Canada français au XIXe siècle: Napoléon Aubin.' *Revue de l'Université Laval* 20:9 (mai 1966), 816–31. [Editor of *Fantasque*.]
– *À la recherche de Napoléon Aubin.* Collection: Vie des lettres canadiennes. Quebec 1969.
Turek, Victor. *The Polish Language Press in Canada: Its History and a Bibliographical List.* Canadian Polish Congress, Polish Research Institute in Canada Survey no. 4. Toronto 1962. [Extensive and detailed 182-page history of Polish-language publishing, accompanied by a list of 118 newspapers and magazines.]
Verzuh, Ron. *Radical Rag: The Pioneer Labour Press in Canada.* Ottawa 1988. [Fine study of proletarian press.]
Vincent, Thomas Brewer. 'College Journalism and Literary Development in Nineteenth-Century Canada.' Unpublished paper.
Waddell, W.S. 'Frank Oliver and the *Bulletin*.' *Alberta Historical Review* 5:3 (Summer 1957), 7–12.
Waite, Peter B. *The Life and Times of Confederation, 1864–1867: Politics, Newspapers, and the Union of British North America.* Toronto 1962.
– *Canada, 1874–1896: Arduous Destiny.* Canadian Centenary Series, vol. 13. Toronto 1971.
Walkom, Thomas Lawrence. 'The Daily Newspaper Industry in Ontario's Developing Capitalistic Economy: Toronto and Ottawa, 1871–1911.' Ph.D. thesis, University of Toronto, 1983.
Wallace, Elizabeth. *Goldwin Smith: Victorian Liberal.* Toronto 1957.
Wallace, W. Stewart. 'The First Journalists in Upper Canada.' *CHR* 26:4 (Dec. 1945), 372–81. [On publishing efforts of Gideon and Silvester Tiffany.]
Watt, Frank W. 'The Growth of Proletarian Literature in Canada, 1872–1920.' *DalRev* 40:2 (Summer 1960), 157–73. Reprint. In McMullen.
– 'Literature of Protest.' In Klinck 1965, 457–7; 1976, 1:473–89.
Whiteman, Bruce. *Lasting Impressions: A Short History of English Publishing in Quebec.* Montreal 1994.
Wild, Roland. *Amor De Cosmos.* Toronto 1958. [Founder-editor of the *British Colonist* (Victoria). See also Woodcock (below).]
Willison, Sir John. *Reminiscences Political and Personal.* Toronto 1919. [See also biographies of Willison – Canadian journalist, editor, and *Times* of London correspondent – by Clippingdale and Colquhoun (above).]
Wiseman, John A. 'Silent Companions: The Dissemination of Books and

Periodicals in Nineteenth-Century Ontario.' *Publishing History* 12 (1982), 17–50.

Woodcock, George. *Amor De Cosmos, Journalist and Reformer.* Toronto 1975. [See also Wild (above).]

Zerker, Sally F. 'A History of the Toronto Typographical Union, 1832–1925.' Ph.D. thesis, University of Toronto, 1982.

– *The Rise and Fall of the Toronto Typographical Union, 1832–1972: A Case Study of Foreign Domination.* Toronto 1982.

Bibliographies, Dictionaries, Directories, Indexes, and Finding Aids

Audet, Francis Joseph. *Historique des journaux d'Ottawa.* Ottawa 1896. [An early attempt at a concise listing of facts.]

Bartlett, Mark, Fiona Black, and Bertrum MacDonald. *The History of the Book in Canada: A Bibliography.* Halifax 1993. [Useful compilation, but many transcriptions are inaccurate.]

Beaulieu, André, and Jean Hamelin. *Les journaux du Québec de 1764 à 1964.* Les cahiers de l'Institut d'Histoire no 6. Quebec and Paris 1965. [2,293 titles alphabetically arranged by town; holdings located in fifty-two Canadian institutions; some historical notes and indexes.]

Beaulieu, André, Jean Hamelin, et al. *La presse québécoise des origines à nos jours, 1764–1975.* 10 vols. Quebec 1973–90. [Massive expansion of their 1965 work; vols 1–4 cover 1764–1910; supremely important compendium of bibliographic, biographical, and related publication data on Québécois serial imprints with useful indexes.]

Bentley, David M.R., with Mary Lynn Wickens, eds. *A Checklist of Materials in 'The Week': Toronto, 1883–1896.* Ottawa 1978.

Blackburn, R.H., et al. *A Joint Catalogue of the Periodicals and Serials in the Libraries of the City of Toronto.* 5th ed. Toronto 1953. [Long out of date, but still useful for locations.]

Bogusis, Ruth, comp. *Checklist of Canadian Ethnic Serials/Liste des publications en série ethniques du Canada.* Ottawa 1981. [Arranged by fifty-five ethnic group headings, but excludes Native and Inuit; generous holdings information; title index.]

Bond, Mary E. *Canadian Directories, 1790–1987: A Bibliography and Place-Name Index/Annuaires canadiens, 1790–1987: une bibliographie et un index des noms de lieux.* 3 vols. Ottawa 1989. [In many ways supplements and updates Ryder (below) but gives holdings only for National Library and National Archives; supplies much basic information.]

Boylan, Heather, comp. *Checklist and Historical Directory of Prince Edward Island Newspapers, 1787–1986.* Charlottetown 1987. [Alphabetical by title; excellent indexes.]

Brown, Mary Markham. *An Index to the 'Literary Garland' (Montreal, 1838–1851)*. Toronto 1962. See especially 'Introduction,' pp. iii–ix. [Update by MacDonald (below).]

Butcher, W.W. *Butcher's Canadian Newspaper Directory*. London, Ont. 1886.

Canadian Encyclopedia. James H. Marsh, ed. Revised 2nd ed. 4 vols. Edmonton 1988.

Canadian Institute for Historical Microreproductions/Institut canadien de microreproductions historiques. *Catalogue of Periodicals in CIHM's Microfiche Collection (as of June 1994)/Catalogue des périodiques dans la collection de microfiches de l'ICHM (à partir de juin 1994)*. Ottawa 1994.

Canadian Library Association/Association canadienne des bibliothèques. *Newspaper Microfilming Project Catalogue/Catalogue microfilms de journaux*. Nos. 1–6. Ottawa 1948–57.

– *Canadian Newspapers on Microfilm: Catalogue/Catalogue microfilms de journaux*. No. 7 and looseleaf supplements. Ottawa 1959–.

Catalogue de la Bibliothèque Nationale du Québec: revues québécoises. 3 vols. Montreal 1981. [Alphabetical by title; covers more than just French-language publications; third volume is four separate indexes.]

Craig, Helen, comp. *New Brunswick Newspaper Directory, 1783–1988/ Répertoire des journaux du Nouveau-Brunswick, 1783–1988*. Fredericton 1989. [670 titles arranged alphabetically by town; holdings located in forty institutions, including the National Library and National Archives of Canada; excellent historical notes and indexes (chronological, publisher, title); continues and extends Harper (below).]

Cukier, Golda. *Canadian Jewish Periodicals: A Revised Listing*. Montreal 1978.

Danky, James P., ed., and Maureen H. Hady, comp. *Native American Periodicals and Newspapers, 1828–1982: Bibliography, Publishing Record, and Holdings*. Westport, Conn. 1983. [Includes some Canadian titles.]

Dictionary of Canadian Biography. George W. Brown, et al., eds. Toronto 1966–93. [Vols 1–11 cover AD 1000–1900; vol. 12 is the index through 1900; vol. 13 covers 1901–10. There is a French edition.]

Dionne, Narcisse-Eutrope. *Inventaire chronologique des livres, brochures, journaux, et revues publiés en langue français dans la province de Québec, depuis l'établissement de l'imprimerie au Canada, jusqu'a 1764–1905*. 4 vols in 2. Quebec 1906. Reprint. New York 1969. [In vol. 1, journals and reviews in French, 1764–1900, 742 titles; vol. 3, journals and reviews in English, 1764–1900, 644 titles. Also published as

supplementary volumes to *TRSC*, series 2, vols. 10 and 12; series 3, vol. 2 (1905–9).]
Directory of Canadian Newspapers for 1900: Being a Catalogue of all Newspapers and Periodicals Published in Canada and Newfoundland. Toronto 1900.
Duke, Dorothy Mary. 'Agricultural Periodicals Published in Canada, 1836–1960.' MLS thesis, McGill University, 1961. [Excellent subject-classified lists.]
Elliott, Robbins L. 'The Canadian Labour Press from 1867: A Chronological, Annotated Directory.' *Canadian Journal of Economics and Political Science* 14:2 (May 1948), 220–45. [Ten of the 239 titles listed published before 1900; some locations indicated.]
Ellison, Suzanne. *Historical Directory of Newfoundland and Labrador Newspapers, 1807–1987.* St John's 1988. [240 titles arranged alphabetically by town; holdings located in fifteen institutions, including the National Library of Canada and the British Library; chronological list by decade; informative historical notes and three indexes (subject and audience, papers published outside St John's, editors and publishers).]
Firth, Edith. *Early Toronto Newspapers, 1793–1867: A Catalogue of Newspapers Published in the Town of York and the City of Toronto from the Beginning to Confederation.* Toronto 1961. [Very brief historical notes; most titles available in the Toronto Public Library's collections.]
Fleming, Patricia Lockhart. *Upper Canadian Imprints, 1801–1841: A Bibliography.* Toronto 1988. [Continues Tremaine (below) for Upper Canada; appendix A: Newspapers (compiled by Elizabeth Hulse) lists and describes 145 early Ontario newspapers; appendix B: Journals (compiled by Fleming) lists and describes extensively fifteen periodicals, and gives locations of copies examined. Six excellent indexes cover all imprints; fully developed descriptive bibliography with meticulous detail.]
– *Atlantic Canadian Imprints, 1801–1820.* Toronto 1991. [Continues Tremaine (below) for Maritimes; includes some serials, but omits newspapers.]
Flitton, Marilyn G. *An Index to the 'Canadian Monthly and National Review' and to 'Rose-Belford's Canadian Monthly and National Review,' 1872–1882.* Toronto 1976. [See especially 'Introduction.']
Gilchrist, J. Brian, comp. *Inventory of Ontario Newspapers, 1793–1986.* Toronto 1987. [Updates and doubles number of Ontario titles in *Union List of Canadian Newspapers* (below); Gilchrist includes holdings of Archives of Ontario and is thus a better source for old titles. Over two hundred pages of entries alphabetically arranged by town; holdings

located in scores of institutions; excellent historical notes and indexes. Limited definition of 'newspaper' and excludes religious titles and languages other than English and French.]

Goggio, Emilio, Beatrice Corrigan, and Jack H. Parker, comps. *A Bibliography of Canadian Cultural Periodicals, English and French, from Colonial Times to 1950*. Toronto 1955. [Brief list of titles examined by compilers.]

Guide to Periodicals and Microforms in the Public Libraries of Metropolitan Toronto. 2 vols. 21st ed. Toronto 1994.

Hare, John, and Jean-Pierre Wallot. *Les imprimés dans la Bas-Canada, bibliographie analytique*. Vol. 1: 1801–10. Montreal 1967. [Continues Tremaine (below) for Lower Canada; regrettably, no further volumes have been published.]

Harper, J. Russell. *Historical Directory of New Brunswick Newspapers and Periodicals*. Fredericton 1961. [Describes and locates 461 titles; largely superseded by Craig (above), but still complementary.]

Heggie, Grace F., and Gordon R. Adshead, eds. *An Index to 'Saturday Night': The First Fifty Years, 1887–1937*. Toronto 1987.

Hulse, Elizabeth, ed. *A Dictionary of Toronto Printers, Publishers, Booksellers, and the Allied Trades, 1798–1900*. Toronto 1982. [Definitive.]

Ingles, Ernest, ed. and comp. *Bibliography of Canadian Bibliographies/ Bibliographies des bibliographies canadiennes*. 3rd ed. Toronto 1994.

Jones, Linda M., comp. *Preliminary Checklist of Pre-1901 Canadian Serials*. 2 vols. Ottawa 1986. Part A: Periodicals; B: Almanacs; C: Annual Reports, Transactions, Proceedings, etc. [Lists without examination more than two thousand periodicals and four hundred almanacs with locations. Commissioned by the Canadian Institute for Historical Microreproductions (CIHM) as part of its preservation filming program.]

Kallmann, Helmut. 'A Century of Musical Periodicals in Canada.' *Canadian Music Journal* 1:1 (Autumn 1956), 37–43; ' ... Concluded' 1:2 (Winter 1957), 21–36.

Kallmann, Helmut, and Richard Green. 'Periodicals.' In *Encyclopedia of Music in Canada*, ed. Helmut Kallmann et al. 2nd ed. Toronto 1992. [Exhaustive list includes thirty-four nineteenth-century titles.]

Komorous, Hana. *Union Catalogue of British Columbia Newspapers*. 3 vols. Vancouver 1987–9.

Landry, Charlotte. 'Franco-Albertan newspapers, 1898–1982: A Guide.' MLS paper, University of Alberta, 1984.

Lewis, Larry C. *Union List of Music Periodicals in Canadian Libraries/Inventaire des publications en série sur la musique dans les biblio-

thèques canadiennes. 2nd ed. Ottawa 1981. [1,783 international entries alphabetically by title, of which a few are nineteenth-century Canadian; gives locations.]

Loveridge, D.M. *A Historical Directory of Manitoba Newspapers, 1859– 1978*. Winnipeg 1981. [423 rural titles; 333 metropolitan Winnipeg titles; 140 'ethnic' titles; locates holdings in eighteen institutions, including the National Library and Archives of Canada, and the British Library; good historical introduction, notes, and indexes; separate newsmagazines list (includes sports, society, literary, drama, etc.) has six pre-1900 titles.]

Lunn, A.J.E. 'Bibliography of the History of the Canadian Press.' *CHR* 22:4 (Dec. 1941), 416–33. [Dated, but still useful for early titles.]

– 'Canadian Newspapers before 1821: A Preliminary List.' *CHR* 25:4 (Dec. 1944), 417–20.

MacDonald, Christine. *Historical Directory of Saskatchewan Newspapers, 1878–1983*. Saskatchewan Archives Reference Series no. 4. Regina and Saskatoon 1984. [Inferior to other provincial union catalogues.]

MacDonald, Mary Lu. 'An Index to the *Literary Garland* Updated.' *Papers BSC/Cahiers SBC* 19 (1980), 79–83.

MacGillvray, George B. *A History of Fort William and Port Arthur Newspapers from 1875*. Toronto 1968. [Title-by-title anecdotal histories of twenty newspapers.]

Manitoba Newspaper Checklist with Library Holdings, 1859–1986. Winnipeg 1986. [Lists approximately nine hundred titles, indexed by subject/theme, language, decade(s) of publication, and title.]

Matthews, Geoffrey J., ed. *Historical Atlas of Canada*. 3 vols. Toronto 1987–93. [Vol. 2 covers nineteenth century.]

[McKim]. *The Canadian Newspaper Directory* [later *McKim's Directory of Canadian Publications*], *Containing: A History of the Rise and Progress of Journalism in Each Province, ... ; Statistics and Tables Showing the Increase in Canadian Newspapers since Confederation; Tables of the Imports and Exports of Materials in the Printing and Publishing Trades; ... ; A Gazetteer of all Canadian and Newfoundland Newspapers, in which is Given the Name of Each Paper, its Editor and Publishers, Date of Establishment; Politics or Class; Frequency of Issue; Subscription Price, Number and Size of Pages, and its Estimated Circulation; ... .* 1st to 31st editions. Montreal 1892–1942. [E.B. Biggar's 'Sketch of Canadian Journalism,' 1st ed., pp. 17–56, is noteworthy.]

McLaren, Duncan. *Ontario Ethno-Cultural Newspapers, 1835–1972: An Annotated Checklist*. Toronto 1973. [Lists and locates five hundred titles.]

Meikle, William. *The Canadian Newspaper Directory, or Advertiser's Guide Containing a Complete List of all the Newspapers in Canada, – the Circulation of Each, – and all Information in Reference Thereto.* Toronto 1858. [Classifies 207 newspapers alphabetically, as well as by county, frequency, and political/religious orientation.]

Mitchell, Mary E. *Periodicals in Canadian Law Libraries: A Union List.* Revised ed. Kingston, Ont. 1994. [English and French holdings of twenty-five law libraries; some nineteenth-century titles.]

Murphy, Lynn, comp., with Brenda Hicks, and Anjali Vohra. *Nova Scotia Newspapers: A Directory and Union List, 1752–1988.* 2 vols. Halifax 1990. [Vol. 1: lists nearly 1,100 titles; vol. 2: excellent historical notes and indexes. Continues and extends Tratt (below).]

Pratt, Maj. A.M. *The Story of Manitoba's Weekly Newspapers [1859–1964].* Winnipeg 1967. [Title-by-title anecdotal histories with extracts.]

Retfalvi, Andrea, comp. *'Canadian Illustrated News,' Montreal, 1869–1883: An Index to Illustrations.* 28 vols. Toronto 1977.

Retfalvi, Andrea, and Ann Hilty, comps. *'Canadian Illustrated News,' Montreal, 1869–1883: An Index.* Toronto 1989.

Roland, Charles G., and Paul Potter. *An Annotated Bibliography of Canadian Medical Periodicals, 1826–1975.* Toronto 1979. [Extends and supersedes H.E. MacDermot's *Bibliography of Canadian Medical Periodicals* (Montreal 1934).]

Rowell, George P. and Co. *American Newspaper Directory Containing a Description of all Published in the U.S. and Territories, Dominion of Canada and Newfoundland.* ... New York 1869–1908. [Annual/Quarterly.]

Ryder, Dorothy E. *Checklist of Canadian Directories, 1790–1950/ Répertoire des annuaires canadiens, 1790–1950.* Ottawa 1979. [Locations given in over ninety libraries across Canada for titles examined; supplemented and updated by Bond (above).]

Smith, Ruell. *Canadian Newspapers in the University of British Columbia Library.* University of British Columbia Library, Reference Publication no. 52. Vancouver 1974.

Story, Norah, ed. *The Oxford Companion to Canadian History and Literature.* Toronto 1967. [Supplemented by Toye (below).]

Strathearn, Gloria. *Alberta Newspapers, 1880–1982: An Historical Directory.* Edmonton 1988. [1,090 titles alphabetically arranged by town; excellent historical notes and indexes, including an enormous biographical index.]

Têtu, Horace. *Historique des journaux de Québec.* Quebec 1875. New ed. 1889. [1875 ed. 51 pages; 1889 ed. 108 pages; variable but often extensive information about titles; earliest title 1764.]

– *Journaux de Lévis.* Quebec 1880. 3rd ed. 1898. [1864 first entry; primarily newspapers.]
– *Journaux et revues de Québec par ordre chronologique.* Quebec 1881. 3rd ed. 1883. [3rd ed. added seven pages; information includes title, date begun and ended; earliest title 1764.]
– *Journaux et revues de Montréal par ordre chronologique.* Quebec 1881. [Sixteen pages of often not much more than name and date.]
Tod, Dorothea D., and Audrey Cordingley. 'A Bibliography of Canadian Literary Periodicals, 1789–1900.' *TRSC*, series 3, 24, sec. 2 (May 1932), 87–96.
Toye, William, ed. *Supplement to the Oxford Companion to Canadian History and Literature.* Toronto 1973. [Supplements Story (above).]
– *The Oxford Companion to Canadian Literature.* Toronto 1983.
Tratt, Gertrude E.N. *A Survey and Listing of Nova Scotia Newspapers, 1752–1957, with Particular Reference to the Period before 1867.* Dalhousie University Libraries Occasional Paper no. 21. Halifax 1979. [Eighty-eight pages of entries plus sixty-six pages of holdings located in seventy institutions; largely superseded by Murphy (above), but still complementary.]
Tremaine, Marie. *A Bibliography of Canadian Imprints, 1751–1800.* Toronto 1952. [Appendix,'Newspapers and Magazines,' lists and describes twenty-three newspapers and two magazines; pioneering work for Canada's 'incunabular' period. Continued by Fleming (above).]
Union List of Canadian Newspapers Held by Canadian Libraries/ Liste collective des journaux canadiens disponibles dans les bibliothèques canadiennes. Ottawa 1977. Supplementary updates issued on microfiche in 1988 and 1991. [Monumental effort to catalogue and locate nearly five thousand different titles across Canada, except British Columbia, without benefit of examination; alphabetical arrangement by province with magnificent index and adequate cross-referencing; good descriptions.]
Union List of Nova Scotia Newspapers: Who Has What, for When, and Where. Halifax 1987. [Issued in difficult format; superseded by Murphy (above).]
Union List of Scientific Serials in Canadian Libraries/Catalogue collectif des publications scientifiques en série dans les bibliothèques canadiennes. 16th ed. 5 vols. Ottawa 1992. [Also available on CAN-OLE database and CD-ROM.]
Union List of Serials in Canada Department of Agriculture Libraries/ Répertoire collectif des publications en série des bibliothèques du ministère de l'agriculture du Canada. Ottawa 1977.

Union List of Serials in Fine Arts in Canadian Libraries/Inventaire des publications en série dans le domaine des beaux-arts dans les bibliothèques canadiennes. Ottawa 1978. [Covers holdings of nearly two hundred Canadian libraries in the National Library's *Union Catalogue of Serials;* valuable checklists of more than three hundred titles; information clearly and simply presented.]

Union List of Serials in Libraries of the United States and Canada. 3rd ed. 5 vols. New York 1965.

Vincent, Thomas Brewer, comp. *An Historical Directory of Nova Scotia Newspapers and Journals before Confederation.* Occasional Papers of the Department of English, Royal Military College, no. 1. Kingston 1977. [Now superseded by Boylan, Craig, and Murphy (all three above).]

– comp. *The 'Amaranth': 1841–1843, Contents Report and Index.* Occasional Papers of the Department of English, Royal Military College, no. 7. Kingston 1984.

– comp. *The 'Canadian Magazine and Literary Repository': July 1823–June 1825.* Occasional Papers of the Department of English, Royal Military College, no. 8. Kingston 1984.

– comp. *Index to Pre-1900 English-Language Canadian Cultural and Literary Periodicals.* Nepean, Ont. 1993. [This CD-ROM indexes articles, stories, poems (titles and first lines), illustrations, and editorials, as well as their authors (where identifiable) in 190 early Canadian cultural, intellectual, and literary periodicals; indispensable research tool for pre-1900 Canadian studies.]

– comp. *A Directory of Known Pseudonyms, Initial Sets, and Maiden Names Found in Selected English-Canadian Magazines, Newspapers, and Books of the Nineteenth-Century.* Kingston 1994. [Identifies over eight hundred pseudonyms; indexed by surname and pen-name; indispensable.]

Vincent, Thomas Brewer, and Ann LaBrash, comps. *The 'Acadian Magazine': 1826–1828, Contents Report and Index.* Occasional Papers of the Department of English, Royal Military College, no. 5. Kingston 1982.

– and Ann LaBrash, comps. *The 'Provincial': 1852–1853, Contents Report and Index.* Occasional Papers of the Department of English, Royal Military College, no. 6. Kingston 1982.

– and Ann LaBrash, comps. *The 'Nova-Scotia Magazine': 1789–1792, Contents Report and Index.* Occasional Papers of the Department of English, Royal Military College, no. 4. Kingston 1982.

Vlach, Milada, and Yolande Buono. *Catalogue collectif des impressions québécoises, 1764–1820.* Montreal 1984. [Informative listing with Quebec locations and eight different indexes.]

Wallace, W. Stewart. 'The Periodical Literature of Upper Canada.' *CHR* 12:1 (March 1931), 4–22; 12:2 (June 1931), 181–3. [Essay plus chronological checklist 1793–1840 of 116 titles; second part is emendations to fourteen titles.]

Wallace, W. Stewart, ed. *The Macmillan Dictionary of Canadian Biography.* 3rd ed. Toronto 1963. [Still indispensable despite *DCB*.]

Wearmouth, Amanda. *Checklist of Yukon Newspapers, 1898–1985.* Whitehorse, Yukon 1987.

Weinrich, Peter. *Social Protest from the Left in Canada, 1870–1970: A Bibliography.* Toronto 1982. [Fifty periodical titles from 1871 to 1900.]

Wilson, Irving, and Frances Wilson, eds. *A History of Weekly Newspapers of British Columbia, 1871–1971.* Vancouver 1972. [Anecdotal, title-by-title listings.]

[Wood]. *T.F. Wood and Company's Canadian Newspaper Directory Containing Accurate Lists of all the Newspapers and Periodicals Published in the Dominion of Canada and Province of Newfoundland.* Montreal 1876.

Young, George, comp., and John S. Lutz, ed. *The Researcher's Guide to British Columbia Nineteenth Century Directories: A Bibliography and Index.* Victoria 1988. [Seventy-five entries arranged chronologically 1860–1900; place and topic index.]

3

India

BRAHMA CHAUDHURI

Introduction

In 1824, William Stevenson, a contributor to *Blackwood's Magazine*, wrote, 'Periodical publications are a surer index of the state of progress of the mind, than works of a higher character.' The Victorian period may be referred to as the golden age of periodical publications not only in Britain but also in its colonies, especially in India. Such publications began because Englishmen at home recognized that 'colonization, to be enduring and beneficent, must be based on intellectual power, and that the English race [could] only prosper as colonists, or as rulers of foreign peoples, through means of their systematic culture and superior moral discipline' ('Education in the Colonies,' 124).

The newspaper and periodical press was unknown in India until the end of the eighteenth century, but that does not mean that the Indians were not curious about news and information from different parts of the country. The bazaar was, and still is, the centre point where the local people gather to listen to and exchange information with the tradesmen, caravans, pilgrims, and wandering vagrants who came from neighbouring towns and from as far as Persia and Afghanistan. The speed with which important news travelled in India was a mystery in itself. It was surprising that the news about a disaster in Manipur in Eastern India in 1891 was talked about in the bazaars of Allahabad and other places in the North long before it reached the general public through the newspapers (Karkaria, 547).

More trustworthy channels of information were, however, the newsletters commonly known as *akhbars*. They were written by *akhbar-navis* or news-writers whose business it was to collect all the news in a particular town, write it down in their letters, and send them to a net-

For a map that includes India, see page 300.

work of correspondents across the country. According to Sir William Sleeman, the King of Oudh paid 3,194 rupees to 660 such *akhbar-navis* in 1856 (Sleeman, 249; see also Karkaria, 548). These *akhbars*, read widely both by the common people and by the British and native rulers, contained news about weather, crops, harvests, religious festivals, social scandals, and political happenings. During the uprising of 1857, Lord Canning, the Governor-General, had to introduce a Gagging Act to prevent the native soldiers from communicating and exchanging information with one another through these *akhbars* (Norton, 328).[1]

Early History of the Press in India

The first newspaper on the Western model, the *Bengal Gazette*, was founded in India in 1780 by an Englishman, James Augustus Hicky. From his addresses to his readers and editorial notices, one learns that Hicky was a printer by profession, and that he had invested some money in merchant shipping. He suffered heavy financial losses in cargo damages; bankrupt and ruined, Hicky surrendered everything he had, his vessel, the remaining cargo, and all his household effects, to his creditors, 'the black Bengal merchants.' In October 1776, he 'delivered up his person at the jail of Calcutta to free his bail, and for the first time in all his life entered the wall of a prison.' But he was not a man to remain idle; inside the jail, he went back to his old profession, set up a printing press, and started paying off his debt (See Busteed, 183–4). William Hickey, a contemporary attorney, writes in his *Memoir*, 'By indefatigable attention and unremitting labour since his release from jail, [Hicky] succeeded in cutting a rough set of types ... Having scraped together by this means a few hundred rupees, he sent order to England for a regular and proper set of materials for printing. While patiently waiting the arrival of these articles, it occurred to Hicky that he might set on foot a public newspaper. ... It met with extraordinary encouragement and he issued the *Bengal Gazette*' (175–6).

But Hicky was more interested in high society gossip and scandals, of which there were plenty. He went too far, however, and made enemies; among those who were directly outraged by his public revelation of social scandals was Warren Hastings, the Governor-General of India. Hastings took immediate steps to prohibit Hicky's paper 'on account of its lately having been found to contain several improper paragraphs tending to vilify private characters and to disturb the peace of the settlement' (Busteed, 190–1). Hicky was confined in the jail and his *Gazette* ceased publication when he was deported two years later.

A future historian, Sir John Kaye, the author of the *History of the Sepoy War*, denounced Hicky's *Gazette* as 'thoroughly worthless' because it was, as he put it in the *Calcutta Review* for 1844, 'full of infamous scandal – in some places so disguised as to be almost unintelligible to the reader of the present day, but in others set forth broadly and unmistakably; and with a relish not to be concealed.' Kaye felt so disgusted with its low moral tone that he would not even quote extracts from it to illustrate his point. 'The most significant passages are too coarse for quotation,' he concluded (1:314–15).[2]

Infamous though Hicky was, there is no denying that his was the forerunner among the six earliest Indian newspapers and periodicals H.E. Busteed mentions in his book, *Echoes from Old Calcutta* (1882): (1) the *Bengal Gazette* (January 1780), (2) the *India Gazette* (November 1780), (3) the *Calcutta Gazette* (February 1784), (4) the *Bengal Journal* (February 1785), (5) the *Oriental Magazine or Calcutta Amusement* (April 1785), and the *Calcutta Chronicle* (January 1786).[3] In 1818, another Englishman, James Buckingham, established what may be called the 'most celebrated periodical of its day,' the *Calcutta Journal or Political, Commercial and Literary Gazette* ('British Indian Literature,' 162). A native periodical in English, the *Brahmanical Magazine*, followed in 1821. It was owned and edited by Raja Ram Mohan Roy, a religious reformer who set out to educate Indian opinion on secular developments in the West and to eradicate age-old Indian socio-religious practices like the caste-system, child marriage, and *suttee*.

From the beginning, the British administrators were apprehensive of the press because they feared that it would eventually lead to political consciousness among the native Indians. Fearless criticism of the colonial administration by journalists like Hicky, Ram Mohan Roy, and others prompted the British Parliament to introduce in 1799 a series of regulations which licensed and attempted to control the press. Native leaders like Dwarka Nath Tagore, Gauri Charan Banerji, and others voiced their protests and sent joint memorandums first to the Supreme Court and then to the Privy Council, but they were unsuccessful in fighting these controls. The government 'tried in every way to discourage them, and even to put them down with a high hand' (Karkaria, 552). Two of the five censorship regulations Hastings issued were:

1.   No paper to be published, at all, until it shall have been previously inspected by the Secretary to the Government or by a person authorised by him for that purpose.

2.   The penalty for offending against any of the above regulations to be immediate embarkation for Europe. (*Parliamentary Papers, East India – Press* 4 May 1858, 4)

The colonial government's attitude toward the press was further reflected in its dispatches to the British Parliament in London: 'The increase of private printing presses in India, unlicensed however [sic] controlled, is an evil of the first magnitude in its consequences ... Useless to literature and to the public, and dubiously profitable to the speculators, they serve only to maintain in needy indolence a few European adventurers who are found unfit to engage in any creditable method of subsistence' (*Parliamentary Papers, East India – Press* 4 May 1858, 5).

Hicky and Buckingham, who openly defied the government censorship, were arrested and deported. Others were effectively subdued and restrained. 'In consequence of the hostility of the authorities, the Press did not make much progress during the first twenty years of the nineteenth century' (Karkaria, 552). The rules which restrained the press from criticizing the East India Company or the British Government continued until 1835, when Governor-General Charles Metcalfe, on Thomas Macaulay's advice, revoked the press laws and liberated the Indian press.

The Indian Press from 1830 to 1850

From 1830 onward, the newspaper and periodical press in India started showing signs of progress again. In his evidence to the Parliamentary Select Committee, Mr James Sutherland, the editor of the *Bengal Hurkaru*, noted that three thousand copies were the 'circulation of the English press in Bengal in 1832' (*Parliamentary Papers. Minutes of Evidence Before Select Committee* [1832], 121). During the formative years of Indian periodicals, from 1830 to 1850, there were thirty-eight in circulation; twenty-five were published from Calcutta, seven from Madras, two from Bombay, and four from other regions. Of these thirty-eight periodicals, there were twelve weeklies, eighteen monthlies, seven quarterlies, and one annual.

It must be mentioned, however, that the missionaries were the most influential force in periodical publication in India, first by establishing the printing presses, and later by introducing newspapers and periodicals, both in English and in vernacular languages. The East India Company disliked the idea of missionaries entering or settling in India, but three of them, William Carey, Joshua Marshman, and William Ward, managed to make their way to Serampur, a Danish settlement near Calcutta, where they founded a Baptist missionary printing press in 1799. These missionaries made it their 'bounden duty' to promote 'the religious and moral improvement' of the people of India through sectarian education and religion. Their object, as the editor of the *Calcutta Christian Ob-*

server announced in its inaugural issue of June 1832, 'was the promoting of a missionary spirit amongst the friends of religion generally in different parts of the country.'

The missionary publications gave rise to controversies and a war of pamphlets. It was pointed out that the 'Christian missionaries were a dangerous and inflammatory class of men who, if they succeeded without exciting a general rebellion, would only contaminate the purity of the Hindoos, and utterly deprave an innocent people' ('Christianity in India,' 616). This anti-missionary sentiment, both in Britain and India, inspired a vigorous secular-religious movement by the followers of Ram Mohan Roy in Bengal, Balashastri Jambhekar and Behramji Malabari in Western India, and humanist reformers in South India (Natarajan, 135).

When the Baptist missionaries of Serampur founded the *Calcutta Christian Observer* in 1832, their aim was to publish sermons, religious essays, and reports concerning the progress and future prospects of their missionary operations. But one-third of this periodical was devoted entirely to English translations of Indian literary works like *Pratapaditya Charit, Rajabali, Sungashan Battrish*, and *Hitopadesh.* 'The pages of this periodical contained,' as the *Calcutta Review* (1844) observed, 'an immense fund of interesting and important information in regard to the languages, literature and cultures of India' (vol. 1, p. 21).

The Rise of Nationalism from 1850 Onwards

During the second half of the nineteenth century, there was a rapid growth of periodicals devoted partly or wholly to literature. They ranged from sporadic monthlies like *Indian Spectator* (1874–5) to *Calcutta Review* (1844–), a monthly magazine which, like the British *Quarterly Review*, published reviews and articles on Indian, English, and European literature. The weekly and monthly periodicals offered Englishmen in India an outlet where they could practise their talent in writing poems, stories, plays, biographies, autobiographies, memoirs, travel accounts, essays, sketches, and so on. This new kind of writing, called Anglo-Indian literature, became so 'extensive' that, in 1869, the *Calcutta Review* introduced a special feature entitled the 'Quarter' to 'make [their] review of contemporaneous literature much more complete than it has been hitherto' (supplement to vol. 49, p. i).

The Mutiny of 1856–7 had far-reaching consequences for Indian journalism. It created a distinction between English-language and Indian-language journals and 'injected a racial colour to British thinking' (Natarajan, 49). There is no evidence that the Indian-owned English journals were interested either in overthrowing the colonial government or in seeing the British residents leave the country. Initially, the British editors of Indian periodicals reacted most vehemently against the mutineers; but later, moderation and good sense prevailed, the first outburst of anger subsided, and a call for a thorough inquiry into the military excesses in India followed.

As the century progressed, periodicals grew in numbers and circulation in Bengal, Bombay, and Madras. The Indians were beginning to recognize that the place to bring effective political pressure to bear was in London and other cities in Great Britain. Periodical essays in support of Indian causes in the 1850s by writers such as John Dickson, John Bright, and Joseph Hume in England and Dadabhai Naoroji and W.C. Banerjee in India led to the formation of the Friends of India and the India Reform Society in London. The emergence of the Irish Home Rule party in 1874, in turn, gave a new impetus to the demand for Indian self-government. The most prominent among the Irish nationalists to take up the Indian question was Frank O'Donnell, who became the London correspondent of Naoroji's magazine, the *Bombay Gazette*. In association with Kristodas Pal, editor of the *Hindu Patriot*, O'Donnell started sending letters to Indian newspapers and magazines to form an Indian nationalist organization. Another magazine, the *Voice of India*, financed and published by Naoroji in India, brought out translations of articles from the Indian vernacular press in 1883. Others, such as Ganendra Mohan Tagore, Keshub Chander Sen, Surendranath Banerjee, Swami Dayanand, and Madame Blavatsky, established their own periodicals, either individually or through organizations of which they were founders, with one purpose in mind – 'to frighten and coerce the English people' (Cumpston, 290).

However, this vast gold mine of English newspapers and periodicals published in India from 1780 to the present still remains uncharted. Until now it has been commonly believed that the *Calcutta Review* was the only Indian periodical which could claim a status equal to a quarterly in England. But there were a few other journals which, though little known until now, received high acclaim from both Indian and British readers. Periodicals such as *Benaras Magazine, Bengal Magazine, Anglo-Indian Magazine, Bombay Quarterly Review, Calcutta Fortnightly Review, Calcutta Magazine,* and the *Indian Spectator* did not lag behind the *Calcutta Review* in any respect; they published articles and reviews on Indian, English, and European literature, and contributed equally, or even more, to a resurgence in cultural and intellectual growth in India by encouraging publication of indigenous articles on literature, history, politics, religion, philosophy, arts, and social life.

It was not hard to determine, however, why these periodicals, which could easily compete in format, language, and coverage with their counterparts in Europe, soon disappeared into oblivion. In writing about his experience in managing the publication of an English periodical in India, the editor of the *Benaras Magazine* writes: 'Had the editor ever foreseen the amount of labour and anxiety which the editorship of a periodical would bring upon him, in addition to sufficiently onerous official duties; ... the serious defections by death and other casualties which he would have from time to time to deplore; and the difficult, and often delicate, offices inseparable from the preparation of a lengthened series of papers for the press; he would have hesitated to assume what the event has proved to be often a very embarrassing position.' One of the most difficult tasks in producing a periodical in India, the editor pointed out, was to maintain its quality so that it could compete with those published in England, and 'yet bear distinct indications of its Indian origin' (preface to vol. 8 [1852]). The reading public was limited and so was the circulation. Unless supported by a church or an institution, a periodical would soon plunge into financial difficulties. The result was the short life-span of periodicals, most of which ceased after only one number; some continued for a year or two; the lucky ones, like the *Calcutta Review* and *Asiatic Society Journals*, survived for years.

Further, the educated class in India was not, as one editor said, 'literary by profession.' An 'intellectual' was either an administrator or a churchman, whereas in Europe there was a whole body of intellectuals to whom literature was a livelihood. Periodical literature could not, therefore, be certain of enough writers or readers to flourish in India as easily as it did in England or Europe.

Pointing out the difficulties faced by an Indian journalist, the editor of another well-known contemporary periodical, the *Calcutta Fortnightly Review*, said in its issue of 19 November 1881:

An Indian periodical has to contend in the first place with the English market which places trashy journals of all sorts before those whose delight is only in Essays and Reviews and in the second place the Indian Dailies, with a view to their own interests, handicap him by publishing gratis for the Sunday reading of their subscribers, interesting tales and extracts from English journals, which of course occupy their time and attention, thereby indisposing them to support the original literature of the land they live in. So that without wishing to detract from the merits of home writers we yet say that in contending with this handicapping, the publishers of original matter in India have vast odds to fight against, and Indian authors will never be able to have their abilities acknowledged so long as the present state of affairs exists.

Of the 123 periodicals listed below, 86 have been examined as closely as possible. The examination of thousands of articles was a task in itself, for it involved patience, hard work, and, at times, tediousness and frustration. Furthermore, there are almost no reference works as there are now for research in British periodicals, to guide the researcher in his endeavours. It was rewarding, however, to find that these magazines were very closely associated with socio-religious movements, educational and literary upheavals, and national awakening in India. A systematic study of these selected periodicals requires examining the contents of each to find out the kinds of articles they published on literature, history, the arts, or professions. One has to determine how a particular periodical gave to its editor, its public, and its network of contributors a forum for the expression of views; and how the individual articles in the periodical reflected the meanings and values of contemporary Indian society.

This detailed examination of the periodicals themselves leaves absolutely no question about their value for research and scholarship. A few examples will illustrate this. Volume 4 of the *Bengal Magazine* was one sample for 1875. The first article in this volume, 'Education in India,' is by a regular contributor with the pseudonym 'Hindustani.' He is critical of the present system of education, which completely ignores the 'sacred tradition of the country.' The writer warns that though the system 'does not breed disloyalty – it generates much ill feeling against those by whom it is supervised and carried out' (141). The second article, 'A Scheme for the Better Government of India' by an anonymous writer, points out how little the English know about the real India. 'The native newspapers are generally not much thought of, and very few of them are ever read by those Englishmen who rule the destinies of India. The native understands the Englishman better than he is known by the latter; but neither of them knows the other sufficiently well for the furtherance of their common interests. Misunderstanding has been the cause of India's ruin' (204).

One section of the magazine reproduces an article 'On the Salaries of Native Civilians' in the popular Lucknow newspaper, *Pioneer*, edited by Julian Robinson. The paper supports the natives who agitate for increased pay and a better style of life. A plea is made for the natives to be allowed to rise in 'civilization,' material as well as moral, 'ere any thing like a free, friendly intercourse between the dominant and the subject classes can take place' (154). Another article on the influence of Western education on the advancement of intellectual life of modern India, 'Progress in Bengal,' urges natives to recognize that the prosperity of a nation depends much upon the intellectual advancement of its women. The early training and formation of ideas of children are left entirely in the hands of their mothers. 'But how can these women,' the writer asks, 'give a healthy tone to the mind when they themselves are brought up in ignorance, and when their knowledge of the world is confined within the four walls of the Zenana?' (372).

The literary section of the magazine offers a chapter of a serial novel, *Rambhadra; or the Mofussil Hakim*, and a story, 'A Simple Story of India,' an article on the works of Ram Prasad Sen in a series entitled 'Literature of Bengal,' a poem, 'The Last day of Pompeii,' and two sonnets, 'Margarete' and 'On the Fly Leaf of Elliot's Horae Apocalypticae.' This particular volume of the magazine also contains a chapter from *Bianca or The Young Spanish Maiden*, an unfinished novel by Toru Dutt. A note from the editor says, 'The gentle hand that had traced the story thus far – the hand of Miss Toru Dutt – left off here. Was it illness that made the pen drop from the weary fingers? I do not know. I think not' (265).

Considering the high mortality rates of journals, the *Bengal Magazine* possessed commanding claims to merit. While many of the magazines lasted fewer than four months, the *Bengal Magazine* survived and improved its quality over a nine-year period. Its founding editor, Lal Behari Dey, the author of *Folk Tales of Bengal*, was a highly respected and influential man of letters. The magazine boasted as contributors some of the outstanding literary men of the age, such as Alexander Duff, Keshub Chandra Sen, Rajendralal Mitra, and Rama Nath Saraswati, and gave first publication to the pioneer of what is now known as Indo-Anglian literature, Toru Dutt. Lastly, the *Bengal Magazine*, in its vigorous campaign for the recognition of Indian intellectuals, encouraged and supported the national movement which sought to come to grips with the many literary, social, and political cross-currents of the third quarter of the nineteenth century.

The works of previous writers such as S. Natarajan, Alok Ray, R.P. Kumar, Mrinal Kanti Chanda, and Ramaswami Parthasarathy shed valuable light on how periodicals were involved in socio-religious movements, educational and literary upheavals, and national awakening. Some others have scanned old Indian journals and newspapers to find materials for their books and articles. Unfortunately, however, the majority of the working scholars are prevented from making full and free use of these newspapers and periodicals; in most cases they have to rely on hackneyed or inadequate secondary sources. There are no adequate tools to tell the researcher what the nineteenth-century periodical holdings are in a particular library, or which periodicals were published in the nineteenth century, or which were reviewing books or publishing articles on education, economic issues, or women's questions. It is essential, therefore, that all those who use or expect to use these periodicals should unite to do something about finding all possible locations of nineteenth-century Indian newspapers and periodicals, compiling descriptive listing, and taking immediate measures to preserve them. The sooner it is done the better, because these journals and newspapers are deteriorating so quickly that after a few years there will be nothing left but piles of crumbled dust.

Scarce though these materials are, they are not getting the special preservation attention they need, nor are they being preserved in microform. The National Library in Calcutta has a well-equipped microfilming department, with highly trained technicians; the rare newspapers and periodicals are held in the same building. However, the impression one gains after talking to staff members of the library is that the reproduction can never be done by the library itself. The library, or a private firm, could easily recoup the expenses of such a project, and no doubt thousands of libraries world-wide would readily be interested in purchasing copies.

Listing of Journals

My year's stay in Calcutta to work on the nineteenth-century periodicals at the National Library was an informative experience in itself. In India, especially in Calcutta, one has to be well prepared for all kinds of unforeseen eventualities like political demonstrations and strikes, unscheduled holidays, bureaucratic delays, and breakdown of electricity. Any one of these disruptions might cause a delay of a day or two. Further, things work in a different way in Calcutta and the researcher needs to be able to cope with unusual circumstances. For example, photocopying just two pages might take two to three hours; it might take three months to obtain microfilm of a particular item. There was no air-conditioning; fans existed but scholars are not allowed to switch them on while handling old periodicals. In India's special kind of intolerable sultry weather, with temperature rising to about forty degrees centigrade, at times it was simply impossible to work inside the periodicals building. There was no alternative, however, because the National Library was the only place in the world where one could get the necessary materials.

The listing of journals that follows is primarily based on the *Catalogue of Periodicals, Newspapers and Gazettes* published by the National Library in 1956. Additions to this primary list were made from the microform catalogue of the India Office Library in London. As many of these periodicals as possible have been examined for their contents and editorial comments. It was not possible, however, for one person to shelf-check each and every item thoroughly. Nor was it possible to visit hundreds of university and public libraries scattered across the vast, populous country. For holdings in major libraries, one relies primarily on the *Union Catalogue of Social Science Periodicals* published for each province separately by the Indian Council of Social Science Research. Visits to major libraries in Delhi, Madras, Bangalore, and Bombay to shelf-check some of the nineteenth-century serials included in these union lists proved futile and frustrating. In the end, it became necessary to concentrate fully on what could be found in the National Library itself. Even though the listing provided here cannot be claimed to be comprehensive or exhaustive, scholars should still find it a useful starting place as a research guide.

The majority of the holdings in the National Library are in incomplete runs. Some of the serials, although listed in the library catalogue, could not be traced for verification. Either they were not on the shelves, or they were in such a pitiable condition that their pages crumbled to dust simply at the touch of a hand. They were 'too brittle to handle,' as the library clerks would write on the requisition slips. In others, pages were falling apart or missing. With the help of an old and experienced library staff member, it was possible to check at least the beginning volumes or issues of these serials.

NOTE ON ANNOTATION

Prices for journals, where known, are given in Rupee (Re.) or Rupees (Rs.). The conversion rate of Indian currency in 1867 was Rs.10 = £1; in 1897 it was Rs.15 = £1. Subject matter was determined after shelf-checking the contents of individual issues of periodicals. Sometimes an annotation, often a quotation from the publication, follows the subject. Holdings are given for two locations only: the National Library (NL) in Calcutta and the India Office Library (IOL) in London.

Some of the periodicals listed are available on microfilm from the British Library Newspaper Library, Colindale, in which case the notation MF appears, followed by dates. Copies of microfilm may be obtained from the library.

Asiatic Researches: or, Transactions of the Society Instituted in Bengal for Enquiring into the History and Antiquities, the Arts, Sciences and Literature of Asia. 1–?, 1788–?; then *Journal of the Asiatic Society of Bengal.* Calcutta: Baptist Mission Press. NL: 1832–1904. Index to *Asiatic Researches.* 1788–1835. Index to *Journal of the Asiatic Society of Bengal.* 1832–56.

Bombay Courier. D. 1–69, 1792–1860; then *Bombay Telegraph and Courier;* then *Times of India. Bombay.* IOL: 1793–1859. NL: 1860. MF: 1793–1846.

Bengal Hurkaru and the India Gazette. D. 1798–1866. Calcutta. Founded by Charles MacLean in 1798. IOL: 1844–66. NL: 1828–36, 1838–66.

Indo-European Correspondence: Or, Indian Catholic Chronicle. W. 1–36, 1826–1902. Calcutta: P.S. D'Rozario and Co. Literature, history, religion (Christianity), missionary news, education. NL: 2–36, 1827–1902.

Oriental Observer: or, General Record of News and Literature. W. 1, 1827; then *Oriental Observer and Literary Chronicle.* Calcutta. Ed. George Pritchard and William Rushton. Fiction, poetry, history, shipping reports, travel, extracts. IOL: 2–7, 1828–33, 1837, 1839. NL: 1–2, 1827–28. MF: 1828–33, 1837, 1839.

Christian Intelligencer. M. 1–37, 1829–65. Calcutta: Church Mission Press. IOL: 1829–65.

Calcutta Magazine and Monthly Register. M. 1–4, 1830–2. Calcutta: Samuel Smith and Co. Current affairs, literature, shipping intelligence, education, law, women's studies. IOL: 1–4, 1830–2. NL: 1–4, 1830–2.

Mirror of the Press: or, The Political and Literary Register. W. 1, 1830. Calcutta. Current affairs, literature, history, extracts. NL: 1, 1830.

Agra Ukbar. Bi-W. 1–15, 1832–46. Agra: Agra Press. Literature, poetry, history, commerce and industries. NL: 12, 1844, 15, 1846.

Calcutta Christian Observer. W. 1–27, 1832–66. Calcutta: Baptist Mission Press. IOL: 1–27, 1832–66.

East Indian United Service Journal and Military Magazine. M. Nos.

1–58, 1832–9. Calcutta: Englishman Press. IOL: nos. 5–58, 1833–9. NL: nos. 5–58, 1833–9.

Englishman. D. 1–112, 1833–1934. Calcutta. Ed. J.H. Stockqueler and Robert Macnaughten. Absorbed *John Bull.* IOL: 2–112, 1834–1934. NL: 1833–40, 1844–51, 1856–7, 1860, 1875–1934. NF: 1834–1906.

Madras Journal of Literature and Science. Q. 1–62, 1833–94. Madras: J.B. Pharaoh. Ed. Captain R.H.C. Tufnell. Published by Madras Literary Society, an auxiliary of the Royal Asiatic Society. Literature, history, antiquities, religion, philosophy, science. IOL: 1833–51, 1856–94. NL: 1836–44, 1856–61, 1864–6, 1878–81, 1886–94.

Madras Literary Gazette, Or Journal of Belles Lettres, Science and the Arts. Q. 1, 1834. Madras: Athenaeum Press. NL: 1, 1834.

Friend of India. W. 1–42, 1835–76; then *Friend of India and Statesman*, 43–9, 1877–83; then *Statesman and Friend of India*, 50–88, 1884–1922; then *Statesman*. Calcutta. Rs. 12 (A). Proprietor: F.A. Cohen. Originally founded and edited as a monthly by William Carey, Joshua Marshman, and William Ward. Literature, history, religion (Christianity), missionary news, education, social customs. 'Contains a brief view of the progress of vital religion in Bengal, among the European part of the community from the earliest part to the present time, to which will be added, an account of the various instructions now formed at this Presidency for the promotion of knowledge and religion.' IOL: 1835–85. NL: 1838–87, 1889–94, 1896–1902. MF: 1835–83, 1894–1923.

Meerut Universal Magazine. M. 1–4, 1835–7. Agra: Agra Press. Literature, history, travel. IOL: 1–4, 1835–7. NL: 2–4, 1836–7.

Spectator. Tri-W. 1, 1837; then *Madras Spectator.* Madras. IOL: 8–20, 1844–56. MF: 1844–56.

Bengal Catholic Expositor. W. 1–26, 1839–64. Calcutta: P.S. D'Rozario. IOL: 1839–62. MF: 1839–53, 1858–64.

Calcutta Christian Advocate. W. 1–15, 1839–53. Calcutta: Baptist Mission Press. IOL: 1–15, 1839–53.

Eastern Star. W. 1–9, 1839–48. Calcutta: Star Press. Rs.20 (A). Printed and published by Edmond Pierre De Beaufort. Proprietor: James Hume. Arts, literature, commercial and shipping intelligence, sports. NL: 9, 1848.

Morning Chronicle and Indian Times. D. 1–18, 1839–56. Calcutta: Star Press. Rs.40 (A). Ed. C.A. Gordon. NL: 1850–1, 1854–6.

Athenaeum. D. 1841–61; then *Athenaeum and Statesman,* 1861–4; then *Athenaeum and Daily News,* 1864–85. Madras. IOL: 1844–85. MF: 1844–85.

Calcutta Journal of Natural History. Q. 1–8, 1841–8. Calcutta: Bishop's College. Botany, zoology, proceedings of the Zoological Society, the British Association and the Asiatic Society of Bengal. IOL: 1–8, 1841–8. NL: 4–8, 1844–8.

Madras Catholic Expositor. M. 1841; then *Madras Roman Catholic Expositor.* Madras. IOL: 2–11, 1842–51.

Bengal Spectator. M. 1–2, 1842–3. Calcutta: Banamali Das. Bilingual, Bengali and English. NL: 1–2, 1842–3.

Calcutta Literary Gleaner, Containing Original Papers, Selections in Prose and Verse from the British Literary Periodicals. M. 1, 1842–3. Calcutta: Baptist Mission Press. NL: 1, 1842–3.

Madras Christian Herald. W. 1–18, 1842–59. Madras: Asylum Press. Rs. 2 (Q). Printed and published by Edmound Marsden. Current affairs, history, religion (Christianity), shipping intelligence. NL: 5–6, 1847–8, 1859.

Bengal Quarterly Sporting Magazine. Q. 1–2, 1843–4. Calcutta: Thomas Rebeiro. Ed. R. Macdonald Stephenson. IOL: 1843–4. LN: 1844.

Oriental Magazine: A Monthly Publication. M. 1, 1843. Calcutta: Lall Bazar Press. Current affairs, literature, serial novels, travel. NL: 1, 1843.

Calcutta Christian Herald. W. 1–3, 1844–5. Calcutta. IOL: 1–3, 1844–5. MF: 1844–5.

Calcutta Review. M. 1844–1912. Calcutta: Calcutta General Publishing Co. Current affairs, literature, history, administration, book reviews. NL: 1–135, 1844–1912. MF: 1844–1902.

Hindu Intelligencer. W. 1–12, 1846–57. Calcutta: Intelligencer Press. Rs.20 (A). Ed. Kasi Prasad Ghose. Literature, history, philosophy, commerce and industries, medicine. NL: 1849, 1853–5, 1857.

Banaras Magazine. M. 1–6. 1848–52. Calcutta: T.J. McArthur. General affairs, literature, history, social customs, Anglo-Indian community, religion (Christianity), sports, book reviews. 'It purports to convey really accurate and important information, on the disciplines, the institutions, and the people of India and the East. Subordinate to these primary designs, it would evince a liking for, and an appreciation of, the amenities of literature.' NL: 1–6, 1848–52.

Bombay Quarterly Magazine and Review. Q. 1–3, 1850–3. Bombay: Bombay Educational Society. Literature, religion, administration, education, social customs, science. 'The criterion of truth examined in reference to the principles and teaching of the church Catholic, and the diverse opinions of dissenting communities.' NL: 1–3, 1850–3.

Eastern Guardian. W. 1–2, 1850–1. Madras: Advertiser Press. Current affairs, literature, shipping intelligence, science, extracts. NL: 2, 1851.

Poona Observer. Tri-W, then D. 1850–1906. Poona. IOL: 1876–1906. MF: 1876–1906.

Citizen. D. 1–6, 1851–6. Calcutta: Citizen Office. Rs.32 (A). NL: 1851–6.

Delhi Sketchbook. M. 1–8, 1851–7. Delhi: Delhi Gazette Press. IOL: 2–8, 1852–7.

Madras Examiner. Bi-W. 1–13, 1852–63. Madras: Catholic Orphan Press. Printed and published by Robert Cralway. Current affairs, military notes, administration, commerce and industries, extracts. NL: 1–3, 1852–4; 13, 1863.

East India Army Magazine and Military Review. Q. I, 1853. Calcutta: R.C. Lepage and Co. 'The officers serve honorable and liberal masters in a profession, the emoluments attached to which are unprecedented and unequalled in any existing Army, but still they ought not to forget, that forbidden to memorialize, debarred from representing their united wishes, they require some such organ, as that it is now endeavoured to establish.' IOL: 1, 1853. NL: 1, 1853.

Hindoo Patriot. W, then D from 6 June 1892. 1853–1903. Calcutta: Hindoo Patriot Press. Rs.10 (A). Ed. Girish Chunder Ghosh and Hurrish Chunder Mukherjee. Current affairs, history, nationalism, politics, administration, trade and commerce. IOL: 1876–89. NL: 1854, 1858, 1860, 1868, 1870–96, 1900–3.

Bombay Quarterly Review. Q. 1–17, 1855–8. Bombay: Smith, Taylor and Co. Arts, literature, history, philosophy, administration. NL: 1–17, 1855–8.

Annals of Indian Administration. A. 1–19, 1855–75. Serampore: Baptist Mission Press. Ed. vols. 3–11, Meredith Townsend; vols. 12–18, George Smith; vols. 19–, George Easton. Printed by J.C. Murray. History, administration, education. IOL: 1–19, 1855–75. NL: 1–19, 1855–75.

Dacca News. W. 1–3, 1856–8. Dacca: Dacca Press. Rs.7 (A). History, nationalism, administration. IOL: 1856–8. NL: 1857–8.

Bombay Standard and Chronicle of Western India. D. 1, 1858; then merged with *Bombay Times and Journal of Commerce*; then *Bombay Times and Standard*; then merged with *Bombay Telegraph and Courier*; then *Times of India*, 1861–. IOL: 1858–61.

Anglo-Indian Magazine: A Soldier's Friend and Home Companion. M. 1–36, 1858–61. Calcutta: Bishop's College. 'We write, not only for soldiers, but for all classes of our Christian community to ensure for it a welcome reception in the Drawing Room and the Barrack.' NL: nos. 1–36, 1858–61.

Madras Times. D. 1858–1914. Madras. Ed. Charles Lawson. Printed and published by J. Smalle. Absorbed *Madras Mail.* IOL: 1858–1914. NL: 1894–1903. MF: 1858–1914.

Indian Punch. M. 1–6, 1859–64. Delhi: Indian Punch Press. History, politics, administration, travel, social scenes. 'The satire of *Punch* in India is a reflexion of mess and club gossip, with a dash of the drawing-room and the field. ... The governor-general is of course a standing joke, and so is the commander-in-chief ... but both Lord Dalhousie and Sir Charles Napier are treated with all due respect' (*All the Year Round* [26 July 1862], 403–4). IOL: 1860–3. NL: 1859–60; n.s. 1861–4.

Madras Daily Times. D. 1859; then *Madras Times.* Madras. IOL: 1859–1914.

Madras Journal of Education. M. 1–29, 1859–87. Madras: Addison and Company. Superseded by *Journal of Education.* IOL: 1859–87.

Madras Standard. W. 1–31, 1860–89. Madras. IOL: 18–31, 1877–89. MF: 1877–89.

Daily Telegraph and Deccan Herald. D. 1–29, 1861–89. Poona. IOL: 16–29, 1876–89. MF: 1876–89.

Indian Mirror. D. 1861–93. Calcutta. Founded by Debendranath Tagore. Ed. Monomohon Ghosh, Satyendranath Tagore, and Keshub Chunder Sen. IOL: 1878–89. NL: 1881, 1891–3. MF: 1878–89.

Times of India. D. 1–42, 1861–1901. Bombay: Times of India Press. Absorbed *Bombay Courier* and *Bombay Telegraph and Courier.* Founded by Luke Ashburner in 1790. IOL: 1861–1901. NL: 1863, 1865–8, 1870, 1872, 1886–1901. MF: 1861–81.

Bengalee. W. 1862–32. Calcutta: Bengalee Press. Rs.10 (A). Ed. Girish Chandra Ghosh and Surendranath Banerjee. Current affairs, nationalism, politics, administration. IOL: 1876–1916. NL: 1891, 1894–6, 1898, 1900–1, 1903, 1905–17. MF: 1871–1932.

Bombay Educational Record. M. 1–22, 1865–85. Poona: Bombay Educational Department. Literature, education. NL: 11–17, 1875–81; 22, 1885.

Asiatic Society of Bengal: Proceedings. M. 1865–1904. Calcutta: Baptist Mission Press. NL: 1865–1904.

Pioneer. Tri-W 1865–9, then D 1869–1975. Allahabad. Rs.38 (A). Founded by George Allen. Ed. Rev. Julian Robinson. IOL: 1865–1933. NL: 1867–97, 1899–1903. MF: 1865–9, 1876–91, 1952–75.

Aligarh Institute Gazette. 1–, 1866–78. Aligarh. Absorbed *Progress* 1876. IOL: 1875–8. MF: 1875–8.

South of India Observer. W. 1867–1914. Ootacamund. IOL: 1877–93, 1897–1900, 1902–14. MF: 1877–93, 1897–1900, 1902–14.

Bangalore Spectator. D. 1–27, 1869–95. Bangalore. IOL: 9–27, 1877–95.

Indian Christian Herald. W. 1–13, 1870–83. Calcutta: Herald Press. Rs.10 (A). Printed and published by P.N. Saha. Current affairs, religion (Christianity), rural scenes. NL: 10–13, 1880–3.

Star of India. D. 1, 1870–1. Bombay. IOL: 1, 1870–1. MF: 1870–1.

Christian Spectator. M. 1–6, 1871–6. Calcutta: Baptist Mission Press. IOL: 1871–6.

Bengal Magazine. M. 1–11, 1872–83. Calcutta: G.C. Hay. Rs.9 (M). Ed. Lal Behari Dey. Literary articles, poetry, education, history, politics, book reviews. 'For the instruction and entertainment of our countrymen ... containing articles on light literature ... to take up all important questions connected with Indian politics & society.' IOL: 1–11, 1872–83. NL: 1–10, 1872–82. *Index,* 1–10 in *Nineteenth Century Studies,* April 1973.

Chameleon. Q. 1–4, 1872–5. Mirzapore: Printed and Published at the Orphan School Press. Rs.5 (A). Ed. Rev. J. Hewlett. Literature, religion (Christianity), travel, rural and urban sketches. 'We have, however, through the kindness of officers commanding Regiments of Bengal Cavalry, been put in possession of material – annuals interwoven with all that is most memorable and romantic in the military history of the English in the East – much of it quite new, which we think cannot fail to be interesting to a large number of Readers.' IOL: 1–4, 1872–5. NL: 1–3, 1872–3.

Indian Antiquary: A Journal of Oriental Research in Archaeology, Epigraphy, Ethnology, Geography, History, Folklore, Languages, Literature, Numismatics, Philosophy, Religion, etc. M. 1–62, 1872–33. Bombay: British India Press. NL: 1–62, 1872–1933. Index to 1–50, 1872–1921 by Lavinia Mary Ausky.

Indian Charivari. F. 1–8, 1872–6; n.s. 1–2, 1877–80. Calcutta: Calcutta Central Press. Rs.20 (A). Ed. T.N. Henry. Current affairs, arts, literature, administration, travel, social scenes, mainly cartoons. 'It is our purpose ... of supplying once a fortnight an illustrated paper, reviewing current topics and matters of interest in a light playful spirit ... its object being rather to promote hilarity and dissipate all depression of spirits and ill-humour. We intend to laugh at and with our small world around us.' IOL: 1–8, 1872–6; n.s. 1, 1877. NL: 4–8, 1874–6; n.s. 1–2, 1877–80.

Law Observer. M. 1–2, 1872–3. Calcutta. NL: 1–2, 1872–3.

Mookerjee's Magazine. Semi-A. 1–6, 1872–6. Calcutta: G.B. Das and Co. Literature, history, religion (Hinduism), social customs. NL: 1–6, 1872–6.

Calcutta Magazine: A Journal of Literature, Politics, Science, and the Arts. M. 1–15, 1873–87. Calcutta: Calcutta Magazine Office. Conducted by Owen Aratoon. Literature, history, administration, social customs. 'Embracing Topics of the Day, Sketches of Eastern life, biographical and historical notes, essays, miscellaneous notices, poetry and serial tales &c, &c, the whole combining useful information and instruction with amusement and recreation.' NL: 1873–5, 1887.

Legal Companion. M. 1–13, 1873–85. Calcutta: Prosunno Coomar Sen. 1–11, 1873–83; 13, 1885.

Bangalore Examiner. Tri-W. 1874–86; then *Daily Post.* Bangalore. IOL: 1877–86. MF: 1877–86.

Indian Spectator: A Monthly Magazine of Literature, Philosophy, History, Science and Politics. M. 1–2, 1874–5. Calcutta: Mookerjee, Gupta and Mitter. Rs.10 (A). Literature, history, politics, administration, social scenes, extracts from other journals. 'Our magazine will be strictly independent.' IOL: 1–2, 1874–5. NL: 1–2, 1874–5.

Theistic Annual. A. 1874–6. Calcutta: Calcutta Central Press. Religion (Brahmo Samaj). NL: 1874, 1876.

Behar Herald. W. 1875–1910. Bankipore. Rs.8 (A). Current affairs, literature, history, Indian National Congress, politics, administration, extracts. NL: 1898–9, 1903–4, 1908–10.

Indian Jurist: A Journal and Law Reports. F. 1–8, 1877–84. Madras: C. Foster and Co., Foster Press. Ed. Edmund Fuller Griffin. Includes supplements. NL: 1–8: 1877–84.

Law Reporter. M. 1–2, 1877–8. Calcutta: Herald Press. Rs.10 (A). Ed. Joy Govind Shome. NL: 1–2, 1877–8.

Anglo-Indian Guardian: A Weekly Newspaper and Review. W. 1878–80. Calcutta: Thomas S. Smith; then *Anglo-Indian: A Weekly Newspaper and Review.* 1880. Calcutta: Calcutta Central Press. Rs.10 (A). Current affairs, fiction, poetry, administration, social customs, Anglo-Indian community, extracts. NL: 1878–80.

Brahmo Public Opinion. W. 1–3, 1878–80. Calcutta: Sadharan Brahma Samaj Press. Rs.6 (A). Ed. Kalinath Dutt. History, religion (Brahmo Samaj), politics, administration, current affairs. NL: 1–3, 1878–80.

Capital. D. 1879–1948. Calcutta. IOL: 1898–1912. MF: 1898–1948.

Indian Herald. W. 1879–82. Allahabad. IOL: 1879–82. MF: 1879–82.

Oriental Miscellany: A Monthly Journal of Politics, Literature, Science and Arts. M. 1–3, 1879–83. Calcutta: H.C. Gangooly and Co. Rs.6 (A). Fiction, poetry, literary gossip, history, religion (Hinduism), politics, administration, social customs. NL: 1–3, 1879–83.

Calcutta Fortnightly Review. F. 1–2, 1880–1. Calcutta: Cones and Co. Re.1 (M). Current affairs, history, politics, administration. 'We intend to divide our journal into two parts; the first of which will contain articles upon politics, current topics, and news; while the second will be devoted to reading of a lighter kind.' NL: 1–2, 1880–1.

Indian Evangelical Review. Q. 1880–92. Calcutta: S.M. Sridhar. Religion (Christianity), missionary news, social customs. NL: 1880–4, 1892.

Star in the East. W. 1, 1880–1. Calcutta: Britannia Press. Rs.6 (A). Printed and published for the Proprietor by F. Mendez. Fiction, religion (Christianity), missionary news, sermons, education. NL: 1, 1880–1.

Students' Magazine: A Monthly Periodical in the Interest of Education. M. 1, 1880–1. Surat: Mission High School. Ed. A.S. Jerris. NL: 1, 1880–1.

Orient: An Anglo-Indian Monthly Magazine. M. 1–6, 1881–6. Bombay: Times of India. Literature, history, politics, administration, social customs, book reviews. 'The magazine is growing steadily and continually in popular esteem, and gaining a more and more secure foothold in India ... even the Bombay government uttered a pleasant word of praise in its report issued from the secretariat, July 14, 1882.' IOL: 1–6, 1881–6. NL: 1–5, 1881–5.

Arya, A Monthly Journal Devoted to Aryan Philosophy, Art, Literature, Science and Religion As Well As To Western Modern Philosophy. M. 1–5, 1882–7. Lahore: R.C. Bary. Religion (Hinduism), philosophy, education. NL: 1–5, 1882–7.

Hindu Reformer and Politician: A Monthly Magazine. M. 1–2, 1882–3. Madras: Madras 'Excelsior' Press. History, religion (Hinduism), politics, IOL: 1–2, 1882–3. NL: 2, 1883.

Indian Spectator and the Voice of India. W. 1–17, 1882–1908. Bombay: Dorabji Sorabji. A column entitled 'The Voice of India' had extracts from various native journals and newspapers. Absorbed *Voice of India.* Literature, history, politics, administration, education. IOL: 1882–9. NL: 1882–1908. MF: 1882–99.

Muhammadan Observer. W. 1–13, 1882–94. Calcutta: Urdu Guide Press. Rs.10 (A). Printed and published by Mursi Abdul Jabbar. Current affairs, religion (Islam), law. NL: 1894.

Purans: A Monthly Amusing Magazine. M. 1–3, 1882–4. Bombay: Kothare and Co. Literature, history. IOL: 1, 1882. NL: 1–3, 1882–4.

Reis and Rayyet: Newspaper and Review of Politics, Literature and Society. W. 1–14, 1882–95. Calcutta: Cornwallis Press. Rs. 12 (A). Ed. Sambhu Chunder Mookerjee. Printed and published by G.C. Chakravarti. Literature, fiction, history, politics, social customs. IOL: 1890–5. NL: 1882, 1996. MF: 1883–6, 1888.

Student's Friend: A Monthly Education Journal. M. 1–6, 1882–8. Bombay. NL: 5–6, 1886–8.

Indian Nation. W. 1883–. Calcutta: D.C. Somoddar. Ed. N.N. Ghosh. Current affairs, nationalism, Indian National Congress, politics, administration. NL: 1894–6, 1898, 1901.

Punjab Notes and Queries: A Monthly Periodical, Devoted to the Systematic Collection of Authentic Notes and Scraps of Information Regarding the Country and the People. M. 1–3, 1883–6. Allahabad: Pioneer Press. Ed. Captain R.C. Temple. Current affairs, history, social customs, extracts. NL: 1–3, 1883–6.

Indian Selector: A Monthly Journal of Politics, Social, Scientific, Religious, Philosophical and Literary Articles Selected from the Best English Periodicals. M. 1–2, 1884–5. Bombay: Printed at the Alliance Printing Press. Ed. N.F. Billimoria. A selection of articles from the *Contemporary Review, Saturday Review, Fortnightly Review, Scientific American, Athenaeum, Academy,* etc. Also included local articles of general interest and a column on literary gossip. IOL: 1884–5. NL: 1884–5.

Anglo-Indian: A Weekly Newspaper and Review. W. 1, 1886. Calcutta: Anglo-Indian Press. Rs. 4 (A). Printed and published by B.M. Halder. Literature, poetry, history, politics, Anglo-Indian community, extracts. 'The domiciled Christian community needs paper representation in the press ... Apart from its purely literary interest the starting of a representative journal has a deep political significance ... an organ as well to instruct and direct their class as to ascertain their wishes and communicate what is being done to meet them.' NL: 1, 1886.

Concord: A Monthly Preview. M. 1, 1887. Calcutta: Concord Club. Rs. 6 (A). Ed. Kali Charan Banurji. Literature, religion (Hinduism), philosophy, education, travel, journalism, press, science. 'It will serve as an organ for a fair, free and full discussion of questions of public utility – seek to educate, influence and direct public opinion on subjects, social, political, intellectual, moral and religious – and concentrate into a focus the thoughts of great thinkers and writers in every department of human affairs.' IOL: 1, 1887. NL: 1, 1887.

English Opinion on India. M. Nos. 1–85, 1887–94. Poona: Arya Bhusana Press. Ed. 1–5, 1887–91, Y.N. Ranade; n.s. 1–2, 1892–4, Vasudeb Balkrishna Kelkar. History, Indian National Congress, politics, administration, parliamentary news. 'Aim is to induce influential Members of Parliament to interest themselves in Indian affairs and to familiarize the British public with knotty and difficult political problems relating to Indian affairs.' IOL: 1887–94. NL: 1887–91.

Indian Engineering. W. 1–2, 1887. Calcutta: Calcutta General Printers Co. Rs.12 (A). Ed. Pat Doyle. Illustrated. NL: 1–2, 1887.

Empress: An Illustrated Magazine. W. 1–37, 1888–1922. Calcutta: T. Black and Co. Rs.6 (A). Arts, serial novels, fashion, sports. NL: 2–37, 1889–1922.

Week's News. 1–4, 1888–91. W. Allahabad: Pioneer Press. IOL: 1–4, 1888–91.

Indian Empire. M. 1–3, 1889–91. Calcutta. History, religion, philosophy, administration. NL: 1–3, 1889–91.

Indian Lancet: A Weekly Journal of Medicine, Surgery, Public Health and of General Medical Intelligence. F. 1–31, 1889–1908. Ed. Lawrence Fernandez. NL: 6–31, 1895–1908.

Allahabad Review. M. 1890. Allahabad: Indian Press. Ed. M. Hameed-Ullah. Poetry, history, religion (Islam), administration, education, law, extracts. NL: 1, 1890.

Indian Medical Record: Monthly Journal of Public Health and Tropical Medicine, etc. Devoted to the Interest of the Medical Profession in the East. M. 1–71, 1890–1951. Calcutta: NL: 1–71, 1890–1951.

Indian Social Reformer. W. 1–17, 1890–1906. Bombay: S. Natarajan. Rs. 5 (A). History, social life. IOL: 4–16, 1894–1906. NL: 9–14, 1898–1903. MF: 1894–1906.

Amrita Bazar Patrika. D. 1–, 1891–1902. Calcutta: Amrita Bazar Press. Ed. Sisir Kumar Ghosh and Motilal Ghosh. Daily newspaper owned and conducted by native Indians. NL: 1891–3, 1897–1902.

North Indian Notes and Queries: A Monthly Periodical Devoted to the Systematic Collection of Authentic Notes and Scraps of Information Regarding the Country and the People. M. 1–5, 1891–6. Allahabad: Pioneer Press. Ed. William Crooke. NL: 1–5, 1891–6.

Archaeological Survey of India, Epigraphia Indica: A Collection of Inscriptions. Q. 1–26, 1892–1942. Ed. Jas. Burgess. Arts, history. 'A record to include not only translation of inscriptions – Sanskrit, Persian, Arabian, and other but lists of them and other miscellaneous antiquarian information including such materials as had been published for the Archaeological survey of western India ... between 1874 and 1885.' NL: 1–26, 1892–1942.

Deccan College Quarterly. Q. 1–9, 1892–1901. Poona. IOL: 1, 1892; 2–3, 1894; 6, 1898; 8, 1900; 1901.

Medical Reporter: A Fortnightly Journal of Medicine, Surgery, Public Health and of General Medical Intelligence. F. 1–5, 1892–5. Calcutta: Medical Publishing Press. Ed. Lawrence Fernandez. NL: 1–5, 1892–5.

Behar Times. W. 1894–1902. Bankipore. Ed. Sachehidananda Sinha. Current affairs, nationalism, administration, journalism, press. NL: 1897–1902.

Calcutta University Magazine. M. 1, 1894. Calcutta: Calcutta University. Conducted by the Secretaries to the Society for the Higher Training of Young Men. Literature, history, biography, religion, education, women's studies, sports. NL: 1, 1894.

Madras Review. Q. 1–21, 1895–1905. Madras: Srinivas Varadachan and Co. Rs.2 (Q). Ed. C. Karunakaran Menon. Literature, history, religion, philosophy, administration, commerce and industries. NL: 21, 1905.

Dawn. M. 1–5, 1897–1902. Calcutta. Literature, history, religion (Hinduism), philosophy, education, science, archaeology. NL: 4–5, 1900–2.

Indian Gardening: A Weekly Journal, Mainly Devoted to Gardening, Agriculture and the Allied Sciences Practical and Scientific. W. 1, 1897. Calcutta: C.J.A. Pritchard at the 'Star' Press. Rs.26 (A). Ed. H. St. John Jackson. NL: 1, 1897.

Mangalore Magazine: The Organ and Record of S.E. Aloysius College. M. 1897–1906. Mangalore: Condialbai Press. Literature, history, education. 'This magazine is published chiefly to further the interests of the college, its graduates and undergraduates and incidentally those of Mangalore and the District of Canara.' NL: 1–3, 1897–1906.

East and West. M. 1–18. 1901–1912. Simla. Ed. Munzar Ali. History, religion (Hinduism), religion (Islam), philosophy, politics, education, rural and urban sketches, law, medicine. NL: 1–18, 1901–19.

New India: A Weekly Record and Review of Modern Thought and Life. W. 1, 1901–3. Calcutta: New India Press. Rs.10 (A). Ed. Bipin Chandra Pal. Printed and published by A.K. Das. Literature, fiction, history, politics, education, book reviews. NL: 1, 1901–3.

Notes

1 During the Indian Mutiny, the native Indian soldiers, known as sepoys, revolted against the East India Company in May 1857. The British regained their control of India and the sepoys by the end of the year.
2 Sir John William Kaye began his career in India as an artillery officer in 1832, joined the Indian Civil Service in 1856, and was appointed Secretary at the

India Office in 1874. A prolific writer, Kaye was a regular contributor to the *Calcutta Review*. He was also the author of the *History of the Sepoy War* (3 vols. 1864–76) and *Administration of the East India Company* (1853).

3 This study is concerned with serial publications in English (including newspapers) printed, published, founded, and edited by British and native Indian in colonial India.

Works Consulted

Barns, Margarita. *The Indian Press: A History of the Growth of Public Opinion in India*. London: George Allen and Unwin 1940.

'British Indian Literature.' *Oriental Magazine* 1 (1843), 157–78.

Bulwer-Lytton, Edward. 'The Value of India to England.' *Quarterly Review* 120 (1866), 200–1.

Busteed, H.E. *Echoes From Old Calcutta: Being Chiefly Reminiscences of the Days of Warren Hastings, Francis and Impey*. 4th ed. London: Thacker, Spink 1908.

Catalogue of Periodicals, Newspapers and Gazettes. Calcutta: National Library 1956.

Catalogue of Printed Books in the Ashutosh Collection. 3 vols. Vol. 3: 'History, Geography, Travels and Biography.' Calcutta: National Library 1978.

Chanda, Mrinal Kanti. *History of the English Press in Bengal: 1780–1857*. Calcutta: K.P. Bagchi 1987.

'Christianity in India.' *North British Review* 13 (1852), 583–620.

Cotton, H.E.A. *Calcutta Old and New: A Historical and Descriptive Handbook to the City*. Calcutta: W. Newman 1907.

Cumpston, M. 'Some Early Indian Nationalists and Their Allies in the British Parliament, 1851–1906.' *English Historical Review* 76(1961), 279–97.

Digby, W. 'The "Struggle for Existence" of the English Press in India.' *Calcutta Review* 63 (1876), 256–74.

'Education in the Colonies and in India.' *Eliza Cook's Journal* 7(19 June 1852), 124–5.

Greenberger, Allen J. *The British Image of India: A Study in the Literature of Imperialism 1880–1960*. London: Oxford University Press 1969.

Hickey, William. *Memoirs of William Hickey*. Ed. Alfred Spencer. 2nd ed. London: Hurst and Blackett 1914.

Karkaria, R.P. 'Beginnings of the Newspaper Press in India.' *East and West* 1 (1902), 546–62.

Kaye, John William. 'The English in India: Our Social Morality.' *Calcutta Review* 1 (1844), 290–336.

– *History of the Sepoy War*. 3 vols. London: W.H. Allen 1864–76

Kumar, R.P. *Research Periodicals of Colonial India: 1780–1947.* Delhi: Academic Publications 1985.

Lent, John A., ed. *The Asian Newspapers' Reluctant Revolution.* Ames: Iowa State University Press 1971.

'A Mutiny in India,' *Household Words* 16 (1857) 154–6.

Natarajan, S. *A History of the Press in India.* Bombay: Asia Publishing House 1962.

National Library, India. *Catalogue of Periodicals, Newspapers and Gazettes.* Calcutta: Government of India Press 1956.

– *Catalogue of Printed Books in the Ashutosh Collection.* 4 vols. Calcutta: Government of India Press 1957–78.

Norton, John Bruce. *Topics for Indian Statesmen.* Ed. G.R. Norton. London: Richardson Brothers 1858.

Parthasarathy, Rangaswami. *A Hundred Years of the Hindu.* Madras: Kasturi and Sons 1978.

Sleeman, Sir William H. *A Journey through the Kingdom of Oudh.* London: Cambridge University Press 1971.

'A Very Black Act.' *Household Words* 16 (26 Sept. 1857), 292–6.

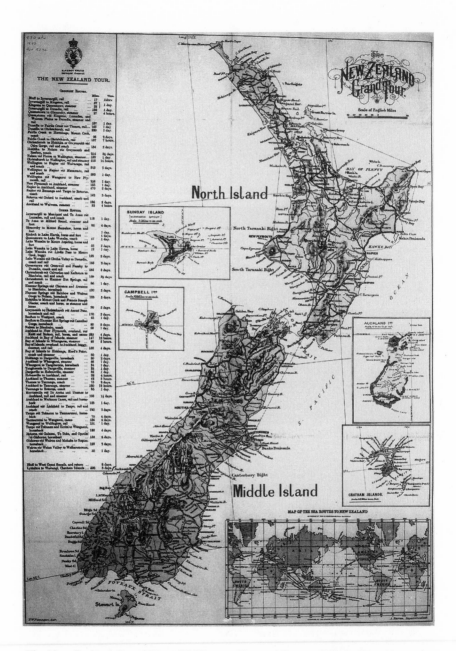

The New Zealand Grand Tour. Wellington, General Survey Office, 1890. Alexander Turnbull Library, Wellington, New Zealand. (ATL Ref: 830atu/1890/Acc. 8294; C16446). Courtesy of the Alexander Turnbull Library.

4

New Zealand

J. REGINALD TYE

Introduction

The following survey has been compiled largely through access to periodicals held in the Alexander Turnbull Library, a research library within the National Library, Wellington; and to newspapers held in the National Newspaper Collection administered by the Turnbull Library. These collections are the country's main repositories. Holdings of early periodicals tend to be incomplete, and may in fact be bound in with others in 'scrapbooks.' A number are available on microfilm. The National Newspaper Collection is substantial, having inherited the holdings of the original parliamentary library. A good number are now on microfilms which include missing issues held in other libraries.

What will be obvious is the multiplicity of titles, and the brevity of their currency, products of the exigencies of settlement: namely the proliferation of smaller centres and the need to disseminate information; the assertion of identity; the thrust of provincial politics; an increasing population; prosperity; and an active group of journalists and printers. Periodicals in particular were affected by the extensive importation of reviews and magazines from Britain, the contents of which maintained a reassuring link with 'Home'; by a small readership for local periodicals cast in the mould of familiar British models; by a small corps of writers; and by a lack of confidence in the significance of their own colonial life. The side effects of university education, the awareness of a significance for New Zealand in world affairs, and a sense of national identity only became apparent in the periodicals of the end of the century, while the potential for a national literature remained embryonic. Nevertheless, the newspapers and periodicals of the century provide an indispensable record of that process.

In 1642 Abel Tasman, the Dutch navigator, sailing eastward from Tasmania, encountered the western coast of New Zealand's South Island (in Maori, Te Wai Pounamu) – throughout the period of colonization often called the Middle Island, while small Stewart Island further south was also named the South Island. Tasman then sailed north, up the west coast of both South and North Islands, the largest in the south Pacific. In 1769, from the opposite direction, Captain James Cook sailed westward, having observed the transit of Venus on Tahiti. He in his turn encountered the east coast of the North Island. Meticulously, under Admiralty instructions, he circumnavigated and charted the coasts of all the islands, great and small, before again sailing west across the Tasman Sea, making landfall on the southeast coast of Australia, similarly charting that coast northwards for two thousand miles. Both territories were taken into possession, in part, on behalf of George III; and thus was set in motion the colonization of 'Australasia,' two potential jewels in the imperial crown, twelve hundred miles apart.

The early development of the two territories was markedly different. New South Wales preceded New Zealand as a colony by some fifty years, and developed as an economic entity through the combination of services for the convict population with internal and external trade, multinational seafaring enterprises, and limited agriculture. With minimum concern for the indigenous people, the initial settlers were predominantly British, whether by immigration or by emancipation. Considerable seafaring traffic developed across the Tasman to and from New Zealand, where small marine servicing settlements also developed. Such contacts were to become increasingly important.

New Zealand's climate, terrain, flora, fauna, and native population were vastly different from its neighbour's. The island had been separated millions of years before by continental drift. Flora and fauna had remained undisturbed by *homo sapiens*, and indeed by any mammalia other than marine, until the arrival of Polynesian adventurers in the first millennium AD. Originally few in number, the Maori developed tribal systems of some complexity, principally in the volcanic North Island. Within the fourteen degrees of the colony's total north/south axis, the climate was temperate, and the land largely covered by podocarp forests. Nevertheless, the land was favourable to cultivation, animal protein was plentiful, and the Maori became skilled gardeners. Land was owned on a tribal basis, and greatly cherished. Over the thousand years of undisturbed occupation, a rich graphic, three-dimensional, and oral culture had developed. Neither ceramics nor metals had, however, been exploited.

Early European contacts, apart from Tasman's and Cook's visits, were principally through Australia, and inimical to the Maori way of life. Escaped convicts, sealers, mercenary sea-captains, and entrepreneurs bearing rum, firearms, and European diseases had a deplorable effect. Partly in dismay, and partly in evangelical zeal, Christian missionaries established bases from 1814 onwards, in both cases with Maori welfare a primary concern. Their ministration was a mixed blessing in the long term, on the one hand achieving a remarkable degree of bilingual, scriptural literacy, assisted by the installation of printing presses, and on the other a radical dislocation of cultural patterns. Missionaries, well intentioned, undoubtedly assisted in subsequent negotiations between Maori chiefs and the British Crown.

In post-Napoleonic Britain there was considerable interest in lands ripe for organized emigration through schemes devised by Edward Gibbon Wakefield and profitable to their promoters; such was the case also in New South Wales, South Australia, South Africa, and Canada. The New Zealand Company was formed in London with the object of acquiring land direct from the Maori, to be subdivided and on-sold to migrants at a sustainable price, reputedly favourable to both parties. The scheme, after making allowance for the profit motive of promoters, was inherently Utopian, drawing inspiration from Wakefield's admiration of the hierarchic society of pre-Victorian England, which formed the basis of migrant selection. The British government distrusted the scheme from its inception, and over the twelve years of the Company's existence there was constant harassment. Nevertheless, five settlements were established during that time. In the North Island, Wellington, conceived as the capital and ultimately so, was founded in 1840; and New Plymouth, to be the provincial centre of Taranaki, also in a Maori heartland, in 1842. In the South Island Nelson, profoundly Anglican and in Maori territory, was founded across Cook's Strait from Wellington in 1842; to the far southeast, Dunedin (New Edinburgh), predominantly Free Church Presbyterian, was founded in 1848 and Christchurch, on the east coast, dedicated to hierarchic Anglicanism, in 1850. All (with the exception of a sixth, Wanganui) were ultimately successful as provincial centres.

The British Empire was far from the minds of the British government. Harassed by lack of money and a shortage of competent administrators, and anxious about the Company's activities and the predicament of the Maori people, it had been forced into annexing lands and negotiating the Treaty of Waitangi, 1840, with Maori chiefs the length and breadth of the colony. There was a general suspicion that the government was saving face, in such a treaty would act as a protection against encroachment by other European powers. The French indeed established a small and charming settlement at Akaroa on the east coast of the South Island in 1840.

William Hobson, RN (d. 1842), having signed the Treaty at Waitangi in the Bay of Islands, had been expected to establish his administration at the town of Russell, across the Bay, notorious for some years under its Maori name, Kororareka, as a sink of iniquity. He chose, however, to operate from Auckland, a considerable distance to the south, which had the benefit of two harbours, east and west, and was flanked by co-operative Maori tribes. The choice was unpopular with white settlers, however, and made more complicated by Hobson's serious illness and eventual death in 1842. The colony was then placed under the control of Willoughby Strickland, to await the arrival of Robert Fitzroy, whose reputation for instability and championship of Maori claims brought intense apprehension. In due course George Grey, with a record of success as Governor of South Australia, was appointed, further antagonizing the settlers, already under attack by Maori in the north and in the south near Wellington. Grey was successful in quelling unrest, however, and eventually acceded to the settlers' demands for representative government by negotiating the Constitution Act of 1852. It provided for a Legislative Council, nominated by the Crown, and a House of Representatives elected by male property owners and settlers over the age of twenty-five, in the six provinces of Auckland, Taranaki, Wellington, Nelson, Canterbury, and Otago, the last five all Company settlements. All provincial centres had immediate access to the sea and beneficent hinterlands. Grey's further achievement was in systematizing land purchase, in huge quantities, from the Maori: thirty million acres in the South Island and three million in the North, later to be on-sold in smaller lots for the benefit of small farmers, while leaving provision for large individual freehold and lease-hold purchase. It was thus that large areas in Hawke's Bay, Taranaki, and the South Island became the basis of the colony's powerful and long-lasting squirearchy.

In Maori affairs Grey's influence was also far-reaching, not least in the well-intentioned policy of assimilation, only recently abandoned. The effect, in the downgrading of Maori culture and language, was profound. These reforms initiated, Grey's final duty before proceeding to South Africa was to call for the first elections to the House of Representatives and to convene its first meeting. He was, nevertheless, to return as Governor (1861–8) to wrestle with the Land Wars.

The establishment of provincial government was the recognition of the fact of settlement. The immigrant population more than doubled in the period 1853–60. Much of it fanned out into additional provinces: Hawke's Bay in the east of the North Island; Marlborough to the east of Nelson; and Southland, south of Otago – all before 1860. Demographically, the profitability of pastoralism resulted in an increasing disparity of immigration between the two islands, reinforced by the difficulty of acquiring land in the North, which was more densely populated by the Maori.

The late 1850s and most of the 1860s saw increasing hostility, interracial, and intertribal. The Maori had divided over the relative merits of financial advantage, as against preservation of culture. The result was warfare, sporadic and widespread, involving the use of imperial troops and colonial militia against at times brilliantly led tribal warriors. The injustice of the wars was much debated among settlers, the Church, the Governor, and the tired British forces. The withdrawal of the last was inevitable, and completed by the 1870s, although skirmishes continued. Pacification was generally achieved by attrition, wholesale confiscation, and radical changes in the disposal of tribal land. The Maori suffered the humiliation of defeat, their demoralization intensified by a fall in numbers so considerable that by the end of the century their race was described as 'dying.' Their one compensation was the right to elect four representatives to the House, from the two islands combined. By contrast, the South Island remained free from open strife, and benefited from the discovery of gold in Otago. This, together with the prosperity of agriculture and pastoral farming, and the concomitant development of commerce, produced a population of some 150,000 in 1870, as against 100,000 in the North, Dunedin containing a quarter of the colony's population.

The Land Wars over, the future of the colony appeared bright. Road and rail communications in both islands improved greatly. The central government had been transferred to Wellington in 1865, and provincial government became increasingly clumsy and subject to unwise local decisions. Accordingly, the system was abandoned in 1876. Nevertheless, the economy was entering a period of considerable uncertainty, largely owing to a decline in the prices for exports, while the Otago gold mines were exhausted. As a panacea, Julius Vogel, premier during 1870–5, and briefly in 1876, launched optimistic programs on the basis of foreign loans, a practice which persisted with dubious results until 1890. It was accompanied by a massive increase in immigrant population, which doubled in ten years. The new wave of settlers was recruited to capitalize on the colony's staple output, primary products. The scheme proved attractive to British farm workers caught up in the rural unrest in the eastern and southern counties of England. Better educated than the earlier labourers, and more familiar with the politics of labour, the new migrants determined to advance themselves as 'yeoman' farmers, the vogue word of the decade. Still others were attracted into small industry. Yet ironically, the colony entered the 1890s with acute unemployment, labour unrest, burgeoning trade unions, and a crippling maritime strike.

Despite these negative aspects, the last decade was to prove one of achievement. The first Liberal government was elected in 1890, a product of an extension of the franchise among the male population, while in 1893 women were granted the vote, the first in the Empire. In 1894 the Industrial Conciliation and Arbitration Act gave at least some protection to the labour force, and in 1898 the Old Age Pensions Act launched social welfare as a state responsibility. In addition, the terms of trade improved, bringing an increase in prosperity to town and country alike. By the end of the century, bluff 'King Dick' Seddon, born at sea between Australia and New Zealand, and a gold miner in both countries, led the colony into the euphoria of imperial unity by joining the Australians alongside the mother country in the South African Boer War, and fed the colony's ambition to become a colonial power in its own right by annexing the Cook Islands.

The Newspaper Press

In the settlement of New Zealand, printing presses played a major role in the transmission of essential information as settlers arrived under the auspices of the New Zealand Company in their main centres of Wellington, Nelson, Christchurch, and Dunedin. Great care had been taken to ensure that both presses and printers with some journalistic experience accompanied the first ships. It is notable that the first issue of Wellington's *New Zealand Gazette* was set up in London in 1839, before the departure of the *Adelaide*, which transported the press, and equally notable that the second issue was set up on a beach in Wellington Harbour and published on 18 April 1840. Across Cook's Straits, the *Nelson Examiner* appeared on 12 March 1842, a mere two months after settlement, the *Otago News* was published rather later, nine months after arrival, and the *Lyttelton Times* (Canterbury) was issued immediately after the landing, on 11 January 1851.

By contrast, the establishment of colonial government in the north of the North Island was turbulent, and fraught will ill-feeling. In the expectation that Kororareka, later Russell, on the Bay of Islands, would be chosen as the centre of colonial government, the *New Zealand Advertiser and Bay of Islands Gazette* was privately launched on 15 June 1840 as the natural vehicle for the Crown Colony decrees. Its fate exemplifies what was to be the common experience of the majority of the newspaper press for decades to come, a division between settler interests and expectations on the one hand and government policy on the other. Its editor was a well-meaning Congregationalist minister-cum-schoolmaster named Barzilai Quaife. In its first issues he both published and attacked the Governor's decrees where they concerned land settlement. In exasperation, the Colonial Secretary called him to account and forced him to accept financial restraint, so rendering the *Advertiser* uneconomic, the more so when the government itself launched its own *New Zealand Government Gazette.* Ironically, it was printed on the original Mission press at Paihia, on 30 December 1840, for the eighteen issues before government was transferred to Auckland. There it survived until April 1842, the government having imported its own press. From then on Auckland became something of a maelstrom as the government moved toward the Constitution Act of 1842, in a flurry of six factionalized newspapers of short duration, only two surviving into the 1850s. Of them all, only the *Southern Cross* survived until 1876. It is, however, also fair to say that in Wellington, the Company's intended capital, of five papers founded in the 1840s, only the *New Zealand Times and Independent* survived into ripe old age, ceasing publication in 1927.

Unquestionably, the pioneer press had a function to perform, principally to inform and act as a forum for political debate among the influential educated settlers, whose preconceptions about the nature of a new society, Utopian, hierarchic, egalitarian, and profitable, found expression. The governing factor was a circulation restricted by the small and scattered population, insecure, with laborious life-styles and limited literacy. The presses themselves, immediately before mechanization, were usually unsophisticated, weighty hand-presses, new or more likely second-hand, imported either from Britain or Australia. Editorship was all-important. In Wellington, Samuel Revans had been chosen by the Company itself on the basis of his experience in Canada as a controversial journalist on the *Montreal Daily Advertiser*, that colony's first daily paper. Revans in fact owned the *New Zealand Gazette/ and Wellington Spectator* (1839–44) until shortly before its failure, having set the not uncommon pattern of transferring his attention to landowning and politics. Revans also set the pattern of balancing losses of publishing a periodical against the establishment of a successful printing house. Of the *Gazette's* two successors, the *New Zealand Spectator and Cook's Straits Guardian* (1844–65) and the *Wellington Independent* (1845–74), the former came into the possession of Robert Stokes, who had gained the patronage of Governor Grey, and the latter, founded by Dr Isaac Earl Featherston, a medical practitioner, was a major force in furthering his political career. In Auckland the practicalities were somewhat similar. There the *New Zealander* (1845–66) had been founded by John Williamson, who shortly thereafter had been joined in partnership by W.C. Wilson; both had been recruited from Sydney to launch the short-lived *New Zealand Herald* (1841–2). Their co-operation with the Governor led to their appointment as government printers. The consequent commercial prosperity enabled them not only to maintain the paper but also to import more sophisticated machinery, including lithographic facilities. In Nelson the *Examiner* (1842–74) was owned jointly by Charles Elliott, an established London printer, and his brother James. Together they were able to operate a general printing establishment, and launched into commerce and livestock breeding. By contrast, the *Otago News* (1848–50) was bedeviled by personalities. Henry Graham, its founding editor and printer, who had been encouraged in the project by the Otago Association, almost immediately crossed swords with the leader of the settlement. The paper foundered shortly before Graham's death in 1851. The necessity of a provincial newspaper was such that the *Otago Witness* (1851–1932) was launched by a co-operative of settlers, before being handed over to William Cutten, son of the settlement leader. Cutten's income from an immigration agency and other business gave the paper initial stability, the press itself proving profitable as a printing house.

Canterbury, the model settlement, was far otherwise. The *Christchurch/ Lyttelton Times* (1851–1929) was funded by a relatively wealthy Oxford printer, complete with sophisticated machinery and accessories, to the extent of £2,500, and a foreman and compositor. The *Times* appears to have been the only founding newspaper to pay its way.

Almost *ab initio*, nineteenth-century New Zealand newspapers tended to be hybrid, containing matter customarily associated with magazines. Certainly, they contained news of local, provincial, colonial, and British interest, together with information on the arrival of immigrants and cargo. There was ample room for contentious, even libellous commentary. In the absence of copyright, items from imported journals were purloined indiscriminately, and to some extent from the colonial press itself. Where copy was scarce, as often happened, space was filled by unpaid feature articles and ad hoc contributions of literary, dramatic, and music criticism. As the population increased, so did the all-important advertising revenue. Inevitably, typesetting left something to be desired, while the quality of the paper was such as to disintegrate rapidly. Thus, early copies are few and far between. Nevertheless, both content and style suggest a well-educated readership, committed in theory and practice to government, landed gentrification, and commerce. Given the composition of immigration and an inherent class structure, circulation was limited; and given the cost of production, the copy price was necessarily high, out of reach of the labouring class. Moreover, given the paucity of news and the unpredictability of communication, regular publication was a problem. Most journals began as weeklies, and figures for the circulation of early issues are instructive. The *Wellington Gazette*, including one reprint, began with a mere 400 copies, falling to an average of 110 for its first year. Circulations in Auckland ranged from 100 to 300, and those for the *Nelson Examiner* amounted to 200. How different from Canterbury, where subscriptions were pre-paid, with a total of 1,000 subscribers among its first four ships.

Predictably, the inception of government by the appointed General Assembly and elected Provincial Councils enhanced the function of newspapers. Inherent was the identification of provincial papers with local politics rather than larger colonial issues. As the country stabilized, and settlement spread outwards into arable and pastoral lands, the comparatively small servicing towns demanded some expression of their identity in print. Whereas in 1858 a total of fifteen such papers had been launched throughout the colony, during the period 1860 to 1880, forty-four were launched in Otago alone. According to G.H. Scholefield, in *Newspapers in New Zealand* (1958), a further fifty were launched throughout the colony in the next twenty years, while ironically eighty-five failed during the same period. One is therefore led to consider the reasons for such a deluge. Undoubtedly there were numerous physical causes. Improved communication by road and rail, less class-oriented subject matter, greater leisure, ready access to more sophisticated printing presses, a corps of entrepreneurial journalists, daily publication, reduction in price, postal concessions, and a rise in news agency all contributed. To meet this variety of interests, a new generation of proprietors appeared in a highly competitive market. There were frequent changes of ownership, and publication became more flexible in function, format, and periodicity. To morning dailies were added those published in the evening, and a proliferation of weeklies resulted, far more akin to magazines.

It was in these circumstances that the New Zealand press, as a genuine fourth estate, came to its majority with the foundation of the United Press Association, operative from 1 January 1880. The Association's function was highly significant, explicitly to promote, lead, and even form 'a healthy public opinion upon political matters.' Membership was open to all newspapers on payment of five hundred pounds, a large sum, as an annual subscription. Its news services were available to members only, a virtual monopoly, since members were also excluded from publishing news from other agencies. Most exclusive of all was sole access to the colony's one international telegraphic cable. The effect of the monopoly was to increase the power of the press in main centres and to discourage non-subscribing publishers. Notably, the monopoly did not preclude political affiliation, but rather enhanced political influence, without the active participation of politicians themselves; nor did it in any way affect intense regional issues.

Clearly, the substantial rise in the number of newspapers implies not merely a substantially increased population but also a literate readership. There are, in fact, statistics which show a consistent rise in literacy, from 63 per cent of the population in 1858, through 71.35 per cent in 1867, 83 per cent in 1874, 89 per cent in 1886, to 91.59 per cent in 1896. The impact of the Education Act (1877) and of more educated migrants is to be seen in the significant rise from the 1870s. A contributory factor in the earlier years had, however, been an inherent concern with education by the settlers themselves. In the Britain they had left behind, the foundation of Mechanics' Institutes had been a major force in self-education. In the main settlements of the colony there was the same concern, and Institutes were founded soon after the settlers' arrival. Thus Nelson's Institute was founded in 1841, with a free reading room; Wellington's was delayed until 1849, but its premises were ultimately elaborate; Dunedin's was opened shortly after settlement, in 1851; and Napier's in 1859. The list could be extended. In addition, for those with an interest in higher education, Athenaeums, which served as centres of culture for Philosophical and Literary Societies, were established. All had small libraries and reading rooms, where there were newspapers and journals. There was, moreover, a natural progression from institutional to public libraries, of which there were 161 by 1874, rising rapidly to 303 in 1886, with a total book stock of 290,000 volumes. The squirearchy later in the century also established libraries for their employees, a benevolent gesture.

Weekly Journals

While the newspapers of the first decade are of interest as repositories of the magazine material, their confirmation as regular dailies made room for the specifically weekly publications of the 1850s, which in spite of format may be legitimately studied as 'periodicals.' The *Auckland Examiner and People,* for instance, had been founded in December 1856 by Charles Southwell, an English journalist of radical tendency, who had been jailed in Britain for blasphemy. His avowed aim was *not* to provide mere news, but to provoke discussion: 'to examine will be our proper function ... critical but just, bold but undogmatic.' Its intended readership was to be 'every class, however humble,' and its content was to range widely over cultural matters, particularly reviews of 'choice works, combining Science,' a recurring interest in New Zealand journals throughout the century, and 'the purely literary.' Strongly biased toward education, Southwell gave whole-hearted support to the Auckland Mechanics' Institute in 1857, which his journal regularly advertised, reporting and reviewing addresses delivered at its meetings. The topics provide a remarkable insight into the considerable and various talents of the speakers, many of them clergy. The standards of the journal's own articles were high, as were those reprinted from British sources such as *The Times* and the *Quarterly Review.* Its satire was generally witty, occasionally in verse, while room was found for 'original' poetry, and serial fiction, which included Edgar Allan Poe's 'The Premature Burial.' Although it was published in newspaper format, the journal's style was modelled on the British *Spectator* rather than the daily press. Despite alterations in format and periodicity, the paper survived its founder by a few issues only, in 1861, but it had clearly served a useful purpose. It is interesting to note that the *Examiner* carried the 'Prospectus' of a quarterly to be entitled 'The Auckland Magazine and Record of Colonial Life and the colonies of Australia, including the Islands of the Pacific,' to be conducted by a Dr Stanhope. The attempt was obviously too grandiose, and no such periodical survives. Almost at the opposite pole was the *Auckland Weekly News* (1861), which survived into the 1930s, with the comprehensive subtitle 'A Journal of Commerce, Agriculture, Politics, Literature, Science and Art,' mainly devoted to practical matters, but with historically valuable supplements. In newspaper format, it was priced at sixpence, printed and published by Charles Williamson, and appears to have had a wide circulation.

Auckland also provided a series of middle-ground journals in the 1860s, among them the *Colonists' Family Herald* (1864–5), the *Penny/Auckland Journal* (1866–7), and the *Auckland Budget* (1867). The *Family Herald,* published from under the wing of the substantial *Southern Cross,* derived its contents mainly from British sources, with occasional articles, stories of adventure, and poetry. With fiction by novelists such as Charles Kingsley and Wilkie Collins, its standards were consistently high.

The *Penny Journal*, subtitled 'A Journal for the People,' in its sixty-one issues provided a diet of news, reviews, serials, 'science' and useful knowledge, family matters, facetiae, and 'poetry.' The provenance of its fiction was largely overseas, with occasional New Zealand writers. Far less reputable was the *Auckland Budget*, 'a Journal devoted to Scurrilous, Abusive, Offensive and Opprobrious comments on Public Men and Social Matters; and Advocating the Uprightness, Sincerity, Justice, Veracity and Rectitude of Everybody Else.' Edited by 'Socrates,' 'Junius,' and Humphry Wilkins Esq., its laboured and prolix humour has some significance as far as the psyche of its readers is concerned.

In the 1870s, the *Southern Cross* launched another middle-ground weekly, the *Saturday Night* (1874–5), also edited by Charles Williamson. By contrast with its predecessor, it aimed 'to enliven the family circle with themes grave and gay,' explicitly rejecting the appellation 'newspaper.' Serials, short stories, and poetry place it among literary periodicals, while 'Fashions of the Season' gave it feminine interest. Male chauvinism was, however, abroad: an article entitled 'Love, honour and obey' counselled its male readers, 'You may rule your wife as you please, good married reader, if you only love and pet her enough.' The source of its failure?

In Dunedin there appeared the *Saturday Review of Politics, Literature, Philosophy, Science and Art* (1864–71), a clear indication of an advancing culture. There followed an intriguing sequence of titles: in 1872, it became the *Saturday Advertiser, Time-Table and New Zealand Literary Miscellany*; in 1875, the *Saturday Advertiser and Public Opinion*. At this stage its ambition was 'to foster a National Spirit in New Zealand, and to encourage Colonial Literature.' Under this title it was distinctly literary, containing serial fiction and short stories by New Zealand writers, set in New Zealand, with Maori scenarios. One issue devoted two whole pages to a remarkable Byronesque idyll in verse, 'Leon and Leonora.' Sad to relate, colonial literature did not flourish, and in July the title was changed to the sybaritic *New Zealand Public Opinion, Sportsman and Saturday Advertiser*, and shortly thereafter it resorted to illustration.

A more provincial journal in the same genre, a new series of the *Hawke's Bay Weekly*, was launched in 1867. Its copy consisted of 'select literature,' 'original poetry,' serials sometimes substantial (for instance 'The Secret of Witmore Chase: a Tale of England and Australia,' written especially by one R.E. Lee), short stories, reprints from British periodicals such as the *St James Gazette*, all in addition to items of local news and editorials of political interest.

Illustrated Journals

Illustrated journalism began in New Zealand with Dunedin's weekly *Illustrated New Zealander* (1866), and more notably the monthly *Illustrated New Zealand Herald for Home Readers* (1868–83). It took full advantage of developments in lithography in its plentiful illustrations, which included many of the colony's scenic splendour. It provides a substantial record of major events and personalities over the period, often with full-page engravings which found their way onto the walls of humbler dwellings. The romanticization of the Maori is evident from finely executed illustrations of indigenous ways of life. Its copy consisted of a mixture of local, colonial, and international news, and evidenced strong links with that other centre of a developing antipodean culture, Melbourne. Its coverage of music, theatre, and sport, together with inevitable fiction and poetry, must have contributed greatly to the enlightenment of the province's general reading public.

Auckland's contribution in the same genre, the monthly *Illustrated Press* (1868–83), provided somewhat similar fare, with an equal indebtedness to Melbourne. In due course it was challenged by the weekly *Auckland Graphic* (1876), modelled on the British Graphic (1869–1932). Auckland's *Graphic* had, however, a commitment to 'the literary and artistic,' and the avoidance of politics. Its contents were essentially family reading, with the customary pabulum of serials, feminine-oriented fiction ('Mira Benson: The Little Music Mistress'), a series of 'Thrilling Incidents in the Life of Sir George Grey (the Governor General),' poetry, 'Sporting and Dramatic,' and rather crude lithographs such as the masculine 'Pakaranga Hunt Club Steeple Chase: The Water Jump' and the sentimental 'Pretty Jane on the Rocks at Gisborne.' Its 'Cartoons of Auckland Life' are of immediate social interest, but in general its early demise was appropriate; neither art nor literature had found its way. In 1880 there appeared Auckland's *Observer*, in the 1890s to become the *New Zealand Observer and Free Lance*, subtitled 'An illustrated journal of interesting and amusing literature,' an example of how newspaper format can make potentially interesting material unattractive. With a religious component ('Round the Churches' and 'Songs and Sermons'), serial fiction ('Did Claud lose?'), 'The Poet's Corner,' and 'Out of Door Sports,' it aimed at a wide readership, but remains remarkably dull, with the exception of its cartoons. Much more interesting was the *Australian and/New Zealand Family Friend* (1888–9). Its ambition was to be 'the largest literary weekly south of the Equator.' It was in fact extremely lively, epitomizing the interests of a middle class of both sexes: serials, well-executed illustrations, snippets of local news, 'Sparks of Wit,' verse, fashion, sport, syndicated material (Mrs Langtry's 'Sketch' of herself), and recollections of early colonial life ('My soldiering days in New Zealand'). Most redolent of the period are its songs and musical scores.

The time was ripe, nevertheless, for the most outstanding illustrated journal of the Victorian era, the Auckland weekly *New Zealand Graphic and Lady's Journal*, launched in Auckland in 1891, with all the resources of photography and photographic reproduction, and a wide range of type-faces. With its publication one has the sensation that New Zealand had emerged from colonial dependence, yet with an increased appreciation of the Colony as part of a great Empire; that it was in an age of self-determined bourgeois affluence, reconciled to the environment, but with a sense of freedom from insurgent Maoridom. By the end of the decade a monument was to be erected in honour of 'the dying Maori race.' In the *Graphic*'s pages one finds an immense variety of material: syndicated British novels such as W.E. Norris's serialized 'Miss Wentworth's Idea,' Kipling's 'The Bottle Imp,' and C.B. Burgin's 'A Would-Be Pilgrim,' alongside Frost Rattray's 'Romance on an Auckland Omnibus' and New Zealand 'Tales.' Inevitably 'poetry' played its part, with one notable tribute to the vanquished Maori in 'Te Morehu's Last Battle.' 'Society Gossip' covered provincial towns as well as major cities, and 'Fashion Notes' included Paris as well as Auckland. Short stories were encouraged by competitors, for insertion in a 'Lady's Story' column.

The most curious phenomenon in illustrated journalism is the widespread imitation of the British comic journal *Punch, or the London Charivari*, launched in 1841. Its first antipodean imitation was the *Melbourne Punch* (1855–1928), and both periodicals circulated in New Zealand. In 1860 the *Taranaki Punch* appeared in the provincial capital, New Plymouth; it was published weekly from 31 October until 7 August 1861, with eight double-column pages for sixpence, obtainable in the main centres of the North Island and in Nelson. Even making allowance for the rudimentary equipment then available, its wood-block caricatures were crude, but graphically convey the tensions of a community embroiled in conflict with dispossessed Maori and their missionary supporters. Its literary contents were largely satiric verse, of little quality.

Later in the decade *Punch in Canterbury* (1865) appeared in Christchurch, far more sophisticated, and closer to its British model in format. Like its Taranaki predecessor, it expressed colonial attitudes to the Maori, but at a comfortable distance, and at a later stage in the conflict. One main feature, a series of humorous dialogues and playlets, is notable for 'The Noble Barbarian, or the Soldier, the Savage, and the Submission: a

Maori Melodrama,' a significant moral fable. After twenty issues it continued under a change of title as the *New Zealand Punch* until its demise on 4 August 1866.

Under the same inspiration, the *Dunedin Punch* appeared on 27 May 1865, continuing after a change of title as the *Otago Punch* from 1 September 1866 until 23 February 1867. A revived version appeared as *Punch, or the New Zealand Charivari* on 18 January 1868, a new series being published in the following May, of undetermined demise. Its targets, even more than those of *Punch in Canterbury*, were largely political, the tone set by a barrage launched against 'the Wellington Bunkum Parliament,' part of a continuing war against North Island pretension. It did, however, have room for sentiment in a memorable 'Psalm of Colonial Life.' In content, style, and graphics it was far ahead of its siblings.

Wellington's own version of the genre came with *Punch, or the Wellington Charivari* for two months, 20 July–14 September 1868. Its style was sophisticated and its contents well executed. Its abrupt termination was apparently due to the departure of its proprietors for Auckland, where they launched *Punch, or the Auckland Charivari*, with its twenty-four issues (14 November 1868–8 May 1869). More closely imitative of the British *Punch*, it ranged widely over personalities, social issues, provincial rivalry, sexism, teetoalism, and Church affairs. The obsession with the genre continued into the next two decades, under a variety of titles: the *National Punch* (1873–4) in Auckland; the *Makomako* (1875–6) in Christchurch; the *New Zealand Punch* (1879–80) briefly, in Wellington; and *Here We Are Again: The Canterbury Punch* (1888–9), which uncharacteristically promised to provide access 'to the most interesting books, periodicals and newspapers of the world,' and 'to instruct and amuse all classes and both sexes.' Neither promise was fulfilled and the century ended with yet another, in Auckland, the *New Zealand Punch* (1898–1900).

Punch was not, however, the only satiric British publication subject to imitation. In London, in 1867, there had appeared the *Tomahawk: A Journal of Satire* (1867–70), edited by Arthur A'Beckett. Much more literary, and based on the tradition of the Noble Savage, it provided a view of the British scene through the eyes of an eponymous North American Indian named Tomahawk. Its merits were grace of style, intellect, and elegant cartoons. In 1870 there appeared an Auckland *Tomahawk: A Saturday Journal of Criticism*, of short duration, bearing little resemblance to its model. But also in 1870, the *Tomahawk: A Saturday Journal of Critical Commentary and Satire* appeared in a most unlikely West Coast provincial centre, Hokitika; Scholefield describes it as an extremely clever journal, edited by a professional journalist. Unfortunately it ended after fifteen issues, and is apparently accessible only in Christchurch city library. Three further *Tomahawks* appear to have been issued, one associated with the *Timaru Herald* on the east cost of the South Island, and two in Auckland, in 1870 and 1899 respectively.

The *Punch* and *Tomahawk* syndromes are clearly worth investigation, particularly in view of New Zealand cartoonists' continuing international reputation.

Periodicals of More Serious Intent

GENERAL

There is a pronounced dichotomy in the orientation of New Zealand periodicals between the secularism of most newspapers and popular journals, and the denominational underpinning of a significant number of weekly and monthly periodicals. Religious 'newspapers' are explicitly excluded (with some exceptions) from R.D. Harvey's *Union List of Newspapers* (1987).

The *New Zealand Magazine* (January–June 1850) was the colony's first secular journal of conventional format, and is extremely rare. It is excellently produced, in green covers and in clear type, published in Wellington. Its motto, *Labour omnia vincit*, is undoubtedly a wry comment on experience. Its aims were unambiguous, that politics should be a leading feature, and that it should be 'a source of amusement to lighten the passing hour.' A quarterly in intent, it consisted of one hundred pages of octavo for an annual subscription of one guinea. There could be no complaint about the range and standard of its contents: in Science, 'The Geology of the Middle Island,' 'Geological Observations on the Book of Genesis,' 'Whales and Whaling,' in fiction, 'Marguerite, a Tale of Brittany,' and 'The Dubutante, a Tale of Parisian Life,' in sentiment, 'Sweethearts and Wives'; in current affairs, 'A Glance at the History of New Zealand as a British Colony' by Walter Mantell; to which were added verse, reviews, and statistics. Edited by W.E. Grimstone, a government official, and laced by verbal sparring between William Swainson, the Attorney-General, and Edward Gibbon Wakefield, proponent of colonization, it has its brighter moments, and its early demise is to be regretted; but the time was clearly not ripe for such ventures.

In Auckland two attempts were made to found traditional magazines in the 1860s. The first was George Chapman's *New Zealand Monthly Magazine* (1862). Chapman had arrived with his brother in Dunedin in

1851, where he founded the Mechanics' Institute. From there he moved to the Australian goldfields, and thence, after a period in Sydney, to Auckland, where he established himself as bookseller and stationer, with a circulating library. His magazine began with high ideals, its contents to be 'literary, scientific and miscellaneous.' It survived a mere five issues, with a mixture of sketches, short fiction of dubious origin, and articles on the history and geology of the country; in all, a courageous effort. Of much greater significance was the *Southern Monthly Magazine* (1863–6) in the same city, in March of the following year; it survived for thirty-six issues with forty-eight pages, later sixty-four, for a shilling, and was modelled along the lines of the British *Cornhill*, itself founded four years before. Its first editorial promised articles on 'subjects interesting to the general reader; which may please the taste to those who read for amusement and stimulate the appetite of those who desire information.' In a retrospect of its first year's operation, the editor recalled his belief that it 'would stimulate and call forth much literary talent hitherto lying dormant' (the first of many such declarations of faith over the generations). In spite of the current land wars, it looked forward to 'a flourishing and settled country in which the industrial arts will flourish, but also the fine arts, and literature far higher than the popular periodical can supply. ... *The Southern Monthly Magazine* will be known as the pioneer of periodical literature in New Zealand.' The last is certainly true. Its interests were literary, and it provided reviews of contemporary New Zealand writing. It had the added charm of delicate lithographed sketches of contemporary Auckland.

The principal centre of serious periodical literature is to be found, however, in the southern city of Dunedin, a phenomenon closely associated with that city's advocacy for the foundation of a University of New Zealand. Inherent in Edward Gibbon Wakefield's settlements was the development of university education, and Dunedin, founded by Scottish Presbyterians of the Free Church persuasion, had some affinities with the Boston of the American Pilgrim Fathers. The Scots had a long tradition of tertiary eduction (St Andrews University had been established in 1411), and the remarkable prosperity generated by the goldfields of Otago, coupled with that of commercial enterprises, gave impetus to a project which would add to the city's prestige. The ferment grew as the decade progressed, though by then similar ambitions operated in the three other main centres. The result was the passing of the University Act of 1870. It provided for the establishment of four university colleges, in which Dunedin took pride of place with its University of Otago in 1869, to be followed by Canterbury University College in 1874, Auckland University

College in 1882, and Wellington's Victoria University College in 1897. The basis of teaching in the earliest of these was moral philosophy and science, disciplines which were to set the tone of the city's intellectual life and foster a series of periodicals of remarkable erudition.

The first such had preceded the university by six years, and was the brain-child of J.G.S. Grant, a graduate of both Edinburgh and St Andrews, and an acerbic individualist. Specifically, his *Saturday Review of Politics, Literature, Philosophy and Science* was modelled on the British *Saturday Review* (1856–1938. Under the distinguished editorship of J.D. Cook, that periodical had achieved a reputation for trenchant criticism. Grant's weekly was published in February 1864 with a stirring denunciation of contemporary journalism as 'clap-trap,' promised 'a series of brilliant articles' in the style of its British forerunner, and continued in a mood of euphoria. 'The cause is great, glorious, almost divine. Dunedin has risen, as if by the wand of a magician, like an exhalation from the quagmire of a stolid village, to the proportion of a grand city that is destined to play the part of Athens in New Zealand' – memorable words when one considers the date of the city's foundation. Its initial issue was of five hundred copies, and it is a tribute to Grant's stamina that he maintained what was almost entirely a personal document for seven years at a high level of discourse, although the original note of optimism degenerated into diatribes against the establishment, deeply religious and doom-laden. The journal does, however, provide social, political, and intellectual documentation of urban colonial life in an almost entirely Scottish settlement, as it moved toward metropolitan status; an example is the serial extracts entitled 'Sibylline Leaves from the Diary of a Philosopher' throughout the issues of 1868 and later. Not satisfied with that, Grant launched a supplementary periodical, the *Delphic Oracle* (1866–70), and went on to publish the *Stoic* (1871–7) – the titles are significant – the *Dunedin Review* (1882–3), and his *Literary Magazine* (1885), all marked by idiosyncrasy. Grant did in fact enter public life in the 1870s as a member of the Provincial Council, and as an unsuccessful parliamentary candidate, dying in poverty in 1903. His difficult temperament is perhaps best illustrated by his verdict on the death of Dickens in 1870: 'The soul sickens, languishes and dies after inhaling the lethal poison of this spurious novel literature.'

More positive notes were struck with the accomplishment of the university. Among its first fruits was the *New Zealand Magazine: A Quarterly Journal of General Literature* (1876–7), founded with high hopes, with an editorial board drawn largely from university personnel, and published in the four main centres. Its 'Introductory' staked its claim as a necessary competitor with 'that host of periodicals that come to us with each mail [from overseas],' and as a provider of space in successive numbers for 'the most contrary arguments from the most thoughtful and farsighted colonists [who] understand how greatly the problems and conditions before them differ from the problems and conditions that beset thinkers in the old countries.' Thus, it welcomed 'the prolonged and searching examination' of matters such as 'capital' and 'labour' as areas for research. 'So long,' it continued, 'as we have fresh thought and valuable argument for or against anything in heaven above or the earth beneath, it will be welcomed: but a mere dray-load of second-hand quiddities this Magazine will not be.' Dangerous sentiments in a Presbyterian environment. Its ambitions were indeed high, since it saw itself in the context of named British journals: the *Contemporary*, the *Quarterly*, *Fraser's*, the *Fortnightly*, and the *Westminster*, three of which were disturbingly radical. Unquestionably it ranked well ahead of any previous New Zealand periodical as it ranged over 'Darwin's Theology,' 'Evolutionist Ethics,' 'The Problem of Poverty in New Zealand,' and political theory. Among its contributors was Robert Stout, later knighted, who became a powerful force in the colony's politics and education, and as Prime Minister. Regrettably, its coverage of literature was minimal and somewhat abstruse; pitched too high, the *Magazine* lasted a mere five issues.

Two years later, the university's influence was again directly obvious in the forty-eight-page *New Zealand Journal of Science* (1882–5) at two shillings a copy by subscription. The monthly was explicit 'devoted to the furtherance of Pure and Applied Science throughout the Colony,' rejecting the 'Popular Science' so much a part of current newspapers and magazines. Its relative longevity was a tribute to its editors, while the extent of its circulation at the time of its demise is interesting: 35 per cent in Otago, 14 per cent in Canterbury, 14 per cent in Wellington (at that stage without a university), 14 per cent in Auckland, 8 per cent in Hawke's Bay, and 7 per cent in Australia. It was revived briefly in 1891.

From the same milieu emerged the *Otago University Review* (1888–93), issued monthly during term time. It covered university activities throughout the colony, and also included articles of significant interest, such as 'Colonial Literature,' where the hope was expressed 'that some day we too may possess a national literature.' A similar aspiration was the basis of its contemporary, less academic periodical, *Zealandia: A Monthly Magazine of New Zealand Literature by New Zealand Authors* (1888–90), committed to bringing forward 'the very large amount of literary talent which is known to exist here,' and the exclusion of the 'altogether superfluous productions of English authors.' True to its aims, its contents were indeed entirely of New Zealand interest and origin: fiction, poetry, essays, and natural history, with specialists 'to meet the requirements of our ladies, our girls, our boys, and our chess and draught players.' And unlike J.G.S. Grant, the editor avowed allegiance in sentiment to Charles Dickens and 'other British master-minds of literature.' What is impressive is that three eminent politicians, Robert Stout, Pember Reeves, and Thomas Bracken – the last two poets – were among contributors. In spite of their eminence, and in spite of twenty-seven agents within the colony and in Australia, *Zealandia* lacked charisma, sickened, and so died. In his farewell the editor had to be contented with the fact that it had been 'a disinterested effort to foster a national literature.' In this it was neither the first nor the last.

The longest lasting of the end-of-century secular periodicals was, in fact, the *Triad: A Monthly Magazine of Music, Science and Art* (1893–1915), edited by Charles Baeyertz, a forceful member of Dunedin's intelligentsia. Its mode was moderate satire – 'Satire's my weapon, but I'm too discreet / To run amuck, and tilt at all I meet' – and met with considerable support. Its coverage of the colony was remarkable, and it is a valuable source of information about New Zealand's cultural life over twenty years. Interesting also is that it placed that culture in the wider context of European, American, and Australian periodicals, unashamed 'to quote copiously.'

There were interesting experiments elsewhere than in Dunedin, as in the case of the *Maoriland Review: A Journal of Fact, Fun and Fiction* (1894), edited by C. Clarke Irons in Christchurch, a little magazine reminiscent of the British nineties. 'We feel,' wrote the editor, 'that a colonial home journal is required ... Both recent settlers and native-born will appreciate our efforts. ... The contents will be selected to please all readers,' to entertain and instruct. Yet a New Zealand short story, 'Verses for Recitation,' 'Savage and Cultural, Ornamental and Decorative Art,' and 'Experiences of Emigrants' were in vain, and it vanished without comment.

In Wellington, the 1880s were also marked by a number of serious-minded periodicals. The *Aeronaut* (1881) (a word at the time associated with balloonists) appeared, published from the Atheneum Hall, an ambitious monthly with an address to the public: 'The want has long been felt of a publication of this description, both as an object of amusement and instruction, and as the vehicle for the circulation of a considerable amount of local talent, which has been dormant from the dearth of opportunity for its dissemination.' Local content indeed there was, including a sentimental poem on Wellington's cemetery, and a short story entitled 'Polly

Plumbridge's Courtship and Marriage,' in a setting 'not 200 miles from the city.' Other stories, however, illustrate the fatal attraction of the 'Old Country,' and the periodical did not survive the year.

In the same decade, two enterprising booksellers, William Lyon and John Rutherford Blair, had better fortune with a sequence of periodicals. The *Era* (1881), in format a newspaper, began with the familiar introduction: 'Wellington has for years been virtually without any publication giving either a reliable or an interesting summary of the week's news.' Strictly liberal, it covered the main interests of the city, including sport, and disavowed trivia such as 'Society' – 'We leave such nasty remarks to Auckland and Canterbury.' Its 'Telegraphic Summary' gave an international dimension, the whole leavened by illustrations and serial fiction. Its format was, however, clearly inappropriate, and its life was all too brief. There followed a somewhat strange venture, largely the product of Blair's own interest in mysticism and eastern religions. *Hestia* (1888) (the name of an important Greek goddess and the word used by the Greeks for the sacred fire distinguishing men from animals) appeared briefly, devoted to 'the Teaching of the Ancient Sages and the Philosophy and Study of Science.' After four issues Blair was forced to admit that it was too restricted to his personal taste, and incorporated it into a third periodical, the *Monthly Review* (1888–90). On this occasion there was an editorial committee which represented several different schools of thought. Didactic in tone, the journal's contents were made up of original articles, excerpts from European and American philosophers, reviews of New Zealand publications of suitable stature, and most significant, a regular Maori feature, by a Maori, about Maori affairs. A minor component was occasional fiction and verse. It was, in all, a significant attempt to found a review along the lines of the British *Contemporary*.

Wellington's weekly *Critic* (1899) was more ambitious, launched with something of a fanfare as 'an illustrated semi-political, social and literary paper,' 'a high-class artistic journal of interest to all sections of the community.' Its editor, Thomas Cottle, 'well-known throughout Australia and New Zealand,' would work with an equally well known artist, Alan Souter; its contents were to be 'illustrated short stories, sketches and verses by New Zealanders, Australians and others.' Wellington had been chosen as 'the postal centre of Maoriland,' a significant use of the word which indicates the sentimental attitude beginning to be adopted toward the indigenous race. 'There is no good reason,' it continued, 'why Maorilanders should depend solely, as at present, upon Australia for their literary market,' a criticism well supported by the presence of so many New Zealand writers in the Sydney *Bulletin* and *Australian Magazine*.

Contributors were indeed to receive 'liberal payment.' Process and pho-
togravure were used for illustrations, which included photographs of
New Zealand troops taking part in the Boer War. In many respects, the
Critic communicates the same *joie de vivre* as the Auckland *Graphic*,
yet it succumbed to the New Zealand malaise. In 'Vale,' in its seventeenth issue, the editor commented, 'The best paper, from the literary
and artistic point of view, which has ever been issued in New Zealand'
had foundered from lack of money, owing to the colony's limited population and, significantly, to 'a most regrettable provincial feeling'; 'a decade
ahead of its time' is something of an understatement.

At the turn of the century, Auckland ventured into competition with
British monthlies such as the *Strand*, founded in 1891. The *New Zealand
Illustrated Magazine* (1899–1905) was embellished with plentiful illustrations of scenery and personalities, line drawings illustrating fiction,
and significant coverage of the Maori people and their culture, from the
point of view of 'Our Empire.' Like the *Graphic*, it mirrored contemporary society and attitudes in its mixture of running features, but its demise was inevitable though delayed. As with almost all New Zealand
magazines, imported periodicals exerted their fatal attractions, and the
Magazine found it impossible to fight, 'with any prospect of success,
against the shoals of English and American magazines [one might add
the Sydney *Bulletin*] flooding the market.' It was, nevertheless, dull.

The monotonous frequency with which the majority of New Zealand's
secular periodicals failed to achieve a sustaining readership was clearly
not due to general illiteracy, and only partly due to life-styles. The conclusion must be that imported British periodicals in particular, from
scholarly reviews through to popular magazines, largely satisfied the
reading public, and maintained a strong cultural hold on New Zealand's
attachment to 'the Old Country.' At the same time, the contents of British magazines in particular tended to be replicated in colonial publications. These are clearly matters for investigation.

RELIGIOUS, TEMPERANCE, AND SUFFRAGE PERIODICALS

A substantial amount of New Zealand's periodical literature was provided by a multiplicity of church groupings, unconstrained by an established church, as in Britain. Such journals had a profound effect on
social attitudes.

The first were those published by missions to the Maori, such as the
Maori Messenger of 1840. The Anglicans published their first *New Zealand Almanac* in 1845, the Evangelicals their *New Zealand Evangelist* in

1848, the Methodists their *Christian Observer* in 1870, the Catholics their *New Zealand Tablet* in 1873, the Congregationalists the *Congregational Magazine* in 1872, the Free Thought and Secular Movement their *Echo* in 1880 and *Freethought Review* in 1883, the New Zealand Mission their *Missionary Record* in 1882, the Presbyterians their *Presbyterian Magazine* in 1866, the Salvation Army their *War Cry* in 1883, and the Theosophists their *New Zealand Theosophical Magazine* in 1900.

Pride of place belongs to the monthly *New Zealand Evangelist* (July 1848–June 1849), published by ministers of the Evangelical Alliance from the office of the Wellington *Independent*, eighteen months before the secular *New Zealand Magazine* (see above). It was deliberately patterned on periodicals in 'the old and settled countries ... to meet the needs of the new colony, where books were scarce, the population scattered, often with little opportunity to attend public worship or to read, and, importantly, too exposed to the secularizing influences of colonial life.' Thus, there were to be articles, reviews, biographies, and anecdotes, all tending to Christian living. The personalia so dealt with are extremely revealing, as are the statistics which led to the foundation of the Total Abstinence Society. In October 1848, for a total Wellington population of 4,500, 15,000 gallons of spirits had been imported in the previous six months, together with 9,000 gallons of ale, beer, and port, exclusive of local manufactured alcohol. As a distraction from such excess, the regular feature 'Christian Amusement' offered 'Gardening,' which does indeed give an insight into the problems of antipodean horticulture. The last issue ends in a burst of spleen, firstly against the prevalence of 'balls,' where 'youth, beauty and fashion are giving animation to the halls of revelry from the noon of night to the dawn of day;' and secondly, against settler society, where 'the manual is at a premium, and intellect at a discount. It is a commodity not wanted in the colonies. It is an impertinent intruder in the levelling system universally prevalent.' However, some seven years later, a third Wellington periodical appeared, the *New Zealand Quarterly Review and Magazine of General and Local Literature* (1857) briefly, from the office of the *Spectator*. Again, it had a religious base. With seventy-two pages at 2s.6d., it was a trim document, obtrusively Anglican, but deservedly perished with its third issue: too expensive, too sectarian, and too academic.

The 1870s saw, as in so many things, a major movement in denominational publications. One of the longest surviving was the Christchurch monthly *New Zealand Church News* (1870–1911), modelled on Anglican periodicals in eastern Australia. Its aim was 'to establish a bond of union and an organ of communication among the scattered members of the

Church of England through the colony of New Zealand'; and, significantly, 'to do away with the sense of isolation' and 'to develop a healthy opinion on matters of common concern.' Its coverage included English, Australian, and New Zealand dioceses, leavened by appropriately religious fiction and verse. It is also of interest on matters outside theology.

In Auckland considerable effort had been put into editing the monthly *Church Gazette* (1869–74), with expectations of 'hearty' lay co-operation. One of its principal objects was to keep New Zealand Anglicanism informed of developments in the Church of England, so reducing dependence on church periodicals from that source. Instead, it made an attempt to escape from doctrinal matters to a family collection of short stories, 'A Page for the Young,' and original 'Select Poetry.' It circulated widely in the North Island. In Auckland also there appeared the monthly *New Zealand Presbyterian Magazine* (1872), a journal representing 'The Presbyterian Church of New Zealand,' alternative to the 'Free Church' migrants to Dunedin. As such it covered the presbyteries of Auckland, Canterbury, Hawke's Bay, Wellington, and Westland. Although it was of brief duration, its twelve issues form an essential document in the church's history. Its 'Children's Corner' is a touching attempt to palliate its rather dour doctrinalism. Dunedin's own *New Zealand Presbyterian/The Christian Outlook: A Family Paper* (1894–8)/*The Outlook* (1898–1987) was a major journal, circulating throughout both Islands. In addition to homiletic material, it contained serials, short stores, and social comment. By contrast, the Auckland Congregationalist *Home Circle: A Magazine for the People* (1895), linked with the Young People's Society of Christian Endeavour, succeeded, in spite of serial fiction and 'Children's Portion,' in being remarkably dull. Not so the *New Zealand War Cry* (1883), the 'Official Gazette of the Salvation Army,' published in conjunction with the foundation of the Army's first corps in Dunedin. At the turn of the century, an ecumenical illustrated journal, the *Young Man's Magazine* (1899–1903), was launched in Wellington, adding science and medicine to the usual fare.

An interesting maverick, the *Comforter* (1890–3), should be added to the list. It provides a study in charisma. Samuel Oakly Crawford, a veteran of the American Civil War who subsequently trained for the Christian ministry, sought refuge in Christchurch in January 1890, having been accused of, and pursued by police in his own country for, no fewer than eight charges of bigamy. In New Zealand he added to his numerous aliases by adopting the name of Worthington, and was later joined by a Mrs Plunkett. With remarkable aplomb, preaching a gospel of pseudo–Christian Science, he attracted a following sufficiently large to fund the erection of a Temple of Truth, reputedly to hold a congregation of sixteen hundred. A year later a school for seven hundred pupils was constructed, followed by a social hall for one thousand persons. His official mouthpiece was the *Comforter*, a rhapsody of self-adulation. As revelations of his past percolated to the city fathers, however, attempts were made to persuade the United States police to apply for extradition. Whether it was gained or not, Worthington fled to Tasmania, returning briefly in 1897, and was subsequently jailed for seven years in 1902. He emerged in New York, to swindle his Presbyterian congregation, and to die in jail in 1917. While St Peter may have had a problem, Christchurch was the recipient of quite useful real estate, the last building being demolished in the 1960s.

New Zealand was not, however, without anti-Christian sentiment, as evidenced by the *Rationalist: A Weekly Freethought Paper* (1885–6) published in Auckland. In format a newspaper, it is catalogued as a periodical. Its four promoters financed the enterprise, and encountered such antagonism after the first fifteen issues that their original printer refused to continue. Their expedient was a common one, to operate their own press. Although anti-Christian and anti-sabbatarian, it continued to receive support from its advertisers, but was doomed. It provides a fascinating commentary on contemporary mores during its all-too-brief currency.

One major issue echoing through the religious journals, as far back as *New Zealand Evangelist* of 1848, was that of alcholism. In the last three decades of the century a whole genre of prohibition journals came into being. The Christchurch *Christian Labourer: A Monthly Temperance Journal* was launched in 1877 'in harmony with the Teachings of God, Science and Experience.' Its first issue attacked not merely drunkenness in Britain and New Zealand but smoking also, and it published a rousing poem, 'Ye British Workmen! England's Hope and Pride.' In Auckland there appeared the weekly *Leader* (1885–), 'published in the interests of Christian and Temperance Work,' with substantial coverage of the Good Templar movement, the Anti-Poverty Society and the Band of Hope. It had strong links with similar movements in Melbourne. Its leading articles, generally on the main theme, were buttressed by serial fiction and the inevitable 'original poetry'; Louisa M. Alcott appears in its pages. On the same lines, Dunedin was served by the *Temperance Herald, Good Templar Record and Blue Ribbon Chronicle* (1878–91), with leading articles, and world coverage of Temperance societies. Its captions could be alarming ('Sin! Sin! Sin!'), and were combined with diatribes against alcoholic sacramental wine and minatory tales of alcoholism.

Further weight was added to the campaign by the foundation of a branch – the first of many – of the Women's Christian Temperance Union in Dunedin in 1885, with a pronounced feminist bias. In Christchurch was published the fortnightly *Prohibitionist* (1890–1906), subsequently the *Vanguard* (1907–54), 'The Organ of the Sydenham Prohibition League,' less overtly religious, but advocating total prohibition. In due course, with an increasing variety of content, it achieved a wide circulation which lasted for more than sixty years. Temperance Union branches reinforced those of the Good Templars and the Bands of Hope, taking under their wing the current agitation for women's suffrage. The logic was simple: alcoholism was predominantly male, and the victims were wives and families.

Most prominent in both suffragist and prohibition movements was Mrs Kate Sheppard, remarkably adept in the organization of rallies and petitions. After the grant of franchise to women in 1893, Mrs Sheppard went from strength to strength. In company with a 'Miss Powell' and a 'Miss Smith,' she launched the monthly *White Ribbon* (1895–1965) under various subtitles: with 'For God and Home and Humanity' as its battle-cry, and 'In the Master's Name,' it was a landmark in feminist journalism. Though published in Christchurch, it carried Kate Sheppard's charisma into the Union's branches in the many large and small towns throughout the country; and with its message as to the extent of the problem and with its world-wide links, it spoke with authority. With singular appropriateness, in the euphoria of the Centennial of New Zealand Women's Enfranchisement, it was Kate Sheppard's image which replaced that of Her Majesty the Queen on the 1993 ten-dollar note.

In Wellington the Evangelical Forward Movement was founded, with the monthly *Citizen* (1895–6) as its journal. Less confined to prohibition, its aim was 'to attempt to bring the cardinal principles of Christianity to bear on the complex conditions of modern society.' The Foundation to which it was attached was modelled on the Mansfield Settlement in London's Canning Town, 'warring in the master's Name against all evil – selfishness, injustice, vice, disease, starvation, ignorance, ugliness and squalor.' It was allied in viewpoint to two well-known radicals, A.R. Atkinson and Sir Robert Stout, in its attack on orthodox political economy. Lady Stout herself contributed an article on 'The New Woman.' Essentially Wellington in provenance, the Movement worked through public lectures on social matters.

In marked contrast was the equally short lived weekly, *Fair Play: An Illustrated Journal for Sensible Men and Women* (1893–4), which declared itself to be 'against prohibition of any kind,' and was determined to attract 'the best known' colonial writers, as well as to serialize British fiction. It was unsuccessful. A similar attitude was taken up in New Plymouth, where the *Stockwhip* was founded in 1899, specifically to counter 'costive' local journals. Light-heartedly it shrugged off teetotalism with 'Pills for Prohibitionists,' published a satiric song complete with music, rejoiced in political cartoons, and serialized 'the Taranki Farmer.' Needless to say, it failed within the year, but it makes a pleasant comparison with its predecessor, the *Taranaki Punch*.

The churches' contribution to the intellectual life of the colony is manifest in a number of denominational journals, roughly at the level of the British *Spectator*. The most notable was the Catholic *New Zealand Tablet* (1873–), located in the stronghold of Presbyterianism, Dunedin, and important as representing an influx of Catholics from Ireland. Excellently edited and produced, it claimed to be 'eminently loyal and respectful to the grand old Church,' with the great object of ascertaining 'what is true and good, and to defend these and the sacred cause of justice.' It was right in its assumption that it had 'a sphere for itself,' and it produced some of the most interesting journalism of the period. Forthright in its criticism, it had a colony-wide circulation. Its commentaries ranged over current affairs, showed a marked interest in Irish politics, with no great love for Britain, and had much to say on such matters as education. Its reviews of current literature were substantial, and its leading articles pitched at a high level of discourse. For lighter reading it provided serial fiction, poetry, and a variety of short notes. In all, it was a formidable accession to colonial journalism.

Denominational balance was to some extent redressed by the *Protestant Ensign: A Record of Religion, Science, Politics, Commerce and Reform* (1887–) aimed, significantly, 'to present the Protestant view of passing events, and keep its aims before the public.' Somewhat later it adopted a more heroic stance, 'to enable the banner of Truth and Freedom to fly freely over our young land.' Published, like the *Tablet*, in Dunedin, it was ably edited, and provided leading articles, verse, fiction, syndicated reprints, and regular features such as 'The Family Circle.' There are times, however, when denominational bias detracts from its general standards, as in the matter of state aid to schools. In June 1889 it produced statistics gleaned from an 1886 census of the aggregate membership of the churches, 502,946 in all. Broken down according to denomination, the statistics reveal 233,369 Anglicans, 80,715 Catholics, 130,643 Presbyterians, 55,292 Methodists, and 3,925 Free Thinkers, figures interesting in themselves. Further analysis went on to identify criminal offending according to denomination: 198 Anglicans, 145 Catholics,

47 Presbyterians, 17 Methodists, and 18 Free Thinkers. On a proportional basis, therefore, Catholics were more prone to crime and should be deprived of their subsidies: a debatable conclusion. Other denominational journals are identifiable in Peter Lineham's *A Religious History of New Zealand: A Bibliography*, third edition, 1989.

The last decade of the nineteenth century saw a great deal of political activity, against the background of considerable labour unrest: the first maritime strike of 1890, although unsuccessful, was ominous. There were also the major achievements of extending the franchise to women and the introduction of Old Age Pensions. New Zealand's social welfare gained an international reputation, influential Fabian socialists visiting the colony in 1898.

This political activity was reflected not merely in the press but in specifically political journals. In Auckland there appeared *Forward! In the Cause of Humanity* (1895–6), with a brief change of title to the *New Zealand Worker: A Social and Democratic Weekly* (February–December 1896). Its aim was to propagate socialism throughout the colony and 'to afford a medium of comradeship and union between all progressionists and workers in the cause of humanity.' Advocating 'Scientific Socialism,' and with a wide range of interest, it makes sound, intelligent, and entertaining reading. In a new series, illustrated by photographs and enlivened by fiction and verse, it nevertheless ended reluctantly, in spite of the need for 'a paper which probes to the root of the political, social and industrial problems of the day.' Somewhat prematurely, the *Auckland Ladies' Political Journal* (1893) appeared for one issue only.

In Dunedin, in newspaper format, there had appeared *New Zealand Life* (1892), professedly apolitical: 'We deal with Life rather than Party,' to make 'a fair and honest effort to put before [the Reasonable Public] fair and honest issues.' A very witty journal, it covered a wide range of social and political issues, laced with fiction and verse, and deserved a longer run. Its defeat was signalled by superimposing 'DEATH' over its frontal masthead 'LIFE,' and the lament, 'We were born before our time ... lack of money, not of matter.' It saw itself as having been defeated by 'party' allegiances. Some four years later, in the same city, the quarto weekly *Democrat* (1896–8) was launched, with avowedly political commitment to the politician Richard Seddon's interest. Part of its attraction lay in its cartoons and half-tone illustrations. Indeed, it encouraged amateurs to submit their own cartoons. Political leading articles, coverage of theatre, housewifery, sport, yachting, and fiction make it an interesting commentary on the decade. Unfortunately, with illusion of grandeur, it was enlarged by four pages in March 1898 and adopted the title of the

English *Sketch* (1893). 'Truth is our Motto,' however, did not prevail, and it faded ignominiously from the scene.

Christchurch, the focal point of affluent settler society, briefly hosted a left-wing monthly, the *Socialist* (August–October 1897), a four-page quarto edited by H.A. Atkinson. Advocating trade unionism, and urging the foundation of a New Party, it lacked compulsion, and was reduced to mere reprints of others' material.

In many ways the most notable political journal proved to be the weekly *Daybreak* (1895–6), an eight-page quarto edited by Louisa Adams and published in Wellington. 'Written by Women for Women about Women,' on behalf of the local Women's Social and Political League, it saw its function as spreading 'knowledge amongst the women of Wellington on the political questions of the day,' most appropriate in the parliamentary centre of government and in the aftermath of women's franchise. Its proud boast was that of 'the first newspaper published in New Zealand, not only in the interests of women, but edited and carried on by the weaker sex,' an echo of the Dunedin Women's Franchise League's expressed objective 'to collect and diffuse information on Social, Economical and Political Subjects.' Indeed, totally serious in content, its copy was made up of leading articles on public and domestic affairs, dealing with such matters as wages, careers (architecture, business), and maternal problems in dealing with boys' upbringing. Although it survived for merely fifty-one issues, it is a critical document in the history of the emancipation of women.

Representative of gratis political publications is Wellington's weekly *Watchman* (1896), 'A Weekly Journal devoted to the interests of Good Government and the General Welfare of the Community.' Published in an election year, it espoused the cause of Sir Robert Stout, provided information on candidates, contained satirical verse and a short story by the British writer G.B. Burgin, and generally supported prohibitionism.

MISCELLANEA

With increasing frequency, periodicals associated with professions, occupations, societies, and pastimes appeared. By no means all of them survive, but wherever an investigation is possible there are always matters of interest.

For instance, the consistent source of New Zealand's wealth has been the production and export of primary products. In Auckland in 1882 the *New Zealand Cattle and Land Buyers Guide* was founded and then retitled the *New Zealand Farmer, Bee and Poultry Journal* in 1885, an illustrated thirty-two page monthly in newspaper format. It gives detailed coverage of agriculture, horticulture, livestock, fruit, and dairy produce; its line drawings of flora and fauna are impressive, while its lighter features of 'Jocosities,' 'Story Teller,' poetry, and serials give another side of rural life, infused with firm support of the British Empire. In Christchurch the literature was more elaborate. The quarterly *New Zealand Country Journal* (1877–98), with seventy-two octavo pages, published by the Canterbury Agricultural and Pastoralists Association, serviced 'Racing, Shooting, Cricket, Boating and many other manly sports' for the house of 'every country gentleman who is imbued with the true spirit' of English country life; it modestly disclaimed 'any extraordinary merit.' In Christchurch also was launched the illustrated *New Zealand Referee: A Journal of Sport, Music and the Drama* in 1884, covering not merely New Zealand but Australian and British events. Under a change of title as the *Weekly Press and Sporting Record* it continued until 1913. Outdoor life had undoubted attractions, as demonstrated by Wellington's *New Zealand Field Journal devoted to Sports and Pastimes* (1896–7). It aimed to provide 'a complete record of all the principal sports and pastimes,' enumerated as 'Chess, Gold, Football, Shooting, Rowing, Yachting, Fishing, Cycling, Gardening, Wrestling, Cricket, Poultry, Pigeons, Billiards, Athletics, and Aquatics'; surely, here was Utopia. As the editor reflected, 'Half a century ago it was deemed impossible that pastimes and business could go hand in hand as a great factor in wealth of the Colony.' Its wealthy directors, all named, claimed the journal as 'the only paper of its kind in the Colony.' As with so many euphoric publications, lack of support caused its closure in July 1897. An interesting combination of outdoor activity and patriotism is to be found in the Christchurch monthly, the *New Zealand Volunteer Gazette and Marksman's Record* (1895–7), largely devoted to military matters, including Australian news. In addition it provided statistics of the colony's volunteer corps, smallest in Wellington at 501, highest in Dunedin, a relic of the Land Wars that was to be utilized in the Empire's involvement in the South African Boer War.

One prestigious extension of outdoor pastimes was the formation of the New Zealand Alpine Club in 1891, which operated throughout the colony's Southern Alps. The *New Zealand Alpine Journal* (1892–), 'A Record of Mountain Exploration and Adventure by Members of the New Zealand Alpine Club,' was conceived as a half-yearly publication, but was in fact somewhat sporadic. Nevertheless it stands as an impressive tribute to the pioneers who opened up the splendours of the territory.

At a more intellectual level, two learned societies published what are listed as periodicals. Under an Act of Parliament, the New Zealand Institute had been established in 1868, into which were admitted a number of incorporated societies. It was thus that papers delivered at their meetings were published annually in the *Transactions of the New Zealand Institute* from 1868 onwards. The extent of their activities is remarkable at such a time. The presence of the Wellington Philosophic Society, the Auckland Institute, the Philosophical Institute of Canterbury, the remote Westland Naturalists' Society, the Otago Institute, and the Nelson Association for the Promotion of Science and Industry underline the colony's early intellectual concerns. And the publication of the *Journal of the Polynesian Society*, a substantial quarterly, from 1892 onwards is a landmark in the wider appreciation of Polynesian culture in the Pacific from Hawaii southward.

At a less exalted level there are relics of the advance of public education in the *Monthly Record and Educational Gazette* (1874–5), published in Wellington, a sixteen-page quarto sponsored by the Education Board for the enlightenment of teachers. The surviving copies have a minimal pedagogic content, but a wide variety of subject matter, such as a serial account of the execution of the martyred King ('The Head of Charles II'), witty letters such as 'A letter from Mr Paul Pry to Dr Pangloss, A.S.S., L.L.D.,' and the inevitable poetry. J.H. Newlyn, its editor, perhaps naïvely, offered 'to insert all Articles, Essays, Lectures, Letters and General Correspondence,' which suggests an educated readership; in vain.

There is one outstanding trade-inspired periodical, of direct interest to bibliophiles: Coupland Harding's *Typo* (1887–97), 'a Monthly Newspaper and Literary Record devoted to the Advancement of Typographic Art.' It is a revelation of the typographical resources available at the century's end to skilled printers. The covers of annual volumes have elaborate borders, delicate vignettes, brilliant colour, and ornate capitals. Each issue, of a mere six pages, supports Harding's declaration of intent: 'It is our design to issue a journal representative of the printing, publishing, bookselling, stationery and kindred interests.' On the completion of 'Our First Volume' he could claim, 'In the whole of the Australian colonies there is no other periodical offering a similar field of interest.' It was unquestionably a major force in New Zealand, and it also circulated in Australia. It gained an international reputation, being published in London as well as in Wellington, whither it transferred in 1891. Its information about the industry and its personnel is indispensable.

MAORI NEWSPAPERS AND PERIODICALS

The distinction between the two categories is best waived in the light of frequent variations in format and irregularity of publication. During the period 1842–1901, at least thirty-six periodicals were published throughout the North Island, and at least one in the South, at some twelve different locations; Auckland is listed as having thirteen, of which four were reincarnations of the first, and Gisborne, Napier, and Wellington four each. The majority of these fall outside the scope of this chapter, being written entirely in Maori.

Politics, the familiar shortage of printing presses, and the limitations of language and readership mainfestly influenced publication. In chronological order, the first and most important was *Te Karere o Niu Tireni: The Maori Messenger* (1842–63), sponsored by the government and (during the period 1842–6) under the editorship of the Protector of Aborigines, Dr Edward Shortland, younger brother of Lieutenant Willoughby Shortland, RN, the unpopular Colonial Secretary. It was manifestly official, its masthead carrying the Royal Arms. Its text was contained in four vertical columns of alternating Maori and English, well-meaning and in a diction reminiscent of the King James Bible. Its second editor was Charles Oliver Davis, who had assisted as interpreter in the Waitangi negotiations, and subsequently became chief government translator. Successive outbreaks of hostilities caused temporary abandonments. Its third incarnation (1855–61) was a sixteen-page two-columned quarto, with an extraordinarily wide coverage of information, including a 'Foreign Intelligence' feature covering Britain, Russia, America, and Turkey, among other countries. It was particularly outspoken on white outrages against 'The Maori People of New Zealand,' – for example, the murder of a 'native woman' by a brutal sawyer. Its somewhat complacent paternalism is manifest in such statements as 'Formerly, before the pakeha [European] came to this island, the Maori people were living in ignorance and killing each other' and in exhortations to Maori parents to have their children educated in English as part of the accepted policy of assimilation. More generally it counselled the Tribes 'to give up injurious superstition.' Again, the linguistic mode was biblical. The paper's final appearance as *Te Karere Maori* (1861–3) was terminated by the increasing hostilities of the Land Wars.

The second such periodical of note was Hugh Carleton's *Anglo-Maori Warder* (1848), in twenty-six issues, published in opposition to government policies, with the Latin tag *Nunquam non paratus* (Never unprepared). A four-column weekly journal, part in English, part in Maori, its projected readership was an over-optimistic five thousand, whom it addressed rather blandly: 'Good morning to you all, kind friends, to all of you to whom this paper may come, to all natives of this country. We who write this are English. We love you, we love our own nation.' It had lofty ambitions, 'to render the Maori a fit and civilized associate of his fellow British subjects.' Carleton was a product of Eton and Cambridge, and abandoned his self-imposed task after six months. Nevertheless, he went on to edit the *Southern Cross*, entered politics, prompted the establishment of universities, and became the first vice-chancellor of the University of New Zealand in 1871.

Some early periodicals are known only by repute. *He Nupepa Maori: Ko Te Ao Marama* [A Maori Newspaper: The World of Enlightenment] is known to have existed at least from September to December 1849. It was published by the *Wellington Independent*, and was edited by one Henry Tacey Kemp, an interpreter from the Bay of Islands. Its aim was 'to foster a spirit of industry among the Natives to acquaint them with the circumstances of their white neighbours.' It would clearly be of interest if discovered.

In 1857 there began an intermittent series of *Wakas* (the word generally used to signify canoe, particularly the large, many-oared war canoe), many completely in Maori, and published in provincial districts where there were substantial Maori communities. The symbol of the 'waka' provided an outstanding, highly significant and politically ominous masthead.

Charles Davis re-entered the field at the time of the Taranaki unrest with his Anglo-Maori publication, *Ko Aotearoa, or The Maori Recorder* (1861–62). Significantly, it was printed at the Aotearoa Office on the one Maori printing press in Auckland, as against the five available to Europeans. Its aim was to instruct and enlighten the Maori people, and in the process, to attack 'the Newspapers' for their antagonism toward 'the Natives.' Although the text is increasingly in Maori, the English sections provide valuable contemporary attitudes to Maori tradition and culture.

The 1860s also saw the development of the Maori King movement in the Waikato, with supportive periodicals. *Te Hokioi e Niu Tirinui* [The Far-Flying Holioi of New Zealand], Maori-edited and Maori-printed at Ngaruawahia, was seen as seditious, and was countered by the government publication *Te pihoihoi Mokemoke i Runga i te Tuanui* in 1863 for five issues, at which point warfare erupted. Both were in Maori, and saw the virtual end of Maori periodicals until the 1870s. Thereafter they steadily increased, the majority totally in Maori. Two, however, come within the scope of this chapter: *Te Korimako* [The Bell Bird] (1882–8), a monthly financed by the American philanthropist W.P. Snow, edited by Charles Davis, and published in Auckland, was addressed 'To the Maori People of Aotearoa extended to all places.' Snow continued, 'I am going forth in search of you. I have seen the evil of the decadence of your manhood,' and he vowed to seek out some means of raising them and establishing 'the ascendancy of good.' Equally, he exhorted Europeans living in the country to support this program. After the first issue, however, there was little in English.

With similar intentions, but with more realistic prospects, the weekly *Te Puke i Hikurangi* [The Hill of Hikurangi] (1898–1907), was for the 'advancement' of the Maori People, coedited by T. Renata and R.S. Thompson, a pro-Maori interpreter. Originally published half in Maori and half in English, it was dedicated to the vindication of Maori rights, and dealt with Polynesian history and ethnology. Again, its abandonment of English makes it generally inaccessible.

The most elaborate of Maori periodicals is a product of the 1890s, the *Jubilee: Te Tupiri* (1898–1900). Dr T.M. Hocken describes it as 'an excellent and loyal paper,' as indeed it was, being founded in the euphoria of Queen Victoria's Diamond Jubilee of 1897. A weekly published in Wanganui, it described itself as 'in the interest of the Europeans and Natives, launched on a sea of colonial journalism.' It was the product of an editorial committee of twenty-four Maori, and committed to an issue of fifteen hundred copies. Setting out the principles of its bilingual contents, the committee addressed its readers: 'We greet you, the tribes and families and chiefs dwelling in your courtyards in our two islands,' and blamed previous failures on half-heartedness. An inspiring leader in the issue of 1 February 1898, 'The Queen's Record Reign,' sang praises of the great Queen, while for some time the masthead was dominated by her portrait. As time passed Maori became the dominant language, but nevertheless the journal has much of interest as the mouthpiece of a subject race.

Guides to Research

PROVENANCE

The main repositories of New Zealand periodicals are those in Alexander Turnbull Library, within the National Library, Wellington; and the Hocken Library, administered within the University of Otago. Turnbull and Hocken were contemporary bibliophiles who bequeathed their collections to their home territories. Another major repository was the General Assembly (Parliamentary) Library, which by 1884 had already accumulated two thousand bound volumes of newspapers. This library was dispersed in 1990, its newspapers passing into the care of the Turnbull Library, Wellington, as part of the National Newspaper Collection. It should be noted that the British requirement that copies of all publications should be lodged in the British Museum, Bodleian, and Cambridge University Libraries, although theoretically applicable to the colonies, appears not to have operated in New Zealand.

The basic bibliography is Dr T.M. Hocken's *Bibliography of the Literature relating to New Zealand* (Wellington: Government Printer 1909), which contains annotated lists of newspapers and periodicals. Invaluable in spite of its obsolescence is the 'Union List of Serials in New Zealand Libraries,' third edition (1969), which in addition to locales covers annuals, learned journals, and government publications. Restricted to newspapers, and excluding religious and temperance journals, is R.D. Harvey's 'Union List of Newspapers Preserved in Libraries, Newspaper Offices and Museums' (1987) held in the Turnbull Library, which formed the basis of the catalogue of the National Newspaper collection administered by the Turnbull Library. L.J. Coard's 'A List of New Zealand Serials to End of 1933 Held in the General Assembly and Alexander Turnbull Library' is useful for its list of annuals. Maori periodicals are covered by the small but significant internal research aid, 'Newspapers in Maori in the Alexander Turnbull Library.' The Turnbull Library's own catalogue of periodicals is in a state of transition, awaiting transfer to the database. Many but by no means all serials are accessible on microfilm.

Smaller repositories were the libraries attached to Mechanics' Institutes and Atheneums, generally used as the bases of public libraries proliferating later in the century. Those in the main provincial centres – Auckland, Wellington, Christchurch, Nelson, and Dunedin – still contain significant series. Holdings in lesser centres seem to have disappeared when storage space became limited. Other repositories are county councils, museums, learned societies, and university libraries. The main religious denominations have their own archives and collections.

STUDIES OF NEW ZEALAND SERIALS

Published material on newspapers and periodicals is comparatively limited.

The first major study was G.H. Scholefield's *Newspapers in New Zealand* (Wellington: Reed 1958), essential to an appreciation of the total scene, covering the general development of the press, its publications, its personnel, and its operation throughout the colony. References to periodicals are incidental, but valuable. Patricia Burns's *The Foundation of the New Zealand Press, 1839–1850* (Ph.D. Thesis, Victoria University 1957) provides a detailed history of the influences at work in the main centres, and the legacy of British newspapers. Patrick Day's *The Making of the New Zealand Press* (Wellington: Victoria University Press 1985) deals with the stress and strain in the development of main centre newspapers until the coming of age with the founding of the New Zealand Press Association in 1880. It provides a useful background for the 'stop-go' predicament of contemporary periodicals. Those newspapers surviving into the twentieth century generally celebrate their centennials as they fall due with brief and not-so-brief histories.

There is very little published material on New Zealand 'Periodicals' per se. What there is tends to be directed toward literary matters, and references are allusive rather than specific. *The Oxford History of Recent New Zealand Literature*, edited by Terry Strum (Oxford University Press 1991), contains four relevant essays: Jane McRae's 'Maori Literature: A Survey,' Peter Gibbons's 'Non-Fiction,' Lydia Wevers's 'The Short Story,' and Dennis McEldowney's 'Publishing, Patronage, Literary Magazines.' The first contains a very useful account of Maori literacy, the politics of Maori periodical publication, and the adaptation of oral tradition to the printed word. 'Non-Fiction' is principally concerned with printed volumes, with occasional reference to periodicals as their source, but provides a wider context in the history of ideas. 'The Short Story' is chiefly concerned with writers, as the most efficient way of dealing with a literary genre so prodigally published in the many journals of the era. Dennis McEldowney's essay, however, provides an important study of logistics, with useful references.

J.O.C. Phillips's 'Musings in Maoriland – or Was There a *Bulletin* School in New Zealand' in *Historical Studies* 20 (August 1983) takes up the question of trans-Tasman cross-fertilization from the popular Sydney *Bulletin*. His analysis shows how substantial was the contribution of New Zealand writers to its pages, and postulates a connection between the *Bulletin*'s popularity and the failure of New Zealand periodicals in competition. Ian Fraser Grant takes up the matter of graphics in his *Unauthorized Version: A Cartoon History of New Zealand* (Auckland: Cassell 1980), an entertaining and informative celebration of satire from the 1840s onwards.

There is a certain amount of unpublished material in the form of theses. In 1951 J.M. Wild submitted 'The Literary Periodical in New Zealand' for a master's degree, now held in the Victoria University Library. It contains a valuable annotated list of some forty-five magazines 'with some claim to be considered as literary,' including comic annuals and temperance magazines. In 1962 Iris Park-Worthington submitted 'New Zealand Periodicals of Literary Interest' for the New Zealand librarians' qualification, a study of thirty-six periodicals aiming 'to show the development of the literary magazine, and to indicate where New Zealand original writing may be found,' now held in the Turnbull Library. Its merits lie in its bibliographical and biographical information. The major contribution to the literary aspect of New Zealand cultural life is Dulcie N. Gillespie-Needham's PhD dissertation submitted to Victoria University of Wellington in 1971, 'The Colonial and His Books: A Study of Reading in Nineteenth Century New Zealand,' with its multiplicity of references. It is accessible in the university library. One specific periodical is the subject of a research essay by Greg Baughen in 'C.N. Baeyertz and *The Triad*,' held in Otago University Library.

HISTORICAL AND CULTURAL BACKGROUND

The following titles are suggested as particularly helpful:

Binney, J., J. Barrett, and E. Olssen, eds. *The People and the Land: An Illustrated History of New Zealand, 1820–1920*. Wellington: Allen and Unwin 1990.

Bloomfield, G.T. *New Zealand: A Handbook of Historical Statistics*. Boston, Mass.: G.K. Heath 1984.

Colless, Brian, and Peter Donovan, eds. *Religion in New Zealand Society*. Palmerson North: Dummors 1980.

McKay, R.A., ed. *The History of Printing in New Zealand, 1830–1940*. Wellington: R.A. McKay 1940. A rare book of Centennial essays.

McLaughlan, Gordon M., ed. *Illustrated Encyclopedia of New Zealand*. Auckland: David Bateman 1990. *The Dictionary of New Zealand Biography 1769–1869*. Wellington: Allen and Unwin 1990.

The New Zealand Journal. London (1840). A primary, contemporary source, available on microfilm.

SUGGESTED RESEARCH

The poverty of research into New Zealand serials, except allusively in the field of politics, suggests a low academic estimation of their significance. There are, however, manifest areas where research would illuminate the settlers' transition from Utopianism through the purgatory of a hostile environment, cultural isolation, and economic stringency to the imperial euphoria of the turn of the century. The inclusion of weekly newspapers and of supplementary issues releases a substantial amount of significant material, particularly in the case of journals published in Auckland and Dunedin, at a level not unworthy of major British reviews. There was an undoubted intelligentsia not afraid of entering into controversy on matters philosophical and religious, over and above routine provincial and colonial politics. At a less exalted level one might investigate the colony's phobia against the Russians and Chinese, while throughout the period the flux in attitude toward the aboriginal people manifest in all classes of periodicals, from the endemically hostile in early years to romantic pity for a 'dying race,' demands examination. In this context, the concept of 'Maoridom' as a kind of settler's paradise forms an ironic comment on the process of colonization. Such a study would be enriched by an analysis of graphic representations of the Maori. Maori periodicals are a separate matter, requiring both knowledge of the language and great sensitivity to their ethnic significance.

The growth of religious periodicals in company with a more sharply defined sectarianism from the late 1860s onwards suggests a division in society and a felt need for more explicit moral suasion. This was brought to a head during the formulation of the Education Act of 1877, whose declared policy that education be free, compulsory, and, notably, secular was a source of continuing concern to the churches. Contemporary with this was the almost global movement to ban the sale of alcohol. In New Zealand the propaganda was overwhelmingly religious, involving the churches both as political and as moral forces in the colony at large and in smaller communities. The moulding of popular attitudes on these and other matters certainly deserves attention, as indeed do the churches' own attitudes to the indigenous people.

The function of periodicals at large in fostering the cultural life of the colony was significant, and has been little explored. There is no study of them as literature in their own right, while they can be accused, owing to their publication of so much syndicated matter and their encouragement of material imitative of the popular fiction of imported magazines, of inhibiting the colony's own creative writing. Routinely, New Zealand writers adopted the class structure and settings of British fiction, with occasional excursions into North America and Australia. Magazine fiction utilizing the colony's own settings, Maori and pakeha, would benefit from analysis against such a background. As to verse, while it is overwhelmingly trite and derivative, there are themes and attitudes, as well as individual items, which may be rescued.

Finally, and with some small exceptions, little study has been made of the printing industry: plant, typography, the processes of illustration, personnel, and economics. Some justice has been done to the early presses, but the phenomenal growth from the 1870s onwards should provide a rich harvest. And there is the abiding problem of the colony's failure to provide any one periodical with which it might identify.

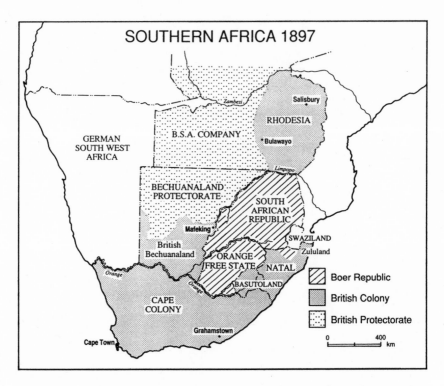

SOUTHERN AFRICA 1897

GERMAN SOUTH WEST AFRICA

B.S.A. COMPANY

Zambezi

Salisbury

RHODESIA

Bulawayo

Limpopo

BECHUANALAND PROTECTORATE

SOUTH AFRICAN REPUBLIC

Mafeking

SWAZILAND

British Bechuanaland

ORANGE FREE STATE

Zululand

NATAL

Orange

Orange

BASUTOLAND

CAPE COLONY

Grahamstown

Cape Town

Boer Republic

British Colony

British Protectorate

0   400
         km

South African Territories, 1895. Map by Philip Stickler, Chief Cartographer, Department of Geography and Environmental Studies, University of the Witwatersrand, Johannesburg. Reproduced by permission.

5

Southern Africa

BRIAN D. CHEADLE

Introduction

Of the four territories which came together as the Union of South Africa in 1910, only two, the Cape Colony and Natal, had been parts of the Victorian Empire, though the Transvaal had been under British annexation for a brief period between 1877 and 1881, and the Orange Free State had been similarly annexed between 1848 and 1853 as the Orange River Sovereignty.[1] Given the historical interrelation of the territories, however, it was obviously essential for this survey to include material from the Transvaal and the Orange Free State for the whole period. To avoid a crippling one-sideness, it was also important to take account of material in Dutch, in Afrikaans (which emerged as a written language toward the end of the century), and in the vernacular languages. A large number of the periodicals and newspapers were bilingual: even the *Cape Monthly Magazine*, the most important English periodical, published some verse in Dutch.

The Southern African territories beyond those which came together to form the Union of South Africa were developed late in the century (with the single exception of St Helena), and there is very little nineteenth-century periodical material from them. Consideration of these areas is thus held over to a brief section at the end, and the survey concentrates on the South African territories.

The dividing line between periodicals and newspapers is often tenuous, particularly in the early periods in each region when newspapers were often the only vehicle for comment and literary expression. The first newspapers at the Cape, for example, the *South African Commercial Advertiser* (1824–69) and the *South African Chronicle* (1824–6), published a good deal in the way of occasional verses and articles of general interest; and good examples of the kind of publication which aimed at being a compromise between a news journal and a literary magazine were *Sam Sly's African Journal* (1843–51), the *Cape Town Mirror* (1848–9), *Excalibur* (1886–90), and the *Cape Register* (1890–3), which described itself as 'a humorous, topical, sporting and critical journal, with cartoons, fashion articles, a London letter, stories, etc.' Later in the century many of the newspapers, including the *Cape Register*, produced special Christmas numbers which are virtually independent annuals. When, as in the Southern African situation, groups of people move off in loosely structured units in an effort to achieve independence, sometimes in a newly developing region the first publications, and often the only publications for a while, are rather broad-ranging kinds of 'government' gazettes and even religious almanacs. Periodicals form a continuum with many other kinds of serial publication, and it is important not to lose sight of the full range. It was not possible in this survey to take account of such additional materials; but as relatively little research has been done on nineteenth-century serials in Southern Africa, it seemed in the interest of researchers to include some account of the work done on newspapers, even though these were excluded from the description of specific titles. As there is very little material at all from the earliest years, the survey is taken back to the time of the first British occupation of the Cape in 1795.

Bibliographies of Victorian Periodicals Published in South Africa, 1824–1900

Unfortunately, the major bibliographical work which covers nineteenth-century South African materials, *A South African Bibliography to 1925*, four volumes (London: Mansell 1979) with a supplementary fifth volume (Cape Town: South African Library 1991), excludes periodicals and newspapers (though it includes much which is of incidental value in this regard). The work is arranged alphabetically by the names of authors and corporate bodies, and it also takes account of Bechuanaland, Basutoland, and Swaziland, but not Rhodesia. Only the supplementary volume has a subject index.

The only bibliographies devoted specifically to nineteenth-century South African periodicals which aim at broad coverage are three typescripted works produced by students of the University of Cape Town School of Librarianship:

South African Periodical Publications, 1800–1875, compiled by C. Daphne Saul (1949).
South African Periodical Publications, 1875–1910, compiled by J.I. Plowman (1952).
South African Periodical Publications, 1875–1910, compiled by G.S. Güldenpfennig (1952).

None of these works is anything like comprehensive, for the period after 1850 in particular. Saul's work is limited to the holdings of six libraries – the Johannesburg Public Library, the Mendelssohn Collection of the Library of Parliament, the Port Elizabeth Public Library, the South African Library, the Jagger Library of the University of Cape Town, and the University of the Witwatersrand Library. Güldenpfennig's work is restricted to holdings of the South African Library, the Mendelssohn Collection, the Johannesburg Public Library, and the State Library. Plowman's work is even further restricted to the holdings of the South African Library and the University of Cape Town Library. Saul and Plowman include almanacs, directories, and yearbooks but exclude newspapers, government publications, and annual reports of societies; Güldenpfennig excludes all of these materials and lists only periodicals published *for the first time* from 1875 onwards. All provide full bibliographical information based on a physical check of the material in the Cape Town libraries, a location guide to the titles listed, and in many cases a brief comment on the content or nature of each periodical. Apart from almanacs, directories, and religious almanacs, Saul lists 63 periodicals, Plowman 76 from the nineteenth century, and Güldenpfennig 68, though there is in each case considerable overlap of material. Overall these three works include 139 different periodical items, and for all their limitations they remain the fullest descriptive listings of nineteenth-century South African periodicals yet published. There is also W.N. Cruywagen's *Bronnelys van Suid-Afrikaanse Tydskrifte* [Source list of South African Periodicals] (University of Pretoria 1949), which is on occasion cited as the sole source of information on certain nineteenth-century periodical items, but neither the University of Pretoria, the State Library, nor any other major South African library can locate a copy of the work.

The comprehensive bibliographical work which *has* been done on periodicals within South Africa at a national level has the grave disadvantage for our purposes of making no distinction between nineteenth-century and later works, and no distinction between works published in South Africa and works published abroad – it is aimed at being a comprehensive union list of all periodical materials held by Southern African libraries. Building on earlier work, in particular that by A.G. Lloyd, and taking account of the returns of eighty-two libraries within South Africa, Percy Freer in 1943 edited the first major work of this kind, the *Catalogue of Union Periodicals* (Pretoria: Council of Scientific and Industrial Research, and National Council for Social Research). Its first volume was devoted to science and technology, and there were supplements to it in 1949 and 1953; its second volume, which covered the humanities, appeared in 1952. The work is cumbersomely arranged in terms of its own system of catchwords, which involves a maze of cross-referencing.

Freer's work was superseded by what has become the computerized enterprise known as *PISAL*, an acronym for *Periodicals in South African Libraries*.[2] *PISAL* is issued by the Council for Scientific and Industrial Research, Pretoria, on microfiche. Information on its development is given in Elizabeth Hartmann's *The History of Pisal and Its Forerunners* (Pretoria: Council for Scientific and Industrial Research Special Report, CSTI 28 1980.

PISAL provides a comprehensive account of the holdings of *all* registered Southern African libraries, including the libraries of the territories from beyond South Africa (other than St Helena) dealt with in this survey. (The holdings of eighty Rhodesian libraries were incorporated in 1976 when *Periodicals in Rhodesian Libraries* was discontinued.) *PISAL* excludes local church and parish magazines as distinct from diocesan and denominational publications, but includes annual reports, government commission reports, house journals, and yearbooks; for the 'very early' period, however, which is to say the nineteenth century, only newspapers were excluded. *PISAL* is an alphabetical listing, and it gives a description of each item (with varying degrees of fullness of detail), a history of the title where known, and an indication of all the known holdings within the region. As *PISAL* was initially the product of independent submissions from 367 public, special research, and academic libraries throughout Southern Africa, it is not a completely standardized work, particularly for earlier periodicals, and it contains some repetition of material. As a regional holdings index it takes no account of items of which no copy is known to exist and no account of holdings abroad. The 1983 edition of *PISAL* contained over 260,000 holding records for some 66,000 serial titles. The 1985 version (on twenty-five microfiche sheets) is now treated as the base, and some, but by no means all, of its records have been taken up into the annual supplements, each of which subsumes all previous supplements (the 1991 supplement is on eighty-six microfiche sheets and contains 85,640 bibliographic records). This means that both the 1985 version and the latest annual supplement might need to be checked when searching for an item, but the hope is that from 1993 all the records will be taken up into a single set of fiches. *PISAL* has until recently been available only on microfiche, but it is now possible to obtain on-line access to it through the South African libraries information network known as Sabinet. International access to Sabinet may be obtained through Uninet and the International X 25 Cloud. Those interested should apply to those systems for further information.

The most comprehensive and most recent checklist of South African serials *in print form* is a commercial publication, *Basil's Comprehensive List of South African Serials*, two volumes (Pinegowrie: Specific Software Series 1990/1). Unlike *PISAL* it includes newspapers, but it too does not separate nineteenth-century serials from the rest and gives no indication of holdings. For the nineteenth century its coverage of newspapers is far more comprehensive than its coverage of periodicals and other serials, which is sketchy and which fails to take account even of a number of the items listed by Saul, Plowman, and Güldenpfennig.

The fullest international bibliography of Southern African periodicals is *Periodicals from Africa: A Bibliography and Union List of Periodicals Published in Africa* (Boston: G.K. Hall 1977), edited and compiled by Carole Travis and M. Alman for the Standing Conference on Library Materials on Africa. This work covers all the territories dealt with in this survey, but once again it does not separate nineteenth-century periodicals from the much vaster bulk of twentieth-century periodicals. This means that a Victorian scholar wishing to consult the South African entry must cull material from sixty-nine densely packed pages. *Periodicals from Africa: A Bibliography and Union List of Periodicals Published in Africa – First Supplement* (Boston: G.K. Hall 1984), compiled and edited by David Blake and Carole Travis, is mainly concerned with extending the record to 1979, and it adds only a handful of nineteenth-century titles. As far as its nineteenth-century South African coverage is concerned, *Periodicals from Africa* includes some periodicals not listed by Saul, Plowman, and Güldenpfennig; but being a compilation by outsiders from information received, it is inevitably deficient, and it arbitrarily includes among its 175 nineteenth-century items at least twenty-five newspapers, several items published in Britain for a British readership, and some annual reports and school and parish magazines. Apart from *PISAL*, these comprehensive bibliographies tend to list continuations of a periodical under a new name as separate items.

As far as South African *newspapers* are concerned, the situation is far more satisfactory, for there is an extremely comprehensive alphabetically ordered *List of South African Newspapers 1800–1982* (Pretoria: State Library 1983). This compilation, based on submissions from eighty different libraries, cross-references variant titles, has an index to towns and cities, and indicates something close to the full range of library holdings within the country, as well as major overseas holdings. Arranged alphabetically, it makes no distinction between nineteenth-century and later material, and, unlike *PISAL*, it excludes material from the other Southern African territories. It includes no fewer than 513 nineteenth-century newspapers (not counting title variants), of which at least 400 are English or bilingual publications. As the introduction acknowledges, however, some of the titles should properly be classified as periodicals, or as religious and mission publications. One of the virtues of this work is that it aims to be more than just a list of holdings: fifty-eight of the nineteenth-century listings are of titles for which no copies are known to have survived. Additional titles are to be found in P.R. Coates's 'Little Known Newspapers,' *Africana Notes and News* (henceforward *ANN*) 17 (1967), 242–7; and in J. Denfield's 'Notes on Some Lost Border Newspapers,' *Quarterly Bulletin of the South African Library* (henceforward *QBSAL*) 19 (1951), 72–9. Items which are included both in *List of South African Newspapers* and in the descriptive list in this chapter are listed in an endnote.[3]

A related work on newspapers brought out by the State Library is *South African Newspapers Available on Microfilm* (Pretoria: State Library 1975). In addition to indicating the dates available for each item, the agency or institution holding the negatives, and the price, this work has informative descriptive entries for most items. It includes fifty-nine newspapers from the nineteenth century. Those more broadly interested in the availability of Southern African newspaper outside the country will consult works such as *African Newspapers in Selected American Libraries: A Union List*, third edition, compiled by Rozanne Barry (Washington: Library of Congress 1965) and A.R. Hewitt's *Union List of Commonwealth Newspapers in London, Oxford and Cambridge* (London: Athlone Press for the Institute of Commonwealth Studies 1960).

As a guide to which Cape newspapers were appearing at any particular date within the nineteenth century there are G.R. Morris's 'A Chart of Cape Town Newspapers,' *QBSAL* 1 (1947), 70–1; R. Barron's 'A Chart of Western Province Newspapers in the South African Library,' *QBSAL* 3 (1949), 79–80; and 'Eastern Cape Newspapers (A Chart),' *QBSAL* 5 (1951). Though these charts are limited to newspapers of which copies are on file in the South African Library, they are virtually a complete record in that the library's Newspaper Collection is by far the largest in the country, particularly for Cape items.

Various specialized bibliographies are more detailed and comprehensive than any of the works yet mentioned, including *PISAL*. The first group of these are bibliographies for particular regions.

Cape Town was until 1831 the only centre in which newspapers or periodicals were produced. The early 'Cape Press,' which is to say books and other materials including periodicals published in Cape Town itself, has been the subject of a valuable series of bibliographical works. By far the most important of these is P.W. Laidler's *The Pre-Victorian Products of the Cape Press* (Johannesburg: South African Library Association 1935), the first comprehensive survey of South African incunabulae. Soon after its appearance a number of further titles were listed by J. Ross in an article in *South African Libraries* 4 (1937), 130–3, but none of the new titles is a serial. Students of the University of Cape Town School of Librarianship brought out a set of three supplements to Laidler's work, extending the survey to 1857. The whole series thus comprises:

The Cape Press 1796–1837, compiled by P.W. Laidler (1935).
The Cape Press 1838–1850, compiled by Joyce C. Mandelbrote (1945).
The Cape Press 1851–1855, compiled by R.M. Schonfrucht (1955).
The Cape Press 1856–1957, compiled by Eunice E. Herbst (1959).

In the main, the three supplementary works are confined to the holdings of the South African Library and the Mendelssohn Collection of the Library of Parliament, though Mandelbrote and Schonfrucht take account of holdings in the University of Cape Town Library, and Schonfrucht includes works from the HAUM Africana collection and the Nederlandse Gereformeerde Kerk (Dutch Reformed Church) archives. All the works in the series contain full descriptions of each item and a holdings record; but they have slightly differing formats. All have a comprehensive index, that for Laidler coming in the form of a separate 'Index to P.W. Laidler's Pre-Victorian Products of the Cape Press' (Johannesburg Public Library 1958). Mandelbrote provides some introductory comments on the quality of the printing encountered, and along with Schonfrucht and Herbst includes an additional index to printers, publishers, and booksellers. Herbst alone treats periodical works separately.

The work on the 'Cape Press' has been complemented by Alfred Gordon-Brown's bibliography *The Settlers' Press: Seventy Years of Printing in Grahamstown 1830–1900* (Cape Town: Balkema 1979). Grahamstown was until the mid-century the only centre in South Africa apart from Cape Town with an active commercial press. Gordon-Brown provides a full bibliographical listing and a highly informative and often entertaining description of all the newspapers and periodicals published in Grahamstown during the century. Still within the Cape, there is N. Monica Southey's much more restricted bibliography, *Kimberley and the Diamond Fields of Griqualand West: A Bibliography* (University of Cape Town School of Librarianship 1946), which is confined to early publications.

For areas beyond the Cape, the Orange Free State is very well served by Karel Schoeman's authoritative *Bibliography of the Orange Free State until 31 May 1910* (Cape Town: South African Library 1984), which includes newspapers and periodicals, as well as a subject bibliography which is particularly useful in that it lists many items of a general nature which are only in part applicable to the Orange Free State. There are, unfortunately, no comparable works for Natal and the Transvaal.

A highly professional specialized bibliography which focuses on a very important subject area rather than on a particular region, and which has an excellent brief introduction, is Les and Donna Swizter's *The Black Press in South Africa and Lesotho: A Descriptive Bibliographical Guide to African, Coloured and Indian Newspapers, Newsletters and Magazines 1836–1976* (Boston: G.K. Hall 1979). The work has a useful description of each item, and here will be found an account of the important early Black newspapers, which have been omitted from the present survey, especially *Imvo Zabantsundu* [African Opinion] (Kingwilliamstown 1884–), edited by John Tengo Jabavu, the most influential organ of Black opinion in the Cape Colony; its competitor, backed by Rhodes, *Izwi Labantu* [The Voice of the People] (East London 1897–1909); and *Ipepo Lo Hlanga* [The Paper of the Nation] (Pietermaritzburg 1898–1904), the first Black-owned newspaper in Natal.

Another more limited specialized bibliography is N. Shackleton's mimeographed *Handlist of the Periodicals in the Collection of the Church of the Province of South Africa* (Johannesburg: University of the Witwatersrand 1961). This handlist of materials in an important collection housed at the University of the Witwatersrand library is worthy of note because it makes clear just how difficult a really comprehensive bibliographical survey of South African nineteenth-century serial material would be. Shackleton lists no fewer than thirty Southern African nineteenth-century church or church-related periodicals of the Church of the Province, many of which are not noted by *PISAL*, and even this is not a complete account, for the Switzers list some vernacular items not included in the collection, and there are some additional items from the Cape listed by *PISAL*. Other such collections are the Methodist Archive and the Papers of the Lovedale Mission, both of which are in the Cory Library at Rhodes University, the former described in J.M. Bernig's *The Methodist Archive Collection* (Grahamstown: Rhodes University 1968). The principal collection of South African Mission material is Sir George Grey's, now in the South African Library.

A different kind of impeccably professional bibliography is Fransie Rossouw's *South African Printers and Publishers 1797–1925* (Cape Town: South African Library 1987), which lists alphabetically the imprints and publications of firms and individuals who worked in South Africa during the first 130 years of the country's printing history, and which also indexes the material geographically and chronologically by province. The work is full of incidental information on the various publishers and their works, and contains much of interest on periodical publications.

Other works in the same field are three bibliographies of the work of early Cape publishers who were, among other things, involved in bringing out periodical material: Joyce Mandelbrote's 'De Lima: A Bibliography,' *QSBAL* 16 (1948), 2–22; J.B. Smit's *Bibliographie van die Drukpersmaatskappy van B.J. van de Sandt de Villiers* (University of Cape Town School of Librarianship 1946); and A.B. Caine and L. Leipoldt's *Bibliography of the Publications of J.C. Juta and Co. 1853–1903* (University of Cape Town School of Librarianship 1954).

For a full listing of Southern African subject bibliographies the first port of call is *A Bibliography of African Bibliographies*, fourth edition revised to 1960 (Cape Town: South African Library 1961), compiled originally by Percy Freer and D.H. Varley, and updated by A.M. Lewin Robinson. A valuable recent listing and description of the material is Reuben Musiker's *South African Bibliography: A Survey of Bibliographies and Bibliographical Work*, second edition (Cape Town: David Philip 1980), which has been updated by Musiker's *South African Reference Books and Bibliographies 1979–83* (Johannesburg: University of the Witwatersrand Library 1983). For even later bibliographies the most recent annual volumes of the *South African National Bibliography* (Pretoria: State Library 1959–91) would have to be consulted. It is most unfortunate that there is as yet no bibliography of materials on printing, the press, newspapers, and periodicals; but a good deal of the most pertinent material is to be found in two journals, *Quarterly Bulletin of the South African Public Library* and *Africana Notes and News*, both of which have very good cumulative subject indexes.

Indexing of Periodicals and Newspapers

The main national periodical indexing enterprise, the *Index of South African Periodicals* compiled by the Johannesburg Public Library, runs only from 1940. Some additional earlier work is card indexed, but only as far back as 1900.

The first attempt to index nineteenth-century periodicals is to be found in *Mendelssohn's South African Bibliography*, two volumes (London: Kegan Paul 1910). The second volume of this major pioneering work has a seventy-two-page section entitled 'Magazines, Etc,' which lists the titles of articles in the complete runs of a number of nineteenth-century serials, twelve of which were published in South Africa during the nineteenth century: *Cape Monthly Magazine* (1857–81), *Cape Quarterly Review* (1881–3), *Cape of Good Hope Literary Gazette* (1830–5), *Eastern Province Monthly Magazine* (1856–8), *Elpis* (1857–60 only), *Folk-Lore Journal* (1879–80), *Nederduitsche Zuid-Afrikaansch Tijdschrift* (1824–43), *Ons Tijdschrift* (1896–1900), *Rhodesian Scientific Association* (1899–1906), *South African Magazine* (1867–9), *South African Philosophical Society Transactions* (1877–1909), *South African Quarterly Journal* (1829–31, 1833–4).

Mendelssohn lists the titles only of what he calls the 'principal South African items,' but some of his omissions are arbitrary – from his list for the very first number of the *Cape Monthly Magazine*, for example, he omits an eleven-page piece entitled 'Shipwreck at Cape Aghullas in 1686.' Throughout his indexing he more often than not ignores items which he takes to be of a merely literary nature, and an obvious example of carelessness is the fact that four of the titles in the list above are unaccountably omitted from his own summary list of titles indexed.

The South African Library has independently indexed on cards (which may be consulted only at the library) the *South African Quarterly Journal* (1829–31, 1833–6), *Cape of Good Hope Literary Gazette* (1830–5), the three series of the *Cape Monthly Magazine* (1857–81), *Eastern Province Monthly Magazine* (1856–8), *South African Magazine* (1867–9), and the *Cape Quarterly Review* (1881–3); and in addition the *South African Journal* (1824), the *Cape of Good Hope Literary Magazine* (1847–8), *Eastern Province Magazine and Port Elizabeth Miscellany* (1861–2), *Orange Free State Monthly Magazine* (1877–80), and *South African Magazine and Review* (1880). A.M. Lewin Robinson's *None Daring to Make Us Afraid* (Cape Town: Maskew Miller 1962), a work which will be described in more detail later, provides in a more accessible form an extremely full discussion of the contents of the *South Afri-*

can Journal, the *South African Quarterly Journal*, the *Cape of Good Hope Literary Gazette*, the *New Organ*, and *South African Grins*.

For the rest, there are two published indexes for individual magazines. The first is M.R. Simmons's *Subject Index to the Cape Monthly Magazine 1857–62* (University of Cape Town School of Librarianship 1962). This index of the non-literary contributions to the first series of this important journal has the added advantage of ascribing authorship to some of the anonymous articles on the basis of names 'written into the copies in the South African Library.' The second such index is Jill D. Wackrill's *Index to the Cape Illustrated Magazine Vol 1 to Vol XII (December 1901)* (Johannesburg Public Library (1963).

A fair amount of attention has been paid to the indexing of periodical illustrations. The most substantial piece of work is E.C.M. Russell's *Subject Index to Illustrations in South African Periodicals 1800–75* (University of Cape Town School of Librarianship 1963), and there is also Carol Searle's *Illustrations in the 'Cape Times Annual' 1896–1923* (Johannesburg: University of the Witwatersrand Department of Librarianship 1971). Indexes of illustrations related to South Africa in certain British periodicals are L.J. De Wet's *Pictures of South African Interest in the 'Illustrated London News 1842–1949'* (Johannesburg Public Library 1956); and a three-part *Index to Pictures of South African Interest in 'The Graphic'* produced by students of the University of the Witwatersrand School of Librarianship, Johannesburg, for 1875–95 (M.J. Evans, 1966), 1896–9 (Carol Ann Matthews, 1967), and January to June 1900 (N.J.R. Roets, 1971). A more focused checklist of illustrated periodicals from abroad is Ryno Greenwall's 'Some Contemporary Illustrated and Satirical Periodicals Which Portray the Anglo-Boer War,' QSBAL 38 (1984), 101–9. *'Vanity Fair' in Southern Africa*, edited by Sonia Clarke (Johannesburg: Brenthurst Press 1991), reproduces some of the main portraits of South African personalities from that magazine. Also of interest is R.F. Kennedy's article on 'Early South African Cartoons' in *Africana Byways*, edited by Anna H. Smith (Johannesburg: Donker 1976), which provides a great deal of information on work in the early periodicals.

As far as the indexing of nineteenth-century South African periodicals in terms of a particular subject is concerned, by far the most substantial work is N.J. Van Warmelo's *Anthropology of Southern Africa in Periodicals to 1850: An Analysis and Index* (Johannesburg: Witwatersrand University Press 1977). This work is minutely detailed and ranges extremely widely through not only local but also international periodicals in a number of European languages. It is arranged by year, and includes an analysis of all the materials relating to the indigenous people of the country in all the important South African periodicals published in the first half of the nineteenth century.

Narrowly focused projects on the historical front are J.G. Kesting's *The Anglo-Boer War, 1899–1902. Mounting Tension and the Outbreak of Hostilities as Reflected in Overseas Magazine Contributions Published January–December 1899: A Bibliography* (University of Cape Town School of Librarianship 1972); and two indexes focused on early accounts of Johannesburg to be found in local and international periodicals, T.R. Shaw's *The Growth of Johannesburg 1886–1939: A List of Articles in Serial Publications* (Johannesburg Public Library 1963), and James Sidney Winter's *First-Hand Accounts of Johannesburg in English-Language Periodicals, 1886–1895* (Johannesburg: University of the Witwatersrand Department of Librarianship 1967).

A major bibliographical task of indexing important early Cape newspapers, the *Cape Town English Press Index*, is currently being undertaken by Peter Ralph Coates. This work is available on microfiche from the South African Library for the years 1871 to 1875. For the years up to 1874 the newspapers indexed are the *Cape Argus* and the *Standard and Mail*, and for 1875 the *Cape Town Daily News* is also included in the index. The project is restricted to Cape Town newspapers, but editorials and news stories from the provincial papers were frequently reproduced in the indexed papers, so that the index provides good coverage of South African news.

Other indexes of early newspapers are *Index of the 'Graham's Town Journal,'* held at the Cory Library, Rhodes University, Grahamstown, which provides a personal-name index only for the period 1831–76 and a somewhat more extended index which takes account of biographical items for the period 1877–97; and Arthur Rabone's *Index of the Graaf-Reinet Herald, Vol. 1, August 1852–August 1853* (Cape Town: Struik 1969).

Studies of the Periodicals

The only attempt to provide a comprehensive overview of South African periodicals comes in the form of contributions by A.M. Lewin Robinson on 'Newspapers and Periodicals' and 'Literary Periodicals' to the *Standard Encyclopaedia of Southern Africa*, twelve volumes (Cape Town: Nasou 1970). Robinson's entries provide useful short introductions to the subject. The encyclopaedia has, too, an overview by B.H.J. van Rensburg of South African 'War Newspapers' in both English and Dutch, and a full account of 'German Newspapers and Periodicals in South Africa' by G.P.J. Trümpelmann. Fuller surveys of Dutch and Afrikaans periodicals are F.C.L. Bosman's *Hollandse Joernalistiek in Suid Afrika Gedurende die 19de Eeue* (Cape Town: Federale Drukpers 1930) and P.J. Nienaber's *Beknopte Geskiedenis van die Hollands-Afrikaanse Drukpers in Suid Afrika* (Cape Town: Nasionale Pers 1943), which emphasizes the emergence of Afrikaans as a written language. On the same topic there is the most comprehensive research project yet undertaken on the newspapers and periodicals, G.S. Nienaber's *Register van Afrikaans Voor 1900* (Pretoria: Suid-Afrikaanse Akademie vir Wetenskap en Kuns 1966–7), which attempts to locate all early written examples of Afrikaans. In passing, this work provides a very useful indication of which English titles contain items in Dutch and Afrikaans – almost certainly a more frequent occurrence than the other way round.

A.M. Lewin Robinson is the author of the only scholarly book-length work on South African periodicals, *None Daring to Make Us Afraid: A Study of the English Periodical Literature of the Cape 1824 to 1834* (Cape Town: Maskew Miller 1962). This very thorough study begins with a useful introduction to the Cape scene in the 1820s, and includes a punctilious bibliographical description and an extensive (indeed at times an over-exhaustive) survey of the contents of all the periodicals (other than the religious ones) produced at the Cape up to 1835. As its title suggests, it also provides a full discussion of the founding of the *South African Journal* by Thomas Pringle and John Fairbairn and of Pringle's rencontre with the Governor, Lord Charles Somerset, which led him to abandon the project. These events are placed against the background of the larger struggle for the freedom of the press in South Africa which led to the banning within its first year of production of the first newspaper, George Greig's *South African Commercial Advertiser* (1824–69), and to its subsequent reinstatement after the matter had been investigated by an already established Commission of Enquiry (only for the paper to be once again banned two years later). The book thus in effect goes a long way toward being a full history of the Cape Press in the early years.

No South African periodical topic has had anything like the treatment accorded to 'the struggle for the freedom of the press.' One side of this story is told first-hand in Pringle's *Narrative of a Residence in South Africa*, introduced by A.M. Lewin Robinson (Cape Town: Struik 1966). Another equally partial early account is L.H. Meurant's *Sixty Years Ago, or Reminiscences of the struggle for the freedom of the press in South Africa and the establishment of the first newspaper in the Eastern Province* (Cape Town: Saul Solomon 1895; facsimile reprint Cape Town: African Connoisseurs' Press 1963). Meurant worked for Greig at the time of the banning, and his work has the great advantage of containing voluminous extracts from many of the contemporary documents. (It also has the added bonus of Meurant's account of his founding of the *Graham's Town Journal*, the first newspaper to be established outside Cape Town.) Further documentation is provided by the facsimile reproduction of George Greig's *Facts Connected with the Stopping of the South African Commercial Advertiser* (Cape Town: African Connoisseurs' Press 1963). The account of the whole affair which sets it most judiciously in a wider context is A.D. Hall's article, 'Pringle, Somerset and Press Freedom,' *English Studies in Africa* 3 (1960), 160–78. The most recent treatment is to be found in H.C. Botha's book-length study *John Fairbairn in South Africa* (Cape Town: Historical Publication Society 1984), a scholarly work with an excellent bibliography, based largely on newspaper research and on a combing of all the government sources.

Gordon-Brown's study of material published in Grahamstown, *The Settlers' Press*, to which we have already referred, provides by far the most informative treatment after Robinson's of any group of South African periodicals. In addition, it has a chapter on the *Graham's Town Journal*, annotated lists of newspapers and almanacs published in the Eastern Cape, and a useful discussion of the Wesleyan Methodist Missionary Press in Grahamstown.

The history of printing, more broadly considered, has had some systematic coverage. Anna H. Smith's *The Spread of Printing, Eastern Hemisphere: South Africa* (Amsterdam: Vangendt and Co. 1971), in the 'Spread of Printing' series edited by Colin Clair, is the most valuable and comprehensive survey, and it largely supersedes the works on the same topic which it lists in its bibliography by Ainslie, Cutten, Lloyd, Morrison, and Varley. Though its topic is Southern African printing in the nineteenth century broadly considered, Smith's work comes the closest to providing an extended overall history of nineteenth-century Southern African periodicals and newspapers. It contains accounts of the beginnings in Cape Town; the Mission Presses; the spread of country presses in the Cape Colony; the early printing enterprises in Natal, the Orange Free State, and the Transvaal; the beginning of printing in adjacent territories; and military printing in South Africa.

Another work which covers much of the same ground more superficially, but which is valuable for the illustrations and photographic material it contains, is Eric Rosenthal's exhibition catalogue, *160 Years of Cape Town Printing* (Cape Town Association of Printing House Craftsmen and the Cape Chamber of Printing 1960). A more important exhibition catalogue is *South Africa in Print* (Cape Town: Van Riebeeck Festival Book Exhibition Committee 1952), which manages to bring together a great deal of information of many kinds in its wide-ranging entries, as does the similar work *South African Printing 1800–1968* (Johannesburg Public Library 1968).

As most of the work on newspapers and periodicals has concentrated on the Cape, an extremely useful contribution is E.B. Nagelgast's article, 'Johannesburg Newspapers and Periodicals 1887 to 1899,' in *Africana Byways* (Donker 1976), edited by Anna H. Smith. This article has the added virtue of containing a very full checklist of the items mentioned, arranged in chronological order though with no separation of newspapers and periodicals: surprisingly, it does not acknowledge Eric Rosenthal's 'Early Johannesburg Printers and Publications,' ANN (1944), and neither work seems to be aware of Dewdney Drew's 'Johannesburg Newspapers,' *Critic* 8 (14 September 1894), 513–15. H.P. Behrens's *The Pretoria Press Story* (Pretoria City Council 1955) fills out the story for Pretoria.

Much of the work which has been done on the early press relates to individual newspapers or newspaper companies. Among the more extended works are Eric Rosenthal's *Today's News Today: The Story of the Argus Company* (Johannesburg: Argus Printing and Publishing Co. 1956), G. Shaw's *Some Beginnings – the 'Cape Times' 1876–1910* (Cape Town 1975), and T. Wilks's *For the Love of Natal: The Life and Times of the 'Natal Mercury' 1852–1977* (Durban: Robinson 1977). Some of the more noteworthy short studies are *Open Testimony: An Introduction to the 'Natal Witness,' South Africa's Oldest Newspaper* (Pietermaritzburg: Natal Witness 1972); Karel Schoeman's '*The Friend* through the Formative Years,' ANN 25:2 (1982); and Conrad Lighton and C.B. Harris's 'Details regarding the *Diamond Fields Advertiser* (1878–1968)' (Pretoria: State Library 1969).

The Black press has understandably received increasing attention during recent years, and here the Switzers' introduction and their extensive primary and secondary bibliography is the first port of call; though mention should be made of Eric Rosenthal's pioneering work, *Bantu Journalism in South Africa* (Johannesburg: South African Institute of Race Relations 1947), as also of D.D.T. Jabavu's life of his father, *The Life of John Tengo Jabavu, Editor of Imvo Zabantsundu, 1884–1921* (Alice: Lovedale Press 1922), which gives an account of South Africa's first Black journalist of note. The Switzers' work is also the best starting point for work from the mission presses, of which the only comprehensive account is P.J. Schutte's *Sendingdrukperse in Suid Afrika, 1800–1875* (Potchefstroom: Pro Rege 1971). Two of the mission presses have published hard-to-come-by histories of their own activities, R.H.W.

Shepherd's *Lovedale, South Africa: The Story of the Century 1841–1941* (Alice: Lovedale Press 1941, revised 1971) and J. Zurcher's *111 Years: Morija Printing Works* (Morija: Printing Works 1972). Since the Switzers compiled their bibliography Karel Schoeman has published a very informative two-part article, 'Die Sendingdrukpers te Beersheba,' *QBSAL* 42 (1988), 119–25 and 167–73.

Another topic which has had informed attention is the political orientation of newspapers. Three valuable contributions here are B.A. Le Cordeur's 'Robert Godlonton as an Architect of Frontier Opinion, 1850–57,' *Archives Year Book for South African History* (1959), which considers Godlonton's role as editor of the *Graham's Town Journal*; Gerald Shaw's *South African Telegraph versus Cape Times* (University of Cape Town Centre for African Studies 1980), which, as its subtitle indicates, is 'an examination of the attempt by the *South African Telegraph*, financed by J.B. Robinson, to challenge the dominance of the pro-Rhodes press at the Cape, August, 1895 to September 1896,' and A.N. Porter's 'Sir Alfred Milner and the Press, 1897–1899,' *Historical Journal* 16 (1973), 323–39. J.D. Bodel's 'Research Value of the "News of the Camp,"' *Historia* 4 (1959), 263–8 is a rather limited attempt to consider how best the periodical material might be used, and Brian Cheadle's 'The Experience of Emigrants to the Cape at Mid-Century,' *English Studies in Africa* 35 (1992), 28–41, suggests how periodical materials might be used to fill in gaps in the historical record.

Finally, there are discussions of the men who edited the periodicals or who made the news. Over and above the items already cited, mention might be made of A.M.L. Robinson's 'Alexander Johnstone Jardine: Librarian and Man of Letters,' *QBSAL* 16 (1962); A.F. Hattersley's 'Sam Sly (William Layton Sammons),' *QBSAL* 9 (1955); B.J. Leverton's 'David Dale Buchanan as Editor of the "Natal Witness,"' *QBSAL* 18 (1963); E.T. Cook's *Edmund Garrett* (London: Edward Arnold 1909), a memoir of the man who edited the *Cape Times* at a critical period before the outbreak of the Anglo-Boer War, and whose own account of events in F.E. Garrett and E.J. Edwards' *The Story of an African Crisis* (London: Constable 1897) is also informative; G. Storey's *Reuters Century, 1851–1951* (London 1951); Elma Kingswell's *Kingswell War Correspondent* (London: Cassel 1938), a life of her father, who was editor of the *Owl* and correspondent of the *London Daily Express*; and, most entertaining of all, Julian Ralph's *War's Brighter Side: The Story of 'The Friend' Newspaper Edited by the Correspondents with Lord Roberts's Forces, March–April 1900* (London: C. Arthur Pearson 1901), which, as an added bonus, reproduces a good deal of the material. For Rudyard Kipling's part in this enterprise there is Susan Gorton's 'Kipling and the Bloemfontein *Friend*,' *Jagger Journal* 2 (1981), 30–3, and the fuller account in René Durbach's *Kipling's South Africa* (Cape Town: Chameleon Press 1988).

In default of a bibliography of work on newspapers, periodicals, and the press, those embarked on a fuller study of press history might well consult the comprehensive checklist produced by C.F.J. Muller and others, *South African History and Historians: A Bibliography* (Pretoria: University of South Africa 1979), and its *Supplement* (Pretoria: University of South Africa 1984). These bibliographies list a number of more specialized items pertinent to press history, including unpublished doctorial theses and masters' dissertations, mainly in Afrikaans and many of them dealing with the early Dutch and Afrikaans press. Beyond that the individual volumes of the *Index to South African Periodicals* (1940–) would have to be combed (an infuriating task, as the entries under 'periodicals' and 'newspapers' in the earlier volumes advise one to 'see also' entries under the titles of individual publications, which is less than helpful, seeing that there are so many from which to choose).

Description of the Periodical Material

Further work on nineteenth-century Southern African periodical material will inevitably have to move in the two directions associated respectively with the *Waterloo Directory of Victorian Periodicals* and the *Wellesley Index to Victorian Periodicals*; the former aiming in the first instance to achieve as comprehensive an alphabetic listing of all serial material as possible, the latter aiming to present a detailed analysis of at least the most important magazines and reviews.

The description of the material which follows falls between the two stools and is not only sketchy but to a large extent derivative (even at times in the phrasing of entries) from the existing secondary sources, in particular *PISAL*. This was inevitable, given the introductory nature of the venture, the constraints of time and space upon the project, and the problems caused both by the range of territories to be considered and by the range of languages involved.

The description affords as comprehensive a list as it was possible to achieve, without extended archival work in a large number of centres, of nineteenth-century South African English and Dutch periodicals (excluding newspapers, reports, government publications, almanacs, yearbooks and directories, and parish, school, and university magazines; but including annuals of general interest, separately produced Christmas numbers of newspapers, and the reports of literary and scientific institutions).

Some descriptive comment is provided on at least the more important items. In default of any adequate history of South African periodicals, a chronological arrangement suggests something of the development of the material. As in *PISAL*, subsequent runs of a journal under a new name are listed under the original title, and it seems worth mentioning that the items numbered 2, 18, 28, 31, 32, 43, 49, 51, 56, 80, 85, 90, 96, 112, 114, 129, 144, 146, 161, 166, 168, 173, 182, 184, 189, and 194 in the descriptive list contain details of subsequent titles, and items 6, 48, and 152 contain indications of the titles of parallel Dutch editions. (Seeming omissions might be sought within these entries and in the endnote listing university, college, and school magazines.)[4] Standing as it does at three hundred items (plus an additional thirty-six indications of subsequent or parallel Dutch titles) and despite excluding parish magazines and also the twenty-two university and school magazines which *PISAL* and most of the lists include (the latter are summarily named in the appendix), the list more than doubles the number of periodical items to be found in any previously published listing: it shows that though much of the material was very ephemeral and has survived only in severely depleted runs, there are many more nineteenth-century periodicals than might have been supposed even from the sum of all the existing published bibliographies, and certainly far more than have ever been comprehensively and independently listed in a convenient form.

The list is intended to be used with *PISAL*, which has much more detailed information on such matters as dates of publication and the extent of the runs. Where an item is not listed in *PISAL* the source for the record is listed; items for which no known copy exists have their dates in square brackets. In supplying dates and other information *PISAL* has been taken as the main authority, despite the fact that the *PISAL* holding dates are not necessarily those when a publication began and ceased. Where further indications were not available, the State Library's *List of South African Newspapers* has been taken as a guide to whether a work should be classified as a newspaper or a periodical. Some overlap has resulted from the decision to include religious items but to exclude commercial items (though even here a few marginal religious items, such as the *Natal Guardian*, 1856–7, a weekly newspaper with strong Anglican leanings brought out in Pietermaritzburg and strongly supportive of Bishop Colenso, were excluded). As previously mentioned, endnote 3 lists items included in the list which *are* also included in *List of South African Newspapers*. Only a few Boer War periodicals which appeared before the turn of the century are included. I am working on a comprehensive discussion and listing of the very varied Boer War serial material in both English and Dutch/Afrikaans; and on alphabetical checklists of all South African nineteenth-century serials.

1 / *South African Journal*. 1824. Cape Town. This was the first literary periodical in South Africa, edited by Thomas Pringle and John Fairbairn and started in monthly tandem with, though largely different in content from, the *Nederduitsch Zuid-Afrikaansche Tijdschrift*. A high literary standard was aspired to, the declared aim being 'to imitate what is excellent and to appropriate whatever is useful,' but the readership was small. Government censure of an article on the settlers in the eastern Cape and the editors' refusal to accept censorship led to its being withdrawn after the second issue, though the Dutch counterpart continued.

2 / *Nederduitsch Zuid-Afrikaansche Tijdschrift* [Dutch South African Journal]. 1824–43. Cape Town. Edited by Dr A. Faure and published bimonthly, it was for some time the only magazine for the Dutch-speaking population and had a devotional emphasis. The issue of May–June 1829 saw the first press illustration in South Africa – an engraving entitled in English 'View of Napoleon's Tomb at St Helena.' Revived after a break as *Zuid-Afrikaansche Tijdschrift* [South African Magazine] 1854–93, a Dutch monthly, its aim being to promote a love of reading among the people. One of its most famous later editors was J.H. (Onze Jan) Hofmeyr. From 1890 it was the organ of the Zuid-Afrikansche Taalbond.

3 / *South African Literary Society – Papers*. 1824–30. Cape Town (Laidler).

4 / *South African Grins*. 1825. Cape Town. 'The Quizzical Depot of General Humbug,' the colony's first satirical paper, containing descriptions in doggerel of the Cape Town scene, lasting for only four numbers.

5 / *The New Organ*. 1826. Cape Town. Fairbairn's second attempt to found a literary periodical. After a single modest and uncontenious issue, which contained a good deal culled from other sources, it was suspended because a licence to publish had not been obtained, and no effort was made to revive it.

6 / *South African Missionary Herald/Zuid-Afrikaansche Zendelings Heraut*. 1828. Cape Town. Seemingly the earliest missionary journal published in South Africa, it contains descriptions of missions in India, the South Seas, the East Indies, and Mongolia as well as local missions.

7 / *South African Quarterly Journal.* First and second series 1829–31, 1833–6. Cape Town. The first South African scientific periodical, edited by Dr James Adamson and Dr Andrew Smith for the South African Institution. It published much of Smith's work on birds, the San and Khoisan people, and African zoology; and J.C. Chase's accounts of expeditions and geographical discoveries.

8 / *Cape of Good Hope Literary Gazette.* 1830–5. Cape Town. A monthly 'devoted exclusively to literature, criticism, science, and the advancement of knowledge,' edited by A.J. Jardine; includes comment on current affairs, reviews, verse, local descriptions, and some amusing woodcuts in volume 4.

9 / *South African Literary and Scientific Institution – Annual Reports.* 1830–5. Cape Town.

10 / *South African Christian Recorder.* 1831–7. Cape Town. A monthly which contains essays, biographical sketches, etc.

11 / *Kaapsche Cyclopedie.* 1833–6. Cape Town. A Dutch 'halfpenny magazine for the people,' with a religious orientation.

12 / *Cape Cyclopaedia.* 1835 and 1837. Cape Town. A religious and educational venture linked to the *Kaapsche Cyclopedie.*

13 / *South African Controversial Adviser.* 1836. Cape Town. Probably a newspaper, though it is not included in *List of South African Newspapers* or in Coates, 'Little Known Newspapers.'

14 / *Iets!* [Something!] 1837. Cape Town. A weekly 'collection of amusing material,' the first of its kind in Dutch at the Cape; it includes much about Piet Retief and his trek.

15 / *Lees-Vruchten* [Fruits of Reading]. 1837–8. Cape Town. A general-interest literary quarterly in Dutch.

16 / *Umshumayeli wendaba* [Publisher of News]. 1837–41. Grahamstown (first ten issues) then Peddie (five issues). The earliest known Black paper, a Xhosa religious quarterly founded by the Wesleyan Methodist Missionary Society. Number 5 contains the text of a treaty concluded at Fort Peddie, 19 June 1838, by Major-General G.T. Napier with chiefs of the Makwane.

17 / *Christian Herald*. 1838. Cape Town. A weekly 'record of the progress of religion and education in South Africa.'

18 / *Honigbij* [Honeybee]. 1838–46. Cape Town. A monthly, the first Church journal in Dutch in South Africa, edited by Dr Abraham Faure of the Nederlandse Gereformeerde Kerk [the Dutch Reformed Church]. Then as *De Gereformeerde Kerk-bode* [The Reformed Church Messenger], 1849–79, a religious weekly; then as *De Christen*, 1880–3; and finally, as *De Kerkbode*, 1884–, adopted as the official organ of the Nederduitse Gereformeerde kerk in 1910. In these successive guises this is by far the longest-running Southern African periodical.

19 / *Fantasticus*. 1839. Cape Town. A Dutch miscellany of which only a single number was published.

20 / *South African Sentinel*. 1839. Cape Town. A weekly review of all the newspapers published in the Colony, edited by C.E. Boniface.

21 / *Echo* 1840. Grahamstown. Though it claims to be 'a literary, scientific and critical magazine,' the only known copy, reconstructed from fragments by Gordon-Brown, suggests that the contents were largely vituperative. The journal was revived in 1869 in Uitenhage for a short spell by the same editor (*SANB*).

22 / *Albany Mirror*. 1841. Grahamstown. 'A monthly journal of literature and science,' intended as a Grahamstown successor to the *Cape of Good Hope Literary Gazette*.

23 / *Cape of Good Hope Pamphlet*. 1841. Cape Town. A miscellany with seemingly only a single issue, sold at 1d. 'for the poorer classes of society.'

24 / *Moboleli Oa Litaba* [Preacher of the News]. 1841–6. Beerseba, OFS. A series of four evangelical tracts published in Sotho by the Société des Missions Évangeliques de Paris.

25 / *Albany Magazine*. 1842. Grahamstown. 'A monthly journal devoted to literature and science' (Gordon-Brown).

26 / *Cape of Good Hope Penny Magazine*. 1843. Cape Town. A weekly.

27 / *Isibuto Samavo* [A Collection of Tales]. 1843–4. Peddie. A religious

and literary quarterly in Xhosa, issued by the Wesleyan Methodist Missionary Society.

28 / *Sam Sly's African Journal.* 1843–51. Cape Town. A zestful weekly, something between a news journal and a literary magazine, owned and edited by W.L. Sammons. Announced as a 'register of facts, fiction, news, literature, commerce and amusement,' it includes considerable information about the War of the Axe, and the effusions of the comic character Kaatje Kekkelbek. A source of information about the current scene and self-appointed gadfly to the community. From 1850 as the *African Journal.*

29 / *Ikwezi* [Morning Star]. 1844–5. Chumie Mission near Lovedale. A devotional and literary magazine issued by the Glasgow Missionary Society in association with the Wesleyan Missionary Society, in Xhosa but with extracts in English, said to include the earliest known writings in the vernacular by a Xhosa writer.

30 / *Cape of Good Hope Christian Magazine.* 1845–6. Cape Town. Monthly.

31 / *Maandwerkje voor de Jeugd* [Monthly Religious Exercises for the Young]. 1845–7. Cape Town. A religious publication continued in 1847 as *Maandwerkje voor Oud en Jong* [... for Old and Young].

32 / *South African Christian Watchman and Missionary Magazine.* 1846–50. Grahamstown. A monthly product of the Wesleyan Mission. Then after a break as *South African Christian Watchman and Wesleyan Record*, 1854–65, Mount Coke.

33 / *Cape of Good Hope Literary Magazine.* 1847–8. Cape Town. Edited bi-monthly by James L. Fitzpatrick. The first attempt after the demise of the *Cape of Good Hope Literary Gazette* twelve years earlier to launch a serious literary periodical in Cape Town. It contains material by three noteworthy visitors to the Cape, George French Angas, Harriet Ward, and the hunter Henry H. Methuen.

34 / *Cape Town Medical Gazette.* 1847. Cape Town. A quarterly, the first of its kind in the country.

35 / *Free Church Witness for the Truth in South Africa.* 1847. Cape Town.

36 / *A Star from the East or The Reflector.* 1848–9. Grahamstown. 'Selections on theological subjects.'

37 / *South African Agricultural News and Farmers' Journal.* 1849–50. Cape Town. Monthly.

38 / *Inkanyezi Yokusa* [Morning Star]. 1850. Durban. A religious and educational monthly issued in Zulu (with some English phrases) by the American Board mission.

39 / *Intellectual Reflector.* 1850. Grahamstown. An ephemeral monthly.

40 / *Isitunywa Sennyanga* [Monthly Messenger]. 1850. King William's Town (Mount Coke). Published by the Wesleyan Mission Press, in English and Xhosa, as a monthly for the 'literary and religious advancement of the Xhosa.'

41 / *Maandelijksche Bezoeker* [Monthly Visitor]. 1850–9. Cape Town. Religious monthlies, also issued at Caledon, Paarl, Tulbagh, Uitenhage, Wellington, and Worcester by the Kaapsche Godsdienstig Traktaatsgenootschap.

42 / *Natal Journal.* 1850. Listed for this date in *Periodicals from Africa* but not in *PISAL* or any other source. (See item 53.)

43 / *South African Church Magazine and Ecclesiastical Review.* 1850–9. Cape Town. A Church of the Province monthly, from 1858 as *South African Church Magazine and Educational Register.*

44 / *Cape Punchinello or Mirror of Wit and Fun.* 1851. Cape Town. A satirical weekly with a few woodcuts.

45 / *South African Miscellany.* 1852. Cape Town. A mix of historic, narrative, and descriptive sketches, tales, and poetry. Only part 1 was published.

46 / *De Verzamelaar* [Gleaner]. 1852–3. Cape Town. Originally a newspaper, it would seem to have been revived for a third run as a Dutch journal (Saul).

47 / *United Musical Society Times.* 1854?

48 / *Cape Temperance Chronicle.* 1855–7. Cape Town. Issued monthly, with a Dutch version, *Het Kaapsche Matigsheidsblad.*

49 / *Eastern Province Monthly Magazine.* 1856–8. Grahamstown. Subsequently as *South African Agricultural Register and Eastern Province Magazine.* 1858–9. A weekly which, in addition to agricultural matters, has papers on 'geology, botany, biography, tales and sketches, reports of scientific societies, map of roads, etc.'

50 / *South African Evangelical Magazine and Church of England Record.* 1856–8. Cape Town. Monthly.

51 / *Cape Monthly Magazine.* 1857–81. Cape Town. First series 1–11, 1857–62, second series 1–18, 1870–9, third series, 1879–81. Announced as a miscellany 'combining amusement with information, and affording equal space to literature, science, the fine arts, and commercial and statistical intelligence,' it aimed in particular 'to illustrate, in its pages, the early history of the Cape Colony.' It also published poetry and serialized several local novels. By far the most important nineteenth-century South African periodical in English and the first to achieve a sustained run. The first series was edited by Alfred Whaley Cole, who became a very successful Cape lawyer, and by Roderick Noble, who was a professor at the South African College; and the second series by John Noble. After the end of the first series and before the magazine's revival, Cole in a sense filled the gap with the *South African Magazine,* 1867–9 – see #77. The third series was succeeded by *Cape Quarterly Review,* 1881–3, which published some important work by the historian George McCall Theal along with book news, poetry, and articles of South African interest. This was the last attempt to sustain a serious journal at the Cape during the nineteenth century.

52 / *Elpis.* 1857–61, 1873–9. Cape Town. A Dutch religious quarterly produced in co-operation with theologians in Holland, aimed at countering the more liberal tendencies of the newspapers *Het Volksblad* and *De Zuid-Afrikaan.* Superseded in 1862 by the newspaper *De Volksvriend* and revived in 1873 after the demise of that newspaper.

53 / *Natal Journal.* 1857–8. Pietermaritzburg. Produced on the press established by the American Board of Commissioners for Foreign Missions. 'A quarterly miscellany of literature and science' – though many of the articles are on religious topics.

54 / *Natal Law Reports*. 1858–. Pietermaritzburg. If one allows for the fact that these have been taken up into the South African Law Reports, this is the longest surviving English serial publication in South Africa.

55 / *South African Ladies' Companion*. 1858. Cape Town. A monthly 'repertoire of the literature of all nations,' the first magazine in the country aimed particularly at women.

56 / *Cape Town Weekly Magazine*. 1859. Cape Town. Later in the year as the *Cape Mercury and Weekly Magazine*.

57 / *Dagster* [Morning Star]. 1859. Philippolis. Only one number of this mission publication appeared.

58 / *De Wekker* [Arouser]. 1859–? Stellenbosch. An orthodox religious monthly – the increase in the Dutch reading public is shown by the fact that it began with a circulation of five thousand.

59 / *De Onderzoeker* [Investigator]. 1860–84. Cape Town. A bilingual religious monthly with a liberal slant.

60 / *Social Reformer*. 1860–3. Grahamstown. Advocates temperance and includes a pictorial tract.

61 / *Eastern Province Magazine and Port Elizabeth Miscellany*. 1861–2. Port Elizabeth. 'A monthly serial devoted to the presentation of accurate information regarding the mineralogy, geology, flora, and general natural features of the Eastern province,' though 'original Tales' would also find a place. It has interesting photographs of Port Elizabeth.

62 / *Ikwezi* [Morning Star]. 1861–8. Pietermaritzburg and the Esidumbini mission. A Zulu religious and educational monthly issued by the American Board Mission.

63 / *North Lincoln Sphinx*. 1861–2. Grahamstown, last two parts at Keiskama Hoek. Regimental periodical of the 2nd Battalion of the 10th or North Lincoln Regiment of Foot. Private circulation only. (Repr. State Lib. 1976: 'It depicts the communal life of soldiers posted to a strange country for the protection of white farmers settled on the border, including stories, essays and poems, and reports of sporting and garrison news.')

64 / *Golden Fleece Gazette*. 1862. Published on board a ship en route to the Cape. Presumably one of the few survivors of a large number of such publications.

65 / *Indaba* [News[. 1862–5. Lovedale. A monthly paper published by the Glasgow Missionary Society for and by Black teachers and students at Lovedale, one-third in English as an educational exercise, otherwise in Xhosa.

66 / *De Natal Bode* [Natal Messenger]. 1862. Pietermaritzburg. A religious magazine with orthodox views (Smith).

67 / *South African Wesleyan*. 1862. Grahamstown. Weekly.

68 / *Church Gazette or Monthly Register for the Diocese of Grahamstown*. 1863. Grahamstown. Church of the Province.

69 / *Cape Farmers' Magazine*. 1864–5. Grahamstown. Monthly information on farming, racing, meteorological tables, etc., and photos.

70 / *Cape Comic News*. 1865. Cape Town.

71 / *Things New and Old*. 1865–6. Cape Town. A literary magazine published twice weekly.

72 / *Church News for the Province of South Africa*. 1866–? Cape Town. A Church of the Province monthly record.

73 / *Omnibus*. 1866. Grahamstown. The only known copy of this journal would seem to have disappeared (Saul).

74 / *City Chronicle*. 1867. Grahamstown. Another ephemeral magazine (Gordon-Brown).

75 / *Kindervriend van Genadendal* [Children's Friend ...]. 1867–? Genadendal. A religious publication for children published by the Moravian mission.

76 / *Mackintosh Journal*. 1867. Somerset East. Though variously listed as a periodical, this was probably a local newspaper.

77 / *South African Magazine.* 1867–9. Cape Town. 'A contribution to colonial literature' edited by A.W. Cole and others after the first series of the *Cape Monthly Magazine* (see #51) had come to an end, part of the effort to maintain a serious literary journal in Cape Town.

78 / *De Bode van Genadendal* [Genadendal Messenger]. 1868–? Genadendal. A religious 'monthly for the Christian family' issued in Dutch by the Moravian mission for its largely Coloured community.

79 / *Celt Gazette.* 1868. Published on board a ship en route to the Cape (*SANB*).

80 / *Orange Free State Mission Quarterly Review.* 1868–75. Cape Town? then Bloemfontein. A Church of the Province publication. Then *Bloemfontein Mission Quarterly Paper*, 1876–1913.

81 / *Echo.* 1869. Uitenhage. An attempt to re-launch, under the same name and by the same editor, a journal which had appeared briefly twenty-nine years earlier in Grahamstown (*SANB*).

82 / *Farm and South African Agriculturalist.* 1869–70. Grahamstown. Weekly.

83 / *Squib.* 1869–70. Cape Town. A humorous weekly with a number of cartoons and a strong political emphasis.

84 / *Cape Town Monthly Magazine.* 1870–80. Cape Town.

85 / *Kaffir Express/Isigidimi SamaXhosa.* 1870–6. Lovedale. Founded by James Stewart, a missionary doctor of the United Free Church of Scotland Mission, originally with four pages in English and four in Xhosa, concentrating on church and racial affairs. In 1876 the two parts were separated, that in English being renamed *Christian Express*, 1876–, that in Xhosa continuing as *Isigidimi SamaXhosa*, 1876–88, the first independent Black paper in South Africa. The former became a national paper with world coverage of missionary work. Continued from 1922 as *South African Outlook*, it is by far the longest-running South African periodical in English.

86 / *Kariega News.* 1870–71. Grahamstown. A weekly sustained for sixty-four numbers by two schoolboys (Gordon-Brown).

87 / *Zingari*. 1870–4. Cape Town. The first illustrated comic weekly in South Africa, and the first to which William Howard Schröder, the most important cartoonist of the period, contributed; something between a newspaper and a journal, its stated aim was 'to be playful without being spiteful, humorous without being vicious.' Best known for its portrait gallery.

88 / *Chumie Banner*. 1871. Alice. Another publishing curiosity printed for a year by an enthusiast of nineteen (Rossouw).

89 / *Clumber Times*. 1871–3. Grahamstown. Edited by 'O. Pah' (Gordon-Brown).

90 / *De Maandbode* [Monthly Messenger]. 1873–94. Burghersdorp. Mouthpiece of the Gereformeerde Kerk [Reformed Church], a different institution from the Dutch Reformed Church. Then *Het Kerkblad* [Church Paper], 1894–9, which was discontinued during the Boer War, but has continued to the present day since its resumption in 1902.

91 / *Cape Spiritualist and Family Medium*. [1874]. Cape Town (Coates).

92 / *White Ribbon*. 1874–? Stellenbosch. Issued by the Womens' Christian Temperance Union of the Cape of Good Hope.

93 / *Debater*. 1875. Grahamstown, Albany Debating Society (Gordon-Brown).

94 / *Fakkel* [Torch]. 1876–. Bloemfontein. A church and school monthly, the journal of the Dutch Reformed Church in the Orange Free State.

95 / *Healdtown Messenger*. [1876–80?]. Fort Beaufort. A religious paper for the Healdtown mission community (Switzer).

96 / *Natal Christian Magazine and Literary Miscellany*. 1876–8. Pietermaritzburg. Journal of the Young Men's Christian Association. Then the *Natal Magazine*, 1878–80.

97 / *uBaqa Lwababtwana* [Light of the Children]. 1877–83. Umvoti. A fortnightly mission news and devotional paper issued in Zulu by the American Board Mission.

98 / *Caldera Clippings*. 1877. Pietermaritzburg. Published on board the colonial mail packet SS *Caldera* during its voyage from London to Natal (*SANB*).

99 / *Cape Templar*. 1877. Cape Town.

100 / *Fun*. [1877]. Cape Town. A serio-comic paper (Coates).

101 / *Lantern*. 1877–92. Cape Town. A weekly with humorous articles, verses, and stories, and some political cartoons – according to Robinson ('Cartoons' in *SAStdEncyc*), a Transvaal edition merged with *Transvaal Truth* (#160).

102 / *Orange Free State Monthly Magazine*. 1877–80. Bloemfontein. A bilingual literary magazine.

103 / *South African Philosophical Society, Transactions*. 1877–1909. Cape Town. Published irregularly, they include some very good illustrations.

104 / *Het Afrikaansche Familieblad* [South African Family Paper]. 1878. Cape Town. Stories and miscellaneous articles (Güldenpfennig).

105 / *Assegai*. 1878. Pietermaritzburg. Listed only in *Periodicals from Africa*.

106 / *De Getuige* [Witness]. 1878–1904. Paarl. A supplement to the newspaper associated with the rise of Afrikaans, *Di Patriot*.

107 / *Good Templar Advocate*. 1878. Kimberley.

108 / *Natal Templar*. 1878–81. Pietermaritzburg.

109 / *Tsetse*. [1878]. Pretoria. Published by *Vokstem*, the first comic paper in the Transvaal (Coates).

110 / *Folk-Lore Journal*. 1879–80. Cape Town. Issued bi-monthly by the South African Folklore Society.

111 / *Mosquito*. 1879–80. Durban. 'A small week-end magazine contain-

ing local news, feuilletons, poems, etc.' seemingly the first of its kind in Natal.

112 / *Oranjevrijstaatsch Familie-Blad* [Orange Free State Family Paper]. 1879–80. Bloemfontein. A magazine supplement to the *Express*, continued as *Express-Familieblad*.

113 / *Cape Baptist*. 1880–2. Cape Town. Monthly.

114 / *Cape Times Christmas Number*. 1880–1906. Cape Town. Superseded by the *Cape Times Annual*.

115 / *Church Chronicle*. 1880–90. Grahamstown. Monthly church news 'for the diocese of Grahamstown and the Province of South Africa.'

116 / *News of the Camp*. 1880–1. Pretoria. 'A journal of fancies, notifications, gossip, and general chit-chat, published [three times a week] in the military camp of Her Majesty's forces defending the beleagured inhabitants of Pretoria' during the first Anglo-Boer War.

117 / *South African*. 1880–3? Listed only in *Periodicals from Africa*. (A newspaper of this name was published from 1892.)

118 / *South African Magazine and Review*. 1880. Port Elizabeth. A monthly with topical articles.

119 / *Wopse*. 1880–1. Cape Town. 'A journal of the wanderings of the Prince Alfred's Own Cape Voluntary Artillery among the Tambookie Campaign.'

120 / *Comet*. 1881. Grahamstown. A slanderous publication 'for men of the world.'

121 / *Illustrated Journal for Ladies*. [1881–?]. Grahamstown. A supplement to Eastern Star (Coates).

122 / *Meteor*. 1881–4. Grahamstown. Trivial chatter (Gordon-Brown).

123 / *Vineyard*. 1881–? Durban. Issued by the Church of the Province in Natal.

124 / *Kindervriend* [Children's Friend]. 1882–? Bloemfontein. Issued by the Dutch Reformed Church.

125 / *Umpire.* [1882]. Cape Town. The first sporting paper in the country (Coates).

126 / *Umwesile* [Wesleyan]. [1882]. Grahamstown. A local church publication of the Methodist Missionary Society in English and Xhosa (Switzers).

127 / *Caplander.* 1883. Paarl. A monthly 'national magazine for the diffusion of popular knowledge in South Africa,' including a list of historical events from the birth of Adam to the birth of the journal (Güldenpfennig).

128 / *Livingstone.* 1883–4. Robertson. A Dutch monthly for the mission in Africa.

129 / *St George and the Dragon.* 1883–4. Grahamstown. Another of the slanderous publications in which the town seemed to specialize. Then the *Society Journal and Court Gazette*, 1884 (Gordon-Brown).

130 / *Zaaier* [Sower]. 1883. Humansdorp. A religious monthly.

131 / *Cape Law Journal.* 1884–1900. Grahamstown. A bi-monthly with digests of cases and articles, 'under the superintendent of the Eastern districts law society.' From 1901 the *South African Law Journal.*

132 / *Cape Musical Monthly.* 1884. Queenstown.

133 / *The Church and Her Missionary Work in the Diocese in Grahamstown.* 1884–90. Grahamstown. Church of the Province.

134 / *Eeuwige Leven* [Eternal Life]. 1884. Cape Town. A Dutch religious magazine.

135 / *Knobkerrie.* 1884–6. Cape Town. 'Light and amusing sketches and reading on the current topics of the day.' The cartoonist Schröder was at least part owner of this comic weekly in the *Punch* style.

136 / *Natal Cricketer's Annual* . 1884–7. Pietermaritzburg.

137 / *South African Illustrated News*. 1884–5. Cape Town. The South African weekly counterpart to the *Illustrated London News*, it published excellent coloured lithographs and work by W.H. Schröder and H. Egersdörfer, as well as Theal's *Boers and Brits*.

138 / *South African Medical Journal*. 1884–90. Cape Town. Monthly.

139 / *War Cry*. 1884–1936. Johannesburg. Issued by the Salvation Army.

140 / *Di Afrikaanse Boer* [Afrikaner Farmer]. 1885. Paarl.

141 / *Sea Serpent*. 1885. Grahamstown. 'A nautical paper published during a voyage in the "Roslin Castle" from England to the Cape' (Güldenpfennig).

142 / *South African Methodist*. 1885–93. Grahamstown.

143 / *Church Magazine for South Africa*. 1886–91. Cape Town. Issued by the Church of the Province.

144 / *Educational Times of South Africa*. 1886–94. Cape Town. A monthly 'review of education, science and literature,' issued by the South African Teachers' Association. Then the *Educational News of South Africa*, 1894–.

145 / *Melon*. 1886–7. Cape Town. 'The South African Comic Paper and "Tit-bits,"' includes cartoons and caricatures.

146 / *Pioneer*. 1886–9. Cape Town. A religious quarterly offering 'a record of women's work in South Africa.' Originally associated with the Cape General Mission, it became *South African Pioneer*, 1890–?, the monthly organ of the South African General Mission.

147 / *Jester or Barberton Skit*. 1887. Barberton. A comic paper from the height of the Eastern Transvaal gold rush; has some crude cartoons.

148 / *Koningsbode* [Messenger of the King]. 1887–? Cape Town. Issued monthly by the Dutch Reformed Church.

149 / *Natal Football Annual*. 1887–8. Durban.

150 / *South Africa.* 1887. Cape Town. 'A monthly magazine of instructive, entertaining and domestic literature' (Güldenpfennig).

151 / *South African Freemason.* 1887–93. East London.

152 / *Agricultural Journal.* 1888–1903. Cape Town. Issued fortnightly by the Cape Department of Agriculture with a Dutch version, *Landbouw Journaal*; from 1903 as *Agricultural Journal of the Cape of Good Hope.*

153 / *Bulletin.* [1888]. Johannesburg. A humourous weekly journal of satire and politics.

154 / *Cape Punch.* 1888. Cape Town. A humorous weekly which includes social and theatrical sketches.

155 / *Cape Smoke.* 1888. Cape Town. A humorous magazine, its title derived from the jocular name for Cape brandy.

156 / *De Gemeente* [Congregation]. 1888–91. Wynberg. A bi-monthly Plymouth Brethren publication.

157 / *Grahamstown Annual.* 1888. Grahamstown. Includes articles on the exhibitions held during the year (Güldenpfennig).

158 / *Ingelosi Yenkosi* [Angel of the Lord]. 1888?–90?]. Mariannhill. A devotional newsletter in Zulu started by the Catholic Mission Fathers, a companion to the 'secular' paper *Izwi Labantu.*

159 / *Temperance News.* 1888–9. Cape Town. The official monthly organ of the Grand Lodge of Western South Africa.

160 / *Truth (Transvaal Truth?).* [1888–9]. Johannesburg. Some cartoons for it by Schröder, but no known copies, have survived.

161 / *Wasp.* 1888. Kimberley. A weekly journal, seemingly at one stage called *Critic.*

162 / *De Zendingbode* [Missionary Messenger]. 1888–9. Cape Town. The monthly magazine of the Dutch Reformed Church Women's Mission Society.

163 / *Golden Age.* 1889–90. Johannesburg. 'A mining, commercial and social journal for the Rand.'

164 / *Inkanyiso Yase Natal* [Natal Light]. 1889–96. Pietermaritzburg. Started as a general and religious monthly by St Alban's College (Church of the Province), partly under Black control as 'the first native journal in Natal,' with a large readership. From 1895, Zulu-owned and -controlled and more strongly critical of colonial policy.

165 / *South African Annual.* 1889. Cape Town.

166 / *Burlesque.* 1890–2. Johannesburg. 'A weekly family and society journal of the times,' edited by Henry Hess. When an interdict was served on it, it immediately resumed as the *Critic*, 1892–6, dedicated to 'exposing social ills' and scathing in its attack on the government and the 'Randlords.' When again suspended, it resumed as the *Transvaal Critic*, 1896–? Suspended once again during the Boer War.

167 / *Buzzer.* 1890–1. Kimberley. 'The South African Telegraph Journal" (*PISAL*).

168 / *Cape Illustrated Magazine.* 1890–1900. Cape Town. An important monthly, edited by Professor J. Gill. It has some very interesting articles, a good deal of poetry, stories and serialized novels, and some good illustrations of South African scenery, but though its prospectus sees the *Cape Monthly Magazine* as its 'prototype,' much of the material is pitched at á more popular level. From May 1900 as *South African Illustrated Magazine.*

169 / *Cape Town of Today.* 1890–2. Cape Town. An annual.

170 / *South African Rambler.* 1890. Cape Town. A light-hearted fortnightly.

171 / *Southern Cross.* 1890–1901. Port Elizabeth. Church of the Province.

172 / *Transvaal Observer Christmas Number.* 1890. Pretoria.

173 / *Witwatersrand Mining and Metallurgical Review.* 1890–1. Johannesburg. 'A monthly journal devoted to the interests of the South African

gold fields,' the first technical journal on the Rand. Then the *South African Mining Journal and Financial News*, 1891–?, 'A journal for investors, mining engineers and managers.' Later became the *South African Mining and Engineering Journal*.

174 / *Cape Times Law Reports*. 1891–1910. Cape Town.

175 / *Fort England Mirror*. 1891–7? Grahamstown. Produced at the local mental hospital (Gordon-Brown).

176 / *Herder* [Shepherd]. 1891–2. Cape Town.

177 / *Press Annual*. 1891–7. Pretoria. The sculptor Anton von Wouw was a cartoonist on the *Press* for some time.

178 / *Railway News*. 1891. Cape Town? Issued by the South African Church Railway Mission (Shackleton).

179 / *South African Catholic Magazine*. 1891–1900. Cape Town. A monthly. From 1901 *Catholic Magazine for South Africa*.

180 / *South African Cricketer's Annual*. 1891–2. Cape Town (SANB).

181 / *Umhlobo Wabamyanu/Mohabo Oa Babatso* [Friend of the Blacks]. 1891–2. Queenstown. A religious paper in Xhosa and Sotho.

182 / *Cape Church Monthly and Parish Record*. 1892–? Cape Town. A Church of the Province monthly, issued together with a supplement *Dawn of the Day*.

183 / *Cosmopole*. 1892. Johannesburg. A Post Office magazine in English and Dutch.

184 / *Eastern Province Magazine*. 1892–8. Grahamstown. A quarterly publication of the Eastern Province literary and scientific society. During its later run the *South African Register and Eastern Province Magazine*.

185 / *Gereformeerd Maandblad* [Reformed Monthly]. 1892–? Stellenbosch. A monthly aimed particularly at ministers.

186 / *Grahamstown Circuit's Wesleyan Methodist Church Record*. 1892–3. Grahamstown.

187 / *Metropolitan Wesleyan Church Record*. 1892–4. Cape Town.

188 / *South African Baptist*. 1892–1918. Cape Town.

189 / *South African Licensed Victuallers' Review and Hotel Courier*. 1892–3. Cape Town. Seemingly for part of its run the *Licensed Victuallers' and Sporting Gazette* and also sometimes listed as the *South African Review and Licensed Victuallers' Gazette*, 1893–6, though it would seem to have become the *South African Review of Sport, Politics, Trade, Travel, Society and the Drama*, 1893–1900. After it had absorbed the *South African Sportsman* and the *South African Wireless Weekly*, it became the longest-lasting weekly journal of its time and circulated widely through the country. The avowed organ of the 'Stalwart' party, its Kaatjie Kekkelbek humorous feature was particularly popular.

190 / *South African Sportsman*. 1892–3. Cape Town. Weekly, absorbed by the *South African Review*.

191 / *South African Wireless Weekly*. 1892–3. Cape Town. Also absorbed by *South African Review*.

192 / *Freedom*. 1893. Pietermaritzburg.

193 / *In Afrikanerland*. 1893. Cape Town. A monthly with topical articles, poems, and an African portrait gallery.

194 / *Jong-Zuid-Afrika*. 1893–6. Paarl. A Taalbond monthly for young people and teachers. Then *Ons Tijdschrift* [Our Magazine], 1896–1901, Cape Town. This illustrated family monthly with separate section for women and children was very popular and had a large circulation throughout South Africa. It in effect replaced *Di Patriot*, which had taken a strong political turn, and it absorbed the Pretoria journal the *Afrikaansch Familieblad*, 1899–1900.

195 / *Moon*. 1893–5. Johannesburg. A weekly general-interest magazine, edited by 'The Tattler' and including political notes, mining news, general and sporting gossip; it also ran annuals in 1893 and 1894, which have good illustrations and photographs.

196 / *Mosupa-Tsela* [Guide]. 1893–? Bethunie, near Rustenburg. In this, its initial series, before resumption in 1914, a religious and general-interest paper produced in Tswana by the Church of Sweden Lutheran Mission.

197 / *Natal Diocesan Magazine*. 1893–1904. Pietermaritzburg.

198 / *Nugget*. 1893. Johannesburg. This 'snapper-up of unconsidered trifles' was an illustrated sporting, theatrical, and social weekly.

199 / *South African Financial Record*. 1893–9. Johannesburg. A weekly journal for investors and businessmen.

200 / *South African Masonic Record*. 1893–4. Cape Town. Monthly.

201 / *South African Medical Journal*. 1893–9. Cape Town. Monthly.

202 / *South African Mining Material Exchange*. 1893–1900. Johannesburg.

203 / *Umhlobo Wa Bantu* [Friend of the People]. 1893–4. Pietermaritzburg. A Church of the Province devotional monthly printed at St Alban's College in Zulu.

204 / *Umsizi Wabantu* [Helper of the People]. 1893. Edendale. A Zulu religious and educational weekly with a column in English, associated with the Edendale Native Training Institution.

205 / *Cape Town Highlanders' Monthly*. 1894. Cape Town (Güldenpfennig).

206 / *Chemical and Metallurgical Society of South Africa Journal*. 1894–1903. Johannesburg.

207 / *Church Magazine of the Diocese of Bloemfontein*. 1894–9. Bloemfontein. Issued by the Church of the Province.

208 / *Freelance*. 1894. Cape Town. A weekly magazine with caricatures and articles (Güldenpfennig).

209 / *Ladies' Magazine*. 1894–5. Johannesburg.

210 / *Link*. 1894–9. Johannesburg. 'The organ of the Praying Band.' Included Christmas issues for 1894 and 1895, the latter combined with *South African Pioneer*.

211 / *Machinery*. 1894–9. Johannesburg. A monthly 'trade journal and magazine of useful information.'

212 / *Mountain Club Annual*. 1894–? Cape Town.

213 / *Pictorial United South Africa*. 1894. Pretoria.

214 / *Afrikanderland*. 1895. Cape Town. A continuation of #193?

215 / *Agricultural Advertiser and South African Farmer*. 1895–1906. Cape Town. Monthly.

216 / *Cape Observer*. 1895. Cape Town. A weekly 'journal of the household.'

217 / *Genade en Waarheid* [Grace and Truth]. 1895. Cape Town. A supplement to *De Volksbode*.

218 / *Johannesburg Sporting Guide*. 1895. Johannesburg.

219 / *Johannesburg Times Annual*. 1895. Johannesburg.

220 / *Newspaper Press Union of South Africa Bulletin*. 1895–1922. Johannesburg.

221 / *Owl*. 1895–1903. Johannesburg, then Cape Town from mid-1896. 'A serio-comic weekly,' from 1897 with a Christmas number. Well known for its political cartoons, it gives a light-hearted but critical review of society and politics at the end of the century.

222 / *Scientific African*. 1895–6. Cape Town. 'A monthly journal of South African science, arts and crafts' (Güldenpfenning).

223 / *South African Agriculturalist*. 1895. Cape Town (Travis).

224 / *South African Jewish Chronicle*. 1895–1903. Johannesburg.

225 / *South African Philatelist.* 1895–6. Johannesburg.

226 / *South African Photographer.* 1895–? Cape Town. Monthly.

227 / *South African Sentinel and Gospel Echo.* 1895–? Cape Town. A Seventh-Day Adventist monthly, published by the International Tract Society, parallel but not identical to its Dutch counterpart *De Wachter* (#229).

228 / *Sun.* 1895. Johannesburg.

229 / *De Wachter* [Sentinel]. 1895–9. Cape Town. See #227.

230 / *Civil Service Journal.* 1896. Cape Town.

231 / *Geological Society of South Africa. Transactions.* 1896–? Johannesburg.

232 / *Hoop der Toekomst* [Hope for the Future]. 1896. Waterval Boven. Issued by personnel of the Netherlands South African Railway Company.

233 / *Methodist Churchman.* 1896–? Cape Town.

234 / *Ons Klyntji* [Our Little One]. 1896–1906. Paarl. A non-political monthly, 'the only magazine in Africaans' and certainly the first with any literary pretension written in the language, its object being to teach the people to write. Suspended during the Boer War.

235 / *Rand Magazine.* 1896. Johannesburg. A general-interest magazine aimed mainly at women.

236 / *Skeptic.* 1896. Johannesburg. A humorous magazine.

237 / *South African Domestic Monthly.* 1896–? Cape Town. A monthly 'magazine for the home,' with social chat, a guide to health and beauty, and suggestions for mothers and housewives.

238 / *South African Educator.* 1896–1903. Cape Town. A monthly circular for teachers, from 1901 the *South African Educator and University Review.*

239 / *Bay Trade Record*. 1897–8. Port Elizabeth. Monthly.

240 / *Citizen*. [1897–8?]. Kimberley. A paper published by the Virginia Jubilee Singers, a troupe of Black American singers touring South Africa, the earliest independent publication for Coloureds (Switzer).

241 / *Heilbode* [Messenger of Salvation]. 1897–1900. George. A monthly for the Christian family.

242 / *Ikwezi* [Morning Star]. 1897–9. Eshowe. A monthly paper for the Anglican diocese of Zululand published entirely in Zulu during these years – later resumed with some English.

243 / *Johannesburg Sceptic and Transvaal Miner*. 1897. Johannesburg. Not mentioned by Nagelgast.

244 / *Johannesburger Bode*. 1897. Johannesburg.

245 / *Racing Calendar and Agricultural Journal*. 1897–8. Port Elizabeth.

246 / *South African Journal of Commerce*. 1897–9. London? This is not listed in the *Waterloo Directory* and was probably produced for the South African market.

247 / *South African Storekeeper*. 1897–1901. Cape Town.

248 / *South African Volunteer Gazette*. 1897–1901. Cape Town. The official monthly organ of the volunteer force in the Cape Colony.

249 / *Templar Mirror*. 1897–9. Johannesburg.

250 / *Transvaal and South African Licensed Victuallers' Gazette and Sporting Review*. 1897. Johannesburg.

251 / *Transvaal Mail and Skeptic*. 1897. Johannesburg.

252 / *Cape of Good Hope Teachers Annual*. 1898–1905. Cape Town. Issued by the South African Teachers' Association.

253 / *Christian Student*. 1898–1904. Stellenbosch. Organ of the Students' Christian Association of South Africa.

254 / *Grahamstown Visitor.* 1898. Grahamstown. A weekly guide to the South African Exhibition held this year in the town (Gordon-Brown).

255 / *Johannesburg Mademoiselle.* 1898. Johannesburg. A 'journal of fashions and society chit-chat, the smart paper for smart women.'

256 / *Life.* 1898. Johannesburg. 'A sub-tropical journal' – a satirical magazine edited by Douglas Blackburn.

257 / *Light from the Line.* 1898–? Grahamstown. Issued by the South African Church Railway Mission (Church of the Province).

258 / *Natal Agricultural Journal and Mining Record.* 1898–? Pietermaritzburg. Issued by the Natal Government Department of Agriculture and Mines.

259 / *Skandinaven.* [1898–1900?]. Cape Town. Directed at Scandinavian businessmen (Ratcliffe).

260 / *South African Globe.* 1898. Listed only in *Periodicals in Africa.*

261 / *South African Journal of Health.* 1898–1904. Cape Town. The monthly organ of the South African branch of the International Medical, Missionary and Benevolent Association.

262 / *South African Red Book.* 1898–9. Cape Town. 'A record of insurance, banking, shipping and commercial affairs.'

263 / *South African Typographical Journal.* 1898–1908. Johannesburg.

264 / *Torch.* 1898–9. Durban. Issued by the Natal Progressive League.

265 / *Visitor.* 1898–1900. Cape Town. Issued by the Seventh Day Adventists South African Congress.

266 / *Zululand Diocesan Paper.* 1898–1900. Eshowe. Issued by the Church of the Province.

267 / *Het Afrikaansch Familieblad* [Afrikaans Family Paper]. 1899–1900. Pretoria. A monthly family magazine which includes war illustrations, and stories and articles of South African interest. Incorporated in *Ons Tijdschrift* from 1900 (see #194).

268 / *Animal Friend.* 1899–1900. Cape Town. Issued by the Cape of Good Hope SPCA (Travis).

269 / *Cape Cyclist.* 1899. Cape Town. Monthly organ of the Green Point Cycling and Athletic Club.

270 / *Christelike Skoolblad* [Christian School Magazine]. 1899–? Pretoria. Issued by the Transvaal Teachers' Association, later as *Kristelike Skoolblad.*

271 / *Gazette of Fashion and Illustrated Dress Guide.* 1899. Cape Town. Issued by Garlicks (*SAL*).

272 / *De Hervormer.* 1899. Pretoria. Two issues of this, the official journal of the Hervormde Kerk (the Reformed as opposed to the Dutch Reformed Church) appeared before it was suspended during the Boer War (*SA Std Encyc*).

273 / *Johannesburg Faces and Places.* 1899. Johannesburg. A monthly illustrated magazine.

274 / *Johannesburg Witness.* 1899. Johannesburg. 'A democratic weekly' edited by J.T. Bain, who was later a trade union leader.

275 / *eKerike e-Katolika* [Universal Church]. 1899. Umtata. A diocesan Church of the Province magazine in Xhosa (Switzer).

276 / *Ladysmith Bombshell.* 1899–1900. Issued during the siege, each of the eight numbers has a full-page cartoon on the front page and some have text illustrations. Reissued as 'a souvenir of the siege.'

277 / *Ladysmith Lyre.* 1899. An illustrated comic paper issued during the siege.

278 / *Lantern.* 1899. Johannesburg. 'A critic of the contemporary scene.'

279 / *Natal Mercury War Specials.* 1899–1900. Durban.

280 / *Natal Volunteer Record.* 1899–1900. Durban (Freer).

281 / *Rambler.* [1899?]. Bloemfontein. A paper connected with the Ramblers Club (Schoeman).

282 / *South African Endeavourer*. 1899–? Cape Town. Organ of the South African Christian Endeavour Union (Ratcliffe).

283 / *South African Museum, Annals*. 1899–. Cape Town.

284 / *South African Saddling Bell Racing Record*. 1899–1902. Cape Town.

285 / *Süd-Afrikanisches Gemeindeblatt* [South African Community Journal]. 1899–1910. Cape Town. A German religious magazine issued by the Deutscher Evangelischer Volksbote vur Süd-Afrika.

286 / *Telephone*. 1899–1900. Cape Town. 'The Cape Town weekly paper of humorous gossip,' with social, political, sporting, and dramatic sections.

287 / *Transvaal Philosophical Society for the Advancement of Science Art and Literature – Papers*. 1899. Johannesburg.

288 / *African Commerce*. 1900. Cape Town.

289 / *Bandolier*. 1900–? Cape Town. The Cape Mounted Police regimental monthly.

290 / *Cape of Good Hope Pamphlet*. 1900. Cape Town. Only one number published (Travis).

291 / *Gram*. 1900. Pretoria (later reissued in London). A 'social magazine' published by the British prisoners of war in the officers' camp in Pretoria.

292 / *Industries*. 1902. Durban. A monthly 'devoted to engineering, mining, and other colonial industries' (Ratcliffe).

293 / *Licensed Victuallers' and Sporting Gazette*. 1900. Cape Town. The fortnightly organ of the Licensed Victuallers' Protection Association, not to be confused with earlier publications.

294 / *Review and Critic*. 1900. Durban.

295 / *South African Catalogue of Books*. 1900. Johannesburg.

296 / *South African Mercantile Gazette*. 1900–5. Johannesburg.

297 / *Transvaal Trader.* 1900. Johannesburg? (Travis).

298 / *Veldt.* 1900. Cape Town. An illustrated monthly with good illustrations of scenery and people.

299 / *Vigilance Papers.* 1900. Cape Town.

300 / *Waterfall Wag.* 1900. Pretoria. Published by British prisoners of war in the camp for other ranks in Pretoria.

Reprints and Anthologies

Very little of the periodical material has been reprinted in more accessible form. The *South African Journal* (1824) has been reprinted in fascimile by the South African Library; and in addition to numerous newspapers the Library has also made *Sam Sly's African Journal* (1843–51), the *Zingari* (1870–5), the *Wasp* (Kimberley, 1888), and the *Owl* (1896–1907) available on microfilm. The State Library has made *News of the Camp* (1880–1) available on microfilm. *Selected Articles from the Cape Monthly Magazine (New Series 1870–76*, introduced by A.M. Lewin Robinson, Van Riebeeck Society, Second Reprint Series no. 9 (Cape Town 1978) reprints a generous selection from this later series of the magazine, largely confined to personal reminiscences of historical events and of travels.

Also of interest is Jennifer Crwys-Williams's *South African Despatches: Two Centuries of the Best in South African Journalism* (Johannesburg: Ashanti Publishing 1989), an anthology which includes twenty-three nineteenth-century items, most of them newspaper accounts of military engagements.

Territories beyond South Africa

As the early material from these countries is so sparse, account has been taken of *all* serial publications. In all cases the lists provided go beyond those in any of the standard bibliographies.

BIBLIOGRAPHIES

The most substantial bibliographies for the territories beyond South Africa are:
Willet S., and D.P. Ambrose. *Lesotho: A Comprehensive Bibliography.* World Bibliographical Series vols. 3 (Oxford: Clio Press 1980).

Hartridge, Anne. *Rhodesia National Bibliography.* Salisbury: Rhodesia National Archives 1977.

Pollak, Oliver B. and Karen. *Rhodesia/Zimbabwe: An International Bibliography.* Boston: G.K. Hall 1977.

Wallace C.S. *Swaziland: A Bibliography.* Johannesburg: University of the Witwatersrand School of Librarianship 1967.

Nyeko, Balan. *Swaziland: A Bibliography.* World Bibliographical Series vol. 24. Oxford: Clio Press 1982.

Swaziland Official Publications, 1880–1972: A Bibliography. Pretoria: State Library, Microfiche edition 1975.

Kitching G.C. *A St Helena Bibliography* limited edition of 20 copies. St Helena: Government Printer 1937.

Balima, M.G. *Botswana, Lesotho and Swaziland: A Guide to Official Publications, 1868–1968.* Washington: Library of Congress 1971.

K.L. Jones's substantive bibliography of Botswana is in progress.

Listings of serials from these territories are included in *Periodicals from Africa,* but they are by no means comprehensive.

DISCUSSIONS OF THE MATERIAL

The only substantial discussion is W.D. Gale's *The Rhodesian Press: The History of the Rhodesian Printing and Publishing Company, Ltd.* (Salisbury: Rhodesian Printing and Publishing Company 1962). This book was written specifically for the company that produced the *Rhodesian Herald,* the *Bulawayo Chronicle,* and the *Umtali Advertiser.* Though it concentrates on the history of these newspapers, it does take account of others in the field, and its first six chapters provide an extremely entertaining and informative account of the Rhodesian press in the pioneering days. On the mission presses and other publishing ventures in Bechuanaland, in addition to the Switzers's bibliography and other works already mentioned, there is I.S.J. Venter's 'The Role of the Press in the Wesleyan Bechuana Mission during the Half-Century 1825–75' (in Afrikaans), *Historia* (1955); N. Parson's 'The Tswana Press – an Outline of Its History since 1856,' *Kutlwano* (Gaborone, Botswana) 3:8 (1968), 4–8; and J.D. Jones's 'Mahoko a Becwana – the Second Tswana Newspaper,' *Botswana Notes and Records* 4 (1972), 112–20.

LISTING OF THE MATERIAL

Some of the items listed, particularly in the case of Bechuanaland, were not published within the boundaries of the territory itself. The main sources are the bibliographies listed above and *PISAL.*

Bechuanaland

1 / *Morisa Oa Molemo* [Shepherd of the Good]. [1836]. Kuruman. Tracts written in Tswana.

2 / *Pulela Ea Lidea Surevanta* [Commentaries of Lidea Surevanta]. 1841. Kuruman.

3 / *Molekoli Oa Becuana* [Bechuana Visitor]. 1856–8. Thaba'Nchu. A religious and general-interest monthly in English and Tswana produced by the Methodist Missionary Society.

4 / *Mokaeri Oa Becuana* [Teacher of the Bechuana]. 1857–9. Kuruman. The oldest Tswana general-interest newspaper.

5 / *Mahoko A Becoana* [News for the Botswana]. 1883–96. Kuruman. A religious and general-interest monthly. This and the other publications in Tswana at Kuruman were from the London Missionary Society Press.

6 / *Griqualand West and Bechuanaland Church Magazine* (Church of the Province). 1884–93.

7 / *Tampan and Bechuanaland Gazette.* 1885? Vryburg.

8 / *Vryburg Advocate and Bechuanaland Gazette.* 1886–7. Vryburg.

9 / *Bechuanaland Government Gazette.* 1887–? Vryburg.

10 / *The Bechuanaland News.* 1888–1908. Vryburg.

11 / *Bechuanaland: Resident Commissioner's Annual Report* (Great Britain, Colonial Office). 1889–? London.

12 / *Bechuanaland: High Commissioner's Proclamations and Notices.* 1891–? Pretoria.

13 / *Mafeking Observer and Protectorate Chronicle.* 1894? Mafeking.

14 / *Mafeking Advertiser.* 1896. Mafeking.

15 / *Mafeking Critic.* 1896. Mafeking.

16 / *Mafeking Mail and Protectorate Guardian.* 1899–? Mafeking

17 / *Koranta Ea Becoana* [Bechuana Newspaper]. 1901–8. Mafeking. A weekly newspaper in Tswana but with some English, edited by Sol Plaatje.

Basutoland

1 / *Basutoland Records.* 1833–68. Cape Town.

2 / *Lenqosana La Lesuto* [Messenger of Lesotho]. 1850. Platberg. A religious magazine in Sotho produced by the Methodist Missionary press.

3 / *Leselinyana la Lesotho* [Little Light of Lesotho]. 1863–? Morija. Written in English and Sotho. The oldest newspaper in Basutoland, founded by a Swiss missionary and taken over by the Paris Evangelical Missionary Society. From the first more than just a religious publication.

4 / *Journal des missions* (Paris Evangelical Missionary Society). 1867–? Morija.

5 / *Orange Free State Mission – Quarterly Paper* (Church of the Province). 1868–75. Then *Bloemfontein Mission Quarterly Paper,* 1875–1912.

6 / *Little Light of Basotholand.* 1872–7. Morija. The English version of *Leselinyana.*

7 / *Basutoland: High Commissioner's Proclamations and Notices.* 1884–96. Pretoria.

8 / *Motsualle Oa Baboleli* [Friend of the Evangelists] (Paris Evangelical Missionary Society). 1889–1905. Morija. A guide for Sunday School teachers in Sotho.

9 / *Basutoland. Governor's Annual Reports* (Great Britain, Colonial Office). 1890–? London.

10 / *Gospel Work in Basutoland* (Paris Evangelical Missionary Society). 1894–? London.

11 / *News from Barotsiland* (Paris Evangelical Missionary Society). 1895–? London.

12 / *Lentswe La Batho* [Voice of the People]. [1899?] Maseru. A Black-owned Sotho paper opposed to the policies of *Leselinyana*.

13 / *Koloyane Kaleidoscope*. 1900. Kolojane. Published for the refugee community during the Boer War.

The *Friend* (Bloemfontein) has always included extensive coverage of Lesotho affairs.

Rhodesia

At times the dates are problematical.

British SA Co.
– *Administrative Accounts*. 1891–?
– *Balance Sheet*. 1891–?
– *Mining in Rhodesia*. 1899–?
– *Report of Annual Meeting*. 1891–?
– *Reports of Extraordinary Annual General Meetings*. 1893–9.
– *Director's Reports*. 1891–?
– *Estimates of Expenditure*. 1898–?
– *Information as to Mining in Rhodesia*. 1899–?
– *Reports on the Administration of Rhodesia*. 1892–?
– *Reports on the Native Disturbances*. 1896–?
– *Report of the Company's Proceedings*. 1892–?

Rhodesia (Southern)
– *Civil Service List*. 1900–?
– *Ministry of Education: Report on Education*. ?
– *Ministry of Justice: Law Reports*. 1899–?

1 / *Nugget*. 1890–1. Fort Victoria. The first Central African newspaper – handwritten.

2 / *Mashonaland Herald and Zambesian Times*. 1891–2. Salisbury. Edited by William Ernest Fairbridge, produced in pen and ink and mimeographed for the Argus Company. It ran for sixty-two weeks, the initial weekly circulation being 180 copies. It was superseded for a short interim by *News and Advertisements* until the *Rhodesia Herald* could be launched.

3 / *Rhodesia Defence Force Journal.* 1891–? Salisbury.

4 / *Tuli Times.* 1891. Tuli. Handwritten and cyclostyled.

5 / *Mashonaland Annual.* 1892. Salisbury.

6 / *News and Advertisements.* 1892. Salisbury. The first printed matter in Central Africa, superseded by the *Rhodesia Herald.*

7 / *Mashonaland Quarterly Paper* (Church of the Province, London). 1892–? It included *Letter for the Children,* 1896–?

8 / *Rhodesia Chronicle and Mashonaland Advertiser.* 1892. Tuli. Its Christmas issue for 1892 was called *Mashonaland Annual,* then the Mashonaland Times.

9 / *Rhodesia Herald.* 1892–? Salisbury. The first substantial newspaper in the territory, supplanting *News and Advertisements* and the *Mashona Herald.*

10 / *Longland's Transvaal and Rhodesia Directory.* 1893–4. Johannesburg.

11 / *Mashonaland Times and Mining Chronicle.* 1893–6. Fort Victoria. Successor to the *Rhodesia Chronicle.*

12 / *Umtali Advertiser.* 1893–5. Umtali. Originally written in pen and ink, and cyclostyled; from November 1894 typewritten and cyclostyled. Then the *Rhodesia Advertiser.*

13 / *British South Africa Company Gazette.* 1894–? Salisbury. Until 28 September 1894 a supplement to the *Rhodesia Herald.*

14 / *Bulawayo Chamber of Commerce: Report of Annual General Meeting.* 1894–? Bulawayo.

15 / *Bulawayo Chronicle.* 1894–? Bulawayo. A daily from 5 May 1897. From 1898 it produced a special Christmas number.

16 / *Catholic Directory of British South Africa.* 1894–? Cape Town.

17 / *Bulawayo Sketch.* 1894–7. Bulawayo.

18 / *Matabele Times and Mining Journal.* 1994–9. Bulawayo. The first newspaper in Matabeleland, cyclostyled until 28 September 1894, when it became the first printed paper in Matabeleland, preceding the *Bulawayo Chronicle* by two weeks.

19 / *Matabeleland News and Mining Record.* 1894. Bulawayo. Then the *Rhodesia Weekly Review.*

20 / *Northern Optimist.* 1894–5. Gwelo. Then the *Gwelo Times.*

21 / *Rhodesia Weekly Review of Men, Mines and Money.* 1894–5. Bulawayo.

22 / *Bulawayo Board of Executors: Report.* 1895–? Bulawayo.

23 / *Bulawayo Observer and Licensed Victuallers' Gazette.* 1895–? Bulawayo.

24 / *[Davis's] Bulawayo Directory and Handbook of Matabeleland.* 1895–9. Cape Town.

25 / *Meph: A Serio-Comic Newspaper.* 1895. Bulawayo.

26 / *Nugget: An Illustrated Magazine.* 1895–7. Salisbury. Edited by Alfred Lyon, its motto was 'Root, Hog or Bust.' Later *Nugget and Rhodesian Critic*, 1898–9, still edited by Lyon but produced in Bulawayo.

27 / *Rhodesia Advertiser.* 1895–9. Umtali. Then *Umtali Advertiser.*

28 / *Rhodesia Weekly Review: A Review of Men, Mines and Money.* 1895–8. Bulawayo.

29 / *Chamber of Mines, Salisbury: Monthly Report.* 1896–? Salisbury.

30 / *Public Opinion.* 1896. Bulawayo. Handwritten and cyclostyled. A newspaper circulated in the laager during the rebellion.

31 / *Rhodesia Railway Mission: Yearbook.* 1896–?

32 / *Rhodesian Landowners and Farmers' Association: Annual Report.* 1896–? Bulawayo.

33 / *Rhodesian Times and Financial News.* 1896–9. Salisbury.

34 / *Bulawayo Caledonian Society: Annual Report.* 1897–? Bulawayo.

35 / *Bulawayo Public Library: Annual Report.* 1897–? Bulawayo.

36 / *Gwelo Times.* 1897–? Gwelo.

37 / *Lomagundi Hornet.* 1897–8. Lomagundi?

38 / *Nellie Reef Development Company: Balance Sheet and Report.* 1897– ? Bulawayo.

39 / *Owl.* 1897. Bulawayo. The first paper in the territory with a regular cartoon.

40 / *Rhodesia.* 1897–? London.

41 / *Rhodesia Chamber of Mines: Annual Report.* 1897–? Bulawayo.

42 / *Bulawayo Memorial Hospital: Annual Report.* 1898–? Bulawayo.

43 / *Bulawayo Presbyterian Church: Annual Report.* 1898. Bulawayo.

44 / *Zambesi Mission Record* (English Jesuits). 1898–? Bulawayo.

45 / *Bulawayo Advertiser and Rhodesia Advocate.* 1899–? Bulawayo.

46 / *Donaldson and Hill's Transvaal and Rhodesia Directory.* 1899–? Johannesburg.

47 / *Free Press Trade, Business and Office Directory of Matabeleland.* 1899. Bulawayo.

48 / *Rhodesian Scientific Association: Proceedings and Transactions.* 1899–? Salisbury.

49 / *Royal Salisbury Golf Club: Annual Report.* 1899–? Salisbury.

50 / *St John the Baptist Monthly Magazine.* 1899. Bulawayo.

Also of interest: *Mozambique Directory* (Lorenço Marques) 1898–?

St Helena

All were published in Jamestown.

1 / *St Helena Monthly Register.* 1810–13.

2 / *Agricultural and Horticultural Society of St Helena – Proceedings.* 1823–31.

3 / *St Helena Almanac and Annual Register.* 1836?–56.

4 / *St Helena: Blue Book.* 1839–?

5 / *St Helena Gazette.* 1845, 1849.

6 / *St Helena: Government Gazette.* 1847–?

7 / *St Helena Chronicle.* 1852–3.

8 / *St Helena Herald.* 1853–60. (*PISAL*).

9 / *St Helena Record.* 1860–1.

10 / *St Helena Guardian.* 1861–? (*PISAL*).

11 / *St Helena Advertiser.* 1865–6.

12 / *St Helena Spectator.* 1866–7.

13 / *Almanac and Annual Register.* 1868, 1883.

14 / *Bug.* 1888.

15 / *Mosquito.* 1888–9.

16 / *St Helena Church News.* 1888.

17 / *St Helena: Report of the Administration* (Great Britain, Colonial Office). 1889–? London.

18 / *St Helena Diocesan Magazine.* 1899–?

19 / *De Krijgsgevangene* [Prisoner of War]. 1901. A Boer prisoners' paper.

Wood's Royal Southern Kalender, Tasmanian Register and General Australasian and East Indies Official Directory (Launceston, Van Dieman's Land,1850) contains directories of officials at St Helena.

Swaziland

1 / *Times of Swaziland.* 1896–? Bredasdorp.

Though it is not a Swaziland publication, *De Kaap Annual* (1896, Barberton) contains a directory of Bremersdorp.

Zululand

1 / *Net: Magazine of the Zululand Missionary Association.* 1897–? London.

2 / *Zululand Governor's Annual Report* (Great Britain, Colonial Office). 1890–6. London.

3 / *Zululand Diocesan Paper* (Church of the Province). 1898–1900. Eshowe.

Southern Africa: Further 'Periodicals of Empire'

Sidney Mendelssohn, in his pioneering South African bibliography, over and above his title-indexing of certain South African periodicals, indexed the titles of articles pertinent to South Africa in the following publications: *Manchester Geographical Society* (1887–1903), *Royal Colonial Institute Proceedings* (1870–1907), *Royal Geographical Society* (1832–1907), and *Scottish Geographical Magazine* (1885–1907). Mendelssohn's attention to these journals may serve as a reminder that many nineteenth-century periodicals not physically published within Southern Africa or primarily intended for a Southern African readership are, in a slightly different but important sense, 'Periodicals of Empire.' Apart from the scientific work of which Mendelssohn takes some account, there are particularly pertinent British publications of a general nature such as the *Colonial Magazine* and *Review of Reviews.* Then too, there is valuable work related to Southern Africa in many of the missionary periodicals: the *Foreign Mission Chronicle of the Episcopal Church in Scotland*

(Edinburgh 1877–99), for example, a work not listed in the *Waterloo Directory*, contains the *Kaffrarian Diocesan Quarterly*; and the *Journal des Missions Évangéliques* (Paris, 1826–) is a major source for Basutoland. The interested researcher wishing to find such material will consult the *Waterloo Directory* or comparable bibliographies under obvious title openings (such as 'African ...', 'Cape ... ', or 'London Missionary Society ...'), but the following periodicals are some that might suggest additional lines of approach: *Alexander's East India and Colonial and Commercial Journal* (London, 1831–42); *American Zulu Mission Annual* (Boston, 1900–); *Anti-Slavery [Monthly] Reporter* (London, 1825–36) and its successor *British Emancipator* (1837–40); *Black and White Budget* (London, 1899–1905), which ran a Transvaal Special during the years 1899–1900; *Mining Journal, Railway and Commercial Gazette* (London 1844–), *Union Line Gazette* (London, 1896–1900) and *War against War in South Africa* (London, 1899–1900).

Conclusion

The main needs are for basic reference tools: the priorities are for an accurate and comprehensive bibliography of nineteenth-century serials such as only the State Library could undertake, with all contributing libraries doing physical shelf-checks, and with major holdings from abroad being taken into consideration; a thorough bibliography of secondary materials on the press, periodicals, and newspapers; and a great deal more in the way of indexing and reprinting of the material. Until these basic tools have been provided it will not really be possible for authoritative analyses of the periodicals to be made, or for the social and literary historians to do full justice to the material. Though valuable work has been done in a number of areas, there are surprising gaps: given the importance of the early missionary activities, for example, it is surprising that there has been no authoritative study of the missionary presses during the century. Given its importance among the periodicals, it is also surprising that there has been no serious assessment of the *Cape Monthly Magazine*, and of why it was not possible to sustain a serious literary magazine in the country after its demise: it may be that later in the century South Africa (by comparison with Australia, say) was too close to Britain in terms of travelling time, with the result that serious readers could readily sustain themselves on imported periodicals without any sense of being much behind the times. It is heartening to see, however, that the first survey of South African literature for some twenty-five years, Malvern Van Wyk Smith's *Grounds of Contest* (Kenwyn: Jutalit

1990), includes a brief section on nineteenth-century literary periodicals which begins to assess the poetry and prose they contain. The same author's *Drummer Hodge: The Poetry of the Anglo-Boer War* (Oxford: Clarendon Press 1978) is the most thorough and impressive attempt to incorporate a consideration of the periodical material in a work of literary history.

Notes

The work towards this chapter was assisted by a grant from the Human Sciences Research Council. I am also grateful for the help I received from various librarians at the University of the Witswatersrand, the South African Library, the State Library, and the Johannesburg Public Library.
1 The following Southern African territories were part of the Empire during the nineteenth century:
1 / The Cape Colony – from 1795 to 1802 and then again from 1806; attained representative government in 1852.
2 / Natal – from 1843, incorporated as a district of the Cape Colony in 1845, made a separate Crown Colony in 1856; attained responsible government in 1893.
3 / Basutoland – annexed by the Cape in 1868, taken over by the British government in 1884.
4 / Bechuanaland – declared a protectorate in 1884, became the colony of British Bechuanaland in 1885 and was transferred to the Cape in the same year; a new protectorate was declared over the land further to the north in 1885 and further extended in 1890.
5 / Zululand – from 1886 in all but name a British Protectorate known as the Zulu Native Reserve, annexed in 1887 and in 1897 made part of Natal.
6 / Swaziland – under joint rule by Britain, the Swazis, and the Transvaal Republic between 1889 and 1894, thereafter administered by the Transvaal until the Anglo-Boer War.
7 / The territories controlled by the British South Africa Company, founded by Cecil Rhodes and Alfred Beit in 1889 under Royal Charter; the main area including Mashonaland and Matabeleland was formally named Rhodesia in 1897.
8 / The island of St Helena in the South Atlantic, even after the death of Napoleon in 1821 and the reduction of the garrison, continued to have some importance as a stopping point on the way to the Cape.
2 The following acronyms are used in the chapter:
ANN – Africana Notes and News
PISAL – Periodicals in South African Libraries
QBSAL – Quarterly Bulletin of the South African Library
SAL – South African Library
SANB – South African National Bibliography

3 The following works in the descriptive list also appear in *List of South African Newspapers: African Journal* (1850–1), *Albany Mirror* (1841), *Bulletin* (1888), *Buzzer* (1890–1), *Cape Baptist* (1880–2), *Cape Punch* (1888), *Cape Punchinello* (1851), *Christian Herald* (1838), *Church Chronicle* (1880–90), *Comet* (Grahamstown) (1881), *The Critic* (1892–6), *Fakkel* (1876–?), *Fun* (1877), *Gazette of Fashion* (1899), *Good Templar Advocate* (1878), *Intellectual Reflector* (1850), *Jester* (1887), *Knobkerrie* (1884–6), *Ladysmith Bombshell* (1899), *Ladysmith Lyre* (1899), *Lantern* (Cape Town) (1877–92), *Life* (Johannesburg) (1898), *Maandbode* (1873–94), *Mosquito* (1879–80), *New Organ* (1826), *News of the Camp* (1880–1), *Owl* (1895–1903), *Racing Calendar and Agricultural Journal* (1897–8), *Sam Sly's* (1843–9), *South African Christian Recorder* (1831–7), *South African Christian Watchman* (1846–50), *South African Church Magazine* (1850–9), *South African Illustrated News* (1884–5), *South African Volunteer Gazette* (1897–1901), *Telephone* (1899–1900), *Transvaal Critic* (1896–?), *De Verzamelaar* (1852–3), *War Cry* (1884–?), *Wasp* (1888), *De Wekker* (1859–?), *Zingari* (1870–4).

4 The following are the titles in chronological order of nineteenth-century university, college, and school magazines listed in *PISAL* or the source indicated: *Students' Oracle, Andrean, Bee, Student, Rhenish College Weekly* (SAL), *College Times, Diocesan College and School Magazine, Maritzburg College Magazine, Union Annual, Graemian* (Gordon-Brown), *Dale College Magazine, Ladysmith School Magazine, Stellenbosch Students' Annual, Grey* (Port Elizabeth), *Grey College Magazine* (Bloemfontein), *Huguenot Seminary Annual, Fancy Fair Journal, Kingswood College Magazine, Studenten Blad: Fac et Spera, St Aidan's College Record, St Michael's Chronicle, South African College Students' Magazine*.

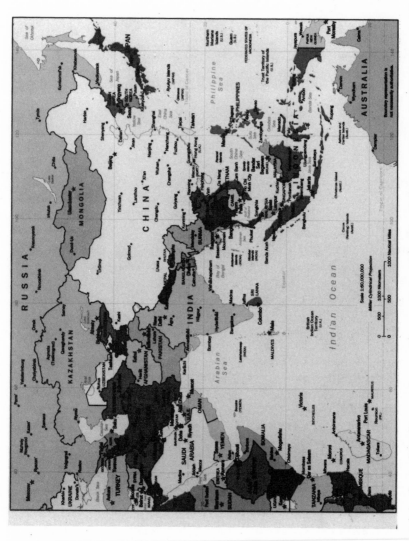

South-East Asia. Central Intelligence Agency Map, courtesy of the Map Collection, University of Washington Libraries.

6

Outposts of Empire

J. DON VANN
ROSEMARY T. VANARSDEL

Introduction

Arthur Ravenscroft comments in his Foreword to *Commonwealth Literature Periodicals* that 'newspapers and literary journals have always existed in the British colonies' (xii), and in some places, such as Jamaica, the journalistic tradition was strong and deep. At the Royal Commonwealth Society Library, for instance, one is able to consult a copy of the *Jamaica Gazette* for 1788 (4:54–97, 2 July–29 November), judged to be probably the only copy extant in the world. It carried general news of the colony, vital statistics, shipping news, plus many advertisements pertaining to the slave trade, to an interested eighteenth-century audience. This chapter is designed to demonstrate that the tradition of periodical publication was as strong in the far outposts of Empire, and in the smallest colonies, as it was in the larger countries.

The organizational framework for the chapter has been adopted from that employed by the annual bibliography of the *Journal of Commonwealth Literature*: Ceylon (now Sri Lanka), Cyprus, Hong Kong, Malaya and Singapore (treated as one entity until the Parliamentary Act of 1965 separated them), Malta, and the West Indies (Antigua, Bahamas, Barbados, British Guiana, Jamaica, and Trinidad). Other British settlements around the globe, such as the Channel Islands, the Isle of Man, Gibralter, the South Atlantic (i.e. the Falklands, St Helena, Tristan da Cunha, and Ascension), the British Indian Ocean Territory (i.e. the Seychelles), and Pitcairn Island in the Pacific Ocean, for a variety of reasons, failed to produce a significant periodical literature. A brief introductory note has been provided at the beginning of each subsection to indicate the chronology of British presence in the colony.

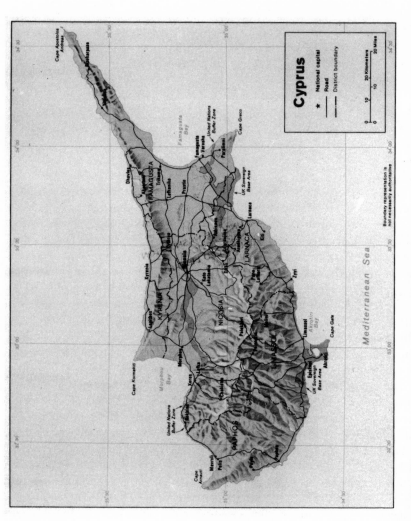

Central Intelligence Agency map, courtesy of the Map Collection, University of Washington Libraries.

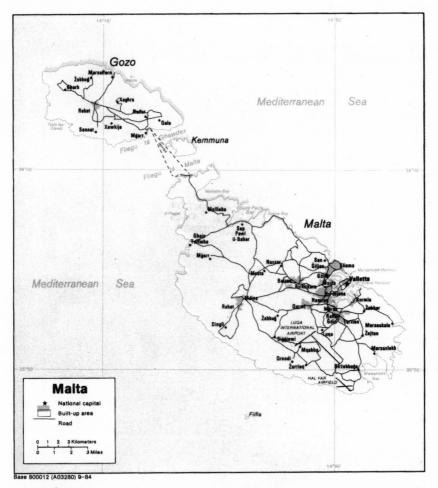

Central Intelligence Agency map, courtesy of the Map Collection, University of
Washington Libraries.

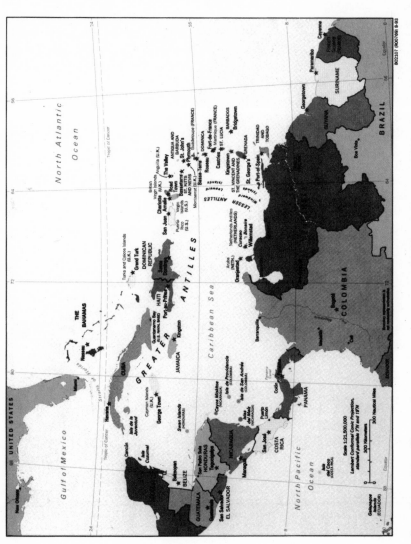

West Indies. Central Intelligence Agency map, courtesy of the Map Collection, University of Washington Libraries.

Who were the British citizens who emigrated to the far outposts of Empire during the nineteenth century? Colonists, settlers, entrepreneurs, expatriates, farmers, soldiers, civil servants, missionaries, teachers, merchants, mariners, and colonial administrators. In the very early days, in the absence of such modern communications as reliable mail service, radio, telegraph, wireless, and so on, how were they able to communicate with each other, and with the outside world? Partly, of course, by slow, uncertain correspondence, but chiefly by means of periodical literature, both newspapers and journals.

By 1870, the British and Indian Telegraph Company laid the first successful direct cable between England and Bombay, later to be extended around the south of India to Singapore, and then split to send one line to meet the Russian cable and the other to Australia. This was accomplished three years before the Atlantic cable was completed, and resulted in an interesting shift in terminology in journals; whereas earlier papers had announced arrival of news by sea with titles such as 'The Latest Packet,' or 'Arrival of Packet,' after the cable columns were titled 'News by Cable,' 'Latest Telegram,' or 'Telegrams.' However, the tradition of newspaper and periodical publication and reading was already firmly established and not to be dislodged by a more modern invention.

Certain problems have arisen in the preparation of this chapter which are not ordinarily present in British periodicals scholarship. The first, and most serious, is the editors' inability to visit national and university libraries to shelf-check titles. In the absence of substantial travel grants, it has been impossible to visit such repositories as the National Library, and the University Library at Malta, for instance, or the university libraries of Cyprus, Hong Kong, Singapore, Ceylon, and the West Indies. (Throughout this essay the editors will adopt the nineteenth-century usage of 'Ceylon,' rather than the modern 'Sri Lanka,' introduced in 1972.) Efforts at long-distance correspondence, in most cases, have proved unsatisfactory. A few excellent bibliographies do exist, such as those for Ceylon, Malta, and the West Indies, and these have been supplemented by on-site visits to the major collections held in British libraries.

A second problem is that of language. H.R. Cheesman, the Malayan bibliographer, emphasizes the importance for the outsider of gaining a clear idea of 'the nature of the environment in which English exists in the region' (*Journal of Commonwealth Literature* [*JCL*] no. 2 [Dec. 1966], 67), namely, as one of four major language groups, Malay, Chinese, Tamil, and English. He also points out that the area was one in which the 1957 census showed that 'nearly half the population was not literate in their own or any other language' (*JCL* no.1, [Sept. 1965], 55).

However, Professor Yasmine Gooneratne, writing of Ceylon, comments on the same subject in a slightly different way. She notes the British self-interest in introducing English early into Ceylonese schools, in order to 'smooth colonial administration; to aid in religious conversions from Buddhism and Hinduism; to transplant successfully English social and political institutions'; and this in spite of the fact that Ceylon also balanced three main language groups, Tamil, Sinhalese, and English. She further states (in 1966) that 'A first-class English education has been available to those who could afford it for the last 150 years' (*JCL*, no.2, [Dec. 1966], 90).

The same difficulty applies to the Mediterranean region, where the national languages of Cyprus and Malta might be mixed with Greek, Latin, Turkish, Armenian, Italian, and numerous other modern European languages, as well as English. Without the opportunity to shelf-check, the authors have at times been unable to determine what proportion of the journal was published in English.

A third problem appears in the prevailing attitudes of the various societies toward literature, criticism, poetry, creative writing, journalism, and the arts. On the one hand, it is deeply touching to read the following proud assertion in the *Singapore Review and Monthly Magazine* for January 1861:

We believe that the progress of a people in material prosperity is intimately connected with their progress in polite letters, science, and art. Ignorance in the higher refinements of life is incompatible, in an enlightened land, with material progress ... the influence of literature on the nation's destiny is ever paramount. (1)

On the other hand, Gooneratne declares that the progress of 'polite literature' was greatly impeded by the 'unmistakable conviction that poetry itself is a luxury in an era of trade and competition' (*JCL*, no. 2 [Dec. 1966], 1). The *Colonial Magazine* (23:1 [Jan. 1852], 1) comments that 'amongst the constant and active occupations of colonial [life], few have time to write.' Some tried to describe scenes where they lived, for families in the homeland, to recount occurrences of interest, or to discuss topics of importance to colonists, but the harsh demands of colonial life left little leisure for literary pursuits.

Authorial identity was a fourth problem facing colonial writers. The introduction to the West Indies section in the first number of *Commonwealth Literature* comments, 'Caribbean writing has tended to concern itself with life in the West Indies or in Britain. ... The dilemma facing West Indian authors confronts all Commonwealth writers – how to escape the essential provincialism of their position without losing the advantages of the exotic. For the West Indian writer, the remote and vibrant quality of Caribbean setting and speech are real advantages.' (no. 1 [Sept. 1965], 72). Gooneratne declared that 'the first steps in the creation of a distinctly Ceylonese literature were made by 19th century British pioneers' and that their work could usefully be anthologized today by drawing on fiction or verse 'that has appeared in periodicals since 1830.' But she cautioned, 'Ceylon offers a classic example of that peculiarly Asian phenomenon, the complex social and cultural pattern that emerges where two cultures that have developed in different directions and at different rates are brought sharply together by political processes' (*JCL* no. 2 [Dec. 1966], 90). Where does that leave the developing artist or journalist in his search for identity?

In other instances, a fifth problem, technology, was sufficient to discourage aspiring journalists and publishers. *Odds and Ends*, published in Hong Kong in 1896, expressed frustration with numerous futile attempts made up to that point to establish an illustrated paper in the colony. Noting that previous journals, the *China Magazine, China Punch,* and *Magpie*, were doomed to very short life-spans, the editor commented, 'The conditions in regard to printing which prevailed in Hong Kong twenty years ago are not materially changed today'; with regard to graphic art, 'the primitive methods of the inventor Fungtau, who lived in the tenth century, are still employed at the present time' (*Odds and Ends* 1:1 [Nov. 1896], 1).

It is worth noting that a number of so-called 'colonial' journals were published in London, for precisely the reason that colonists lacked the time for literary work. Often staffed and written by people who were themselves ex-colonists, or retired military or civilian personnel who had served in colonial administration, they purported to have the best interests of the colonists at heart. The *Colonial Magazine* was one of these, and in 1852 its editor, William Henry Giles Kingston (1814–80), the well-known and prolific author of children's (especially boys') fiction in the late nineteenth century, proclaimed its editorial objectives as follows: '[to give] the colonists an organ of their own, [to] express their wishes, their intentions, and expectations to the brethren at home; [and to be a] work useful to intending colonists' (23:1 [Jan. 1852], 1).

The following is a selected sampling of this type of journal, offering information about births, marriages, deaths, prices, stocks, foreign funds, and shipping intelligence, interspersed with the occasional poem, witty observance, or bit of philosophy. These titles, originally held in the collection of the Royal Commonwealth Society (henceforth RCS), are now, with the Library's relocation, at Cambridge (see Acknowledgments), and supplemented by holdings of the Cambridge University Library (henceforth CUL). This is by no means intended as a definitive list.

Simmonds Colonial Magazine and Foreign Miscellany. RCS has vols. 5–7, 9, 11; CUL vols. 1–16:61, 1844–9). Then, *Colonial Magazine and East India Review* (RCS has vols. 16–18, 21–3; CUL has vols. 16:63–23:102, 1849–52). Edited by W.H.G. Kingston. Then, merged with the *Asiatic Review* to form the *Colonial and Asiatic Review* (CUL has vols. 1–2, 1852–3).

Colonial Magazine and Commercial Maritime Journal. Vols. 1–8, 1840–2. (RCS and CUL both have the full eight vols.) Then, *Fishers Colonial Magazine* (RCS has vols. 1–4, n.s. vol. 1; CUL has vols. 1–4, n.s. vols. 1–2, 1842–5).

Asiatic Journal and Monthly Miscellany. (CUL has third series, vols. 1–4, 1843–5); then, *Asiatic and Colonial Quarterly Journal* (RCS has vols. 4–5; CUL has vols. 1–7, 1846–9).

Two sources have been fundamental to preparation of this chapter. First *Commonwealth Literature Periodicals, A Bibliography,* including periodicals of former Commonwealth countries, with locations in the United Kingdom. This material was prepared by a Working Party on Library Holdings of Commonwealth Literature from the Commonwealth Institute in London, and was compiled and edited for publication by Ronald Warwick (London: Mansell 1979). The basic focus of that work differs from the present essay, inasmuch as the Working Party concentrated chiefly on twentieth-century periodicals and was concerned with the role periodicals played in developing a national literature in English, whereas this survey seeks to draw a Victorian, or nineteenth-century, portrait. But the book does include some nineteenth-century periodicals, making it an important starting point for the researcher.

The second vital source is the *Journal of Commonwealth Literature,* established in September 1965, and still flourishing in 1994. Its initial statement of mission observed, 'This journal will concern itself with imaginative writing in English in various parts of the Commonwealth.' It was the outgrowth of the first international conference on Commonwealth literature held at the University of Leeds in 1964, and was originally conceived as an annual, published by Heinemann Educational Books for the university. The first issue contained an annual bibliography (for 1964) of work world-wide on Commonwealth literature, a practice which continues to this day and has proved to be one of its most valuable features. The journal's early publishing history was irregular, but it never failed to produce an annual bibliography, even though the intervals were sometimes uneven. When, in 1970, Oxford University Press succeeded Heinemann, it became a semi-annual, and in 1974 a triennial publication; the editor announced: 'When the first issue of this journal was being prepared for the press, the editor naively wondered whether the *Journal of Commonwealth Literature* would not exhaust its area of study within five years. By the fifth year the "Annual Bibliography" had grown by fifty-six pages, and the editor was having to turn down articles he would have liked to print ... simply for lack of space' (8:1, [June 1973], 1). It continues to be the chief and most reliable source for up-to-date information on Commonwealth literature.

Finally, a word needs to be said about the remarkable collection of colonial periodicals housed at the Royal Commonwealth Society Library, formerly located at 18 Northumberland Avenue, London, which while there meshed most fortuitously with collections also held in London at, respectively, the British Library, the British Newspaper Library at Colindale, the Commonwealth Institute, the India Office Library, and the Institute for Commonwealth Studies. Founded in 1868, its collections of books, manuscripts, photographs, maps, newspapers, and periodicals span two centuries, and provide a unique repository of rare items unavailable elsewhere. Its collection now consists of approximately three hundred thousand printed works and over seventy thousand photographs. In the early 1990s, however, the Royal Commonwealth Society was experiencing severe financial difficulties and facing possible sale of the library, piecemeal, by auction. Indeed, some of the more valuable items were packed off to auctioneers, including the remarkable Claude Delaval Cobham collection on Cyprus. Cobham was Commissioner of the Lanarca District in Cyprus for twenty-eight years, from 1879 to 1907, and a book-lover and collector who amassed priceless treasures pertaining to Cyprus.

A three-million-pound appeal was launched in 1992, however, with the Prince of Wales as Patron, and the support of many prominent and wealthy friends of the library as well as ordinary readers and individuals; the success of this fund-raising drive allowed the collection to be moved to the Cambridge University Library, in 1993, where it became part of the public domain. Fortunately, its very knowledgeable librarian, Miss T.A. Barringer, also removed to Cambridge in 1993 to continue in her post as its head officer. Her expert knowledge of the archive makes the riches of the library much more readily accessible to the researcher. The sections in this chapter on Ceylon, Malaya, Malta, Singapore, and the West Indies would be much less complete without her help, and the resources of this remarkable library.

One further piece of good fortune occurred as a result of the fundraising when items earlier sent to the auctioneers, such as the Cobham Collection on Cyprus, were reprieved and reunited with the rest of the Royal Commonwealth Society Library, thus keeping this priceless archive intact. (For a full account of the evolution of this collection, and of its move to Cambridge, see T.A. Barringer, 'The Rise, Fall and Rising Again of the Royal Commonwealth Society Library,' *African Research and Documentation* no. 64, [1994].)

The editors consider that much more work remains to be done in this field and intend to continue their explorations of this fascinating subject. High on their agenda will be efforts to find funding for necessary site visits to conduct shelf-checks in national and local libraries. These are avenues which will yield much additional information and enrich our understanding of British colonial periodical literature in the nineteenth century.

Bibliography

Bibliography of Malaya. Comp. H.R. Cheesman. Published for the British Association of Malaya. London: Longmans, Green 1959. 'Being a Classified List of Books Wholly or Partly in English Relating to the Federation of Malaya and Singapore.'

Clarke, Prescott. *'The Development of the English-Language Press on the China Coast, 1827–1881.'* Unpublished MA Thesis, University of London 1961.

Cole, George Watson. *Bermuda in Periodical Literature*. Boston: Boston Book Co. 1907. Cole has collected articles in periodicals published anywhere relating to Bermuda. His book is a valuable storehouse of information.

Commonwealth Literature Periodicals. Ed. Ronald Warwick. London: Mansell 1979.

Cundall, Frank. *Bibliotheca Jamaicensis. Some Account of the Principal Works on Jamaica in the Library of the Institute*. Kingston: Institute of Jamaica 1895. Contains some passing references to periodicals.

á Fonseka, Lyn. 'Index of Contents of Journals.' *Royal Asiatic Society*, Ceylon Branch, 37:102 (1946), 112–203. This article indexes the contents of vols. 1–36, nos. 1–100, 1845–1945.

Gooneratne, Yasmine. *English Literature in Ceylon, 1815–1878. Ceylon Historical Journal*, 14; Ceylon: Tisara Press 1965.

Goonetileke, H.A.I., comp. *A Bibliography of Ceylon: A Systematic Guide to the Literature on the Land, People, History and Culture. Published in Western Languages from the Sixteenth Century to the Present Day.* 5 vols. Zug, Switzerland: Inter Documentation, vols. 1 and 2, 1970; second unchanged edition 1973; vol. 3, 1976; vols. 4 and 5, 1983.

Gore, J.F.W. *Index to the Journals and Proceedings of the Ceylon Branch of the Royal Asiatic Society.* Vols. 1–11, nos. 1–41, 1845–90. Colombo: Acting Government Printer 1895.

Gorman, G.E., and J.J. Mills. *Guide to Current National Bibliographies in the Third World.* 2nd rev. ed. London: Hans Zell 1987.

The Growth of the New Empire, 1783–1870. Ed. J. Holland Rose et al. Cambridge 1940. Vol. 2 of *The Cambridge History of the British Empire.*

Guide to Malay Periodicals, 1876–1941. Comp. W.R. Ruff. Singapore: Eastern Universities Press 1961.

Guide to Western Manuscripts and Documents in the British Isles Relating to South and South East Asia. Comp. Mary Doreen Wainwright and Noel Matthews. London: Oxford University Press 1965. Published for the School of Oriental and African Studies.

Hadler, Jerome S. *A Guide to Source Materials for the Study of Barbados History.* Carbondale: Southern Illinois University Press 1971. ('Newspapers,' pp. 116–18).

A Handbook of Library Holdings of Commonwealth Literature in the United Kingdom. Comp. and ed. Gail Wilson. London: Commonwealth Institute Working Party 1971. Supplement on *Holdings in some European Libraries.* Ed. Donald Simpson. 1974. (Sections on Austria, Belgium, Denmark, France, Germany, Italy, Malta, Norway, Spain, Sweden.)

Hewitt, A.R. *Union List of Commonwealth Newspapers in London, Oxford, and Cambridge.* London: Athlone Press for the Institute of Commonwealth Studies 1960.

Journal of Commonwealth Literature. London: Heinemann Educational Books and the University of Leeds, 1965–. Annual bibliographies beginning 1965, for 1964.

Journal of the Malayan Branch of the Royal Asiatic Society. vol. 4, 1927, iii–101. Singapore. 'Consists entirely of "Index to the Journal of the Straits Branch of the Royal Asiatic Society, 1878–1922."' Comp. C.E. Wurtzburg, with Preface.

– Vol. 19, 3 Dec. 1941, 125 pp. Singapore Printers, Ltd.: 'Consists entirely of a "Descriptive Catalog of the Books relating to Malaysia in the Raffles Museum and Library, Singapore."' Comp. P. Daniel, with Preface.

– Vol. 21, 3 Oct. 1948. viii + 66 pp. Singapore: Malaya Publishing House,

Ltd. 'Consists entirely of "Index to the Journal of the Malayan Branch of the Royal Asiatic Society 1923–47."' Comp. C.A. Gibson-Hill, with Introduction.

Lim, Patricia Pin Huen. *Newspapers Published in the Malaysia Area, with a Union List of Local Holdings.* Singapore: Institute of Southeast Asian Studies 1970.

Makepeace, Walter. 'Institutions and Clubs,' in *One Hundred Years of Singapore*, ed. Walter Makepeace et al. London: John Murray 1921, 2:278–97. The first part of the chapter contains a brief history of the periodical press.

Newspaper Directory of China (including Hong Kong). Shanghai 1935.

Pactor, Howard S. *Colonial British Caribbean Newspapers, A Bibliography and Directory.* New York, West Port, Conn., and London: Greenwood Press 1990.

'Periodicals and Newspapers in Ceylon,' in [J. Capper] *Ceylon Miscellany* (1853), 3–8; 1:2 (1853), 213–14. Reprinted in *Journal of the Dutch Burgher Union of Ceylon* 31 (4 April 1942), 137–52.

Sapienza, Anthony F. *A Checklist of Maltese Periodicals and Newspapers in the National Library of Malta (formerly the Royal Malta Library) and the University of Malta Library.* Valletta: Malta University Press 1977.

Serials of Hong Kong. Comp. L.B. Kan, and Grace H.L. Chu. Hong Kong: 1981.

Ceylon

First ruled by the Portuguese, then the Dutch, Ceylon was conquered by the British in 1795–6. At the Treaty of Amiens, 1802, it was officially ceded to Britain and remained a British Crown Colony throughout the nineteenth century. In the twentieth century, in 1972, it became the Republic of Sri Lanka, but this chapter retains the nineteenth-century nomenclature.

Listings in this section are drawn from 4 sources:

BL	*British Library Catalogue*
RW	*Commonwealth Literature Periodicals*, ed. Ronald Warwick
G	Gooneratne, *Bibliography*
RCS	Library, Royal Commonwealth Society

Major reliance has been placed on the bibliography compiled by Yasmine Gooneratne, *English Literature in Ceylon, 1815–1878*, primarily because she was working in, and with, the libraries of Ceylon. She is acknowledged world-wide as the leading authority on nineteenth-century Ceylonese periodicals in English. In addition, she published a bibliography of the year's work annually, from 1965 to 1978, in the *Journal of Commonwealth Literature*. There is one problem with her bibliography, however; she does not give a termination date. This omission has been remedied to some extent by consulting the other three references, and by shelf-checks when possible, but for many titles it is impossible to supply a final date without visiting Ceylonese libraries, which the editors were unable to do. Copies of titles held in British libraries have been examined.

Ceylon Government Gazette. 1802. G.

Colombo Journal. 7 Jan. 1832–Dec. 1833. G, BL.

Colombo Religious and Theological Magazine. 1833. G.

Observer and Commercial Advertiser. 1834. G.

Colombo Religious Tract Society Magazine. 1835. G.

Ceylon Chronicle. 3 May 1837– 3 Sept. 1838. G, BL.

Ceylon Miscellany. 1837. G.

Colombo Academy Miscellany. 1837. G.

Friend. 1837. First series. G.

Ceylon Herald and General Advertiser. 1838–43. Published twice weekly, Tues. and Fri. 12s. per quarter. Predominantly news of England. G, BL.

Colombo Magazine. M. 1:1–3, Jan.–March 1839. General news, shipping information, obituaries, marriages, births, poetry, and serial fiction. Designed to stimulate literary talent through tales, narratives, aphorisms, scientific discussions, essays, poetry, religious topics; politics avoided. RW, RCS.

Ceylon Magazine. M. 1, no. 1–2, no. 13, 1840–2. Colombo. Emphasized religion and morality, but also polite literature: essays, tales, memoirs, poetry. Addressed topics of Ceylon, such as history, scenery, capabilities. Followed discovery and improvements in science and art; also presented extracts from other periodicals. G, RW, RCS.

Journal of the Ceylon Branch of the Royal Asiatic Society. 1845–. Semi-A. 1 guinea (A). First meeting, 7 Feb. 1845, 'to promote inquiries into the History, Religion, Literature, Arts, and Natural Philosophy of Ceylon, together with the social condition of its present and former inhabitants.' In 1971 the title was changed to *Journal of the Sri Lankan Branch of the Royal Asiatic Society.* G, RCS.

Ceylon Examiner. 1846. G.

Ceylon Times. 1846. G.

Monthly Examiner. M. 1846. Colombo. News and advice for planters. BL.

Young Ceylon. M. 1850–2. Colombo. Ed. G.F. Nell. Reviews, essays, poetry. 'Started in 1850 by a group of enterprising young Ceylonese,' for the purpose of producing Ceylonese criticism of contemporary British literature. It contained articles on such subjects as: 'Dickens and the *Edinburgh Review*,' by Dandris de Silva Guneratne; and articles on Carlyle and Tennyson from a Ceylonese perspective by C.A. Lorenz. G, BL.

Ceylon Medical Miscellany. 1853 G.

Students' Magazine. 1860. G.

Muniandi. F. 1869. Colombo. Is. Humour magazine containing cartoons, quips, riddles. G, BL.

Friend. M. 1870. Second series. Colombo. 3d. Editorial statement: 'Our design is to discuss religious and social questions in a Christian spirit, to present accurate information of the work of the Protestant churches in Ceylon and the world at large, and to publish articles respecting religions, literature, and customs of the people of the island.' G, RW, RCS.

Ceylon Quarterly Magazine. 1871. G.

Ceylon Literary Register. M. 1–7, 1886–93. Colombo. Published as a supplement to the *Ceylon Observer.* Then, *Monthly Literary Register and Notes and Queries for Ceylon.* 1–4, 1893–6. G, RW

Appuhami. 1890. G.

'Save the Children.' Our Children's Friend. Alternate months (six per

year); 1891–93. Colombo. 6 cents. Children's religious magazine with inspirational essays, poetry, stories, and puzzles. RW, BL

'Willing Hearts.' A Ceylon Christian Monthly Magazine. M. 1892–3. Colombo. Rs. 1.50 (A). Contains sermons, Bible lessons, testimonials from converts. RW, BL.

Ceylon Evangelist. M. July 1893–Dec. 1894. 20 cents. Advertised itself as 'A monthly publication devoted to the exposition of all Bible Truths.' An evangelical publication given to the augmentation of Christian dogma. BL.

Ceylon Review. A Monthly Magazine of Literary and General Interest. M. 1–3, 1893–6; n.s. 1, no. 1–7, no. 20, 1897–1902. Colombo. Ed. J. Scott Coates. RW.

Sunbeam. A Monthly Periodical for the Young Folks. M. March–July 1893. Colombo. Poetry, essays, humour, reviews of literature, results of university entrance exams. RW, BL.

Period. An Illustrated Monthly Review and Index. M. 1, no. 1–9, Oct. 1896–June 1897. Colombo. G, BL.

Youth. M. 1896. Colombo. 20 cents. A literary magazine with serial fiction, poems, quips, riddles, cricket and football information. Begun by the Fourth Form boys of St Joseph College, 'to encourage literature in all its branches.' RW, BL.

Cyprus

The third largest island in the Mediterranean, Cyprus was known to have been inhabited in the Neolithic Age, and was the scene of constant incursions throughout history. On 4 June 1878, after a long period of unrest and decline, Great Britain, by Treaty with the Sultan of Turkey, took over occupation and administration of Cyprus, thus assuring Turkey of protection from Russia. On 16 November 1914 Cyprus was annexed to the British Crown when war with Turkey broke out.
    Sources for this section are:

BL   British Library Catalogue
RW   Commonwealth Literature Periodicals, ed. Ronald Warwick
RCS   Library, Royal Commonwealth Society

Cyprus. A Weekly Journal of Agriculture and Commerce. W. 29 Aug.–24 Oct. 1878. Larnaca. 5 pence. A standard newspaper of little interest, except that the last issue (24 Oct. 1878) says, 'We intend printing a Special Edition on Saturday next containing the latest telegrams by the submarine cable.' Unfortunately, the special issue is not in the British Library or in the other two references mentioned above. BL.

Cyprus. An Independent Newspaper. 12 July 1880–18 Aug 1882. Larnaca. 3 pence (W). Regular news from Egypt, Turkey, and Greece. Shipping news. An occasional poem. BL.

Cyprus Herald. W. Nos. 1–270, 1881–7. Limasol. 2 piastres. Legislative reports, cricket results, 'London Letter' with news from home. BL, RCS.

Cyprus Times. F. Nos. 1–84, 1881. 3 pence. All local news BL, RCS.

Hellenic Times. F. Nos. 1–10, 1 March–10 May 1884. Nicosia. 2 piastres. Ed. O. J. Passonides. Editorial statement in initial issue says, 'This paper is a means of communicating whatever is of any interest from Europe to the Greeks in this country, serving as a bridge of intercourse and good understanding between English and native Greeks.' No. 1 was published in separate parts in English and Romanic, with an appendix titled *The Helicon.* BL, RCS.

Times of Cyprus. W. Nos. 1–406, 6 March 1886–2 Jan. 1895. Larnaca. 2 piastres. Local, legislative, and sporting news, occasional poetry and serialized stories. BL.

Owl. F. Nos. 1–11, 1 Sept. 1888 – March 1889 Nicosia. Ed. Max. Ohnefalsch-Richter. The editorial statement in the first issue says, 'Any scientific papers which have directly, or indirectly, any bearing on Cyprus, ancient or modern, will be published.' The journal, in fact, carried only archaeological papers, with one on linguistics. Excellent illustrations. BL.

Owl: a Weekly Newspaper and Review. W. Nos. 1–255, 1 Sept. 1888–1 Sept. 1896. Nicosia. Ed. E. Clarke. BL, RCS.

Journal of Cyprian Studies. 1889. Ed. M. Ohnefalsch-Richter. BL, RCS.

Hong Kong

Official British occupation of Hong Kong dates from 1841, when the Chinese ceded it to Britain (later confirmed by the Treaty of Nanking,

1842), but it previously had served as a base for English ships during the first Opium War of 1839–42. Before the occupation, it had been mainly a fishing village and haven for vagrants. Its deep, sheltered, and accessible harbour on the main pathway to China contributed to its growth, during the nineteenth century, to one of the world's greatest ports.

As one scans Hong Kong journals, certain general themes emerge: first, the price of opium was generally a standard feature in commodity reports; second, the English-language newspapers of Singapore and Hong Kong were unanimously outraged by reports suggesting a slave trade; and, third, the shipping news often listed names of passengers arriving in the colony. The third point could be useful to a researcher tracing movements of persons known to have been in the area during the nineteenth century.

Sources for Hong Kong are:

BL   British Library *Catalogue*
RCS   Library, Royal Commonwealth Society
UHK   University of Hong Kong Library

Hong Kong Register. 1827–60. 25 Hong Kong dollars (A). A commercial paper. It is startling to the modern reader to see opium listed among the commodities, along with rice and cotton. BL.

Overland China Mail. M. 29 Jan. 1845 – 31 Dec 1861; Jan. 1863–. 4 Hong Kong dollars (A). Shipping, markets, local news, essays explaining Chinese culture to English residents. BL.

Overland Friend of China. M. 25 April – 28 Sept. 1847; 29 Nov. 1849 – 28 Sept. 1859. 50 Hong Kong cents. Shipping, local, and overseas news; poetry and essays. BL.

Friend of China and Hong Kong Gazette. Tri-W. 4, no. 56, 12 July 1854; 10, no. 77, 24 Sept. 1851; 17, no. 24, 24 March 1858. 12 Hong Kong dollars (A). Mainly shipping news. BL.

Hong Kong Monthly Magazine. M. Vols. 1, 2, 4, 5, 6, July, Aug., Oct., Nov., Dec., 1857; vols. 7–12, Jan.–June 1858. 75 Hong Kong cents. Ed. Mrs Annie E. Beecher. Essays, poems, fiction. UHK.

China Overland Trade Report. F. 11 Sept. 1858 – 31 Dec. 1861; 31 March – 14 Dec. 1863; 14 June 1864 – 11 Jan. 1871; 3 Jan. 1878 – 19 Jan. 1888. 6 Hong Kong dollars (A). Reports on exports, imports, prices – strictly commercial. BL.

Hong Kong Mercury and Shipping Gazette. D. Nos. 1–162, 1 June – 4 Dec. 1866. 2 Hong Kong dollars (M). Much financial news, especially banking. Publishes an occasional poem. BL.

China Punch. F. 1, nos. 1–24, 28 May 1867–28 May 1868; nos. 2–3, Dec. 1872 – Jan. 1873. 10 Hong Kong dollars (A); 50 cents a copy. Ed. Mr. Punch (pseudonym). Satires, humorous essays, illustrated with caricatures. UHK.

Notes and Queries: on China and Japan, A Monthly Medium of Intercommunication for Professional and Literary Men, Missionaries and Residents of the East Generally. M. 1, no. 1–2, no. 12, Jan. 1867–Dec. 1868. 4 Hong Kong dollars (A). Ed. N.B. Dennys. Essays, news from home. UHK.

Daily Advertiser. Nos. 2–30, 1871; 2 Jan. 1872–30 April 1873. 2 Hong Kong dollars (M). Shipping news, 2 pages of ads, occasional serialized fiction, poetry. BL.

China Review: or, Notes and Queries on the Far East. Bi-M. 1–25, 1872–1901; series 2, 1–4, 1919–22. 6.50 Hong Kong dollars (A). Ed. N. B. Dennys. Essays, reviews. UHK.

Hong Kong Catholic Register. F. 1, no. 15– 3 no. 17; 4, no. 13, 11 May 1878 – 27 Dec. 1879; 27 Nov. 1880. Then, *Catholic Register*, 6, no 28 – 10, no. 27, 17 May 1883–17 Sept. 1887. 50 Hong Kong cents (M). Religious news from Rome and from missions. Announcements of religious activities. BL.

Hong Kong Telegraph. D. 16 June 1881–. 16 Hong Kong dollars (A). Share prices, shipping news, legislative reports, local events, news from England, occasional poetry. BL.

Odds and Ends. An Illustrated Journal published every other month. 1, nos. 1–5, Nov. 1896–Aug. 1897. 1 Hong Kong dollar per copy, 5 Hong Kong dollars (A). Conducted by J. P. Braga. Contents include 'Books Published in Hong Kong: 1888–1896,' plus games, calendar, reviews, short stories. Also, descriptions of botanic gardens, hospitals, and sports events. RCS, UHK.

Malaya and Singapore

Although Malaya was early dominated by the Portuguese and Dutch presence, the French wars in 1795 gave the British the opportunity to capture Malacca, and in 1819 they succeeded in founding a settlement at

Singapore. At the Treaty of London, 1824, the Dutch agreed to cede all of Malaya to Britain, while the British agreed to cede all of Sumatra to the Dutch.

Singapore, founded in 1819 by Sir Thomas Stamford Raffles, was sparsely populated at the beginning of the nineteenth century. Separated from Malaya only by the Straits of Johore, it was a free port governed by the East India Company. With the opening of the Suez Canal in 1869, however, the port's activities were transformed. A vast system of docks to accommodate the shipping trade soon made it a centre for world commerce.

The periodical literature of the time was so intertwined between Malaya and Singapore that it is difficult, and perhaps not useful, to try to separate the two. The problem of language is also difficult, each area recognizing four tongues: Chinese, Malay, Tamil, and English. This study, of course, is concerned only with periodicals in English.

The two most important bibliographies of nineteenth century periodicals for the area are *Bibliography of Malaya*, comp. H.R. Cheesman, and *Commonwealth Literature Periodicals*, ed. Ronald Warwick. Neither of these two works attempts to separate the two literatures; this listing, therefore, follows their direction.

Sources for this section are:

BM	*Bibliography of Malaya*
BL	*British Library Catalogue*
CUL	Cambridge University Library
RW	*Commonwealth Literature Periodicals*, ed. Ronald Warwick
RCS	Library, Royal Commonwealth Society

Major reliance has been placed on the Cheesman bibliography, compiled in Asian libraries, but the same caveat applies as in the case of Ceylon; missing information is not available without personally visiting libraries in Malaya and Singapore.

Prince of Wales Island Gazette. W. 1805–27. Local news, shipping, extracts from English newspapers, occasional poetry. BM, BL.

Indo-China Gleaner. 1817–22. BM.

Malay Magazine. Q. No. 1, Jan. 1821. Malacca. 'Containing Translations and Treatises on Various Subjects, as History, Biography, Natural Philosophy, Religion, Miscellanies, etc., to be published quarterly. Profits, if any, to be applied to charity among indigent Malays – to support education and employment.' RCS.

Singapore Chronicle. F, then W. 1824–37. Established by Frederick James Bernard in 1824, this was the first newspaper published in Singapore (See Makepeace). Shipping, financial news, local events, European news. BM.

Malacca Observer. F 1826–9; W 1888–90. BM.

Pinang Register and Miscellany. W. 1827–8. BL, BM.

Singapore Free Press. W. 1835–69; 1884–, excluding Japanese occupation. Ed. William Napier, 1835–46; then, Abraham Logan. See Centenary Number, 8 Oct. 1935. BM.

Periodical Miscellany and Juvenile Instructor. M. 1837. Malacca. Printed at the Anglo-Chinese College. A monthly magazine with educational and inspirational articles, poetry, and travel narratives to teach young Orientals English, introduce them to Western culture, and indoctrinate them into Christianity. BM.

Straits Chronicle. W. 1838. Singapore. BM.

Malacca Weekly Register. W. 1839–40. BM.

Weekly Register. W. 1841. Malacca. 'Conducted by Hugh A. Edwards.' Weekly local and periodic foreign news. This is clearly a newspaper, even though its size is that of a magazine, approximately nine inches by twelve. BL.

Straits Messenger. W. 1842. Singapore. BM.

Overland Singapore Free Press. M. 1845–7? 50 cents. BL.

Straits Times and Singapore Journal of Commerce. W 1845–58; then, D. Ed. R.C. Woods, 1845–61; John Cameron, 1861–67; John Marshall, T.C. Cargill, Arnot Reid, 1889–1900. Editors' names from Makepeace. BL, BM.

Journal of the Indian Archipelago and Eastern Asia. A. 13 vols: 1–9; n.s. 1–4. 1847–62. Singapore. Ed. J.R. Logan. Articles mainly signed. Local topics include history, arts and industry, agriculture (cotton, nutmegs, cloves) archaeology, piracy and the slave trade, Cambodia in 1851, transport. Illustrated with maps. Valuable for historians, cultural historians, description of geographers. BM, RCS, RW.

Singapore Local Reporter. 1852. BM.

Straits Guardian. W. 1856. Singapore. BM.

Chermin Mata, the 'Glass Eye.' Subtitled *'A Quarterly Magazine of Literature and Instruction.'* Q. 1858. Singapore. BM.

Singapore Review and Monthly Magazine. M. 1, Jan. 1861. Its aim was to be a first-class monthly. 'We believe that the progress of a people in material prosperity, is intimately connected with their progress in polite letters, science, and art. Ignorance in the higher refinements of life is incompatible, in an enlightened land, with material progress; ... the influence of literature on the nation's destiny, is ever paramount.' An ambitious publication, it contains literary essays, theatrical reports, serial fiction, and poetry. Illustrated with maps. Also, long lists of incidental information, such as: arrivals and departures; shipping news; meteorological tables; quotations on goods and merchandise such as shirtings, damask, brocades, velvet, thread, sarongs, etc. Ed. E.A. Edgerton. BM, RCS.

Singapore Daily Free Press and Transcript. D. ?1863–7. BM.

Straits Produce. [Malayan Punch.] Published irregularly: no. 1, Christmas, 1868; no. 2, Jan. 1870; no. 3, Christmas, 1893; no. 4, 4 July 1894; no. 5, April 1895; revived 1922–33. Singapore. A humour magazine with cartoons, quips, and comic poetry. A collection of cartoons from *Straits Produce*, titled *Dream a While*, was published in Singapore, 1933. BM.

Malacca Weekly News. W. 1872–5. BM.

Journal of Eastern Asia. 1875. Ed. J. Collins, Government Printer, Singapore. BL, BM.

Malayan Royal Asiatic Society Journal. Straits Branch, Royal Asiatic Society (SBRAS). A. 1878–1922; then Malayan Branch Royal Asiatic Society (MBRAS), no. 1, 1923–, excluding Japanese occupation. BM, RCS, RW.

Straits Advocate. 1880. BM.

Straits Intelligence. 1883–6. Singapore. Eurasian newspaper. BM.

Singapore Eurasian Advocate. 1888–91. BM.

Straits Eurasian Advocate. W. Jan. 1888 – Dec. 1889. Singapore. 20 cents. BL.

Selangor Journal. F. 1–5. 1892–7. Kuala Lumpur. Ed. John Russell, Supt., Government Printing Office, Kuala Lumpur. BM.

Straits Chinese Magazine. Q. 1–8, 1897–1904. Singapore. 50 cents. Subtitled '*A Quarterly Journal of Oriental and Occidental Culture.*' Ed. Lim Boon Keng and Song Ong Siang. Contains literary essays, poetry, and general news, all dealing with the two cultures. BM, CUL.

Malta

Since the time of the Phoenicians, the island of Malta has stood as a crossroads in the Mediterranean. In June 1798 Napoleon conquered it by treachery and the Maltese people, caught up in a British/French war, appealed to Britain for protection. On 9 February 1799, the British flag was hoisted, and at the Treaty of Amiens, 1802, Great Britain was recognized as Sovereign. In 1813, at their own request, the Maltese people were acknowledged as British subjects.

The main sources for Malta, outside the country, are:

BL   British Library *Catalogue*
AS   *A Checklist of Maltese Periodicals and Newspapers*
RW   *Commonwealth Literature Periodicals*, ed. Ronald Warwick
RCS   Library, Royal Commonwealth Society

Within Malta, there are two collections rich in nineteenth-century periodical literature in English: one is housed in the National Library of Malta, Valletta (formerly the Royal Malta Library), the other in the University of Malta Library.

Malta Government Gazette. Irregular. Nos. 1–1986, 1816–1964. (Formerly, *Gazetta del Governo di Malta*, 1813–16.) Valletta. Contents identified in *Malta Penny Magazine* (5 Oct. 1839); 'According to an article on "the fine arts in Malta" inserted in the *Malta Government Gazette* of May 2nd, 1838.' AS.

Mediterranean Literary Register. Irregular. Nos. 1–24, 1827–8. AS, RW.

Harlequin, or Anglo-Maltese Miscellany. Irregular. Nos.1–115, 1838–40.

Valletta. Ed. James Richardson. Price varies: 3d., then 2d., then 4d. A vigorous campaigner for religious freedom for Protestants. BL, AS.

Valletta Journal of Literary and Miscellaneous Information. M. Nos. 1–4, 1838. Valletta. AS, RW.

Clown. W. Nos. 1–28, 1839–40. Valletta. Ed. James Richardson. 1st issue (31 Oct. 1839) 'respectfully dedicated to Miss Victoria Price.' AS.

Malta Penny Magazine. W. Nos. 1–120, 1839–40. Valletta. Ed. James Richardson. Published Saturdays and sold by M. Weiss, 97 Strada Forni. 4 large pages. Historical articles on Malta and the Mediterranean, poetry, natural history, Arabic inscriptions on Malta, architecture, music, science, dress, classical subjects, geography. Religious in tone; moral earnestness. Aphorisms and filler: i.e., 'As daylight can be seen through small holes, so little things show a person's character' (22 Feb. 1840). Lavishly illustrated with engravings of pen-and-ink drawings and local maps. BL, AS, RW, RCS.

Mediterranean Magazine for the Diffusion of Useful Knowledge. W. Nos. 1–20, 1842–3. Valletta. AS.

Beacon, or Malta Weekly Record; then, *Malta and Mediterranean Weekly Record.* W. Nos. 1–71, 1855–7. Ed. nos. 1–44, Samuel Lowell; nos. 45–71, Charles F. Stevens: 'A political, literary, naval and military, legal, mercantile and miscellaneous intelligencer.' AS.

Public Opinion. W. Nos. 1–2361, 1867–1908. Valletta. Price 3d., then 6d. 'Established with the view of laying before our Rulers and the British Public the views and the aspirations of the well-wishers of the Maltese.' BL, AS. The editor listed five points the paper would advocate:

1. The moral and intellectual improvement of all classes of the population, by means of a sound system of education.
2. The promotion of their physical and material prosperity, through the encouragement of Agriculture and Commerce.
3. The gradual development and extension of the political liberties that we have already obtained from Her Majesty's government.
4. The strictest economy in the expenditure of public money, in order that the Government may be enabled to construct such public works as may be considered absolutely necessary to remunerate fairly all public servants, and to provide efficiently for the security of life and property.

5. Whatever may have a tendency to strengthen the ties which happily unite these Islands to the Crown of Our Most Gracious Sovereign, Queen Victoria.

Enterprise. W. Nos. 1–12, 1878. Valletta. The British Library holds a copy numbered '17.' BL, AS.

Malta Standard. W. Nos. 1–1202, 1880–96. Valletta. 6d. Occasional literary essays, poetry, travel literature, short fiction. An interesting feature is a directory of English residents. BL, AS.

Critic. W. Nos. 1–6, 1884. Valletta. 'Our task ... will be to criticize the Journals, and their contents.' AS.

Weekly Malta. W. Nos. 1–45, 1884–5. Valletta. Price 6d. Contains some poetry. An anti-reformist paper. An editorial statement announces its intention to publish an English-language newspaper reproducing 'all the articles on important subjects appearing in the local papers printed in Italian and belonging to the National Party' (20 Sept. 1884, p. 1). BL, AS.

West Indies

The main sources for the West Indies are:

BL   British Library *Catalogue*
NLJ   National Library of Jamaica
Pactor   *Colonial British Caribbean Newspapers*, comp. Howard S. Pactor
RCS   Library, Royal Commonwealth Society
UWI   Library, University of the West Indies

While there is some similarity between the Pactor bibliography and the present essay, the objectives of the two studies are different: Pactor seeks to identify all newspapers published in the West Indies from earliest times to the present, whereas this work seeks to isolate periodicals, belonging principally to the nineteenth century, which contain some measure of literary or artistic content. The separate goals account for substantial differences in the two lists. For one thing, Pactor lists newspapers published on smaller islands, such as Dominica, Grenada, Montserrat, Nevis, and so forth, whereas the present editors could find no extant journals in those areas addressing literary or artistic concerns. In addition, Pactor's research has been limited to libraries in the Americas while research for this project has taken advantage of the resources of British libraries, including those of the Royal Commonwealth Society and the British Library, both of which are rich in West Indies material.

Prices cited are those that appeared on copies of the journals; apparently both decimal and sterling symbols were used.

ANTIGUA

Discovered by Columbus and named after a church in Seville, Antigua, previously uninhabited, was settled by the British in 1632.

Weekly Record. W. 1813–40; then, *Antiguan Weekly Register*, 1840–82. St John's. BL.

Antigua Free Press. W. 1824–31. $6 (A). St John's. Ed. 1825–30, Robert Priest; 1830–1?, James Scotland. Local and international news, regular poetry. BL.

Antigua Herald and Gazette. W. 1832–59. St John's. $6 (A). Local and international news, parliamentary reports, literary essays. 'Poet's Column' is a regular feature. Pactor says, 'Also known as Weekly Herald,' and gives dates as 1832–59. BL.

Antigua Observer. W. 1849–1903. 6d. St John's. Ed. 1843, A.C. Hill; 1845, Mr Jewet; Daniel Ward Scarville was editor when it ceased publication in 1903. Local and European news, occasional poetry, short fiction, essays. BL.

Antigua Times. W. 1850–83; 1897–9. St John's. Price 3d. Standard features, including passenger lists from ships, occasional poetry. BL.

Antigua New Era. 1870–May 1875; then, the *New Era*, 1875–83. St John's. BL.

Antigua Standard. Published on the 1st, 10th, 16th, and 26th of each month. 2 July 1833–1902. Price 4d. 'Intercolonial News' about various colonies, sporting news, 'Review for Home Readers' for those who had returned to England, regular column entitled 'Original Poetry.' BL.

Record. W. 1887–8. St John's. 10s. (A). Mostly local news, occasional poetry and short fiction. BL.

Carib. A West Indies Magazine. 1, nos. 1–6, 1895. St John's. 1s. Ed. Miss F. Cassin. Poems, essays, serialized fiction. Institute of Commonwealth Studies.

BAHAMA ISLANDS

Columbus landed in the Bahamas in 1492, a landfall which marked European discovery of the New World, but the Spaniards made no attempt to settle them. In 1644–5, English religious dissidents from Bermuda attempted to settle, followed by Captain John Sayles, who led about seventy settlers; in 1717, Captain Woodes Rogers became first Royal Governor, brought troops, crushed piracy, and established order. In 1834 slavery was abolished, and there were no more political struggles. Tourism is the only important industry.

Bahama Gazette. W. 1812–15; 1819. Nassau. BL.

Bahama Argus. 1831–2; 1834–7. Nassau. BL.

Observer. Bi-W. 1837–40. Nassau. In addition to the standard news, this paper carried a regular poetry column. BL.

Bahama Herald. 1849–51; 1852–7; 1858–60; 1862–3; 1864–6; 1877. Nassau. BL, Pactor.

Nassau Guardian. 1844–55; 1857; 1863–1988. Nassau. BL, Pactor.

Herald, 1849–77. Nassau. BL, Pactor.

Nassau Times. 1869; 1873; 1875–6; 1877–88. Nassau. BL, Pactor

Freeman. 1887–9. BL.

Bahama News. 1898–1901. Nassau. BL.

BARBADOS

From 1620 to 1624, the British settled this previously uninhabited island. The year 1834 saw the abolition of slavery.

Barbados Mercury and Bridgetown Gazette. 8 Jan. 1805–49. Bridgetown. BL, Pactor.

Barbadian. Bi-W. 1, no. 2, 18 Dec. 1822–8 Dec. 1861. Local and international news, column entitled 'Review for Home Readers,' apparently aimed at those who had been in the colony and had returned to England; short fiction, occasional poetry, essays. BL.

West Indian. Bi-W. 4 Nov. 1833–30 June 1885. Bridgetown. $4 (A). Ed. 1833–6, Samuel Hyde. Local and international news, market reports, shipping, news from other colonies, occasional poetry, literary essays. BL.

New Times. 23 April 1836–8 March 1839? Ed. Samuel Prescod. In addition to regular news features, it contained information on education, gardening, etc., in short, maintaining the amenities of home in a far-flung colony. BL.

Barbados Globe and Colonial Advocate. Bi-W. N.s. 4 Sept. 1837–8 April 1840; 1 Nov. 1875–1926. Bridgetown. Local and home news, news of other colonies, shipping reports. BL.

Liberal. Bi-W. 1837–64. Bridgetown. Standard news, occasional poetry and essays. BL, Pactor.

Official Gazette and General Advertiser. 1840. Bridgetown. BL.

West India Magazine. M. No. 1, May 1840. Bridgetown. Publisher, I. Bowen. Poetry, reviews, literary pieces. UWI.

Barbados People and Windward Islands Gazette. Bi-W. 23 March–22 Aug. 1876. Inland, $1 (A); Intercolonial, $2 (A). (This suggests a large circulation.) Local news, many extracts from other newspapers, some historical essays. BL.

Barbados Agricultural Gazette and Planters' Journal. M. ?1878–87. 5s. (A). Published by the Council of the Barbados General Agricultural Society. An intelligently written, progressive agricultural magazine. BL.

Barbados Herald. 3 April 1879–25 July 1896. Bridgetown. BL.

Barbados Bee. W. 1, no. 1–2, no. 14, 1887–8. Bridgetown Ed. E.G. Sinkler. Illustrated comic magazine. Pactor.

BERMUDA

Bermuda, a group of islands, was first visited by a Spaniard, Juan de Bermudez, in 1515, and settled by the British in 1612. In the nineteenth century it was important as a military and naval base, with shipbuilding and saling the foundation of its economy.

Bermuda Gazette. W. 1821–7. Then, *Royal Gazette, Bermuda Commercial and General Advertiser* 1828–1903. $6 (A). St George. Local and international news. Column entitled 'Poet's Corner,' essays, short fiction. BL.

Bermudian. A Commercial, Literary, and Political Weekly Journal. W. 1833; 1839–40; 1858; 1871–3; 1875. Hamilton, Bermuda. Local and international news, poetry, short fiction. BL.

Bermuda Colonist. W. 1865–1915. £1/1s. (A). St George. Local, foreign news, regular serial fiction on p. 1, essays, poetry, much humour. BL.

Bermuda Chronicle. 1866. St George. BL.

BRITISH GUIANA

Technically considered part of the British Caribbean, although situated on the South American continent, British Guiana was formed in 1831 by uniting the settlements of Demerara, Essequibo, and Berbice. Its prosperity was adversely affected by the abolition of slavery in 1834, but remedied somewhat by immigration from the East Indies in the mid-nineteenth century, and later by the general rise in prosperity in the whole of the British West Indies area.

West Indies Quarterly. Q. 1–2, 1885–7. Demerara. Ed. Rev. H. Scotland (Jamaica); Rev. A. Caldecott (Barbados); Ven. J. Clark (Antigua); Rev. G.H. Butt (Berbice). Religion, politics, literature. UWI.

JAMAICA

Columbus landed on Jamaica, the largest island in the West Indies, on 3 May 1494; it remained under Spanish control until 1655, when the British captured and held it. The Royal African Company, founded in 1672, established Jamaica as one of the greatest slave marts in the world. Abolition of the slave trade, 1807, and of slavery, 1833, seriously affected the economy. The October 1865 uprising at Morant Bay was ruthlessly suppressed by Governor Edward John Eyre, who was called home and dismissed. His successor, Governor John Peter Grant, a successful and enlightened leader, established the banana trade.

Journals

Jamaica Magazine. M. 1–4, no. 1., 1812–13. Kingston. Containing original essays, moral, philosophical, and literary; together with biographical and political sketches taken from European publications. BL.

Jamaica Journal. No. 1, 1818. Kingston. Ed. Mr Rippingham. A miscellany consisting of 17 chapters. Gives accounts of the struggle for some civilization. BL.

Jamaica Quarterly Journal and Literary Gazette. Q. 1818–19. Kingston. 'Conducted by a Society of Gentlemen.' Provides twelve sheets of letter press for each number containing letters, essays, extracts, natural history, poetry, local vital statistics, and list of subscribers. BL.

Trifler. W. 1, nos. 1–13, 26 April 1822–22 March 1823; 2, nos. 1–13, 29 March–21 June 1823. Kingston. 'Open to all parties and influenced by none.' BL.

Buckatoro Journal. [?Buccatorro]. M. Nos. 1–6, 1823. Kingston. Content is very local, concerning topical issues. Account of a public circumcision. BL.

Jamaica Journal and Kingston Chronicle. W. 1–4, 1823–6. Kingston. Contents include much of the debate over the abolition of slavery, news from London, shipping information, occasional poetry, reviews of books, and a section 'Apprehended Slaves,' with descriptions of those runaway slaves who had been captured. BL.

Watchman and Jamaica Free Press. W. 1, no. 1, 1832(?)–5, nos. 56–104, 13 July–28 Dec. 1833. Largely concerned with colonial news and business, the slavery question, foreign news packets, correspondence, general notices, vital statistics, shipping news, passenger lists. Occasional poetry. BL, RCS.

Sheridan's Jamaica Quarterly Magazine. Q. (1, no. 1, Jan. 1834, was announced in *Watchman and Jamaica Free Press* for 13 July 1833. No actual copy has been traced.) It was to contain biography, short fiction, poetry, reprints from British periodicals, accounts of balls, theatricals, sporting events, and a quarterly digest of public events. Vital statistics. RCS.

Jamaica Journal of Arts, Science and Literature. No. 1, Oct. 1837. UWI.

Jamaica Monthly Magazine. M. April 1844. Kingston. UWI.

Jamaica Quarterly Journal of Literature, Science, and Art. July, Oct. 1861. $5 (A). Ed. James Gall. 'Containing original and Communicated Articles in Literature, the Arts, Medicine and Surgery, Law and Equity, Social Science, Agriculture, Natural History, Chemistry, Botany, Geology, Architecture and Engineering.' RCS, UWI.

West India Quarterly Magazine. Q. No. 1, Aug. 1861. Kingston. 20s. (A). Ed. Hugh Croskery. Medicine, science, literature, commerce, art, and agriculture. UWI.

Victoria Quarterly. Q. 1, no. 1–4, no. 4, 1889–92. Kingston. Ed. J.C. Ford. A publication of the Victoria Institute. Reviews, literary pieces, science. RCS, UWI

York Castle Quarterly. Q. No. 1, 1889. Kingston. Editorial says it is 'the first venture,' 'a boys' magazine; one written by boys and for boys,' 'a chronicle of our doings.' It is the organ of York Castle High School 'on top of a Jamaica mountain.' Founders: the Conference of the Wesleyan Church; high school established in 1876. BL.

Journal of the Institute of Jamaica. Q. Subtitled *'For the Encouragement of Literature, Science, and Art.'* 1, Nov. 1891–3; 1894–9. Kingston. Institute of Jamaica, Date Tree Hall, East Street. The Institute of Jamaica appears to have been a kind of 'cultural institute' which provided a library, lectures, and meetings. The periodical came with membership and constituted, more or less, a 'Proceedings,' or record of the activities of the Institute. No price is given for either membership or a subscription. RCS, UWI.

Trifler. M. 1894. St Ann's Bay, Jamaica. UWI.

Newspapers

Falmouth

Trelawny and Public Advertiser. Bi-W. 1785?–29 Dec. 1887. 24s. (A).
Standard news content and literary essays. BL.

Falmouth Post and General Advertiser. Bi-W. ?1834–31 Aug. 1877. £2
(A). All news and ads. BL.

Jamaica Witness. M. 1876–87. (From 1 Jan. 1883 published at Kingston.)
2s. 6d. (A). A Presbyterian paper, all religious news, mainly of missions, strongly temperance and anti-Catholic. Contains much inspirational poetry. BL.

Falmouth Gazette and Jamaica General Advertiser. Bi-W. 1, no. 1–10,
no. 100, 3 Jan. 1879–29 Dec. 1888. £1 4 s. (A). Produced by the former editor
of the defunct *Falmouth Post.* A standard newspaper with occasional
poetry. BL.

Kingston

Colonial Standard. D. 1849–50; then, the *Colonial Standard and
Jamaica Dispatch* 1850–29 June 1895. £2 (A). Standard news content,
short fiction, historical essays, travelogues, occasional poetry. BL.

Gall's 'Packet' News Letter. [Frequent title changes.] 1872–27 March 1899.
$5 (A). 'Containing a Succinct Summary of Jamaica, West India, Central
and South American News, Specially Prepared for Transmission by the
British Mail Packet "Nile" to Europe.' Reports on political developments,
weather, shipping, and markets, probably aimed at former residents of
the colonies and investors. BL.

Budget. Tri-W. 1877–1886; then, the *Evening Budget,* 1887–8; then, the
Tri-Weekly Budget, 1888. Some news but mostly advertising. BL.

Evening Express. D. Nos. 27–652, 11 June 1884–31 Dec. 1888. 24s (A).
News plus poetry and short fiction. BL.

Montego Bay

Cornwall Chronicle and County Gazette. ?1772–11 Dec. 1839. 14 (A).
(Only one issue available.) A standard four-page paper. BL.

Jamaica Standard. Bi-W. ?1836–40. Local and international news, some poetry. BL.

Spanish Town

Colonial Reformer. W. 1839–13 Feb. 1841. A progressive paper, it was especially critical of American slavery. Contained occasional poetry and some short fiction. BL.

St. Jago de la Vega Gazette. 1839–40. News plus poetry and literary essays. BL.

TRINIDAD

Columbus landed at Trinidad, the most southerly and second largest island of the British West Indies, in 1498, and it was subsequently fought over by the French, Dutch, and Spanish. In 1797 Sir Ralph Abercomby claimed it for Britain, after which it was formally ceded to the British at the Treaty of Amiens in 1802.

Trinidad Sentinel. 1856–3 Oct. 1864. A standard four-page paper with political news, letters to the editor, etc. BL.

Trinidad Monthly Magazine. M. 1871. Port of Spain. A monthly containing articles of general interest, serialized fiction, and poetry. BL.

Trinidad Review. W. 1, nos. 31–65, 28 Feb.–23 Oct. 1884. 20 cents. Concentration on local news, very little international. Occasional poetry. BL.

Union Magazine. 1892. Port of Spain. 6 cents. Published by the Church of England Union for Men, this monthly magazine contained articles on gardening, science, and travel, as well as original poetry. BL.

Progress. 'A Monthly Journal of Advanced Thought.' M. 1893–4. Port of Spain. 4 cents. Ed. E. Dos Santos. A progressive secular magazine with articles on agnosticism and free-thinking, strongly anti-clerical. The articles show much conflict with established religion, especially evangelicals. BL.

Monthly Magazine for the Parishes of Holy Trinity, All Saints, and St Margaret. M. 1896–8. Port of Spain. News of activities in the three parishes, including services and obituaries. Occasional poetry. BL.

Notes on Contributors

Brahma Chaudhuri teaches at the University of Alberta. Fluent in both Hindi and Bengali, he has published widely on the work of Charles Dickens. His work has appeared in *Dickens Quarterly, Dickensian, English Language Notes, Études Anglaises,* and other journals. He is editor of *Annual Bibliography of Victorian Studies* and *Victorian Database on CD-ROM,* and currently is working on a book on Sir Philip Francis and Madame Grand.

Brian Cheadle is Professor and Chair, Department of English, University of the Witwatersrand. His work on Dickens and Shakespeare has appeared in *Dickens Studies Annual, Themes in Drama, Notes and Queries, English Studies in Africa,* and other journals. He is working on a comprehensive checklist and study of the highly varied Boer War periodicals, both in English and Dutch/Afrikaans; and also on a checklist of all nineteenth-century South African serials, including such items as almanacs and reports.

N. Merrill Distad, Assistant Director of Libraries at the University of Alberta, is a former editor of *Victorian Periodicals Review* (1978–84) and a past president of the Research Society for Victorian Periodicals (1985–7). Currently, he is editor of the *Bulletin of the Bibliographic Society of Canada/Société bibliographique du Canada* (1991–); author of *Guessing at Truth: The Life of Julius Charles Hare, 1795–1855;* as well as numerous scholarly articles. LINDA MIRON DISTAD is a professional editor with more than a score of books to her credit, and a devotee of historical research.

J. Reginald Tye, retired Reader in English at Victoria University, Wellington, New Zealand, was a founding member and president of the Australasian Victorian Studies Association. He is author of *Periodicals of the Eighteen Nineties: A Checklist of Literary Periodicals Published in the British Isles at Longer than Fortnightly Intervals, 1890–1899* (1974), a special publication of the Oxford Bibliographical Society; he has also published *The Image Maker: The Art of James Berry* (1984). His scholarly articles have appeared in *Nineteenth Century Fiction,* the *Dickensian,* the *Gissing Newsletter, English Literature in Transition, New Zealand Libraries,* and the *Turnbull Library Record.* Most recently his 'Periodicals of the 1890s' appeared in *Victorian Periodicals: A Guide to Research* 2 (1989).

Rosemary T. VanArsdel, distinguished professor of English, emerita, at the University of Puget Sound, is coeditor, with J. Don Vann, of *Victorian Periodicals: A Guide to Research,* vols. 1 and 2 (1978, 1989) and *Victorian Periodicals and Victorian Society* (1994). She is coeditor, with Gordon S. Haight, of *George Eliot: A Centenary Tribute* (1982). A founding member, and past president, of the Research Society for Victorian Periodicals (1981–3), she served on the editorial boards of the *Wellesley Index to Victorian Periodicals, 1824–1900* (5 vols., 1966–89) and the *Union List of Victorian Serials in North American Libraries* (1985). She is author of numerous articles on Victorian and Edwardian studies in scholarly journals in North America and the United Kingdom, and is a member of the Editorial Board of *Victorian Review.*

J. Don Vann, Regent's Professor of English at the University of North Texas, former secretary of the Research Society for Victorian Periodicals, and associate editor of *Studies in the Novel,* was the original editor of the annual bibliography in *Victorian Periodicals Review.* He is coeditor, with Rosemary T. VanArsdel, of *Victorian Periodicals: A Guide to Research,* vols. 1 and 2 (1978, 1989) and *Victorian Periodicals and Victorian Society* (1994). He is author of *Victorian Novels in Serial* (1985) and has published books on Graham Greene, Samuel Beckett, and Henry James, as well as articles on Dickens, Browning, and other Victorian authors.

Elizabeth Webby, Professor of Australian Literature at the University of Sydney, has for the past twenty-eight years been carrying out research into the literary and theatrical culture of nineteenth-century Australia. Her publications include *Early Australian Poetry* (1982); *Colonial Voices*

(1989); *Modern Australian Plays* (1990); and, as joint editor, *Happy Endings* (1987); *Goodbye to Romance* (1989) and *The Penguin Book of Australian Ballads* (1993). She has also published numerous book chapters, articles, and reviews, and been a contributing editor of *The Penguin New Literary History of Australia* (1988) and *A Feminist Companion to Literature in English* (1990). Since 1988 she has been editor of *Southerly*, Australia's oldest literary quarterly. She is a member of the editorial boards of two major current projects, the *Academy Editions of Australian Literature* and *The Book in Australia*, and of several international journals.

Index